More Addiction  from Wiley Ps

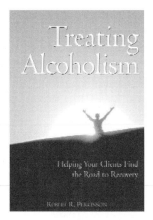

0-471-65806-5, $34.95

Full of practical information on assessing, diagnosing, and treating alcohol addiction. Includes sample treatment plans, alcohol screening tests, non-chemical addiction tests, resource listings, and a sample behavioral contract to use with adolescents.

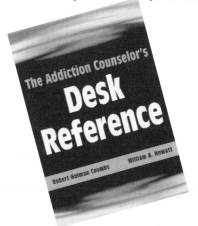

0-471-43245-8, $35.00

Includes detailed definitions and practical illustration of addiction-related terminology, addictive disorders and behaviors, descriptions of treatment models and techniques, and more.

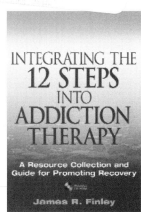

0-471-59980-8, $45.00

Learn how 12-Step, peer therapy programs work and how to integrate 12-Step methods into traditional therapy. Combines an in-depth discussion of the 12-Step Way with detailed treatment resources.

0-471-48483-0, $34.95

Includes assessment scales, tables, checklists and diagrams; features such as "Dos and Don'ts" and "Important Things to Remember;" problem-solving scenarios, "Self-Improvement Techniques;" and suggested resources.

0-471-47946-2, $39.95

Get specific information on working with varied clients in diverse settings and practical advice on treatment techniques and professional development. Features engaging examples and exercises, popular assessment instruments, group counseling techniques, and more.

0-471-70381-8, $50.00

Contains more than 70 forms for addiction treatment as well as clinical documentation updated for HIPAA, JCAHO, and CARF compliance. Includes a CD-ROM with all forms and presentations for easy customization and printing.

WILEY

Now you know.

wiley.com

To order call toll-free 1-877-762-2974
or online at www.wiley.com/psychology
Also available from Amazon.com, BN.com, and other fine booksellers.

The Wiley
Concise Guides
to Mental Health

Substance Use Disorders

The Wiley
Concise Guides
to Mental Health

Substance Use Disorders

Nicholas R. Lessa,
M.S.W., M.A.

Walter F. Scanlon,
Ph.D., M.B.A.

John Wiley & Sons, Inc.

WILEY

Copyright © 2006 by John Wiley & Sons, Inc. All rights reserved.
Published by John Wiley & Sons, Inc., Hoboken, New Jersey.
Published simultaneously in Canada.

Library of Congress Cataloging-in-Publication Data:

Scanlon, Walter F.
    Substance use disorders / by Walter F. Scanlon, Nicholas Lessa.
        p. cm. – (Wiley concise guides to mental health)
    Includes bibliographical references.
    ISBN-13: 978-0-471-68991-1 (pbk.)
    ISBN-10: 0-471-68991-2 (pbk.)
    1. Substance abuse. 2. Substance abuse–Treatment. I. Lessa, Nicholas, 1957– . II. Title.
III. Series.
    [DNLM: 1. Substance-Related Disorders–therapy. 2. Social Work, Psychiatric–methods.
WM 270 S283s 2006]
    RC564.S28 2006
    616.86–dc22

Printed in the United States of America

10 9 8 7 6 5 4 3 2 1

To
Our respective families

We cannot control the direction of the wind, but maybe we can adjust our sails
–Emmerich Vogt

CONTENTS

Section Three: Treatment

SERIES PREFACE

The *Wiley Concise Guides to Mental Health* are designed to provide mental health professionals with an easily accessible overview of what is currently known about the nature and treatment of psychological disorders. Each book in the series delineates the origins, manifestations, and course of a commonly occurring disorder and discusses effective procedures for its treatment. The authors of the *Concise Guides* draw on relevant research as well as their clinical expertise to ground their text both in empirical findings and in wisdom gleaned from practical experience. By achieving brevity without sacrificing comprehensive coverage, the *Concise Guides* should be useful to practitioners as an on-the-shelf source of answers to questions that arise in their daily work, and they should prove valuable as well to students and professionals as a condensed review of state-of-the-art knowledge concerning the psychopathology, diagnosis, and treatment of various psychological disorders.

Irving B. Weiner

PREFACE

The world of substance dependency and abuse is multidimensional. With its global economic and political manifestations notwithstanding, it is a national concern that impacts every strata of society. No one is immune to its devastation. Alcohol-related vehicular deaths, drug-related crimes, domestic violence, and drug overdoses attest to its seriousness. And because of their attention-getting sensationalism, these consequences of Substance Use Disorders (SUDs) are the problems society becomes aware of. But they are the tip of the iceberg—we need to reach and treat those users who make the news—and we also need to reach and treat those who have not made the news—yet!

Early intervention based on proven treatment methods is the key to achieving that objective. While the past 100 years reveals a variety of clinical and administrative efforts to deal with alcohol and other drug problems in the United States, the dawn of the twenty-first century will, hopefully, become a period of clinical innovation and intervention. As the scientific community continues to study and better understand the biology and physiology of addiction, the behavioral treatment community works on etiologically sound treatment applications.

The *Wiley Concise Guide to Mental Health: Substance Use Disorders* is divided in 12 chapters that cover, to a greater or lesser degree, six related subgroups: users, family, society, suppliers, law enforcement, and helping professionals. The users, those individuals afflicted with Substance Use Disorders, are the driving force behind this book. Many of them will eventually find their way to treatment, while others will continue to attempt to meet life's challenges through mood-altering drugs. Still others will fail in recovery, not for a lack of motivation—it is *our* job to motivate them—but for lack of treatment options.

The need to continue to improve upon the existing treatment alternatives and provide more opportunities for recovery is the impetus for most works in the field. In that way this book hopes to find itself in the good company of many excellent works that have brought us to where we are today in treatment. And as every author hopes to advance the cause of treatment in some meaningful way, we, too, humbly hope to achieve that objective. By offering a treatment guide that reduces often otherwise complex concepts to simple terms, we hope to play some part in providing more opportunities for recovery.

While mood-altering substances have been around for thousands of years, the concept of *drug addiction* did not emerge until the beginning of the nineteenth century. Up until that time, the world seemed to be in a state of mass denial. In Chapter 1, we discuss the importance of this revelation and how it relates to the challenges in treatment that still exist. With the focus on definitions, treatment, and misconceptions about mood-altering substances, the progression of Substance Use Disorders is examined in this chapter as well as the criteria that define *abuse* and *dependence*. Because Substance Use Disorders are viewed by most professionals as biological, psychological, social, and spiritual disorders, we thoroughly explore spirituality as a factor in addiction and recovery in Chapter 9. The disease controversy and treatment as a science are also discussed. Other controversies, including gender differences in treatment, outpatient treatment versus inpatient treatment, and the role of the professionally trained recovering person as a treatment provider are also reviewed.

The wise words of George Santayana, a Spanish-born American author, "Those who cannot remember the past are condemned to repeat it," prompted our starting Chapter 2 with a brief 100 year history of drug use in our society. While viewing drug use in its historical perspective may not be essential to becoming a good clinician, it allows the clinician to better understand why it remains a problem that is not likely to go away. The legal classification of psychoactive substances and laws to better control the availability of designer drugs were legal attempts to reinforce the war on drugs. The legal classification of drugs approaches the problem from a criminal-justice perspective while the general or pharmacological classification of drugs serves the medical and treatment communities. We also discuss in this chapter the mood-altering properties of specific drugs and drug classifications, together with their synergistic, tolerance, and withdrawal potential.

Everything we know today about the treatment of Substance Use Disorders comes out of our successes and failures of yesterday. The theme in Chapter 3 is that in order to treat any disorder, we must first know exactly what we're treating. Unlike yesterday's hit-and-miss program-model attempt to treat the person with a Substance Use Disorder, today's treatment is far more individualized and precise. Using *DSM-IV-TR* diagnostic criteria and American Society of Addiction Medicine levels of care, this chapter discusses assessment methods, tools, and applications in developing treatment plans. Case studies are used to test their application, emphasizing the importance of collateral information, mental status, employment history, and family impact on the client. As in the treatment of any malady, the more information the clinician has, the better the chance of an accurate diagnosis and treatment plan.

In Chapter 4 we talk about levels of care and their importance in providing appropriate treatment services. Chapter 4 is a detailed description of those levels of care and the services provided for each of them. Outpatient and inpatient treatment facilities, including intensive outpatient programs, day-hospital facilities, methadone maintenance treatment, inpatient rehabilitation programs, extended-care facilities, halfway houses, and therapeutic communities are explained, and their historical relevance reviewed in this chapter. Because overtreating the patient may be as ineffective as undertreating the patient, knowing exactly what services are provided on each level of care is essential to good treatment planning and successful outcomes.

Physical tolerance and withdrawal symptomatology take us to the medical aspect of Substance Use Disorders. Chapter 5 deals with the importance of medical detoxification on the continuum of care. A biological understanding of intoxication and maintaining biological balance (homeostasis) are important to a safe detoxification. The goals of detoxification, treatment protocols, assessment tools for alcohol and other drug withdrawal, Breathalyzer readings, and opioid maintenance therapy are discussed in this chapter. The science of agonists and antagonists are also discussed. While medical detoxification can be managed on any level of care, this chapter provides the tools to determine the appropriateness of outpatient versus inpatient detoxification. The value of counseling at this acute phase of treatment is also talked about.

Medical conditions can often complicate treatment. Such conditions may have preceded the Substance Use Disorder or may be the consequence of substance use and abuse. While most Substance Use Disorders can be life-threatening at some point, untreated serious medical problems can be particularly dangerous. Chapter 6 reviews such risks, including cardiovascular diseases directly related to drug abuse; liver disease, including hepatitis C; other blood-borne diseases, such as HIV and AIDS; as well as pulmonary and respiratory diseases. Lung cancer is on the rise in addicts who smoke marijuana and crack cocaine, while more and more IV drug users are found to be developing liver cancers. This chapter will also discuss chronic pain and the addicted patient.

Coexisting mental disorders, if left untreated, are certain to inhibit recovery. In Chapter 7 the reader will learn how to assess and take appropriate action if other mental health problems are present. This includes understanding comorbidity and its treatment implications, assessing for Psychotic Disorders, Mood Disorders, Anxiety Disorders, and Personality Disorders. Substance treatment professionals need to assess and refer for consultation those patients that exhibit symptoms of mental health disorders. This calls for recognition of symptomatology and the ability to differentiate between Substance Use Disorder symptoms such as mild anxiety and depression from symptoms that may point to a concomitant mental health diagnosis.

A Substance Use Disorder affects not just the identified patient, but also family members and other loved ones. Conversely, the family environment often enables continued substance use, abuse, and dependence. The family will frequently undermine recovery. Chapter 8 will explore both the importance of family in treatment as well as the deliberate exclusion of family involvement. Family dynamics will be examined, including family mental health, family alcohol and drug use, family rules, and family resistance to recovery. An accurate family history is important to treatment planning and ongoing recovery. The difference between recovery and abstinence is also reviewed, as well as the role of the workplace in ongoing recovery, the social environment, and the culture of addiction from which the person with a Substance Use Disorder emerged. Moderation management, a controversial approach to recovery, will be discussed.

We refer to spirituality as the neglected dimension. While it is probably impossible to experience spirituality when in the throes of a Substance Use Disorder, it has become the fourth dimension when describing the components of a Substance Use Disorder: biological, psychological, sociological, and spiritual. Spirituality in some form may become an important dimension in recovery. Chapter 9 will discuss various aspects of spirituality: resistance to it, gravitation toward it, and surrender to it. Ego versus humility, irresponsibility versus discipline, and resentment versus forgiveness are some of the topics to be discussed. Under any other name, recovery is, in and of itself, a spiritual experience.

Chapter 10 is all about the use of structured intervention in getting the identified patient to accept the help he or she needs. The myth of *hitting bottom*, a belief that prevails in both the treatment community and in the general population, is explored in this chapter. We continue to hear, "They are not going to stop drinking or stop using drugs until they hit bottom." The identified patient often has already hit bottom but does not yet know it. The intervention is a pretreatment strategy that serves to present this reality to him or her in a receivable way.

The notion that significant others need to wait around as the person with a Substance Use Disorder spirals downward has served to foster denial among individuals, families, the medical community, and helping professions. Unlike most other illnesses, resistance to treatment is a feature of Substance Use Disorders; the simplest (but least helpful) response to resistance is denial: "We can't help them until they're ready for help." An intervention, however, dispels this myth and raises the bottom through a collaborative effort of support and loving leverage involving family, friends, and employers. Several intervention models are explored in this chapter.

In Chapter 11 we address what has been the essence of treatment for individuals with Substance use Disorders—behavioral change. This chapter is aimed at developing effective counseling skills and treatment strategies. Using motivational interviewing and motivational enhancement therapy as the foundation for this chapter, emphasis is placed on change rather than abstinence. While abstinence is the desirable goal in most Substance Use Disorder diagnoses, our contention is that skillfully moving the client to the next level of behavioral change will prove far more effective in most cases than demanding abstinence. Treatment readiness, stages-of-change strategies, resolving ambivalence, teaching coping skills, and preventing relapse are a few of the important concepts covered in this chapter.

Relapse prevention therapy is the core of effective treatment and relapse is as much a part of recovery as it is of the disorder. Chapter 12 is dedicated exclusively to relapse prevention both as a separate function as well as an integrated component of treatment. Many of Marlatt and Gordon's concepts associated with relapse and relapse prevention, including high-risk situations, self-efficacy, and the abstinence violation effect are explored in this chapter. Gorski's integration of the fundamental principals of Alcoholics Anonymous with the Minnesota treatment model is also explored. While both the Gorski and Marlatt and Gordon models have more similarities than differences, their differences are important to understand.

As a profession emerges, it develops technical language to facilitate communications. Medicine and psychiatry, for example, have professional reference resources such as the *Physician's Desk Reference* and the *Diagnostic and Statistical Manual*, respectively, that serve to standardize communications. The social work profession, in addition to using these resources, developed language that reflects not just the person and his or her malady, but also the *person-in-environment.*

The treatment of Substance Use Disorders, a relative newcomer to the helping professions, borrows from these disciplines and has also developed a substance-specific language. Because it is a relatively new profession, its vocabulary continues to emerge. Words like *dependency* and *abuse* have specific diagnostic criteria that standardize their use. *Chemical dependency*, however, is a vague nebulous term that does not differentiate abuse from dependence. In other words, as a technical term it lacks technical accuracy. In an effort to encourage the use of unambiguous language, we chose to use *Substance Use Disorder* in this book's title rather than *chemical dependency.*

Alcoholism is another word that fails the technical accuracy test. Is a person diagnosed with Alcohol Abuse afflicted with alcoholism? Or is that word reserved for those who are alcohol dependent? How about an *alcoholic*? Would either diagnosis of Alcohol Dependence or Alcohol Abuse qualify as alcoholic?

Addict, another word that defies definition, comes from the noun *addiction.* Is a marijuana smoker who meets the diagnostic criteria for Cannabis Abuse an addict? Or is that word reserved for Cannabis Dependence? The word *addiction,* in fact, does not necessarily indicate a Substance Use Disorder. A person who is medically dependent on a prescription opioid, for example, may not necessarily meet the criteria for a Substance Use Disorder, as defined in the *DSM-IV-TR.* The term *drug abuser* is also a generic description and does not separate dependence from abuse.

While the terms *chemical dependency, alcoholic, alcoholism, drug abuser,* and *addict* are likely to remain with us, we have used them only where they are appropriate, such as in a historical context. We have taken the liberty, however, to use certain words and terms interchangeably. *Patient, client,* and *identified patient* will all mean the same thing—a person who is in treatment, should be in treatment, or will soon be in treatment.

An SUD is an equal gender disorder. When considering all the different substances that one can abuse or become dependent on, it is difficult to assess with absolute certainty whether there are more women or more men with SUDs. Men, for example, abuse more alcohol, but women may abuse as much amphetamine and cocaine. It would follow then that pronouns used throughout this book would represent both genders; for example, "him and her," "he and she," or "his and hers." We use this form in many instances. But where doing so would detract from the continuity of a paragraph, section, or chapter, we chose to revert back to the "him," "he," and "his" pronouns representing both genders. We hope that in the name of clarity, you accept our apology.

The terms *substance abuse professional, counselor, therapist, social worker, psychologist,* and *health-care professional,* depending upon the nature of the text, might also be used interchangeably. *Addictions counselor* and *chemical-dependency counselor* might be used in a historical perspective.

While the words *sobriety* and *sober* were in the past associated with alcohol, it is not unusual to see them representing any person with a Substance Use Disorder who is drug- and alcohol-free. The diagnostic classifications that fall under Substance Abuse and Substance Dependence, such as Cannabis Dependence, Alcohol Abuse, Heroin Dependence, and so on, will not be represented in any form other than these *DSM-IV-TR* classifications.

We like to think of the founding of Alcoholics Anonymous (AA) on June 10, 1935 as the beginning of treatment as we know it today. But in reality, AA is not treatment—it is self-help. And there was a lot of treatment available before William Griffith Wilson (Bill W.) and Robert Holbrook Smith (Dr. Bob) founded the program that changed the way we think—not just about *alcoholics,* but about the power of the human spirit. It is just that most of the help that was available in those early days was whimsical and ineffective. Miracle tonics, magical formulas, aversive methods, geographical cures, and other radical measures gave lots of hope but offered little success in helping individuals who were struggling with alcohol and other drug problems. The twenty-first century, however, is promising. Twelve-step programs are as popular as ever, science is on the cutting edge of pharmacological innovation, and behavioral therapies continue to reshape themselves to meet the needs of the substance treatment community. While the dream of a magic pill to end all drug abuse and dependence is not likely, our optimism and understanding of behavioral and pharmacological treatment today is as exciting as those early days of Alcoholics Anonymous when Bill W. and Dr. Bob shook hands for the first time.

ACKNOWLEDGMENTS

This book could not have been written without the many lessons learned from the literally thousands of teachers I have had over the years—my patients. I wish to also acknowledge my mentor, Lee Kassan, for his assistance and encouragement, and my coauthor, Walter Scanlon, for without his collaboration, this book would have remained a dream.

My gratitude goes out to my family, friends, and business partners, Robert Smith and Vincent Casolaro, for their love and support during this endeavor. And finally, my dedication to my daughter, Samantha, and my wife, Laura, who remain my hope and strength.

Nicholas R. Lessa

While we authors assume credit for the final document, a book is really a collaborative effort involving many others. Taking an idea and turning it into a readable work is a process requiring the input of lots of people. This input comes in the form of hands-on assistance, personal support, and ongoing encouragement. Without the help and patience of family, friends, and colleagues, this book would probably not have been possible. I am especially grateful to Farida Parakh for her personal support, professional perspective, and experience on several levels of care. Her reviews and feedback on several drafts served to ensure that this book would reach its targeted audiences.

Professional organizations serve several functions, including personal and professional support. I thank my colleagues and friends in the New York City chapter of the Employee Assistance Professionals Association and the National Association for Addictions Professionals for always being available. In addition to Nicholas Lessa, my colleague, good friend, and coauthor, my thanks go to several other friends and associates who read drafts, offered ideas, or just made me laugh in the thick of it all, including Anita Yulsman, Kathleen Sullivan, Barbara Beattie, Vincent Casolaro, and Farias Parakh.

Finally, I thank all the recovering, and yet to recover, men and women who, wittingly and unwittingly, made this book possible.

Walter F. Scanlon

ABOUT THE AUTHORS

Nicholas Lessa is a managing partner and chief executive officer of Inter-Care, Ltd., a comprehensive alcohol and drug treatment center in New York City. Mr. Lessa has been a leader, trainer, and innovator in the treatment of Substance Use Disorders for more than 20 years. He has developed and implemented training programs covering a wide range of clinical and program management topics. Mr. Lessa has worked with many training and treatment centers over the years, including the Narcotics and Drug Research Institute, the Alcoholism Council of New York, and the New York City Department of Mental Health, Mental Retardation, and Alcoholism Services. He is currently an adjunct associate professor at New York University, and maintains a private practice. Mr. Lessa holds master's degrees in both psychology (MA) and social work (MSW). He is also a New York State Credentialed Alcoholism and Substance Abuse Counselor (CASAC).

Walter Scanlon is a program/workplace consultant with 25 years management and clinical experience in behavioral health care, including the treatment of Substance Use Disorders, employee assistance program (EAP) development, and structured intervention services. The principal of Walter Scanlon Management (WSM), Dr. Scanlon has taught, trained, and presented nationally; he is an adjunct professor at Marymount Manhattan College and City College of New York. Dr. Scanlon is widely published in the areas of substance abuse, employee assistance, criminal justice, and related areas, including two books, the latest titled *Alcoholism and Drug Abuse in the Workplace: Managing Care and Costs through Employee Assistance Programs* (1991). Dr. Scanlon has held clinical and EAP management positions at Beth Israel Hospital, the Port Authority of New York and New Jersey, and Freeport Hospital. As the principal of WSM he has provided EAP services for Alcoholics Anonymous World Services, Hazelden New York, Verizon Communications, and American Express. He currently serves as a consultant to the New York City Police Department. Dr. Scanlon holds a PhD in Psychology, a Master's of Business Administration (MBA), and is credentialed as a Certified Employee Assistance Professional (CEAP), a New York State Credentialed Alcoholism and Substance Abuse Counselor (CASAC), a national Substance Abuse Professional (SAP), and a Master's Addiction Counselor (MAC).

Introduction

THE WILEY
CONCISE GUIDES
TO MENTAL HEALTH

Substance
Use
Disorders

CHAPTER 1

Substance Use Disorders: Definitions, Treatment, and Misconceptions

W hile the use and abuse of psychoactive substances predates the printed word, it was not until 1821 that the Western world was presented with an extraordinarily new concept: drug addiction. It was then that Thomas De Quincey created a minor sensation with his autobiographical *Confessions of an English Opium Eater* (Jonnes, 1999, p. 15). Describing in disturbing detail his "tortured love affair with laudanum"—a liquid form of opium dissolved in alcohol—De Quincey's work confronted, perhaps unwittingly, English men and women of that period with the consequences of drug use. Although opium usage was a common remedy for "sundry aches and pains," the Western world seemed to have been in a state of mass denial.

De Quincey's unsettling tale was the earliest documents to reveal the truth about drug use in a somewhat clinical manner. He invented the concept of recreational drug use, making it absolutely clear that opium's value in society is more than medicinal or spiritual (Boon, 2002, p. 37). In doing so, he got society to consider two additional facts: Drugs are fun, and drugs are addictive. While many probably dismissed De Quincey's *Confessions of an English Opium Eater* as "his problem," it begged the soul-searching questions—Am I using drugs for pain or for pleasure? Are the consequences of my drug use negative or positive? Can I stop anytime, or am I dependent?

Almost two centuries later, we are asking these same questions. But because the answers are as elusive as they are important, such questions now take the form of qualifying criteria. The criteria are as quantitative as they are qualitative, rendering not simply the answers to such questions but the type and severity of the problem. While a diagnosis is just the first step in the treatment of a Substance Use Disorder (SUD), it is impossible to develop an effective treatment plan without first establishing what's being treated. A good start is to differentiate between recreational use and problematic use.

The Progression of Substance Use

Progression is viewed as either an increase in consumption or an increase in problems. Often imperceptible to the user, the psychoactive substance assumes an ever-more important role, and problems mount. The word *psycho* relates to the mind, and *psychoactive substances* are drugs that alter the mind. Acting on the central nervous system (CNS), such drugs are often referred to as *mood-altering substances*.

While innocent experimentation may prove harmless for many, for others it serves as an introduction to recreational drug use. Although we have observed cases where individuals had established an almost instantaneous problematic relationship with alcohol or other mood-altering substances, the progression to an SUD is more likely to happen in three stages. As the sidebar shows, we have discovered that each stage is totally independent of its succeeding stage. What separates one stage from the next? For example, when does experimental use progress to recreational use? Does using a substance for the second time mean one is now a recreational user? Does missing 1 day from work constitute problematic use? How about 1 day per month? Or perhaps one DWI? Progression is not always predictable, yet when the user arrives at the next stage, it was almost as if it *were* predictable.

Initially, psychoactive substance use is begun either for *medical* or *experimental*

SUD Progression

1. Stage one, *experimental use,* usually occurs in the preteen, teen, and adolescent years. The cocaine epidemic of the 1980s, however, challenged this notion. The 21 to 35-year-old age group accounted for countless new users throughout that decade. Not all who experiment progress to recreational drug use.

2. Stage two, *recreational drug use,* does not necessarily lead to problematic patterns of use. Ninety percent of the population, for example, enjoys alcoholic beverages without serious incident.

3. Stage three, *problematic substance use,* represents those who meet the criteria for an SUD.
   a. Substance Abuse
   b. Substance Dependence

(This is further discussed in the next section.)

Experimental Substance Use

Mary was offered marijuana at a party when she was 22 years old. She had never tried marijuana before. In fact, she never tried any other illicit substance in her life. Her parents instilled in her a fear of drugs. She, however, was curious about the drug. Several of her friends smoked marijuana and did not seem negatively impacted by regular use of it. She told herself, "Why not?" She tried marijuana at the party and did not like the effects. Mary never smoked marijuana again.

reasons. A substance may be prescribed by a doctor for the treatment of a physical or psychological condition. It is then discontinued once the acute condition has improved. The prescribed substance may be taken for longer periods of time if the condition being treated is chronic in nature. This pattern of use may or may not be problematic, depending on the patient's ability to discontinue the medication once it is no longer medically warranted. Problematic use patterns of this type are known as *low-dose dependencies.* Some physicians, when prescribing psychoactive substances, underestimate the addictive qualities of the substances being prescribed. This can be especially problematic when the patient has a genetic predisposition to addiction. While trusting the training and experience of the medical professional is usually a good idea, we cannot always assume that the doctor knows best under these circumstances.

When the start of substance use is *experimental,* the substance is initially used out of curiosity for its mood-altering qualities. The person tries the substance to assess its effects. If the substance is not considered pleasing or beneficial in some way, the substance is likely to be discontinued. However, if the substance is considered to be rewarding, it may be continued. The determination on whether to continue using the substance is based upon a variety of psychological, social, physiological, and perhaps spiritual factors, such as prior beliefs or lack of understanding on the danger of the drug or past experiences with other substances. Experimental use is not considered problematic. One government study on adolescent drug use conducted many years ago showed that the vast majority of adolescents experiment with some form of mood-altering substance at some time during their adolescence. It considered experimental use of mood-altering substances to be a kind of rite of passage for adolescents. The study went on to say that the small minority of adolescents who did *not* experiment were found to display more psychopathology, as a whole, than did the experimenters. This is, obviously, a controversial finding that may have reflected a particular period in time.

If the person continues to use the substance

Progression of an SUD

Stage	Dynamic	Control
Experimental	Curiosity	Full
Recreational	Fun	Choice
Abuse	Denial	Limited
Dependence	Addiction	Impaired

Recreational Substance Use

> John is a 36-year-old accountant. He began drinking beer at age 17. He has now become an aficionado of wine. He has a collection of expensive wines in his custom-built wine cooler. John likes to have dinner parties with friends about once a month when he presents several wines from his cooler. John appears to drink responsibly. He seems to know when he has had enough to drink and can easily refuse offers for more alcohol. He has not displayed any negative consequences (e.g., physical, social, occupational, or financial) around his wine drinking.

beyond the stage of experimentation, he or she is considered to be in the *recreational* stage of use. Recreational use typically involves using in the company of others, for example, in social situations such as parties, to enhance pleasurable situations. (This is not to say that problem use cannot occur while attempting to enhance pleasurable situations.) Sometimes the substance may be used when alone, such as when a person enjoys an alcoholic beverage during a meal. Recreational substance use involves significant choice and control. For example, the person who uses alcohol recreationally may decide not to drink on a particular occasion and, as a result, abstains during that occasion. Or a person who recreationally uses marijuana at a party decides only to have two puffs on a joint and is okay with that choice. The recreational user does not display any negative consequences regarding the substance use—socially, legally, occupationally, or physically. Sometimes the person may not be aware of the consequences of use (e.g., an alcohol user damaging his or her liver) or may deny the consequences (e.g., how cocaine use is affecting the marriage). Under these circumstances, the use is not considered to be recreational—it has begun to become problematic.

Substance Abuse

> Peter is a 46-year-old building engineer. In our initial interview, he has been drinking alcoholic beverages since he was 15 years old. He began using cocaine when he was 18 years old. Peter is the first to admit he is a heavy drinker, but he would resist identifying himself as an alcoholic. He regularly drinks on the weekend and occasionally during the week. At least once weekly, usually on Friday nights, Peter uses cocaine along with his beer drinking and shots of tequila. Most Friday nights there are no problems related to his partying. Once in a while, though, Peter gets himself into trouble. He has been arrested twice for Driving While Intoxicated (DWI) and arrested once for assault after a bar fight. Additionally, Peter's girlfriend recently left him, complaining about his drinking and irresponsible behavior. Peter will admit that he has missed a few Mondays at work because of hangovers. He also began missing clinic appointments and dropped out of sight for 9 months. Peter remains ambivalent about stopping but is back in treatment.

Individuals recovering from SUDs often have difficulty accepting that some people can use psychoactive substances without consequence. Because they were unable to do so, they assume that others cannot as well, or they assume that recreational users will ultimately develop into problem users. While this is possible, it cannot always be assumed to be the case. Experimental and recreational users are not considered to have SUDs and may never progress to that point.

The next stage in the progression of use is known as the stage of *abuse*. We've observed that during this stage, the person may occasionally experience negative consequences associated with the use of the substance. Because the negative consequences only occur intermittently, the person has difficulty admitting to problem use. The person may justify the negative consequences as bad luck or as isolated incidents. Sometimes, the substance abuser actually admits to problem use. The person in this stage may occasionally consume too much of the substance and has to deal with the resulting consequences. The main point is that the person is not regularly experiencing negative consequences of use nor regularly experiencing loss of control and choice over use. Because of this, the person may have more difficulty admitting to the presence of an incipient problem.

The person in this stage usually finds the substance to provide a useful purpose beyond a social one. For instance, the cocaine user may associate cocaine use with an enhanced ability to make effective business presentations. The alcohol user may associate alcohol use with an enhanced ability to cope with the stresses of the household. The sedative user associates use with improved sleeping. In some cases, the benefits of use are not always conscious to the user. Many users cannot explain why they continue to use a substance despite the negative consequences associated with the substance.

The final stage in the progression of use is known as *dependence*. In this stage, the person exhibits signs of needing the substance for physical or psychological relief. There is a loss of control, and the ability to make rational choices—to use

---

Substance Dependence

Mary is a 44-year-old single female living alone. She is employed as an administrative assistant. Her drinking has progressed to the stage of Alcohol Dependence. She has a nightly ritual of visiting the neighborhood liquor store and purchasing a quart of vodka. On weekends she will purchase even more. She drinks in isolation and usually to oblivion. While at work, she thinks about getting home to drink. She has tried to moderate her drinking with little success. Miraculously, she makes it to work most days and is quite productive. There have been complaints by coworkers that she sometimes smells of alcohol, but her boss is too uncomfortable to discuss it with her. Recently she has been complaining of stomach pain and decided to go for a physical exam. The doctor discovered that she is in an early stage of liver damage. She continues to drink despite her medical concerns.

or not to use—becomes more difficult. As consequences emerge, the individual may be more apt to admit to experiencing substance-related problems. Depending on the substance, the person may also become physiologically dependent. At this point the primary reason for using may be to avoid withdrawal symptoms. Pleasure, the original reason for using, becomes elusive.

It should be noted that Substance Abuse does not always lead to Substance Dependence. While we use the word *progression* to underscore the progressive nature of the substance-related problems, it does not necessarily mean that the quantity of the substance ingested has also increased. The quantity (or quality) of problems may increase but the level of consumption may stay the same. A substance abuser that frequently drives a vehicle while under the influence poses a serious problem whenever he or she drinks—even if it occurs infrequently.

Defining the Substance Use Disorders (SUDs)

There was a time in the not-too-distant past when a cookie-cutter approach was used in the treatment of Substance Use Disorders. Even when we provided individual counseling, the message was the same: Your problem is alcoholism or drug addiction, your goal is abstinence, and your success lies in establishing a re-

---

Substance Abuse: *DSM-IV-TR*

A maladaptive pattern of substance use leading to clinically significant impairment or distress, as manifested by *one (or more)* of the following, occurring within a 12-month period:

1. Recurrent substance use resulting in a failure to fulfill major role obligations at work, school, or home (e.g., repeated absences or poor work performance related to substance use; substance-related absences, suspensions, or expulsions from school; neglect of children or household).

2. Recurrent substance use in situations in which it is physically hazardous (e.g., driving an automobile or operating a machine when impaired by substance use).

3. Recurrent substance-related legal problems (e.g., arrests for substance-related disorderly conduct).

4. Continued substance use despite having persistent or recurrent social or interpersonal problems caused or exacerbated by the effects of the substance (e.g., arguments with spouse about consequences of intoxication, physical fights).

The symptoms have never met the criteria for Substance Dependence for this class of substance.

Source. (*DSM-IV-TR*, APA, 2000)

---

lationship with a 12-step program. If the patient did not comply, he or she was deemed unmotivated and needed to hit his or her bottom to get motivated. There was no differential diagnosis attempted. In other words, there was no attempt to assess for an additional diagnosis that might explain why the patient was relapsing, for example, anxiety or depression.

While such a limited treatment approach may work in some cases, it misses all those individuals who need a more comprehensive treatment plan. It ignores the individual treatment needs of not only those who are presenting concurrent psychiatric problems, but also those who simply need an alternative treatment approach.

In today's treatment environment, the more enlightened approach is to individualize treatment through assessment and diagnosis. Although there are likely to be many similarities in treatment plans, it is the individual differences that separate successful outcomes from failures. As in medicine, we are not expected to formulate a treatment plan before we determine exactly what is being treated. And to determine what is being treated, we are likely to depend on what is considered to be the bible of mental-health disorders: the *Diagnostic and Statistical Manual of Mental Disorders (DSM-IV-TR)*. The two sidebars are for Substance Abuse and Substance Dependence. The manual, however, includes every conceivable psychiatric disorder, including those that will often coexist with SUDs, for example, Anxiety Disorders and Mood Disorders.

SUDs fall into two main categories: *Substance Abuse* and *Substance Dependence*. Such categories, while not perfect, provide us with a standard to assess and diagnose patients for SUDs. These criteria necessary to diagnosis or rule out such disorders are taken directly from the *Diagnostic and Statistical Manual of Mental Disorders, fourth edition, text revison* ([*DSM-IV-TR*] American Psychiatric Association, 2000). While Substance Abuse and Substance Dependence are both defined as a "maladaptive pattern of substance use leading to clinically significant impairment or distress" (pp. 197 and 199), the qualifying criteria for each are different. Dependence is viewed as being more advanced than abuse; therefore, its qualifying criteria are greater. And although an earlier diagnosis of abuse can later change to a dependence diagnosis, the reverse is not true. A dependence diagnosis may change to "dependence, in partial remission," but not back to abuse. It's kind of like a pickle—it can never change back to a cucumber! As for the difference between abuse and dependence, dependence is simply more clinically advanced than abuse. This does not mean a less favorable prognosis (treatment outcome), however. In fact—as we will discuss later—a diagnosis of abuse may sometimes be more difficult to treat than a diagnosis of dependence. Other factors, including the behavioral consequences, are at least as important. An individual diagnosed as dependent, for example, may present few problems, while another person diagnosed with abuse might get arrested every time he or she drinks.

A Biopsychosocial and Spritual Disorder

An SUD has biological, psychological, social, and spiritual components directly involved in its development. Some individuals present predominant biological factors leading to Substance Abuse and Substance Dependence, suggesting a physiological predisposition. With others, psychological and social influences may be contributing factors. More typically, individuals with SUDs are likely to present a unique mix of all three factors, forming an etiological basis for such a diagnosis. In other words, this may be a person who began drinking socially, discovered that alcohol also reduced stress, and ignored a family history of substance-related problems. The spiritual influence, a concept more difficult to qualify,

---

Substance Dependence: *DSM-IV-TR*

A maladaptive pattern of substance use, leading to clinically significant impairment or distress, as manifested by *three (or more)* of the following, occurring at any time in the same 12-month period:

1. Tolerance, as defined by either of the following:
   a. A need for markedly increased amounts of the substance to achieve intoxication or desired effect.
   b. Markedly diminished effect with continued use of the same amount of the substance.

2. Withdrawal.
   a. The characteristic withdrawal syndrome for the substance.
   b. The same (or a closely related) substance is taken to relieve or avoid withdrawal symptoms.

3. The substance is often taken in larger amounts or over a longer period than was intended.

4. There is a persistent desire or unsuccessful efforts to cut down or control substance use.

5. A great deal of time is spent in activities necessary to obtain the substance (e.g., visiting multiple doctors or driving long distances), use the substance (e.g., chain-smoking), or recover from its effects.

6. Important social, occupational, or recreational activities are given up or reduced because of substance use.

7. The substance use is continued despite knowledge of having a persistent or recurrent physical or psychological problem that is likely to have been caused or exacerbated by the substance (e.g., current cocaine use despite recognition of cocaine-induced depression, or continued drinking despite recognition that an ulcer was made worse by alcohol consumption).

Source. (*DSM-IV-TR,* APA, 2000).

Self-Medication

> Barbara always thought of herself as a very sensitive person—perhaps a little high-strung. She would have liked to have been more social in college, but parties made her feel anxious. Besides, she didn't drink. At 37 she began to find it difficult to get off to sleep. Her days were becoming more and more stressful for lack of sleep at night. One of Barbara's coworkers suggested she try having a "Hot Toddy" before she went to bed—also suggesting that she double the whiskey in the recipe. It worked—and three jiggers of whisky worked even better! It wasn't long before Barbara also discovered that a couple of fancy drinks in the daytime also helped her to feel more relaxed and less anxious.

may incorporate family values, religion, character, or one's perceived place in the universe. This will be covered in more detail in Chapter 9.

As will be discussed in later sections, the scientific community has been aware for some time that physiological or genetic factors may play a role in the development of SUDs. Exactly what that role is, however, is not fully understood. For example, we are not quite sure which physiological defects or vulnerabilities are actually passed on. Genetic marker studies attempt to link Alcohol Dependence to other traits known to be inherited. Doing so might establish a genetic basis for the disorder. The mapping of the 23 pairs of chromosomes that make up the human genome may soon shed more light on this subject, as well as provide scientific insight into other devastating diseases. Initially, such information will be important to the prevention of SUDs and ultimately lead to improved treatment strategies.

Self-medicate is a term used to describe the practice of using a substance to relieve pain—psychological or physical. Alcohol is such a substance. While the intent may have been to enjoy the pleasure of a social drink, its sedating qualities will also quiet the distressing symptoms of psychiatric conditions that may exist. Similarly, a medication prescribed for back pain might provide a sense of well being long after the pain is gone. What had been prescribed as a short-term remedy for medical trauma is discovered to also alter the mood in a pleasurable way. Psychoactive substances function as coping mechanisms—albeit destructive when misused—to compensate for fragile personality traits. Anxiety, depression, trauma, obsessive-compulsive disorders and social stress are just a few of the types of disorders responsive to a variety of psychoactive substances—legal and illegal. The original intent of the individual may be recreational or medicinal, but the symptomatic relief rendered may drive the individual to misuse the substance.

Social influences include all those factors not identified as physiological or psychological. The individual's environment, both family and nonfamily, plays a role in the development of SUDs. Where heavy drinking is the family norm, the rate of alcohol- or drug-related problems will be higher. In neighborhoods where alcohol and drug use is prevalent, the chance that an individual will experiment and eventually develop a problem is higher. A small town in northern Canada was devastated by the alarmingly high use of mood-altering substances. The abuse and dependence rates topped 75 percent—the adults were addicted to alcohol and the children to "huffing" gasoline and other inhalants.

There seems to be a relationship between substance use and work environments. Some occupations are associated with higher alcohol and drug consumption. Heavy alcohol use and illicit drug use is high among waitstaff, bartenders, and construction workers, while low among technicians and professional specialty workers (SAMHSA, 2005).

Although we are aware of biological, psychological, and social factors influencing SUD development, it is not easy to determine what the primary factor in any given case might be. The evolving understanding of the etiology of SUDs, however, is also aiding in the treatment of other addictive disorders (e.g., gambling, weight loss) and psychiatric disturbances (e.g., Personality Disorders, obsessive-compulsive disorders, Mood Disorders, etc.). And while we do not yet have this down to a science, one of the objectives of this book is to provide readers with a variety of assessment procedures to better help understand such influences.

An SUD is not only caused by biological, psychological, social, and spiritual factors, but it can also damage them. We are aware that SUDs can harm the biological systems of the body (e.g., cardiovascular, gastrointestinal, CNS, etc.). We are also aware of their psychological and social consequences (e.g., causing depression and shame and destroying families). As previously discussed, the pattern of damage caused by the SUDs varies from patient to patient. One person may develop more damage to biological systems; the next may have more psychological damage, while the next will suffer greater social or spiritual consequences. Treatment, to be covered in later chapters, will address such issues.

Because each patient we treat is expected to have a unique mix of these components leading to an SUD, as well as a unique assortment of consequences

Biopsychosocial

Biological: Connected by direct genetic or physical relationship rather than by adoption or marriage

Psychological: Directed toward the will or toward the mind, specifically in its conative function

Social: Of or relating to human society, the interaction of the individual and the group

Spiritual: Of, relating to, consisting of, or affecting the spirit

caused by an SUD, it follows that we need to treat each person uniquely. This is the basis of individualized treatment. Using the same approach for all patients may lead to positive outcomes for some patients, provide little relief for others, and may actually be detrimental to others. By assessing each component separately to determine causative as well as consequential factors, we can begin the process of individualized treatment, thus pinpointing specific areas needing attention.

The Disease Controversy

Merriam-Webster's Collegiate Dictionary (2003) defines *disease* in three ways. First, its synonymous reference is "trouble: to agitate mentally or spiritually." One does not have to look far to find a relationship between "trouble" and an SUD. The second definition is "a condition . . . that impairs normal functioning and is manifested by distinguishing signs and symptoms." The *DSM-IV-TR*'s criteria for SUDs include a definitive set of signs and symptoms. One such criterion is continuing to use in spite of social and interpersonal problems. The third definition is simply "a harmful development."

If we were to use only Webster's definitions, we would have enough information to define an SUD as a disease. Other definitions of disease from various sources include "uneasiness; distress," or a feeling of "dis-ease." We can easily associate SUDs with this definition. It is quite clear that SUDs lead to uneasiness and distress. A disease is also a destructive process in the body, with specific cause(s) and characteristic symptoms. It is clear that the abuse of psychoactive substances can be destructive to the body. Unlike many other medical diseases, the specific cause(s) of SUDs is not yet definitive. However, science has made great strides in understanding the causative factors involved in this disorder.

Disease or not, SUDs are a departure from good health, and the consequential damage is likely to be physical, psychological, and social. As for the spiritual

---

Disease Concept Is Not a New Idea

Benjamin Rush (1746–1813)—a member of the Continental Congress, a signer of the Declaration of Independence, and a physician-general of the Continental Army—suggested that chronic drunkenness was a progressive medical condition. Rush's first professional recognition of the problem of alcohol involved the level of drunkenness among soldiers of the Continental Army—an issue of concern to George Washington as well. In 1777, Rush issued a strong condemnation of the use of distilled spirits, which was distributed to all soldiers. While a fully developed disease concept of alcoholism would not emerge until the 1870s, Rush's writings stand as the first articulation of a disease concept of alcoholism by an American (White, 1998, pp. 1–2).

Spirituality

> One of the great gifts of spiritual knowledge is that it realigns your sense of self to something you may not have even ever imagined was within you. Spirituality says that even if you think you're limited and small, it simply isn't so. You're greater and more powerful than you have ever imagined. A great and divine light exists inside of you. This same light is also in everyone you know and in everyone you will ever know in the future. You may think you're limited to just your physical body and state of affairs—including your gender, race, family, job, and status in life — but spirituality comes in and says "there is more than this."
>
> *Source.* Adapted from *Spirituality for Dummies* (Janis, 2000).

aspect of the damage, many recovering individuals describe themselves as being "spiritually and morally bankrupt" prior to entering treatment. When asked to explain what this meant, they would talk of a deprivation and despair. Some described themselves as stripped of compassion, devoid of goodness, having a loss of empathy, incapable of forgiveness, lacking in understanding, being totally self-involved, selfish, and even evil. One recovering person used the Latin dictum to express her relationship with alcohol: *Spiritus Contra Spiritum,* interpreted to mean, "Alcohol Precludes Spirituality."

Drug addiction and alcoholism are diseases recognized by the World Health Organization and by the medical community at large. However, the notion of an SUD being an illness is still a matter of heated debate in this country. There are two predominant views regarding the causation of SUDs: the *disease model* and the *moral model.* The disease model suggests that a person, without choice, acquires a disease of addiction or alcoholism innately. It is not a learned behavior, but inherited. The disease model assumes that an addict or alcoholic has some defect in the ability to control the use of mood-altering substances. Consequently, addicts and alcoholics who attempt to control their use of such substances are likely to fail. It is assumed to be incurable.

The most prolific resistance to the concept of the disease model is that it absolves the substance user of any responsibility. It is argued that even those who have this inherent defect in the ability to control their substance use still have a responsibility not to use a substance over which they have no control. If a diabetic knows that consuming sugar can be harmful but consumes it anyway, he or she must bear the responsibility of that choice. Individuals who meet the *DSM-IV-TR* criteria for an SUD cannot deny that they initiated the use of the very substance over which they have no control.

Another popular view is that SUDs are self-inflicted bad habits and are based on weaknesses of character or willpower. This has become known as the moral model; substance abusers are viewed as lacking the discipline to resist temptation. This model views intemperance as bad or immoral behavior. It places the onus of responsibility for developing an SUD squarely on the user. This model fails to acknowledge any predisposing factors that may contribute to this disorder.

Because we believe SUDs comprise a variety of causative factors, the term should include elements of the disease model *and* moral model. As previously stated, some people with substance abuse disorders (PSUDs) are predominantly affected by biological or genetic influences leading to the disorder. These individuals seem to have some physiological defect in their ability to control the use of mood-altering substances. Although we have not yet been able to identify these biological defects (due to undeveloped measurement tools for genes and brain chemicals), once discovered they would provide significant credibility to the disease model.

Other individuals, who have never before shown a defect in the ability to control mood-altering substances, are introduced to a new drug and suddenly lose control. For these individuals, the primary cause of their Substance Abuse may be the innate power of a particular substance itself, such as cocaine or heroin. They may, at some point, discontinue the substance that caused the problems and return to nonproblematic use of other mood-altering substances, such as drinking socially, thus refuting the disease model.

Still others seem to lose control in a sporadic fashion. Their substance use does not appear as severe as that of the diseased person. These individuals appear to have more control and choice over their use and, consequently, more responsibility for the negative consequences associated with use. They appear to consciously choose a path of intemperance and the negative consequences associated with that choice. They also appear to more closely resemble the description provided by the moral model. There is no probable single cause or prototype for an SUD. It is the goal of clinicians to assess and identify the unique causative factors for each individual we treat so that we may provide the most effective treatment approach possible.

Treatment in Brief

Addiction Treatment as a Science

Addiction treatment encompasses elements from medicine, psychology, social work, sociology, and spirituality. It is no longer a field of recovering paraprofessionals looking to share their experience, strength, and hope. Those days are long gone. This field is evolving into a science requiring special skills for standardized assessment procedures, skills for diagnosing and treating psychiatric disorders, skills for level-of-care decisions, and an understanding of pharmacological and psychotherapeutic approaches.

Over the last several decades, there has been tremendous growth in the understanding and treatment of SUDs. The primary method of treatment in the past was behavioral (getting patients to conform to a particular way of behaving through positive and negative reinforcement) and often accomplished through

Therapeutic Communities

> Drug-free therapeutic communities (TCs), got their start indirectly through AA. In 1958 Charles E. Dederich, a former AA member, established Synanon in California as a drug-free treatment center for drug addicts. This was an innovative approach, utilizing a powerful encounter component to treat the hard-core drug addict. Other therapeutic communities that followed, including Daytop, Phoenix House, Odyssey House, and Project R.E.T.U.R.N, were also structured on the Synanon model. Therapeutic communities have since modified their treatment approach to meet the needs of the changing drug culture (Scanlon, 1991, p. 13).

humiliating confrontational methods (e.g., in old-style therapeutic communities, wearing signs like "I'm a big crybaby," or receiving harsh punishments for not conforming to house rules). While such approaches were effective in reaching a percentage of PSUDs, those successes were primarily limited to inner-city heroin addicts. Today, we have gained a greater understanding of the biological, psychological, social or environmental, and spiritual components encompassing this disorder, leading to greater treatment effectiveness.

Does Treatment Work?

According to the federal government's Center for Substance Abuse Treatment (CSAT), individuals receiving alcohol and other substance use disorder treatment exhibit a wide range of benefits. These benefits include a decline in criminal activity by two-thirds after treatment, declines of approximately two-fifths in the use of mood-altering substances, a one-third reduction in hospitalizations, and significant improvements in other health indicators (SAMHSA/CSAT, 1993–2004), and this does not even account for the improvements treatment brings to job productivity, mental health, and family.

Common Misconceptions in the Treatment of SUDs

An Addict Is an Addict Is an Addict?

As previously discussed, the causative factors for SUDs are varied. One of the objectives of this book is to provide an understanding of the many causative factors of SUDs and, hence, the variety of ways of treating them. Treating all substance abusers (or addicts) similarly had been an early mistake in our field—a mistake that is, unfortunately, still perpetuated. No two people with substance abuse disorders are exactly the same. They may have similarities, but the causative and consequential factors for each person are unique.

As we now know, there are at least four main factors involved in the development and manifestations of SUDs: biological factors, psychological factors, social or environmental factors, and spiritual factors. In time, we may even identify additional factors. The strength or influence of each of these factors, uniquely combined for each person, produces a multitude of different cases, each needing individualized attention. We had two new intakes in our orientation group that exemplify the importance of individualizing treatment.

Genetic Influences Eddie, a 29-year-old crack addict with a seemingly outgoing personality and a long treatment history, jokingly announced that he was born to a proud family of alcoholics and drug addicts. We were to learn that both his father and grandfather were alcoholics, and his three brothers all had SUDs. Eddie's mother, who he described as an "angel," didn't drink at all.

In spite of the initial impression that Eddie presented, we were also to later learn that the social and psychological consequences of this genetic malady were not a laughing matter. Eddie's father was unavailable emotionally, the numerous physical altercations between Eddie's parents caused personal trauma, and Eddie carried the burden of guilt for not protecting his mother from his father. He said he often felt depressed.

Eddie also talked about other social and emotional consequences of genetic and social influences, including physically abusing his wife and mistreating his children. Raised in a family wrought with drugs and violence, Eddie's choices were no surprise. Eddie's mother, however, had been a regular at Sunday mass. When asked about his own spirituality, he said he feels life has been unfair and suggested that perhaps he had been chosen by God to pay for the sins of his family. Eddie continues in outpatient care and had one relapse early on in his current 13 months of treatment.

Gender Differences Susan, a 45-year-old Caucasian woman with fingers stained from decades of cigarette smoking, presented us with a very different picture. She came to our program seeking continuing care following inpatient treatment for Alcohol Dependence. Susan admitted to developing a tolerance to alcohol, losing control over alcohol use, and being preoccupied with alcohol. She continued to drink despite recurring consequences, including physical and social problems. Susan admitted to consuming as many as two bottles of wine per day, usually drinking alone at home. (Women tend to drink more heavily in solitude, while men drink more heavily in social situations.)

Susan's recent discharge was her second inpatient rehabilitation within a 2-year period of time. She reported having a problem with alcohol for about 19 years and added that she was "taking several medications" for anxiety. At the time of her intake, Susan said she felt very anxious. Her longest period of sobriety ended 5 years ago when she remained alcohol-free for 12 months. Susan denies ever using illicit drugs.

Susan was divorced 4 years ago, and her 29-year-old son lives with her. She describes her relationship with her father as "distant," and her relationships with six siblings—four of them male—not much better. She revealed that her mother, who died 17 years ago, was also an alcoholic. Susan is an office manager and has been with the same company for the past 9 years.

It is not difficult to see the differences in these two individuals. Their genetic and social histories are miles apart; their substance choices are not likely to find them in the same environments; and their gender, age, and collateral problems bear little resemblance. To treat Eddie and Susan using a similar treatment approach would be wrong. These are two cases with very different roots and developing factors. Each of them has different treatment needs and different issues to attend to. While there may be many similarities in their treatment planning, addressing their differences is critical to the likelihood of successful outcomes.

Just Go to Meetings; Motivation Will Follow?

Treatment programs currently emphasize the belief that action steps are necessary for treatment to be effective. Treatment providers emphasize the importance of attending 12-step support groups, obtaining a sponsor at 12-step meetings, making 90 meetings during the first 90 days of sobriety, having aftercare following inpatient treatment, and so on. Treatment programs teach cognitive-behavioral skills to cope with urges and cravings, how to handle difficult emotions, and how to prevent relapse. While these action strategies are valuable for the motivated patient, they are of little use for the patient still ambivalent about discontinuing the use of psychoactive substances.

Treatment providers, as well as managed care companies who demand these services, have not yet become aware that the first and most crucial step toward change is for the patient to develop an internal desire or commitment to change. This step must precede the initiation of action strategies. To begin action steps prior to developing a commitment to change is likely to lead to failure. (This will be explored further in subsequent chapters.) Many clinicians *assume* that their patients are truly committed to change and proceed from that belief. In reality, many patients initiating treatment—possibly the majority—have not sufficiently resolved their ambivalence about changing their substance-using behavior. They still perceive many benefits from their use despite acknowledging consequences attached to continued use. To ignore the patient's conflict (ambivalence) over continued use is to ignore the crux of the problem.

Relapses are often indicators of unresolved ambivalence about sobriety. Rather than being explored, and hopefully resolved, patient relapses are often punished. They are often discharged from treatment programs or cut off from insurance payments by managed care organizations for noncompliance with treatment objectives, for example maintaining continuous sobriety. Even Alcoholics Anonymous (AA)—its success in keeping millions of its members in sobriety notwithstanding—can be hard on those who relapse. It's not that its members aren't supportive of a fellow member that picks up a drink, but length of continuous sobriety is a measure of success in AA, and the relapser must begin counting days again. There is an innate sense of failure in losing the continuous sobriety that

Ambivalence

> Ambivalence is a common human experience and a stage in the normal process of change. Getting stuck in ambivalence is also common, and approach-avoidance conflicts can be particularly difficult to resolve on one's own. Resolving ambivalence can be a key to change, and, indeed, once ambivalence has been resolved, little else may be required for change to occur. However, attempts to force resolution in a particular direction (as by direct persuasion or by increasing punishment for one action) can lead to a paradoxical response, even strengthening the very behavior they were intended to diminish (Miller & Rollnick, 2002, p. 19).

had been achieved. Marlatt calls this the *abstinence violation effect* (Marlatt & Gordon, 1985, p. 41). The failure can be so devastating that it often provides an excuse to continue drinking after a slip.

Many patients enter treatment under duress (e.g., coercion from an employer, spouse, courts, or child protective services). They do not initiate the change process on their own. Consequently, we cannot assume that they are truly motivated for change. However, the assumption that they are is commonly made, and patients are taught skills for remaining sober before they have even reached a sincere commitment to *getting* sober. Even those who voluntarily enter treatment cannot be assumed to have sufficiently resolved their ambivalence about using drugs and alcohol. Ambivalence, in fact, is very much a function of early to middle recovery and an important concept for the treatment professional to be aware of.

More Treatment Is Better than Less?

One's progress in resolving ambivalence toward change is much more important than the quantity of action steps taken prior to resolving the ambivalence. Making the decision to change is more significant than the number of treatment groups one attends or how many consecutive days one attends 12-step meetings. The quality of one's commitment to recovery is more crucial than the steps taken prior to or following that commitment. We have not found, for example, that those who attend an outpatient treatment program four times a week resolve their ambivalence faster than those who attend two times per week. And attending an outpatient program for 3 hours per day is not necessarily more effective than attending for 90 minutes per day. This is not to say that those who attend more treatment groups, or those who attend more 12-step meetings, do not do better than those who attend fewer support groups. We believe they do. However, the reason for their success is based not on the quantity or frequency of services attended but on their degree of motivation for change. Those who voluntarily attend treatment services or support groups more frequently do better because they are simply more motivated and committed to change than those who are not willing to attend as frequently. It becomes the "chicken-or-the-egg" dilemma. Does the higher frequency and duration of support services lead to positive behavioral changes, or are those attending simply more committed to change? The latter is probably true.

Yet in a recent study published in the *Harvard Mental Health Letter* (2003, p. 7), stating one's motivation for change does not necessarily ensure a commitment to change. The authors of the study, McKellar, Stewart, and Humphreys, suggest that "expressed intentions, especially in substance abusers, are not a reliable test of commitment to change behavior." (Based on this study, it might appear that the road to hell is, indeed, paved with good intentions.) The study, which measured the effectiveness of AA, further reported that those in the study who attended 12-step meetings, "whatever their earlier [stated] feelings," such meetings helped *create* that commitment to change (2003, pp. 302–308). While verbally committing to treatment is a good start, following through with action is a true demonstration of motivation.

Inpatient Treatment Is Better than Outpatient Treatment?

It would follow then that a critical factor in treatment effectiveness is not the services per se, but one's level of commitment to change. Inpatient programs are often perceived as leading to greater success toward recovery than outpatient programs. Following discharge from inpatient treatment, however, patients often experience a *pink cloud* period. We have found that they appear fully committed to abstinence and promise to work on their recovery—wholeheartedly. Their resolve is sincere. But this level of confidence has not yet passed the litmus test. That determination to remain clean and sober needs to survive real-world challenges. Without the reinforcement and safety of the inpatient facility, fortitude can quickly change to ambivalence. That high level of motivation begins to wane as the idea of one last high becomes more appealing.

Early recovery's challenges threaten what appears to be a solid grounding in sobriety. But ambivalence—literally, "of two minds"—gives cause to reconsider that earlier resolve. The treatment plan formulated while an inpatient begins to seem less achievable on the street. The commitment to 90 12-step meetings in 90 days is broken, and high-risk situations, by chance or choice, start to emerge. The ambivalence—to use or not to use—becomes lopsided, and the desire to use begins to seem like a good idea.

While any number of factors might impact one's recovery, the concept of ambivalence is the sum of sobriety's pros and cons. It is the vague, nebulous intrusion that emerges in the form of rationalization and justification. The real reason why ambivalence began to appear after discharge is because it was never really resolved—or perhaps never even addressed—while an inpatient. The person was probably taught action strategies for maintaining abstinence from drugs or alcohol but did not understand nor learn how to begin to resolve his or her ambivalence toward change. While relapse-prevention strategies are important to recovery, ambivalence toward change requires ongoing monitoring. Even if the ambivalence of change *had* been the focus of inpatient treatment, it has to be dealt with through ongoing care. Change is the essence of recovery, and resolving ambivalence is the essence of change. For the PSUD, managing ambivalence is critical to managing recovery. No matter how long a person remains at an inpatient facility, ambivalence is an ongoing concern that can be effectively managed only after discharge in an outpatient treatment setting.

Inpatient treatment is necessary when a patient is unable to maintain sobriety without a protective environment. It is also important in stabilizing a medical or psychiatric condition. But such a setting is not a panacea for developing successful sobriety in the ambivalent patient. Ambivalence is resolved through experience, not through education in a protective environment. The educational experience provides a foundation, but the application of positive change in an outpatient setting reinforces recovery. If not outpatient treatment, then a commitment to a 12-step program or some other form of reinforcement will be necessary. This might include a spiritual or a secular program with a focus on lifestyle change.

Effective Treatment Must Include 12-Step Meetings?

Twelve-step meetings include any support groups that utilize the 12 steps originally developed by the founders of AA. These meetings now include support groups for myriad disorders and life problems, from Substance Abuse to baldness. For our discussion, we will be focusing on 12-step meetings that involve SUDs. These include Narcotics Anonymous (NA), Cocaine Anonymous (CA), Marijuana Anonymous (MA), as well as AA meetings.

Before the founding of AA, there was little help available for those whose drinking impacted negatively on their lives. Social services were available for

---

Alcoholics Anonymous

Cofounded by recovering alcoholics William Griffith Wilson (Bill W.) and Robert Holbrook Smith (Dr. Bob) in Akron, Ohio on June 10, 1935, Alcoholics Anonymous is an international fellowship of men and women who have had a drinking problem. It is nonprofessional, self-supporting, multiracial, apolitical, and available almost everywhere. There are no age or education requirements. Membership is open to anyone who wants to do something about his or her drinking problem. In the fall of 1935, a second group of alcoholics slowly took shape in New York. A third appeared in Cleveland in 1939. It had taken over 4 years to produce 100 sober alcoholics in the three founding groups. There are now more than 2 million members throughout the world. In addition, hundreds of other self-help groups have been started on the principles of Alcoholics Anonymous, including Narcotics Anonymous, Cocaine Anonymous, Marijuana Anonymous, and Overeaters Anonymous.

families, but little was done for the family member who had the problem. Family members would pray for the afflicted, and religious conversions often resulted in abstinence, but neither treatment nor self-help groups existed at that time. On June 10, 1935, all of this changed. William Griffith Wilson and Robert Holbrook Smith, members of the Oxford Group, a nondenominational, conservative membership organization, founded the program that became the prototype for all 12-step programs—AA (Kurtz, 1979). Alcoholics Anonymous now has a membership of more than 2 million worldwide and is considered the flagship program of all self-help programs. One might even advance the notion that had it not been for the founding of Alcoholics Anonymous, our advances in treatment and recovery might not have been realized.

While attendance in 12-step meetings is important to initiating and supporting behavioral change, they are not for everybody. The ability to share one's experience, strength, and hope in a meeting does not come easy for many. Some people resist the religious implications of the meetings and the organization's religious underpinnings. There are still others who report that the war stories actually increases their desire to get high. Individuals with more serious psychiatric disorders are often uncomfortable in group settings—individual counseling is almost always indicated before any kind of group activity is considered.

Mandating 12-step meetings is often counterproductive. Forcing individuals to attend AA, NA, or MA against their will is likely to increase their resistance to attending such programs in the future. Courts, employers, and managed care organizations sometimes require attendance as a condition of the individual's probation, employment, or continued insurance coverage. One school of thought is that leveraging individuals—the use of such force—to attend such meetings eventually leads to an acceptance. The adage, "bring your body, the mind will follow," applies to this notion. While this may, at times, be true, it more commonly leads to the reverse effect. Once the coercive force has ended, the person ceases to attend and perceives the experience in a negative way. While this may appear to contradict the Harvard study previously cited, it really doesn't. The Harvard study stated that unmotivated individuals who attended AA meetings eventually developed the motivation to remain sober. Although unmotivated, however, these individuals attended voluntarily and were not *required* to attend.

In the absence of alternatives, such referrals may appear to be appropriate. But the ideal, and perhaps the more effective approach is to refer the individual to a treatment program or addictions specialist that will explore resistance, discuss ambivalence, and motivate the individual toward change. The prospect of becoming substance-free is a daunting one, and the resistance to such an initiative is complex. While abstinence is an achievable goal for most individuals on any given day, continued recovery is a process that begins with a willingness to change. Before such change is possible, the idea of such change has to become feasible. This is the first function of a treatment provider. When the notion of recovery becomes less daunting, the action steps necessary to achieve that goal become possible. If 12-step meetings are to be in the treatment plan, it is here that the individual will be more receptive.

To Work in This Field You Have to Have "Been There"?

A treatment study by the National Institute on Drug Abuse (NIDA) finds a declining trend in both recovering counselors and certified counselors in the field between 1995 and 2001. The study also showed an increase in master's-level counselors during those same years (NIDA, 2001). *Certified counselors,* as defined in this study, are those who are state credentialed or state certified but do not hold a master's-level degree. In most treatment facilities, a recovering counselor without credentialization or certification is usually working toward that goal. While NIDA's findings underscore increasing academic demands to qualify as an SUD counselor, many professionals in the field hold state certification, master's degrees, *and* are themselves recovering.

Being in recovery from an SUD is not essential to being an effective clinician in this field. While having such an experience may serve to establish a unique credibility among patients, it can also be a handicap. Being in recovery without the benefit of education and training above and beyond personal experience may narrow the counselor's treatment perspectives. Recovering clinicians are sometimes limited by their own treatment experience, depriving the patient a full range of possible treatment options better known to the trained and experienced professional. As in any profession, rigid, dogmatic beliefs can be counterproductive to growth. What worked in the counselor's personal treatment may not necessarily be what works in the treatment of his or her patients.

Being an SUD Professional

Self-Disclosure

As for sharing personal experience with the patient, there are no hard and fast rules on this subject. Kinney and Leaton, however, add a cautionary word about the technique of self-disclosure (1991, p. 252). The authors consider self-disclosure to be a *counseling technique* and "as such, it requires the same thoughtful evaluation of its usefulness as any other counseling tool." It may seem only natural to allay some of the client's nervousness or resistance with the news that the clinician has been there and knows how the patient feels. The recovering counselor also becomes proof of successful recovery. But what seems natural, Kinney and Leaton go on to say, "may be totally inappropriate or even countertherapeutic. Therapists need to remember that their *professionalism* is important to the client, particularly in the early days of treatment—that professionalism is comforting" (1991, p. 253).

When the counselor self-discloses appropriately and ethically, it can be a model of hope for the client and become extremely useful (Bissell et al., 2003). On the other hand, it should be very clear to the counselor why he or she believes

Peck on Psychotherapy

We are now able to see the essential ingredient that makes psychotherapy effective and successful. It is not "unconditional positive regard," nor is it magical words, techniques, or postures; it is human involvement and struggle. It is the willingness of the therapist to extend himself or herself for the purpose of nurturing the patient's growth—willingness to go out on a limb, to truly involve oneself at an emotional level in the relationship, to actually struggle with the patient and with oneself. In short, the essential ingredient of successful deep and meaningful psychotherapy is love (Peck, 2003, p. 173).

this action will benefit the client. When self-disclosure is employed, it should be very specific and relevant to current discussion (Bissell et al., 1987–2000). In other words, such action should make a clinical point, by example or reference. Sharing one's experience, strength, and hope is not likely to be of therapeutic value and might even undermine the relationship between the client and the counselor. While the counselor might be well-intentioned, it could be interpreted by the patient as *one-upmanship,* for example, "My story is worse than yours, so why can't you get clean and sober like me?"

Miller and Rollnick state that there could even be a compromise of a counselor's ability to provide "critical conditions of change" because of overidentification (2002, p. 7). If the clinician elects to self-disclose, such action should result in increased credibility, hope, wisdom, or inspiration.

Counselor Prerequisites

In addition to the academic and profession-specific credentials often required to get a job in this field, the SUD professional should possess other qualities. These include a genuine concern for the well-being of others, the ability to consistently manage personal emotions, an openness to new ideas, and the personal discipline to read and keep up with changes in the field. Good communications skills, including speaking and writing, are also important. As for counseling skills, Carl Rogers regarded accurate empathy, unconditional positive regard, and genuineness as more significant than any specific therapeutic techniques (Rogers, 2004). In other words, whatever approach to treatment the counselor embraces, being empathic, respecting the client, and being sincere should never be compromised. M. Scott Peck (2003) takes this one step further. He states that "love," not positive regard, is an essential ingredient of successful deep and meaningful psychotherapy.

Empathy Research indicates that counselor empathy can be a significant determinant of clients' response to treatment (Miller & Rollnick, 2002, p. 7). Empathy includes "such therapist characteristics as warmth, respect, supportiveness, caring, concern, sympathetic understanding, commitment, and active interest" (p. 25). Perhaps empathy can be taught, but for most practitioners in this field it is probably more of an inherent quality. Before starting a career in this field, it might be wise to do a serious self-inventory, preferably with a therapist present, and explore the reasons for choosing this profession—or choosing any helping profession for that matter.

Control of Emotions As discussed in the preceding section, an important personal quality for working in this field is the ability to be even and consistent in our display of emotions. Working with families and individuals with SUDs can be emotional work—frustrating, physically draining, and even anger provoking. Our patients are often emotionally inconsistent and may not have dealt with their true feelings in years—relying on mood-altering substances to avoid the discomfort. Now they are turning to us to provide the emotional consistency they lack. And their ideals and values may not be compatible with those of the SUD counselor. Nevertheless, the counselor must always be respectful, regardless of the patient's beliefs, values, character flaws, and physical or mental disabilities. Being respectful of others and of oneself is a lesson from which even the most challenging patient is likely to learn.

Openness Being open to new ideas is another important quality for the clinician treating addictions. Rigid views and closed-mindedness are always countertherapeutic, limiting the patient's potential for growth and recovery. This field is in a process of perpetual evolution, with scientific and behavioral breakthroughs developing regularly. A clinician who is resistant to change will not grow as a professional and will not remain current on developments in the field. As in any profession, ongoing education is not only recommended, but it is also required in order to maintain clinical certification.

Communications and Organizational Skills Finally, clinicians in this field are required to do a great deal of writing, including chart notes, treatment plans, progress reports, and clinical summaries. They must also discuss cases in clinical team meetings with colleagues and talk with referral sources, community resources, employee assistance programs, and managed care organizations. The ability to communicate effectively on several organizational levels is also important—an often overlooked function that comes with the job. And besides having good communications skills, SUD professionals need to have excellent organizational and time-management skills to stay on top of administrative and paperwork demands, case conferences, and regulatory agency requirements.

With all of its requirements and challenges, or perhaps because of them, this is a profession filled with rewards, opportunities for growth, and advancement. As with any career choice, the question must be asked: Is this the right job for me?

References

Bissell, et al. (1987–2000). In Dual Relationships and Self Disclosure. Essay Database: www.essays.cc Retrieved October 9, 2005.

Boon, M. (2002). *The road of excess.* Cambridge, MA: Harvard University Press.

DSM. (2005). Answers.com. Retrieved October 5, 2005, from www.anserx.com

How effective is Alcoholics Anonymous? (2003, December). *Harvard Mental Health Letter,* p. 7.

Janis, S. (2000). *Spirituality for dummies.* Hoboken, NJ :Hungry Minds/Wiley.

Jonnes, J. (1999). *Hep-cats, narcs, and pipe dreams: A history of America's romance with illegal drugs.* Baltimore: Johns Hopkins University Press.

Kinney, J., & Leaton, G. (1991). *Loosening the grip: A handbook of alcohol information.* St. Louis, MO: Mosby Year Book.

Kurtz, E. (1979). *Not God: A history of Alcoholics Anonymous.* Center City, MN: Hazelden.

Marlatt, G. A., & Gordon, J. R. (Eds.). (1985). *Relapse prevention: Maintenance strategies in the treatment of addictive behaviors.* New York: Guilford.

McKellar, J., Stewart, E., & Humphreys, K. (April 2003). Alcoholics Anonymous involvement and positive alcohol-related outcomes: Cause consequences, or just a correlate? In *How effective is Alcoholics Anonymous?* (December 2003). *Harvard Mental Health Letter, 20,* 7.

Merriam-Webster's collegiate dictionary (11th ed.). (2003). Springfield, MA: Merriam-Webster.

Miller, R, & Rollnick, S. (2002). *Motivational interviewing: Preparing people for change.* New York: Guilford.

National Institute on Drug Abuse. (2001). *Research Grant RO1-DA-13110.* Rockville, MD: NIH-NIDA.

Peck, M. S. (2003). *The road less traveled* (Rev. ed.). New York: Simon & Schuster.

Rogers, C. (June 2004). In What Is Supportive Therapy? *Harvard Mental Health Letter, 20,*(12).

SAMHSA. (2005). [Chart]. Percentage of full-time workers, age 18–49, reporting current illegal drug and heavy alcohol use, by occupation categories, 1994 and 1997. Retrieved October 5, 2005, from www.samhsa.gov

SAMHSA/CSAT. (1993–2004). TIP Series 44. *Substance abuse treatment for adults in the criminal justice system.* Rockville, MD: U.S. Department of Health and Human Services.

Scanlon, W. F. (1991). *Alcoholism and drug abuse in the workplace: Managing care and costs through employee assistance programs.* New York: Greenwood.

White, W. L. (1998). *Slaying the dragon.* Bloomington, IL: Chestnut Health Systems/ Lighthouse Institute.

CHAPTER 2

Understanding Mood-Altering Substances

A Brief History

In 1972, more than 30 years ago, a Consumers Union report stated that the illicit drug scene in the United States was "rapidly becoming intolerable." The report originated 5 years before in an effort to better understand what appeared to be an emerging problem in the United States. It went on to say that heroin, marijuana, LSD, cocaine, amphetamines, and barbiturates had become readily and increasingly available on the illicit market in many parts of the country; the use of illicit drugs, especially by young people, appeared to be increasing year by year (Brecher, 1972, p. ix).

The report was a massive study of the pharmacology, sociology, and history of mind-affecting drugs in our society, including society's legal responses. And while it underscored the seriousness of the problem at that time, it described an

Drug Warfare 1909

Last week the United States Senate passed the Anti-Opium Bill. When it was brought up in the House, immediate consideration was prevented by certain leaders, chiefly because the bill, if passed, would involve a loss in revenue! The bill forbids the importation into the United States, after April 1, 1909, of smoking opium in any form or any preparation or derivative thereof. Opium, other than smoking opium, may be imported for medicinal purposes only, under regulations which the Secretary of Agriculture is authorized to establish. Transgressors of the law are to be punished by the forfeiture of the property and a fine of a sum not exceeding five thousand dollars or less than fifty dollars, or by imprisonment for any time not exceeding two years, or both (Warfare Against, 1909).

earlier era—the nineteenth century—in even graver terms: "dope fiend's paradise." The period affectionately referred to as the *Gay 1890s* might also be known as the unregulated 1890s. Citing that period as a time when mood-altering chemicals were as easily available as aspirin is today, over-the-counter patent medicines often contained opium or morphine. Marketed as treatment for an assortment of maladies including women's problems, coughs, diarrhea, pain, and consumption, these cure-alls included such brand names as Mrs. Winslow's Soothing Syrup, Darby's Carminative, Godfrey's Cordial, McMunn's Elixir of Opium, and Dover's Powder. In fact, one wholesale drug house boasted of more than 600 proprietary medicines and other products containing opiates (Towns, as cited in Brecher, 1972). And while most raw opium was imported from foreign sources, a great deal of it was homegrown. It had been reported that opium from white poppies was cultivated in Massachusetts, Vermont, New Hampshire, Connecticut, Florida, Louisiana, California, and Arizona (Hays, as cited in Brecher, p. 4). Opium was also produced in the Confederate states, including Virginia, Tennessee, South Carolina, and Georgia, during and perhaps after the Civil War (Culbrith, as cited in Brecher, p. 4).

Drug use during the middle of the twentieth century may have been "rapidly becoming intolerable," but reported drug use during the nineteenth century is almost unbelievable. Although much of the credit for reducing drug accessibility can be attributed to laws, regulations, and controls implemented during the early decades of the twentieth century, such laws also served to disguise the problem. Where the medical community used to manage addiction problems, the new laws, as important as they were, changed the problem of addiction to a criminal justice problem. The Pure Food and Drug Act of 1906, the first such law, was for preventing the manufacture, sale, or transportation of adulterated or misbranded or poisonous or deleterious foods, drugs, medicines, and liquors, and for regulating traffic therein, and for other purposes. Prior to this law, makers of food and drug products were not required to list their ingredients (Brecher, p. 47).

The Harrison Narcotics Tax Act of 1914, the second most important law, was (is) "An Act to provide for the registration of, with collectors of internal revenue, and to impose a special tax on all persons who produce, import, manufacture, compound, deal in, dispense, sell, distribute, or give away opium or coca leaves,

---

Drug Use in the Workplace

The 2003 survey findings show that more than three-quarters of adults who have a serious substance abuse problem are employed, which challenges the stereotype that the typical drug user is poor and unemployed. More specifically, of the 19 million adults age 18 and older characterized with a serious alcohol or drug problem in 2003, 77 percent—or 14.9 million people—were employed either part time or full time (SAMHSA News, 2004).

their salts, derivatives, or preparations, and for other purposes." In plain English, the act, under penalty of law, no longer allowed a vendor to lawlessly "sell, barter, exchange, or give away" the aforementioned substances (Brecher, p. 49).

In all fairness, the extent of addiction at the turn of the century was far beyond the control of the medical community. Governmental involvement was probably necessary. But such involvement was also the beginning of what was to become a vast criminal enterprise involving the import, manufacture, sale, and use of mood-altering substances. As the legal availability of psychoactive substances began to diminish, new illegal channels of distribution began to emerge. Also, the science of psychopharmacology began to play an important part in the development of exciting new ways to reach altered states of consciousness never before possible.

Today's concern with the use of mood-altering substances is different from both that of the *intolerable* 1970s and *unregulated* 1890s. Based on both anecdotal and government reports, it would appear that experimental users are younger now than they were at any time in our history. And the potential availability of mood-altering substances has also changed. While foreign importation, domestic cultivation, and regional processing plants were more than adequate to flood the marketplace with an assortment of drugs in the past, today's kitchen and trailer park laboratories have introduced a new array of mood-altering possibilities never before possible. While the pharmacological classifications of the drugs have remained constant over the decades, the range and variety of designer drugs and club drugs have grown. And although poly-drug use has always been a concern, the combinations of drugs used today are far more creative. Combining such drugs as Viagra and ecstasy (referred to as *hammer-heading* because of the pounding headache it can cause) to produce a feeling of well-being without compromising sexual performance is one such recipe.

The Legal Classifications of Psychoactive Substances

The Drug Enforcement Administration (DEA), an agency of the U.S. Department of Justice established in 1973, has the primary task of attempting to reduce the supply of illicit drugs produced domestically or entering the United States from abroad. The DEA also regulates the legal trade in narcotic and dangerous drugs, manages a national narcotics intelligence system, and works with other agencies to support drug traffic prevention.

The agency, under the Comprehensive Drug Abuse Prevention and Control Act of 1970, established a schedule that qualified drugs according to their perceived potential for abuse and the danger in their use. The ranking from *one* (being the most dangerous) to *five* (the least dangerous) also changed the requirements for writing prescriptions—the higher the number, the less paperwork involved. Drugs that are on schedule 1, according to this system, are not only dangerous but are also illegal and cannot be manufactured, sold, or prescribed

Schedule of Drugs

- Schedule I: High potential for abuse. No current medical use. (Heroin, methaqualone, cocaine, marijuana).
- Schedule II: High potential for abuse. (Narcotics, amphetamines).
- Schedule III: Some painkillers (OxyContin, hydrocodone).
- Schedule IV: Benzodiazepines (Valium, Xanax, Librium).
- Schedule V: Other prescription drugs.

Source. Comprehensive Drug Abuse Prevention and Control Act of 1970.

for any medical purpose. Heroin and cocaine, for example, are schedule 1 drugs. There are few exceptions to this law, one being the continued exploration of such drugs for research purposes.

Federal Analog Act of 1986

Prior to the passing of this law, *designer drug* control was beyond the reaches of the law. Possession of drugs that were different in chemical structure, even just slightly, from known controlled substances was not considered illegal. Drugs like ecstasy, for example, were legal. The Federal Analog Act of 1986 was passed to address this serious oversight. Section 203 of this law states that, "A controlled substance analogue shall, to the extent intended for human consumption, be treated, for the purposes of this title [Title I: Enforcement] and title III ["Interdiction"] as a controlled substance in schedule 1." The law addresses a chemical compound that is structurally similar to another but differs slightly in composition (as in the replacement of one atom by an atom of a different element).

Under provisions of the Federal Analog Act of 1986, the DEA was granted powers that effectively allowed the agency to outlaw every designer drug on the street, including those not yet created. While this law appears to be a good idea, not everyone was or is happy about it. The law, in fact, triggered a storm of protests—from legal chemists, who felt it restricted their research, and from behavioral therapists, who saw promise in the then-legal designer stimulant methylenedioxymethamphetamine (MDMA), better known as ecstasy, as a tool in or adjunct to therapy. This debate continues as of this writing.

Drug Classifications and Their Importance

Humans have found ways to alter their mood since the beginning of recorded time. Evidence of fields harvested for marijuana date back to 4,500 B.C.E., and coca chewing (coca is the plant from which cocaine is derived) has been around more than 5,000 years. Opium, the cause of wars between England and China, is one of the oldest drugs known to man. If history is a predictor of the future, it is likely that the search for altered states of consciousness will always be with us. People have both enjoyed and suffered in their pursuit of such substances and probably always will.

As history shows, the U.S. government has played an active role in its attempt to manage the problem through laws and sanctions. Its first efforts date back more than 100 years, and current policies are shaped by existing legislation—historic and new. While discussion on the pros and cons of specific policies might be a lively read, such discussion is beyond the scope of this book.

What is important for those in the field of chemical addiction, however, is a working understanding of drug classifications. Why? First, those treating SUDs need to stay on top of the names and effects of different substances as they are introduced to the marketplace. To both organize and make drug names easier to remember, mood-altering substances are divided into categories or classes along with those producing similar effects. For example, substances that relax are placed into one classification and those that excite are placed into another. Second, understanding the effects of each substance may help us to understand why a person chooses a particular substance as his drug-of-choice. Third, understanding the effects of intoxication and potential side effects of each substance greatly improves our assessment acumen. With this knowledge, addiction professionals can quickly identify symptoms and behaviors associated with one or any combination of substances. Also, such an understanding will provide the addiction professional with the ability to quickly know when medical detoxification is necessary as well as withdrawal symptoms that might be expected.

General Classifications of Psychoactive Substances

Psychoactive substances are chemicals that have specific effects on the mind, usually in the dimension of altering mood. Most substances that are abused are mood-altering. They usually affect the mental state of the person ingesting them. One is not likely to see BenGay addicts entering treatment programs because BenGay is an ointment without mood-altering qualities. Psychoactive substances are often categorized by their prevalent mood-altering qualities. Because many of these substances have similarities with other substances, they are not universally categorized in the same way. We've divided these psychoactive substances into several distinct classes endorsed by the National Institute on Drug Abuse (NIDA; 2000):

- Depressants
- Stimulants
- Opioids and Morphine Derivatives
- Hallucinogens
- Cannabinoids

- Dissociative Anesthetics
- Anabolic Steroids
- Inhalants

Depressants or Sedative Hypnotics

Depressants are a class of substances that promote a relaxed state of mind. This category includes alcohol, sedatives, hypnotics, and other anxiolytics. *Alcohol,* found in beverages such as beer, wine, and liquor, is technically known as *ethyl alcohol.* Ethyl alcohol is the most common depressant used in our society. Sedatives derive their meaning from the word *sedate,* meaning calm, quiet, or composed (Webster's, 2001). Sedatives are also known as *tranquilizers.* The most commonly used sedatives or tranquilizers on the market today are called benzodiazepines. These include Valium, Xanax, Ativan, Librium, and Halcion. Physicians commonly prescribe benzodiazepines for the relief of anxiety.

The term *hypnotics* is derived from its root, *hypno,* meaning "to sleep." They are used medically as sleeping pills. The most common hypnotics fall into a group of substances known as *barbiturates.* Barbiturates are medications usually ending in the suffix *al.* Barbiturates include Phenobarbital, Seconal, Tuinal, Nembutal, and Amytal. Other depressants include gamma-hydroxybutyrate (GHB), known on the street as *G, liquid ecstasy,* (although having nothing in common with the drug known as ecstasy), and *grievous bodily harm.* Rohypnol (flunitrazepam), known on the street as *roofies* or *forget-me pill,* and GHB have been associated with sexual assaults due to their sleep-inducing, depressant qualities and potential for memory loss. When used for this purpose, they are usually slipped into the drinks of unsuspecting victims.

To understand how depressants at higher levels of intoxication affect a person, we will present alcohol intoxication as the example. Low levels of depressants generally lead to *relief from anxiety.* Higher dosages result in a state of *disinhibition.* Disinhibition allows the usually reserved, shy, or inhibited person begin to shed inhibitions and act in an uncharacteristic manner. For instance,

Stages of Intoxication: Depressants

Relief from anxiety: A general feeling of well-being

Disinhibition: Little concern with what others think

Muscle relaxation: Slurring and loss of coordination

Memory impairment: Hazy recall and blackouts

Sleep: Natural cutoff—"You've had enough."

Anesthesia: Only in emergencies

Coma: The stage before death

this state leads a bashful person to approach the opposite sex, leads the passive person to become very assertive, and causes the usually quiet and reserved person to become loud and boisterous. The next significant effect of higher doses of alcohol is *muscle relaxation*. Because of the muscle relaxation, one's coordination also becomes impaired. During this state of intoxication, the individual may begin slurring words due to muscle relaxation. The next stage of intoxication leads to *memory impairment*. The parts of the brain controlling memory retention seem to be affected, at least temporarily. This is the stage when blackouts occur, which lead to brief lapses in memory that can be minutes or days long. The next level of alcohol intoxication produces *sleep*—the body's natural cutoff system to communicate that you have had enough. (Individuals who have ingested large quantities of alcohol prior to falling asleep may actually be getting more intoxicated while sleeping.)

The liver can only process a finite amount of alcohol per hour. If a person has consumed a large amount of alcohol in a short period of time, it must sit in the stomach until the liver is able to process it. The liver can only process 1 ounce of pure ethyl alcohol per hour. (One drink is usually measured as 12 ounces of beer, 5 ounces of wine, or 1.5 ounces of 80-proof liquor.) If large quantities of alcohol are consumed just *prior* to falling asleep, the blood-alcohol level will continue to rise, and intoxication will increase while sleeping. The next level of alcohol intoxication is the stage of *anesthesia*. During the Civil War, if anesthetics were not available during a surgical procedure, alcohol was used as an anesthetic. However, using alcohol as an anesthetic is very dangerous because too much can lead to the next level of intoxication—*coma*. At high doses, the combination of alcohol and depressants can lead to coma. Karen Ann Quinlin, the comatose woman who fueled a national controversy in 1976 on the proper time to pull the plug, had ingested such a fatal mix. She went into a coma and was placed on a respirator after ingesting alcohol and barbiturates, never to regain consciousness. The final level of depressant intoxication is *death*. The part of the brain controlling breathing stops functioning, leading to death.

Tolerance and Withdrawal Several other important points need to be mentioned regarding the use of depressants. First, depressants is one of only two classes of substances that can lead to physiological dependence, the other being opioids. Physiological dependence involves two criteria, *tolerance* and *withdrawal*. *Tolerance* is defined as "a need for markedly increased amounts of the substance to achieve intoxication or the desired effect" (APA, 2000; p. 197). Looking at it from another perspective, tolerance is defined as "markedly diminished effect with continued use of the same amount of the substance" (p. 197). For instance, the individual who used to get a desired effect from drinking two beers now needs three beers to get the same result. Another example is the person who needed one sleeping pill for sleep and now requires two sleeping pills. The second criterion for physiological dependence is *withdrawal*. *Withdrawal* consists of a characteristic withdrawal syndrome in the absence of the substance or the need to

Biological Basis of Chemical Addiction

All mood-altering drugs with abuse potential acutely enhance brain-reward mechanisms. "Getting high" is just such an enhancement. Neuronal circuits deep in brain (limbic system), including medial forebrain bundle and nucleus accumbens, are critical in expression of reward. Limbic-directed functions include eating, avoiding being eaten, and reproducing. These are essential functions necessary for survival. The addict, in search of his drug, is attempting to avoid "being eaten." He is attempting to survive. While *survival* may have a different meaning today than it once had, humans have brought predation to profound levels of complexity and efficiency. Pleasure and survival are two sides of the same coin. In other words, the human brain has a pleasure center—including groups of cells that mediate mood and well-being. Various drugs act on different levels of this circuitry. For the addict, *getting high* and *survival* are synonymous.

take a substance to avoid withdrawal symptoms. For depressants, characteristic signs of mild to moderate withdrawal include tremor, anxiety, nausea, insomnia, sweating, and increased pulse rate. Severe withdrawal includes delirium, dementia, psychotic disturbance, grand mal seizures, and possibly death. It is also worth noting that an alcohol hangover is considered a mild form of alcohol withdrawal.

Synergistic Effect The second point about depressants is that they have an additive effect—or a synergistic effect—meaning any combination of depressants increases, sometimes exponentially, the overall potency. As in the Karen Ann Quinlin tragedy previously mentioned, combining alcohol with other substances significantly increased the overall effect of both drugs, leading to a dangerous and, in this case, lethal dose. Even alcohol alone at high levels, for example, may lead to loss of consciousness, coma (chances of possible brain damage), and death from respiratory shut down.

In addition to having a potentially fatal effect during intoxication, depressant withdrawal can also be potentially fatal. Agitation, fever, and life-threatening convulsions may occur in severe cases. Third, as with all classes of substances discussed, the depressants are also psychologically addictive. All mood-altering substances can lead to a psychological dependence. A psychological dependence is exhibited through obsession, compulsion, and strongly held beliefs about the importance of these substances in one's life.

Stimulants

Stimulant drugs have the opposite effect of depressants; they excite rather than relax, increasing brain and psychomotor activity. Such drugs include, but are not limited to, cocaine, methamphetamine, MDMA, amphetamine, caffeine, nicotine, and other substances.

Primate Social Strata Determine Cocaine Addiction

Monkeys at the bottom of the social dominance hierarchy are more prone to cocaine addiction, say researchers. But they caution against making direct comparisons with humans.

"The positive spin on our findings is that enriching the environment can produce large and robust changes in the brain," says Michael Nader at Wake Forest University. "These lower the propensity for using drugs."

But he rejects the simplistic interpretation that the changes he has identified might underlie any link between cocaine use and social exclusion in humans.

Dopamine is a chemical messenger that is released at junctions between nerves. The pathway transmits pleasure and pain sensations and is directly affected by drugs such as cocaine and ecstasy, which boost dopamine levels.

The monkeys were trained to self-administer cocaine. While both dominants and subordinates used the drug, only the subordinate monkeys became addicted (Nader, 2002).

Cocaine Cocaine is a powerful stimulant. Known in its pure form as cocaine hydrochloride, it can be either inhaled (snorted through the nose) or smoked in a more pure and potent form known as *crack* or *freebase*.

Methamphetamine Methamphetamine is commonly known on the street as *speed, crystal meth, crank,* and *ice*. Methamphetamine can be used in pill form, snorted, smoked, or injected. It is longer acting than cocaine.

MDMA Methylenedioxymethamphetamine, or MDMA, is a substance that continues to grow in popularity among younger adults. It has many street names including *ecstasy, X, XTC, E, M, Adam, Bean,* and *Roll*. Methyl-enedioxymethamphetamine can cause mild hallucinogenic effects in addition to the usual expected effects of a stimulant.

Amphetamine Amphetamines, including Dexedrine and Biphetamine, are similar in chemical structure to methamphetamine but usually less potent. Its street names, both current and past, include *Dex, Uppers, Bennies,* and *Black Beauties*. Amphetamines were commonly used for diet pills because of their appetite suppressant qualities until they were discovered to have mood-altering qualities—and the potential for psychological dependence.

Methylphenidate Another common stimulant is methylphenidate, or Ritalin, a medication used for the treatment of Attention-Deficit/Hyperactivity Disorder (ADHD). In recent years, several alternatives to Ritalin have emerged. While there was some fear that such drugs might find their way to the black market and be sold illegally, its limited "get high" qualities also limited its potential for abuse.

Caffeine Caffeine is also a commonly used stimulant, with mild potency, often overlooked in discussions about stimulants. Based on our current criteria defin-

Caffeine: Drug of Abuse?

> The widespread use of culturally sanctioned caffeine-containing foods presents an intriguing paradox. On one hand, it is the experience of most regular caffeine users that caffeine produces only rather subtle effects that are generally so well woven into the fabric of daily experience that they are not clearly differentiated from the changes in mood and behavior associated with normal experience. On the other hand, caffeine is arguably the most robust form of drug self-administration known to man (Griffiths & Mumford, 2000).

ing SUDs, caffeine can be abused, and dependency can also develop. It may cause withdrawal symptoms (mostly headaches) after cessation of heavy use, and regular users develop tolerance and experience cravings when ceasing use. Regular users can also become emotionally and mentally dependent upon their daily caffeine (coffee, soda, etc.). Some recent studies suggest that coffee and tea in moderation may have some therapeutic value. Caffeine tablets are commonly sold in over-the-counter products and can be found in various medications.

Nicotine Another substance often overlooked in discussions about stimulants, despite its popularity and high incidence of disease-producing fatalities, is nicotine. Nicotine, commonly associated with relaxation, is often overlooked as a stimulant. It is the primary chemical in tobacco and is believed to be involved in the death of more than 430,000 U.S. citizens per year—more than alcohol, cocaine, heroin, homicide, suicide, car accidents, fire, and AIDS combined. Tobacco use is the leading preventable cause of death in the United States. The National Cancer Institute (NCI) reports that among current smokers, 57 percent of all male deaths and nearly 50 percent of all females deaths are attributed to smoking (NCI, 1997). The National Institute on Drug Abuse states that smoking accounts for one-third of all cancers, including cancers of the lungs, mouth, pharynx, larynx, esophagus, stomach, pancreas, cervix, kidney, ureter, and bladder, as well as its association with lung diseases and coronary heart diseases (NIDA, 1998).

Stimulants are used medically to treat ADHD, obesity, and narcolepsy. Recreationally, stimulants are used to heighten alertness, sharpen awareness, decrease fatigue, increase wakefulness, lengthen attention span, and lead to the mental state known as *euphoria* (a state of well-being, exhilaration, buoyancy, and vigor). In high doses, stimulants can lead to insomnia, anxiety, restlessness, hypervigilance, heart failure, and stroke. With overdose, stimulants can lead to psychotic symptoms, including paranoid delusions (e.g., "The police are after me.") and auditory hallucinations.

Stimulants are highly addictive psychologically, leading potentially to an insatiable appetite for more. Cocaine, a most potent stimulant as previously stated, is especially likely to cause psychological dependence. Individuals dependent on cocaine will go to great lengths for more. This psychological dependence can also be found in many animal studies involving cocaine administration. Monkeys given the choice between food, sex, and cocaine almost invariably choose cocaine. Studies performed with mice show they will continue running across an electrified grid to get more doses of cocaine. As the voltage of the grid is increased, mice will continue to brave higher electrical shocks for more cocaine, even to the point of electrocution.

There has been controversy over whether stimulants can lead to physical dependence. Some researchers claim that stimulants lead to tolerance, as evidenced by wanting increasing amounts of the substance while using it. Others suggest that the insatiable appetite for stimulants is technically not tolerance because the person does not automatically need increasing amounts to get the same effect on subsequent occasions of use. For example, a regular sedative user may eventually need higher amounts of sedatives to get the desired effect following days of use. The stimulant user does not need increased amounts on following days of use. They choose to continue using heavy amounts of stimulants at one sitting due to compulsion rather than tolerance. The same controversy applies to withdrawal symptoms and stimulants. Some researchers suggest that stimulant dependence does not produce withdrawal. Other researchers suggest that, although the withdrawal symptoms are not affecting physical states (e.g., body tremor, nausea, diarrhea), stimulant withdrawal affects the parts of the brain controlling psychological processes leading to depression, anxiety, fatigue, paranoia, and aggression when the substance is discontinued.

In our role as substance treatment professionals, we believe the line that divides physical and psychological dependence is not always clear. The withdrawal symptoms of each are subjective, and the degree of suffering that an addict may be experiencing can be underreported or grossly exaggerated. While there are some physical signs of withdrawal that can be visually observable, such as tremors, diarrhea, or vomiting, other symptoms, such as muscle ache, anxiety, and depression, cannot easily be determined with certainty through observation. And although stimulant withdrawal symptoms, such as extreme craving, acute anxiety, and depression, are perceived as psychological, they are experienced physically. Such withdrawal symptoms are *not* felt just above the neck but are, in fact, communicated throughout the body by way of the brain, spinal cord, sympathetic nervous system, and parasympathetic nervous system. Emotional distress *is* emotional pain. The brain and spinal cord are all part of the same complex that we call a person. Pain, whether it is emotional or physical, is experienced both emotionally and physically. The discontinuation of a mood-altering chemical is always a painful experience, whether the pain is driven by physical withdrawal or emotional dependence.

Opioids and Morphine Derivatives

Opioids Opioids, also known as opiates or narcotics, are generally used for the relief of physical pain. Some clinicians suggest that opioids are also effective for treating emotional pain. The term *opioid* comes from the word *opium,* a natural substance taken from certain varieties of the poppy plant. Incidentally, poppy seeds—the kind often used to garnish baked bread products—are closely related to poppy plants. In some instances, eating poppy seeds prior to a urine toxicology screen may test positive for opioids. As for mood-altering qualities, there are none—except, perhaps, for the pleasure of biting into an oven-fresh bagel or kaiser roll.

Opium, in its pure form, is not commonly used in this country. Chemists have been able to develop more powerful opioids by adding other chemicals to it (semisynthetic opioids). A common semisynthetic opioid includes heroin (one of the most potent opioids). Chemists have also been able to produce completely synthetic forms of opioids such as Codeine, Fentanyl, Demerol, Methadone, Dilaudid, Percocet, and Percodan.

Opioids are used medically as analgesics, anesthetics, antidiarrheal agents, and cough suppressants. Besides their medical uses, opioids can also lead to a state of euphoria, including a sense of calm and tranquility. Opioids can be administered through injection, swallowed in pill form, snorted, and smoked.

Opioids are highly addictive and can lead to both a psychological and physical dependence (i.e., tolerance and withdrawal). Signs of withdrawal include restlessness, insomnia, nausea, diarrhea, muscle aches, vomiting, and fever. A common misconception about withdrawing from opioids is that it is potentially fatal. Opioid withdrawal, although painful and uncomfortable, is not life threatening, as found with the depressants. Signs of intoxication on opioids include sedation, slurred (but different from drunk) speech, constricted pupils, staggering gait (nodding), and nausea. Signs of overdose include confusion, respiratory depression and arrest, unconsciousness, and coma.

History of the Poppy

The lore of the opium poppy can be traced back to the oldest records of human history. Originally, the plant was native to the Eastern Mediterranean. It was domesticated and spread throughout Europe during the Neolithic (Stone) Age. Ancient texts on herbalism, referring to *poppy tea,* document the plant's usage during this time period. Opium was well known to the Greek, Roman, Mesopotamian, and Assyrian cultures. Amazingly, it was unknown in ancient China and India. Opium's popularity in these countries (and later in Western countries) is a comparatively recent development (Allen, 2000).

Contempt for Drugs

> And now acknowledge this principle, which is the sole justification for the taste for drugs: what users ask for, consciously or unconsciously from drugs, is never these dubious sensual delights, this hallucinatory proliferation of fantastic images, this sensual hyperacuity, stimulation, or all the other nonsense which those who know nothing about "artificial paradises" dream about. It is solely and very simply a change of state, a new climate where their consciousness will be less painful.

(Gilbert-Lecomte, as cited in Boon, 2002, pp. 68, 69)

Hallucinogens

Hallucinogens, also known as psychedelics, alter sensory perception and are generally used as mind expanders. They may increase alertness, vividness, and clarity at low doses but also lead to mental confusion, paranoia, disorientation, and psychotic disturbance (e.g., delusions and hallucinations) in high doses. Hallucinogens can be both natural and synthetic. Naturally produced hallucinogens are generally milder than synthetically manufactured ones. Naturally produced hallucinogens include mescaline (i.e., peyote, buttons, mescal, and cactus) and psilocybin (i.e., magic mushrooms). One of the most powerful synthetic hallucinogens is lysergic acid diethylamide (LSD). Lysergic acid diethylamide is also known as *acid, blotter, sunshine, microdot,* and a host of other brand names.

There are no current medical uses for hallucinogens. They are used only for recreational purposes. Besides the altered state of sensory perception, these drugs can lead to nervousness, sleeplessness, loss of appetite, numbness, tremors, weakness, and *rehabituation*—a word that has entered the lexicon describing when the familiar experience becomes a novel experience. Former LSD users also report *flashbacks* when not using the drug—a reliving of an exciting moment of revelation or dread.

Cannabinoids

Cannabinoids are substances that include the psychoactive chemical delta-9-tetrahydrocannabinol (THC). Cannabinoids include the substances marijuana and hashish. Both substances come from the hemp plant known as *Cannabis sativa.* Marijuana and hashish are usually smoked but can also be eaten or drunk in special brews. Hashish, also known as *hash,* is usually more potent than marijuana (due to higher levels of THC) and is made from the dried, caked resin of the hemp plant flower. It is generally smoked in pipes. Marijuana, also known as *pot, grass, weed, reefer,* and *herb,* is a mixture of dried flower buds and leaves from the hemp plant. According to the New York State Office of Alcoholism and Substance Abuse Service, it is the most widely used illicit drug in the country

(OASAS, 2005). Marijuana is smoked in pipes or rolled into cigarettes known as *joints.* Growing in popularity is smoking marijuana *blunts,* which are cigars that have been emptied of tobacco and refilled with marijuana, sometimes in combination with another drug, such as crack cocaine (NIDA, 2004). Federal and local law enforcement crackdowns impact the availability of marijuana. To make up for decreasing supplies, creative methods to increase potency have emerged. Hydroponically grown marijuana, for example, is marijuana produced with a process that can produce very high THC levels—marijuana's psychoactive chemical. Such innovation raises not just the potency but also the price.

In low doses, cannabinoids act similar to the depressants, producing sedation, euphoria, a feeling of well-being, and elation. At higher doses, they act more like hallucinogens, leading to an altered sensory perception, particularly of distance and time. For some users, marijuana can have adverse reactions ranging from mild anxiety to panic and paranoia (OASAS, 1999). Marijuana has been found to be effective medically in the treatment of glaucoma and as an antinausea medication following chemotherapy treatment. The use of marijuana for medical reasons is currently being debated in the Supreme Court. Regular marijuana use has been associated with signs of physiological dependence, including tolerance and withdrawal (irritability, sleep disturbance, and increased anxiety). Regular use of marijuana has also been associated with respiratory problems, impaired memory and learning, a decrease in motivation and drive levels, and lower testosterone levels in males.

Dissociative Anesthetics

Dissociative anesthetics get their name from their ability to disrupt functions of consciousness, memory, and perception, similar to Dissociative Disorders (e.g., amnesia, fugue, and depersonalization), as well as their ability to produce the feeling of being numbed (anesthetic) and outside of one's body (dissociative). They include the substances phencyclidine (PCP) and ketamine (Ketalar SV).

Phencyclidine (PCP) Phencyclidine (PCP), also known as *angel dust,* is an anesthetic developed in the 1950s but discontinued in 1965 because of its problematic side effects. Phencyclidine is a white powder that can be snorted, swallowed as a pill, or smoked. When smoked, it is applied to leafy material such as mint, marijuana, or oregano (NIDA, 2004). It is used for its sedating and out-of-body effect. Users of PCP report feelings of strength, power, invulnerability, and a numbing effect on the mind. Although PCP is not known to lead to physiological dependence, it is psychologically addictive. High doses of PCP can cause seizures or coma, and can mimic psychotic symptoms such as delusions and hallucinations. Phencyclidine overdose has also been associated with violent behavior and suicide. Chronic use of PCP can lead to cognitive impairment, such as memory loss and difficulties with speech and thinking. There seems to be a high incidence of PCP use among individuals with psychotic disturbances.

The Cranberry Myth

It was once believed that PCP use *caused* long-term psychotic disturbance. PCP users were often told to drink cranberry juice to remove the lingering effects of PCP use. Where this remedy originated is a mystery to us. Cranberry juice had no effect on removing the psychotic disturbance found in these individuals. It was eventually realized that some people with Psychotic Disorders seem to have a special affinity for PCP. While we know that PCP intoxication can mimic a psychotic disturbance, it also appears that individuals with Psychotic Disorders seem particularly drawn to PCP use. So it appears that PCP, rather than causing long-term psychotic behavior, is particularly attractive to individuals who may already be psychotic. The reason for this attraction remains unclear. As for the cranberry juice, it does nothing for psychosis but does have nutritional value—and it tastes good, too.

Ketamine Ketamine, also known as *K, Special K,* or *cat Valiums,* is another dissociative anesthetic gaining popularity in the club scene. It was originally created as a human anesthetic but frequently used as an animal tranquilizer, thus the street name cat Valiums. Ketamine is a liquid that can be transformed into white powder for snorting, smoking, or injecting. At low doses it produces mild, dreamy, out-of-body sensations. At higher doses, it acts more like a hallucinogen. High doses can lead to delirium, depression, respiratory depression, and respiratory arrest. When mixed with depressants, such as alcohol, sedatives, or hypnotics, it can become potentially fatal. Ketamine is highly addictive psychologically (DanceSafe, 2005).

Anabolic Steroids

Anabolic steroids are synthetic substances related to the male hormones (androgens). They promote the growth of skeletal muscle (anabolic effects), the development of male sexual characteristics, increased energy, and a state of euphoria (NIDA notes, 2000). Anabolic steroids have been used primarily to improve performance in sports, especially bodybuilding (weightlifting). There are more than 100 different types of anabolic steroids available. Because they require a prescription in the United States, most steroids taken are illegal and used without medical monitoring. Some of the more commonly abused oral steroids include Anadrol (oxymetholone) and Oxandrin (oxandrolone). Injectable steroids are Deca-Durabolin (nandrolone decanoate) and Durabolin (nandrolone phenpropionate).

Steroid use disrupts the normal production of hormones in the body, causing both reversible and irreversible changes (NIDA notes, 2000). It has been associated with reduced sperm production, shrinking of the testicles, baldness, masculinization of the female body, breast development in men, acne, heart attacks, strokes, and liver cancer. Psychologically, anabolic steroid abuse has also been associated with aggressive behavior, mood swings, distractibility, forgetfulness, and confusion. Withdrawal from anabolic steroids has also been associated with mood swings, fatigue, restlessness, loss of appetite, insomnia, and reduced sex drive (NIDA notes, 2000).

Inhalants

Inhalants are volatile solvents that produce chemical vapors inducing psychoactive, mind-altering, experiences (NIDA, 2000). These substances are almost always inhaled. Inhalants are divided into four general categories: volatile solvents, aerosol, gases, and nitrates. *Volatile solvents* are liquids that vaporize at room temperature. They include products commonly used for household and industrial purposes, such as paint thinners and removers, dry-cleaning fluids, degreasers, gasoline, glues, correction fluids, and felt-tip marker fluids. *Aerosols* are sprays that contain propellants and solvents, such as spray paints, deodorant and hair sprays, vegetable oil sprays, and fabric protector sprays. *Gases* include medical anesthetics and gases used in household or commercial products, such as ether, chloroform, halothane, and nitrous oxide (laughing gas). *Nitrates* are primarily used to dilate blood vessels and to relax the muscles, such as amyl nitrate (*poppers* and *snappers*), butyl nitrate (also known as poppers), and cyclohexyl nitrate. The effects of using inhalants are often similar to the effects from alcohol and other depressants: slurred speech, poor coordination, euphoria, and dizziness. Some users experience light-headedness, hallucinations, and delusions. Nitrates are pri-

---

Instant Death

Norman is in recovery for 35 years. He said he got clean and sober after more than 17 years of addiction to alcohol and other mood-altering substances. In telling his story, Norman recalled an event that happened a long time ago. He and his friend, Peter, had just come from seeing the movie *The Man with the Golden Arm* and were heading home when Peter said, "Let's get high." They both were 13 at the time. Having heard that cleaning fluid, if sniffed (inhaled), would make them feel good, they bought a bottle, went into a building basement, and poured the substance onto handkerchiefs. The active ingredient at that time was carbon tetrachloride—an ingredient no longer used in anything. Norman felt a euphoric rush with the first sniff. That rush quickly changed to a deafening buzzing sound and then to a cold metallic feeling that seemed to fill his lungs. He turned to Peter, who had a vacant expression on his face that suddenly changed to a giggle and finally to a deep guttural groan as he tumbled, head first, hitting the hard concrete basement floor. The coroner's office said he was dead before he hit the ground. The cause of death was cardiac arrest. Norman was devastated by his friend's death, yet his substance use continued for almost 2 more decades. When asked why, he had no answer but said, "Both my parents were heavy drinkers—maybe there's something to the family predisposition thing."

marily used to enhance sexual performance and pleasure. They have been very popular in the gay community.

Most inhalants are extremely toxic and can cause long-term brain damage similar to such disorders as multiple sclerosis. Inhalant abuse has been associated with cognitive abnormalities, damage to the heart, lungs, liver, and kidneys, asphyxiation, suffocation, choking, and fatal injury from accidents and from a syndrome known as *sudden sniffing death* (NIDA, 2000).

Conclusion

The enormous range of mood-altering chemicals can be matched only by the ingenious ability to find and create more. Both the desire to experience euphoria and the means to achieve that objective have been around since the beginning of time. It is likely that neither this need nor the ability to fulfill it will ever disappear. Even if every drug and substance in this chapter were to be eliminated from the face of the earth—and we know this is not possible—there would be plenty of known and unknown substances that would take their place. As of this writing, there are mysterious little-known-about herbs and plants that are both legal and available. One such substance is Salvinorin A (a psychoactive component of *Salvia divinorum*), a plant found in Mexico and known to be used by the Mazatec Indians, perhaps as *entheogens* (for religious purposes). This substance has been described as the "most potent naturally occurring psychedelic known"; it has the potential for inducing "experiences" beyond those of other psychedelic substances (Turner, 2003). Yet as of this writing, this mood-altering substance is not illegal under the Federal Analog Act of 1986.

Recognizing that both substance use and SUDs will always be a part of our culture—the government's war on drugs notwithstanding—and that education and treatment are as much of our culture as the drugs themselves, the rest of this book will focus on those two disciplines. While education and treatment are usually viewed as two separate approaches, they are really two sides of the same coin. Treatment is not possible without education, and education is not practicable without treatment. So we urge the reader to think education when we talk treatment, because however we describe it, recovery is both a treatment experience and a learning experience.

References

Allen, J. W. (2000). Opium poppy cultivation. Retrieved from http://www.erowid.org/plants/poppy/opium_poppy_cultivation/opium_poppy_cultivation1.shtml

American Psychiatric Association. (2000). *Diagnostic and statistical manual of mental disorders* (4th ed.; Rev. ed.). Washington, DC: Author.

Brecher, E. M. (1972). *Licit and illicit drugs: The Consumers Union report.* Boston: Little, Brown, and Company.

Comprehensive Drug Abuse Prevention and Control Act of 1970 (PL 91-513).

DanceSafe. (2005). Drug information. Retrieved from http://www.dancesafe.org/documents/druginfo/index.php

Federal Analog Act of 1986/Controlled Substance Analogue Enforcement Act of 1986. P. L. 99-570. Sub Title E, Title 1. Retrieved from http://www.erowid.org/psychoactives/law/law_fed_analog_act.shtml

Federal Food and Drugs Act of 1906. (The Wiley Act). (1906). P. L. 59-384. 34 Stat. 768 (1906). Retrieved from http://www.fda.gov/opacom/laws/wileyact.htm

Gilbert-Lecomte, R. (1974). *Oeuvres completes*. (2 vols.). Paris: Gallimard. In M. Boon, *The road of excess* (pp. 68, 69). Cambridge, MA: Harvard University Press.

Griffiths, R. R., & Mumford, G. K. (2000). *Caffeine : A drug of abuse*. Rockville, MD: National Institute on Drug Abuse.

Harrison Narcotics Tax Act of 1914. P. L. 23, 63rd Congress.

Nader, M. (2002). Low rank monkeys more prone to cocaine addiction. Retrieved from http://www.newscientist.com/article.ns?id=dn1810

National Cancer Institute. (1997). Changes in cigarette-related disease risks and their implications for prevention and control–Monograph 8. Rockville, MD: National Institutes of Health.

National Institute on Drug Abuse. (1998). *Nicotine addiction report*. NIH Publication No. 01-4342. Rockville, MD: National Institutes of Health.

National Institute on Drug Abuse. (2000). About anabolic steroids. *NIDA Notes, 15*(3).

National Institute on Drug Abuse. (2000). Commonly abused drugs. Retrieved from http://www.drugabuse.gov

National Institute on Drug Abuse. (2004). NIDA infofacts: Science-based facts on drug abuse and addiction. Retrieved from http://www.nida.nih.gov/infofacts/infofaxindex.html

National Institute on Drug Abuse. (2005). NIDA Research Report–Inhalant abuse. NIH Publication No. 00-3818. Rockville, MD: National Institutes of Health.

New York State Office of Alcoholism and Substance Abuse Services. (2005). Retrieved from http://www.oasas.state.ny.us/admed/drugs/drugs.htm

SAMHSA News. (November–December 2004). 2003 survey. Workplace statistics. Retrieved October 12, 2005, from http://alt.samhsa_news/VolumeXII_6/text_only/article9txt.htm

Schaffer Library of Drug Policy. (2004). Harrison Narcotics Tax Act of 1914. Retrieved from http://www.druglibrary.org/schaffer/history/e1910/harrisonact.htm

Turner, D. M. (1996). Salvinorin–The psychiatric essence of salvia divinorum. Retrieved October 12, 2005, from http://www.erowid.org/library/books_online/salvinorin/hist.shtml

Warfare against opium-smoking in America. (1909). *Outlook, 91,* 275. Retrieved from http://www.druglibrary.org/schaffer/history/opiumwarfare1909.htm

Webster's new world college dictionary (4th ed.). (2001). Forster City, CA: IDG Books.

Assessment

THE WILEY
CONCISE GUIDES
TO MENTAL HEALTH

Substance
Use
Disorders

CHAPTER 3

Assessment, Diagnosis, and Treatment Planning

A Historical Perspective

An accurate assessment is the first step toward an effective treatment outcome. It is the necessary groundwork for establishing a diagnosis, developing a treatment plan, and implementing appropriate treatment strategies. An unsound or incomplete assessment will negatively impact professional credibility, lead to improper treatment, cause early dropout, or possibly result in personal injury. Imagine going to a doctor for sharp abdominal pains and, after a cursory examination, being diagnosed with gas pains, only to later discover that you actually had appendicitis. Substance abuse clinicians have an important responsibility, as do medical doctors, to provide the most accurate assessment possible. Patients trust our judgment and expertise to provide the best care that we can.

When we first entered the field, there was little emphasis on assessments. In the 1970s and 1980s, assessments were usually performed by inexperienced paraprofessionals, whose main objective (it seemed) was to ensure that inappropriate patients were not admitted, for example, the mentally ill and the violent. Little to no formal training was provided for staff in the 1970s, primarily because few were knowledgeable enough to conduct such training. Medical and psychological assessment techniques that focused on SUDs were in their infancy. The paraprofessional staff often had more experience and more knowledge than the degreed professional staff who supervised them. In one New York City hospital-based program, the professional-degreed staff were trained by the recovering paraprofessional staff so that they could qualify, after training, as their supervisors. Psychiatrists, psychologists, and social workers received little or no academic training in the treatment of SUDs, yet were placed in supervisory

What Is a Trained Clinician?

A trained clinician is a person who has the education and experience necessary to get the job done. It is a person who relies not on just his personal experience to assess or treat a client, but draws also from a body of knowledge through education, training, and experience. A master's or doctorate degree in a related discipline is not a prerequisite, but it serves to broaden the clinician's perspective. Conversely, a degree is only as good as the training and experience that it complements. That training and experience must be specific to the assessment and treatment of SUDs. We have known good substance treatment counselors who were severely limited by their lack of education, and we have known degreed professionals who were equally limited by their lack of SUD assessment and treatment skills. As in any profession, a foundation of knowledge should be established so that specific skills may be learned and applied. The assessment and treatment of SUDs necessitates such skills, and a broad knowledge base facilitates their application.

positions. There was a limited body of knowledge and treatment decisions were often arbitrary or excessive. By the 1980s, inpatient treatment became the treatment of choice, and residential programs were charging premium rates. All health care costs were rising at the time, but the rising cost of alcohol and drug treatment became a target for cost cutting. Managed care companies (MCOs) stepped in and began to reduce cost by demanding treatment accountability through precertification, recertification, and utilization review. But their rationale for denying treatment was no better than the existing rationale for accessing treatment. Neither the treatment community nor the managed care community had an adequate body of knowledge to defend their decisions. Ironically, as things turned out, the criteria currently used to determine levels of care is the same for both the treatment communities and managed care communities.

While the MCO gatekeeper policies may have limited access to treatment for some, it also caused the treatment community to take a hard look at itself. These companies placed constraints on the liberal policy of allowing treatment on demand—not that treatment was denied, but the level of care was determined through comprehensive assessments. Instead of permitting their subscribers to utilize their substance abuse benefits as they wished, MCOs came to expect treatment to be individualized for each patient. The concept of standard length of treatment was quickly vanishing. It was replaced by a medical model providing individualized assessments that had to *prove* the medical necessity for treatment. Initially, many clinicians in the field resented these changes. But despite initial resistance, MCOs forced those in the field to improve their assessment and diagnostic skills and, in so doing, improved the overall effectiveness of treatment.

The Modern Day Assessment

Today's chemical dependency assessment is highly standardized and objective. The process employs focused areas of questioning, specific diagnostic criteria, and precise criteria for patient placement. Substance Use Disorder evaluations are now based on a biopsychosocial assessment, incorporating the biological, psychological, and social factors that may play a role in a patient's disorder, negatively or positively. There is now a demand for trained clinicians experienced in performing such assessments. While the field continues to assess itself and develop more effective assessment and treatment tools and strategies, its efforts to date have greatly improved treatment outcome effectiveness for our patients.

Five Essential Questions

There are five essential questions to be answered in determining treatment for an SUD. These questions need to be answered fully and accurately when assessing for an SUD:

1. Does the person have an SUD?
2. If so, how severe is the disorder?
3. What level of care is needed?
4. What are the goals of treatment?
5. What services would best achieve such goals?

Assessment Question 1: Does the Person Have a Substance Use Disorder?

The answer to this question has been much too frequently assumed to be in the affirmative. Many clinicians have taken this for granted when a potential patient enters the office for an SUD assessment. Just because a person uses mood-altering substances does not automatically mean he or she has an SUD. Through a variety of questioning techniques, the clinician must provide evidence that an SUD is present. The patient's propensity to minimize actual use is a factor in selecting the instrument to be used and interviewing style employed.

The Face-Valid Approach The simplest method for determining if a person has an SUD is a *face-valid approach*, where the patient is asked whether he or she has experienced the symptoms of a particular disorder. If a person admits to having a number of relevant symptoms, then it is likely that the person has the disorder in question. For instance, a substance dependence disorder is characterized by physiological dependence, loss of control, and preoccupation with use, to name a few possible symptoms. If a patient admits to such symptoms, we are likely to be looking at a diagnosis of Substance Dependence. As for a substance abuse disorder, continued use in spite of adverse consequence alone will render such a diagnosis. When using this approach, it is easiest to format the criteria for

Face-Valid Questions

Michigan Alcoholism Screening Test: (The Brief MAST)

1. Do you feel you are a normal drinker?

2. Do friends or relatives think you are a normal drinker?

3. Have you ever attended an AA meeting?

4. Have you ever lost friends or girlfriends or boyfriends because of drinking?

5. Have you ever gotten into trouble at work because of drinking?

6. Have you ever neglected your obligations, your family, or your work for 2 or more days in a row because you were drinking?

7. Have you ever had delirium tremens (DTs), severe shaking, or heard voices or seen things that weren't there after heavy drinking?

8. Have you ever gone to anyone for help about your drinking?

9. Have you ever been in a hospital because of drinking?

10. Have you ever been arrested for drunk driving or driving after drinking?

A "yes" answer to any question opens the door for further exploration. To reach a definitive diagnosis, additional assessment techniques are recommended.

Substance Abuse and Substance Dependence into questions. We like to begin with questions assessing for the more severe SUD—Substance Dependence. This is because a substance dependence disorder always precludes a substance abuse disorder. If the diagnosis is Substance Dependence, then there cannot be a diagnosis of Substance Abuse. To determine if a patient has a diagnosis of Substance Dependence on heroin, for example, we can go down the list of *DSM-IV-TR* symptom categories and ask directly about each one. For example:

- Have you ever developed a tolerance for heroin, needing more of it to get the same effect than you once did?

- Have you ever experienced withdrawal from heroin or taken a similar substance to relieve or avoid withdrawal?

- Have you often taken heroin in larger amounts or over a longer period than was intended?

- Have you had unsuccessful efforts to cut down or control your heroin use? Have you had a persistent desire to cut down or control your heroin use?

- Have you spent a great deal of time around your use of heroin, for example, obtaining it, using it, or recovering from it?

- Has your use of heroin caused you to give up or reduce other important activities in your life (e.g., social, occupational, or recreational)?

- Have you continued using heroin despite knowing it has caused or may increase an ongoing physical or psychological problem (e.g., AIDS, heroin-induced depression)?

In order to meet a diagnosis of Substance Dependence, a patient must respond in the affirmative to at least three of these seven questions, and the symptoms must have occurred at least once during the same 12-month period. Notice the simple language used in asking these questions: It is important that the patient understands what is being asked.

The criteria for Substance Abuse can also be formatted into questions:

- Has your use of heroin resulted in a failure to fulfill major role obligations at work, school, or home?

- Have you used heroin in situations in which it is physically hazardous?

- Have you had recurrent heroin-related legal problems?

- Have you continued using heroin despite having persistent or recurrent social or interpersonal problems caused or increased by the effects of heroin?

Unlike Substance Dependence, to meet the diagnosis of Substance Abuse, only one of these questions—not three—needs to be answered in the affirmative, with symptoms occurring at least once within a 12-month period.

In addition to, or instead of, formatting the *DSM-IV-TR* diagnostic criteria for Substance Dependence and Substance Abuse into questions, you can obtain one of the many standardized diagnostic and screening instruments now on the market, such as the Michigan Alcohol Screening Test (MAST), the Drug Abuse Screening Test (DAST), the Alcohol Use Disorders Identification Test (AUDIT), the Alcohol Use Inventory (AUI), or the Triage Assessment for Addiction Disorders (TAAD).

A favorite instrument of ours is the Substance Use Disorders Diagnostic Schedule (SUDDS). This is a comprehensive assessment instrument for determining an SUD. It has formatted the symptom categories of Substance Dependence and Substance Abuse into detailed questions and developed a checklist for determining specific SUDs.

Assessment instruments need to meet two criteria if they are to be effective: *validity* and *reliability*. *Validity* refers to whether an instrument measures what one wants it to measure. In this case, we want to be sure the instrument will assess alcohol or drug problems, not another mental health problem. While this information may be important, we would go to the appropriate instrument for that additional information (McNeece & DiNitto, 2005).

Reliability is when the instrument produces the same results with the same person at different times and under different circumstances. If a MAST or a Substance Abuse Subtle Screening Inventory (SASSI) were administered to a client today during a visit to an outpatient clinic, one would expect the same or very similar results if it were administered to the client next week at his or her home (McNeece & DiNitto, 2005).

Non-Face-Valid Questions

Selected SASSI True or False Questions

1. Most people would lie to get what they want.
2. I usually go along and do what others are doing.
3. I was always well behaved in school.
4. My troubles are not all my fault.
5. I have lived the way I should.
6. It is better not to talk about personal problems.
7. I am very respectful of authority.
8. I have sometimes been tempted to hit people.
9. I frequently make lists of things to do.
10. I like doing things on the spur of the moment.

Unlike the preceding face-valid example, the objective of non-face-valid questions is not obvious.

Whatever assessment instruments you use, also keep in mind that time, environment, ease of use, and cost-effectiveness are important considerations. The cost of the instrument needs to be weighed against the amount of time it takes to administer it. If an instrument is inexpensive but it takes staff 4 hours to administer it, then you better look around for a different one. But whatever the cost of the instrument, never encourage making illegal copies of it instead of purchasing it! You might never get caught, but it is illegal, unethical, and tacky. In a profession where we are attempting to demonstrate honesty, do we want to deprive the developers of such instruments their rewards? (Yes, unfortunately, we have observed both individuals and agencies engage in such unprofessional behavior.)

Non-Face-Valid Questioning The problem with a face-valid approach is that it assumes the individual is answering these questions honestly. Unfortunately, in our field we are often assessing individuals who enter our offices under some form of coercion (e.g., pressure from work, home, courts, etc.). We cannot always assume they are willing to tell us the truth about the extent of their substance use. As a result, our job as diagnostician is further complicated. Unlike clinicians diagnosing other medical and mental disorders, we must perform detective work to find evidence of an SUD in many of the patients we are assessing.

When working with a patient who has a vested interest in concealing the extent of his substance use, using a face-valid approach may not be helpful. In this case, employing non-face-valid questions would be preferable. Non-face-valid questioning attempts to find evidence of a disorder without directly asking about the symptoms of that disorder. Consequently, it is more difficult to conceal relevant information.

In addition to the standardized non-face-valid assessment tools, there are several sources of information that one can draw from to construct non-face-valid questions. These include the following:

- Physical health problems
- Family history of drug or alcohol problems
- Criminal arrests
- Cigarette use or other substance use
- Collateral information

Because these areas of questioning are not directly or obviously related to the symptoms of an SUD, highly guarded patients are more apt to answer them truthfully.

Specific questions on current or past physical health matters are important. The answers will help the clinician determine or rule out the existence of an SUD. We know pancreatitis, ulcers, liver disease, or other gastrointestinal disorders may be associated with Alcohol Abuse or Alcohol Dependence. Inquiring about the frequent use of antacids or other heartburn medication can also provide clues to gastrointestinal disorders. Information about hepatitis, abscesses, sexually transmitted diseases (STDs), or HIV status may provide clues about IV drug use. Sinusitis or other nasal problems may provide clues to intranasal abuse of cocaine or other inhaled substances.

Because we are aware of a genetic susceptibility to SUDs, it is important to investigate family history. The closer the blood relationship between patient and the identified family member with the problem, the greater the likelihood of its impact on the patient. For example, the patient with the substance dependent mother or father is at higher risk than the patient whose cousin was rumored to have a problem. It is helpful to obtain a family history of drug and alcohol use among parents, siblings, aunts, uncles, and grandparents.

An inquiry into criminal arrests can also lead to substantial information related to an SUD. Any arrests for driving while intoxicated (DWI) or driving while ability impaired (DWAI) lend credibility to the possibility of an alcohol use disorder, especially a repeated history of arrests. Additionally, complaints for domestic violence, assaults, or other forms of disorderly conduct usually occur under the influence of a mood-altering substance and lend credibility to an SUD diagnosis. Child neglect charges or loss of child custody are also associated with the possibility of an SUD.

Because most PSUDs smoke cigarettes, it is worth asking about current or past cigarette use. This is not to say that everyone who smokes cigarettes has an alcohol use disorder, but the probability is higher. It is always important to ask of cur-

A Law Enforcement Applicant

Mr. Smith was a 21-year-old male applying for a position in law enforcement. He had just completed college. Mr. Smith said he drank no more than once or twice monthly, one or two beers per occasion. He said he had been drunk only one time in his lifetime but admitted to drinking 12 or 13 beers at "a lot" of frat parties throughout his college years. Mr. Smith admitted that his father was in recovery.

The record showed that Mr. Smith had been disciplined for loud parties at the dorm, received a summons for public urination, and had been suspended for a fight involving alcohol. He was also in possession of a false ID. Mr. Smith was placed on academic probation in his junior year and graduated with a grade point average of 2.0.

The collateral information on Mr. Smith did not support his self-report of one or two drinks per occasion. His high consumption rate at frat parties indicates he had developed a tolerance for alcohol, and existing documented behavior supports a probable problem. While public urination and fistfighting are not proof positive of a drinking concern, together with the other inconsistencies, these incidents cannot be ignored.

Mr. Smith was determined to be at risk for an SUD and was not hired by the law enforcement agency.

---

rent or past substance use, of course. Oftentimes this type of questioning leads us to other possible substances of abuse.

It is helpful, whenever possible, to gather information about the individual being assessed by other sources (e.g., referral sources, family members, employers, schools, etc.). Such sources can be valid resources for crucial information supporting or negating a patient's drug use. We often ask the patient's permission (documented with a signed release form) to call a spouse while he or she is in our office in order to verify his extent of drug use. It is better to substantiate this information before the patient has an opportunity to collaborate a story with the spouse.

In addition to using these types of non-face-valid questions, it is advisable to employ a non-face-valid assessment instrument for SUDs. There are only two non-face-valid instruments for SUDs on the market; the McAndrew scale of the Minnesota Multiphasic Personality Inventory (MMPI), and the SASSI. Because the McAndrew scale is part of the MMPI, it is sold only to clinicians trained in psychological testing. Therefore, it may be inaccessible to most workers in the substance treatment field.

The SASSI, however, is a more accessible instrument. Although it also requires training, it can be self-administered by patients, can be scored in minutes, and claims a 93 percent accuracy rate in diagnosing the probability of a substance dependence disorder, even with patients that may be less than forthcoming. Addi-

Selected Screening Instruments

The Alcohol Use Disorders Identification Test (AUDIT)
National Computer Systems, 1-800-627-7271

The Minnesota Multiphasic Personality Inventory, 2nd Edition (MMPI)
1-800-627-7271 or http://www.ncspearson.com

The American Society of Addiction Medicine Patient Placement Criteria for the Treatment of Substance-Related Disorders, 2nd Edition-Revised (ASAM PPC-2R)
1-800-844-8948

The Substance Abuse Subtle Screening Inventory, 3rd Edition (SASSI-3)
The SASSI Institute, 1-800-726-0526

The Substance Use Disorders Diagnostic Schedule (SUDDS)
Evince, 401-231-2993

Michigan Alcoholism Screening Test (MAST)
Substance Abuse and Mental Health Services Administration (SAMHSA), 1-800-729-6686

Triage Assessment for Addiction Disorders (TAAD)
Evince Clinical Assessments, 401-231-2993

tionally, the SASSI provides clinical interpretations for other personality factors, including patient defensiveness, self-esteem, codependency issues, and probability of legal problems (see Box on selected screening instruments for selected instruments).

Assessment Question 2: If an SUD Does Exist, How Severe Is the Disorder?

If you determine that the answer to Question 1 is no, (the patient does not have an SUD), the assessment is over. Well, it's over in terms of an SUD, but you may need to refer the patient to a more appropriate resource that could meet his or her needs. However, if the patient has been determined to have an SUD, then Question 2 asks us to determine the severity of the SUD. By determining severity, we will also be able to answer Question 3: What level of care (or intensity of treatment) is needed? In most cases, the greater the severity of the SUD, the greater the intensity of treatment needed.

The Six Dimensions The method for determining the severity of an SUD that we have found useful is the *six dimensions,* developed by the American Society of Addiction Medicine (ASAM; 2001), the *Patient Placement Criteria for the Treatment of Substance-Related Disorders* (Mee-Lee et al., 2001). The ASAM is an organization of medical doctors who specialize in the treatment of addictive disorders. It is an organization that acts as an innovator in our field and is regularly working to improve the scientific methodology of our industry.

The six dimensions, also known as the *primary problem areas,* were developed after reviewing the assessments of many substance abuse treatment centers from around the country. The ASAM found these six dimensions to be the most commonly evaluated during initial SUD assessments. These include the following:

1. Acute Intoxication and/or Withdrawal Potential

2. Biomedical Conditions and Complications

3. Emotional/Behavioral or Cognitive Conditions and Complications

4. Readiness to Change

5. Relapse/Continued Use or Continued Problem Potential

6. Recovery/Living Environment

Dimension 1: Acute intoxication and/or withdrawal potential. This dimension refers to the assessment of present or potentially hazardous consequences of physiological drug dependence (withdrawal) and the risks associated with acute intoxication (hurting oneself or others). The need for hospitalization may depend solely on the assessment of this dimension.

Dimension 2: Biomedical conditions and complications. This dimension assesses the severity of physical illnesses, other than withdrawal, that need to be addressed or other chronic medical conditions needing attention. Severity on this dimension may also warrant hospitalization.

Dimension 3: Emotional/Behavioral or cognitive conditions and complications. This dimension assesses potential psychiatric conditions and psychological, behavioral, cognitive, or emotional problems needing attention.

Dimension 4: Readiness to change. This dimension assesses the patient's motivation or readiness to change addictive or abusive substance use.

Dimension 5: Relapse/Continued use or continued problem potential. This dimension assesses the patient's probability of continuing or reverting back to problem use of substances or continuing to experience problems related to a mental health condition.

Dimension 6: Recovery/Living environment. This dimension assesses the safety of the patient's environment (i.e., family, friends, roommates, coworkers, neighborhood, etc.) and potential resources for successful recovery from an SUD.

Assessing these six dimensions enables the clinician to determine the proper level of care for treatment, the goals of treatment, and the services needed to meet the goals.

Assessment Question 3: What Level of Care Is Needed?

Assessing the six dimensions in Question 2 helps us to answer Question 3: What level of care is needed? The levels of care (LOC) we will be discussing are taken directly from the ASAM PPC-2R. Each patient entering treatment for an SUD will be placed into one of the following levels of care:

Level 0.5—Early Intervention

Level I—Outpatient Treatment

Level II—Intensive Outpatient/Partial Hospitalization Treatment

Level III—Residential/Inpatient Treatment

Level IV—Medically Managed Intensive Inpatient Treatment

Early Intervention (Level 0.5) Early intervention is a pretreatment level of care and, therefore, given the designation of being only half a level. Early intervention is for the intervention of a person who may be at risk for an SUD but does not meet the criteria for either Substance Abuse or Substance Dependence. It may also include "those for whom there is not yet sufficient information to document an SUD" (Mee-Lee et al., 2001, p. 2). This may include an employee who has tested positive for drug use on the job but exhibits no other signs of an SUD, or a teenager who admits to using drugs but is not presently exhibiting signs of an SUD. Early intervention is more about educating the patient than treating the patient. The goal is to increase a patient's awareness about the dangers of using mood-altering substances. This LOC is usually performed in an outpatient setting, such as a clinical office, school, work site, community center, or an individual's home.

Outpatient Treatment (Level I) Outpatient treatment is performed in a nonresidential setting encompassing less than 9 contact hours per week. This LOC is utilized for the treatment of SUDs with mild severity or for continuing care following inpatient treatment. Settings for outpatient services include private offices and clinics.

Intensive Outpatient Treatment/Partial Hospitalization (Level II) This level of care encompasses two separate modalities: intensive outpatient and partial hospitalization services:

■ *Intensive Outpatient Treatment:* Intensive outpatient treatment, also known as IOP, consists of structured outpatient treatment from 9 to 20 hours weekly. This LOC is utilized for the treatment of SUDs with mild-to-moderate severity.

■ *Partial Hospitalization:* Partial hospitalization is also a structured outpatient setting consisting of treatment for 20 or more hours per week. This LOC includes day programs in which the patient may attend from, say, 9 A.M. to 3 P.M., 5 days per week. This level of treatment is considered to be more equipped than IOP to handle more severe medical and psychiatric problems.

Residential/Inpatient Treatment (Level III) This is the most confusing LOC because it encompasses four subcategories. The common element is that this LOC involves placement in a safe and stable living environment with some degree of clinical or medical monitoring.

The following are the four subcategories in this LOC:

■ *Level III.1: Clinically Managed Low-Intensity Residential Treatment.* This level is a halfway house type setting. Its focus is on developing recovery skills, relapse prevention, and the start of a positive support network. It is often used in conjunction with outpatient services.

■ *Level III.3: Clinically Managed Medium-Intensity Residential Treatment.* This level is used for patients with more severe medical, emotional, or behavioral problems. It is characterized by an extended care facility, such as a nursing home.

■ *Level III.5: Clinically Managed High-Intensity Residential Treatment.* This level is utilized for those patients with significant living skills problems beyond SUDs, such as unemployment, antisocial behavior, psychological problems, and impaired social functioning. The treatment is more habilitative than rehabilitative. It is characterized by the therapeutic community treatment model, such as Phoenix House.

■ *Level III.7: Medically Monitored Inpatient Treatment.* This level provides 24-hour professionally directed medically monitored care in an inpatient setting. It is addressed to those patients whose "biomedical, and emotional, behavioral or cognitive problems are so severe that they require inpatient treatment" (Mee-Lee et al., 2001, p. 76) but not so severe that they need the services of an acute care general hospital or a medically managed inpatient treatment program.

Medically Managed Intensive Inpatient Treatment (Level IV) This is the most intensive LOC available. This LOC "is appropriate for patients whose acute biomedical, emotional, behavioral and cognitive problems are so severe that they require primary medical, psychiatric and nursing care" (Mee-Lee et al., 2001, p. 127). This would include treating patients who present with acute suicidal ideation, along with the need for acute medical detoxification, severe intoxication or withdrawal problems, severe biomedical problems, and severe mental health problems. The focus of treatment is the medical stabilization of the patient in an environment with the full resources of a general acute care or psychiatric hospital.

In the first edition of the ASAM PPC, detoxification was handled solely in a Level IV treatment setting. However, this was revised in the second edition. It is now considered customary, under the proper criteria, to detoxify patients at any level between Level I and Level IV. This will be discussed further in Chapter 5, Dimension 1, Acute Intoxication and Withdrawal Potential.

Assessment Question 4: What Are the Goals of Treatment?

Questions 4 and 5 are related to treatment planning. In Question 4, we are attempting to identify the goals of treatment. The goals of treatment are usually

Adversarial Factors in Establishing Rapport

- Drug-abusing patients often do not enter treatment on a voluntary basis.
- Patients often maintain highly dysfunctional presuppositions about therapy.
- Patients often are not very open and honest, at least at the start of therapy.
- Patients may be currently involved in felonious activities, thus presenting confidentiality dilemmas.
- Patients view their therapist as part of the system, not as an ally.
- Patients have a difficult time believing that their therapists really care about their problems.
- Patients look askance at therapists whom they perceive to differ from them markedly in term of demographics and attitudes.
- Therapists may maintain negative presuppositions about drug abusing patients.

Source. (Beck, Wright, Newman, & Liese, 1993, pp. 54–55).

divided into short-term goals and long-term goals. Short-term goals are usually very specific and measurable. The length of a short-term goal varies, depending on the LOC. For example, a short-term goal in a detox may be expected to be achieved in 1 day, in an inpatient rehab it may be expected to be achieved in 4 weeks, and in an outpatient program it may be expected to be achieved in 90 days. Long-term goals are usually more generalized and less likely to be totally achieved during the current course of treatment. An example of a long-term goal may be to maintain a drug-free lifestyle.

It is surprising to observe, throughout the years in this field, clinicians' lack of emphasis on detailing specific goals of addiction treatment. Treatment has been regularly performed without individualizing treatment goals for the patient. Many programs have been using a cookie-cutter approach to treatment planning, offering the same goals of treatment for every patient. Without specific goals, treatment wanders and lacks direction; it is difficult to know if a patient's treatment has been successful. Managed care has been instrumental in holding clinicians accountable for developing specific and measurable goals for each patient's course of treatment. It holds SUD clinicians accountable for detailing a specific plan of treatment, as it would any other mental health or medical professional.

A good place to begin identifying specific and individualized goals of treatment is by reviewing the patient's problems in the six dimensions identified in Question 2: How severe is the SUD? For example, if the patient exhibits moderate withdrawal symptomology in Dimension 1 in the form of hand tremors, agitation, and high blood pressure, a possible goal would be to significantly reduce withdrawal as measured by elimination of hand tremors and agitation and stabilization of blood pressure. In Dimension 3, the patient may exhibit symptoms of depression in the form of depressed mood, insomnia, indecisiveness, and weight loss. A goal may be to decrease depression as measured by a decrease in depressed mood, improved sleep, improved decision making, and weight gain or loss. In Dimension 4, the identified problem may be a lack of awareness of the negative consequences of his substance use. A possible goal would be an improved awareness of the negative consequences of use, as evidenced by an increase in verbalizations about the negative consequences of use.

The idea is to use information accumulated in the severity factors of the six dimensions (problem areas) to formulate specific goals of treatment. By using this approach, we develop a very individualized list of treatment goals for the patient. Of course, treatment goals can be developed beyond the six dimensions. For instance, goals related to vocational or educational deficits may be established.

Whenever possible, the development of individualized treatment goals should be collaborative between the patient and clinician. Having the patient involved in his own treatment planning will encourage a successful achievement of those goals. Collaboration will also avoid setting goals that the patient finds either undesirable or unachievable. In our program, we have patients complete their own version of a treatment plan based on the Happiness Scale found in *Clinical Guide to Alcohol Treatment: The Community Reinforcement Approach* (Meyers & Smith, 1995). This helps to determine mutually agreed-upon goals.

Another important point is that individualized treatment goals may differ for each patient depending on the LOC that is chosen. For instance, a patient in need of Level IV detox will most likely have goals around his medical needs (e.g., stabilization of vital signs, improved sleep patterns, reduced agitation, etc.). Treatment goals around the patient's vocational deficits would probably not be a priority at this LOC. On the other hand, a patient entering a Level I outpatient program may provide a reasonable environment to address vocational deficits.

Another common error of clinicians in the field of substance abuse treatment is failing to address agreed-upon, individualized goals during treatment. Many clinicians have their own agenda when entering patient sessions and often ignore the set goals; or the clinician may downplay the importance of the developed goals; or the clinician may play a very passive role in the session, allowing the patient to set the agenda. Clinicians have the responsibility and need the discipline to stick to the agreed-upon goals during sessions. Once these goals are addressed, the session can proceed to other matters if time permits. Of course, in unusual circumstances, such as crisis situations (e.g., family dispute, job firing, etc.), there can be exceptions to this rule.

Assessment Question 5: What Services Would Best Achieve the Goals?

There is a concept discussed in the ASAM PPC-2R called *unbundling*. Essentially, unbundling seeks to provide the appropriate combination of specific services to match a patient's needs. It seeks to provide an array of service options in order to provide individualized treatment. It works counter to the previous system of providing a set list of services (bundling) based upon the treatment setting, for instance, only providing medical care in an inpatient setting or only providing family therapy in an outpatient setting. It is now considered more advantageous to provide the patient with a variety of treatment services in all levels of care.

A recent study (McLellan et al., 1998) compared a standard addiction program of twice-weekly outpatient group counseling to a program offering supplemental social services (e.g., medical, housing, parenting, and employment services) in addition to the group counseling. The study concluded that patients in the enhanced program showed significantly less substance use, fewer physical and mental health problems, and better social functioning than those in the standard program. This study seems to reinforce the importance of providing an array of services *or* unbundling in addiction treatment.

There is no right approach to determining the specific services needed to achieve the stated goals of treatment. Sometimes a determination is based upon experience, and at other times it is based upon common sense. There are times when we will choose a specific group for a patient based upon the makeup of the group, for instance, choosing a group of very supportive members (as opposed to confrontational members) to aid an emotionally fragile patient. At other times, we will choose a specific service based solely on the patient's need (e.g., a coping skills group for a patient with poor coping skills). With experience, we believe one's clinical acumen for choosing the most appropriate services for a patient improves.

As also stated in Question 4, deciding on the specific services to provide a patient should be made in collaboration with that patient whenever possible. This will more likely ensure the success of the prescribed treatment plan. Collaboration places a greater responsibility on the patient to achieve success.

Applying the Assessment Tool to a Case

This chapter presented the five essential questions of a proper SUD assessment and the methods for obtaining the answers to these questions. Developing the skills to adequately answer these questions will improve the overall effectiveness of the patient's treatment and provide a clear direction for treatment planning.

Now let's take the preceding five essential questions to answer in determining treatment of an SUD and develop a sample Assessment Summary Form that will facilitate their application. The following is a case study. Our job is to answer each of the five questions by reviewing the case and simply using our assessment skills to fill in the appropriate blanks.

Sample Assessment Summary Form

DSM-IV-TR Multiaxial Evaluation

AXIS I:

AXIS II:

AXIS III:

AXIS IV:

AXIS V:

Severity Ratings in the Six Dimensions

(Scale: NONE, MILD, MODERATE, and SEVERE)

1.   4.

2.   5.

3.   6.

Level Of Care (LOC) Determination

(Based on preceding findings)

Treatment Goals and Services

Dimension Goals   Services

The initial treatment plan is determined in a sequential assessment process through the application of the *DSM-IV-TR* Multiaxial system, the Severity scale, the LOC, and, finally, the treatment goals and services.

Psychosocial Assessment Summary

Identifying Information David is a 22-year-old single, Caucasian male who is very thin and casually dressed. He appears cooperative but answers questions slowly.

Presenting Problem The patient reports "money problems due to the use of drugs." However, the primary reason for this assessment is a court order due to his recent legal difficulties. Upon some questioning, David admits to his legal difficulties and reports plans to cooperate with the recommendations of this evaluation.

Substance Use History David reports primary difficulty with crack cocaine. He reports first use of cocaine at 15 years old and says it became a problem at 18 years old. He reports daily use of crack for the past 3 months, averaging $50 per day. His symptoms of use include using more than planned, a preoccupation with use, financial difficulties due to use, and family concern.

David also reports use of marijuana several times per week, averaging one joint per occasion, and infrequent use of LSD and ecstasy. He denies these substances ever becoming a problem, despite acknowledging that these substances have caused legal problems and a deterioration of school performance. David claims a dislike for alcohol and uses it one time per month or less.

Assessment Tool David's SASSI results suggest a "high probability of having a substance dependence disorder." The results of the SUDDS suggest Cocaine Dependence, Marijuana Abuse, and Hallucinogen Abuse.

David does not display any signs of physical withdrawal symptoms.

David denies any previous history of drug or alcohol treatment. He denies ever attending a 12-step meeting.

Medical History David describes his general medical condition as fair. He is complaining of shortness of breath and an erratic heartbeat. He appears underweight and possibly malnourished. David claims he has little or no appetite because he works around food all day. He has practiced unsafe heterosexual sex during the last year and has not been tested for HIV because "I am afraid of the results." He denies any previous hospitalizations.

Psychiatric History David has reported cruelty to animals and difficulty maintaining attention. He recently saw a psychiatrist for two sessions, under a court order for cruelty to animals, which occurred last summer. The psychiatrist recommended he enter an inpatient drug treatment program. He denies any other psychiatric treatment or psychotherapy.

Mental Status Examination David exhibited slow speech with a ruminative quality. His mood was moderately anxious, and his affect was varied. His concentration seemed severely impaired, and his insight was poor. David has a short attention span and poor abstracting ability that could interfere with his ability to participate in treatment.

Current Social Information David currently lives with his mother. He is satisfied with his current living situation. He is not involved in any intimate relationships outside his relationship with his mother, which appears enmeshed. He reports having few friends and spending most of his time alone using drugs. He claims his mother is supportive. She appears to be enabling his continued drug use. David spends most of his salary on drugs and does not pay his mother for rent or food. He reports pawning many of his belongings to obtain money for drugs.

Childhood and Family of Origin Information David was raised by his mother, along with his two siblings. His parents were divorced when he was 3 years old. His father was rarely around as he was growing up. He reports anger at his father for the neglect. David's mother had difficulty raising him and, at age 11, placed him with family friends for 2 years. David describes these foster parents as uncaring. By sixth grade, his grades deteriorated. He began using drugs in the seventh grade. David dropped out of school in the tenth grade and has not sought any further education or training.

Work History David is employed full time as a fast-food worker. He has been working in this position for 8 months. He reports no other job history. His salary is spent primarily on drugs.

Legal History David has a history of being charged with assault, drug possession, vandalism, and cruelty to animals. His legal history dates back to early adolescence and includes two periods of probation at ages 14 and 17.

Assessment Findings for David

Based upon the biopsychosocial assessment presented in the preceding, we would formulate the following case: David appears to meet the symptom criteria for a substance use disorder as delineated in the free-form interview (e.g., daily use, using more than planned, preoccupation with use, financial problems, and family concern) as well as in the SASSI and SUDDS results.

Because David appears to meet the criteria for an SUD, we would next determine the severity of his SUD.

- *On Dimension 1:* There are no apparent signs of withdrawal potential that need monitoring, but a review of his vital signs would be advised. "None" would be the level determined here.

- *On Dimension 2:* David reports shortness of breath, erratic heartbeat, and poor appetite, and appears underweight and malnourished. These signs would suggest to us a "Moderate" level of severity on Dimension 2.

- *On Dimension 3:* David's cruelty to animals, labile affect, and apparent cognitive deficits, including slow speech, short attention span, and poor insight, suggest a "Moderate" to "Severe" score.

- *On Dimension 4:* David does not appear very motivated toward treatment. However, he seems willing to comply with the assessor's recommendations. We would rate David's treatment resistance severity on Dimension 4 as "Moderate."

- *On Dimension 5:* David's daily use of cocaine for the past 3 months suggests a "Severe" relapse potential.

- *On Dimension 6:* Given his mother's supportive but enabling behavior, we would rate this dimension as "Mild."

Given this severity profile, we would suggest treatment at Level III.3 (Clinically Managed Medium-Intensity Residential Treatment). Level III.3 provides a slower pace of treatment for those with a cognitive impairment that David seems to display. Level III.3 also is geared to treat more severe medical or psychiatric problems. Furthermore, this level also handles more severity in the areas of treatment resistance, relapse potential, and recovery environment that David is experiencing. Level II treatment might have been considered for David, but his likelihood for relapse suggests inpatient treatment. Also, given the leverage provided by the courts, we would like to take advantage by providing the protective environment afforded by Level III.3.

The following is a sample of a completed Assessment Summary Form for David:

Completed Sample Assessment Summary Form for David

Multi-Axial Evaluation

AXIS I:

    Cocaine Dependence

    Poly-Substance Abuse

    Rule-out Conduct Disorder

    Rule-out Cognitive Disorder

AXIS II:

    Deferred

AXIS III:

    Shortness of breath

    Erratic heartbeat

    Malnutrition

Axis IV:

    Economic problems

    Health problems

    Legal problems

Axis V:

    50

Severity Ratings in the Six Dimensions

Scale: (NONE, MILD, MODERATE, and SEVERE)

Dimension 1: None/Mild

Dimension 2: Moderate

Dimension 3: Moderate/Severe

Dimension 4: Moderate

Dimension 5: Severe

Dimension 6: Mildly unsupportive

Level of Care Determination

Level III.3 (Medically Managed Medium-Intensity Residential Treatment)

Treatment Planning: Goals and Services

Treatment Planning Goals and Services Guide

Dimension	Goals	Services
1	Does not apply	Does not apply
2	a. Diagnose shortness of breath	a. Medical evaluation
	b. Assess seriousness of erratic heartbeat	b. Medical evaluation
	c. Increase body weight by 2 pounds weekly	c. Nutritional consultation
	d. Obtain HIV test results	d. HIV pretest counseling
3	a. Rule out Conduct Disorder	a. Psychological or psychiatric evaluation
	b. Rule out Cognitive Disorder	b. Neuropsychological evaluation
4	a. Gain a greater understanding and acceptance of his SUDs	a. Group therapy, individual therapy, drug education, and 12-step meetings
	b. Begin 12-step meeting participation	b. Arrange and encourage meetings
5	a. Remain substance-free over the next 90 days	a. Group therapy, individual therapy, 12-step meetings, and urine monitoring
	b. Develop alternate leisure plans	b. Recreational therapy
6	a. Explore codependency or enmeshment issues with mother	a. Begin family therapy with mother and patient
	b. Explore vocational or educational aspirations	b. Vocational counseling

Assessment, Diagnosis, and Treatment in Conclusion

Patient and Collateral Interviews

A skilled clinician will use many different techniques, tools, and strategies to collect information. While screening instruments are important, they should never be used exclusively. In fact, screening tools should be applied so that they may seamlessly fit into the complete assessment process. The following is a detailed listing of areas to explore as well as selected questions to be asked when conducting an assessment.

Drug History and Current Patterns of Use When did alcohol or other drug use begin? What types of alcohol or other drugs does the individual currently use? Does the person use over-the-counter medications, prescription drugs, tobacco, and caffeine? How frequently are the substances used and in what quantity?

Substance Abuse Treatment History Has the individual ever received treatment for an SUD? If so, what type of treatment (inpatient, outpatient, methadone maintenance, 12-step programs, etc.)? Were these treatment experiences considered successful or unsuccessful and why? Has the person been sober and experienced relapse or has he or she never attained recovery?

Medical History and Current Status What symptoms are currently reported by the patient? Are there indicators of infectious diseases or STDs? Has the individual been tested for HIV and other infectious diseases? Are there indicators of risk for HIV or other diseases for which testing should be done? What kind of health care has been received in the past? The causes and effects of various illnesses and traumas should be explored.

Patient and Collateral Information

Drug history and current patterns of use

Substance abuse treatment history

Medical history and current status

Mental status and mental health history

Personal status

Family history and current relationships

Positive support systems

Crime or delinquency

Education

Employment

Readiness for treatment

Resources and responsibilities

Mental Status and Mental Health History Is the individual orientated to person, place, and time? Does he or she have the ability to concentrate on the interview process? Are there indicators of impaired cognitive abilities? What is the appropriateness of responses during the interview? Is the person's affect (emotional response) appropriate for the situation? Are there indicators from collateral sources of inappropriate behavior or responses by the person? Is there evidence of extreme mood states, suicidal potential, or possibility of violence? Is the individual able to control impulses? Have there been previous psychological or psychiatric evaluations or treatment?

Personal Status What are this person's critical life events? Who constitutes his or her peer group? Does the individual indicate psychosocial problems that might lead to an SUD? Does the person demonstrate appropriate social, interpersonal, self-management, and stress management skills? What is the individual's level of self-esteem? What are the person's leisure time interests? What are his or her socioeconomic level and housing and neighborhood situations?

Family History and Current Relationships Who does the individual consider his or her family to be; is it a traditional or nontraditional family constellation, for example, non-blood relationship, institution, relative other than parent as primary caretaker? What role does the individual play within the family? Are there indicators of a history of physical or sexual abuse or neglect? Do other family members have a history of an SUD, health problems or chronic illnesses, psychiatric disorders, or criminal behavior? What is the family's cultural, racial, and socioeconomic background? What are the strengths of the family, and are they invested in helping the individual? Has there been a foster family or other out-of-home placements?

Positive Support Systems Does the person have hobbies, interests, and talents? Who are his or her positive peers or family members?

Crime or Delinquency Have there been previous arrests or involvement in the criminal or juvenile justice system? Has the person been involved in criminal or delinquent activity but not been apprehended? Is there evidence of gang involvement? Is the person currently under the supervision of the justice system? What is the person's attitude about criminal or delinquent behavior?

Education How much formal education has the person completed? What is the individual's functional educational level? Is there evidence of a learning disability? Has he or she received any special education services? If currently in school, what is the person's academic performance and attendance pattern?

Employment What is the individual's current employment status? What employment training has been received? What jobs have been held in the past, and why has the person left these jobs? If currently employed, are there problems with performance or attendance?

Readiness for Treatment Does the patient accept or deny a need for treatment? Are there other barriers to treatment?

Resources and Responsibilities What is the individual's socioeconomic status? Is the person receiving services from other agencies, or might he or she be eligible for services?

As stated in the first section of this chapter, proper assessment leads to accurate diagnosis and, ultimately, to effective treatment planning strategies. Without an accurate diagnosis, developing an effective treatment plan is not possible. While there may be varying styles and preferences for assessing and diagnosing the client's needs, most important is that the approach be based on established and proven criteria. Not only is a comprehensive assessment going to prove essential to establishing treatment goals, it is simply good clinical practice. Even when a client is already known to the agency or treatment facility, a full history should be taken (again). Based on the collective information, both past and present, a revised diagnosis can be established. Substance Use Disorders are not static—they are dynamic illnesses that require a dynamic treatment approach. Inconsistencies in patient self-reports are common, and modifications in biopsychosocial information gathered can often be expected.

References

American Psychiatric Association. (2000). *Diagnostic and statistical manual of mental disorders* (4th ed.; Rev. ed.). Washington, DC: Author.

Beck, A. T., Wright, F. D., Newman, C. F., & Liese, B. S. (1993). *Cognitive therapy of substance abuse.* New York: Guilford.

Bohn, M. J., Babor, T. F., & Kranzler, H. R. (1995). The Alcohol Use Disorders Identification Test (AUDIT): Validation of a screening instrument for use in medical settings. *Journal of Studies on Alcohol, 56*(4), 423–432.

Graham, J. R. (1999). *MMPI-2: Assessing personality and psychopathology* (3rd ed.). New York: Oxford University Press.

Harrison, P. A., & Hoffmann, N. G. (1989). *SUDDS: Substance Use Disorders diagnostic schedule manual.* St. Paul, MN: New Standards.

McLellan, T. A., Hagan, T. A., Levine, M., Gould, F., Meyers, K., Bencivengo, M., & Durell, S. (1998). Supplemental social services improve outcomes in public addiction treatment. *Addiction, 93*(10), 1489–1499.

McNeece, C. A., & DiNitto, D. M. (2005). *Chemical dependency: A systems approach* (3rd ed.). Boston: Pearson Education.

Mee-Lee, D., Shulman, G. R., Fishman, M., Gastfriend, D. R., & Griffith, J. H. (2001). *Pa-*

tient placement criteria for the treatment of substance-related disorders (2nd ed.; Rev. ed.). Chevy Chase, MD: American Society of Addiction Medicine.

Meyers, R. J., & Smith, E. S. (1995). *Clinical guide to alcohol treatment: The community reinforcement approach*. New York: Guilford.

Miller, G. A. (1985). *Substance abuse subtle screening inventory (SASSI): Manual*. Bloomington, IN: Spencer Evening World.

Selzer, M. L. (1971). The Michigan Alcoholism Screening Test: The quest for a new diagnostic instrument. *American Journal of Psychiatry, 127,* 1653–1658.

Wanberg, K. W., Horn, J. L., & Foster, F. M. (1977). A differential assessment model for alcoholism. *Journal of Studies on Alcohol, 38,* 512–543.

CHAPTER 4

Levels of Care:
What Happens Where?

I n Chapter 3 we discussed diagnoses, assessing patient needs, and planning early treatment based on clinical findings. As part of that process, because we needed to understand the various treatment options, we also introduced the American Society of Addiction Medicine (ASAM) levels of care (LOCs). These LOCs include the following:

- Level 0.5—Early Intervention
- Level I—Outpatient Treatment
- Level II—Intensive Outpatient/Partial Hospitalization Treatment
- Level III—Residential/Inpatient Treatment
  - Level III.1—Clinically Managed Low-Intensity Residential Treatment
  - Level III.3—Clinically Managed Medium-Intensity Residential Treatment
  - Level III.5—Clinically Managed High-Intensity Residential Treatment
  - Level III.7—Medically Monitored Inpatient Treatment
- Level IV—Medically Managed Intensive Inpatient Treatment

Levels of Care Described

This chapter attempts to further clarify LOCs, specifically what kinds of clinical interventions and clinical activities are provided at and within each LOC. For example, a *residential halfway house* is different from a *residential rehabilitation program* although each provides inpatient care. A *partial/day-hospital program* is different from an *intensive outpatient program* although each provides outpatient care.

Early Intervention: Level 0.5

This is a level of care for the person who may be at risk for an SUD but may not meet the diagnostic criteria for either Substance Abuse or Substance Dependence. Sometimes called *secondary prevention,* it is an opportunity to address risky behavior or identify the potential for an SUD before it reaches a stage where a higher level of treatment becomes necessary, for example, Level II, Intensive Outpatient Treatment.

High School Drinking and Drug Use Drinking in high school and junior high school, for example, can either be experimental or it might signal an incipient problem. Schools, families, and community efforts are critical to addressing, containing, reducing, or preventing alcohol- and drug-related problems in adolescence. Early intervention can focus on an individual or target a specific high-risk population. The failing academic performance of a single student might flag a problem, or the collective behavior in a school might call for educative intervention. Just as education on substance use and abuse is an important responsibility at all LOCs, it is also an essential part of early intervention. As Figure 4.1 shows, almost 9 percent of the adolescents between the ages of 12 and 17 meet the diagnostic criteria for use or abuse. That's the bad news—an appropriate level of care would probably be indicated for this population. The good news is that 91 percent of this population did not meet the criteria for abuse or dependence. But this does not necessarily mean that this larger group is free of experimentation and incipient substance-related problems; many in this group might, in fact, benefit from early intervention. A comprehensive education program on drug

One-Year Prevalence of Substance Abuse/Dependence by Drug: Estimates for Adolescents (ages 12 to 17), 2002

Drug	Percentage with Past-Year Abuse or Dependence on Listed Substance		
	Total with Abuse or Dependence	Dependence	Abuse
Alcohol and/or Illicit Drugs	8.9%	4.4%	5.6%
Alcohol (with or without illicit drugs)	5.9%	2.1%	3.7%
Alcohol and Illicit drugs	2.5%	0.8%	0.6%
Illicit drugs (with or without alcohol)	5.6%	3.2%	2.4%

Figure 4.1 *Adolescent substance abuse/dependence.*
Source: Office of Applied Studies (2003).

and alcohol use, including what children should understand before completing high school, should include but not be limited to the following:

- Both the immediate and long-term physical effects of specific drugs
- The possible fatal effects of combining drugs
- The relationship of drug use to other diseases and disabilities
- The effects of alcohol and other drugs on the fetus during pregnancy
- The fact that drug use is not a victimless crime
- The effects and possible consequences of operating equipment while using alcohol and other drugs
- The impact that drug use has on society
- The extent of community intervention resources

College Drinking and Drug Use Another opportunity for early intervention is in college. A study shows that 6 percent of college students meet criteria for a diagnosis of Alcohol Dependence (also referred to as *alcoholism*), and 31 percent meet the clinical criteria for Alcohol Abuse. A study published in the *Journal of Studies on Alcohol* reported that almost 40 percent of the students in this survey met the criteria for Alcohol Abuse or Alcohol Dependence (Knight, et al., May 2002)!

While most of these college students will reduce their drinking significantly upon completing their studies and entering the world of work, early intervention will have accounted for a large percentage of these spontaneous remissions. As previously discussed, such interventions may be individual or collective: a student or a student body. The fact that such binge drinking rates are so high in college, however, indicates that there is too little money and energy invested in this important LOC.

Because college binge drinking rates are higher among students living away from home, the responsibility for early intervention falls upon the community and the school. Professors and administrators should be trained to identify the indicators of alcohol or drug problems among its students. This does not mean that they should become diagnosticians but that they need to take action where the problem is evident. Such action might be the implementation of educational and counseling services. Early intervention services would include the following:

- Student assistance programs (SAPs) where students can take personal problems, including incipient alcohol or drug concerns, for help
- Clearly written policies on behavioral problems, including available assistance
- Ongoing education on all aspects of the possible consequences of substance use, as outlined in the preceding
- Assistance that will engage parents, if necessary, that is within the state's guidelines on confidentiality issues

Working, Drinking, and Drug Use Still other opportunities for early intervention can be found in the workplace. An employee qualifying for early intervention is not necessarily young or in immediate danger of health-related problems. But when drug or alcohol use affects one's livelihood, it becomes as serious as any other consequence of use or abuse. (See case in Box titled Candidate for Early Intervention.) Employees who are in safety-sensitive positions, for example, are drug tested randomly, and even experimentation or recreational drug use may result in job loss. Employees who fall under the provisions of the Federal Department of Transportation, for example, such as interstate truck drivers, railroad engineers, or airline pilots, are required to comply with zero tolerance regulations.

While all the LOCs discussed in this chapter are important to treatment planning and recovery, early intervention is probably *the* most important. Not only are success rates likely to be higher when the problem is addressed early on, but also the LOC required and the cost of such treatment are both likely to be lower. The lower the LOC, the lower the cost of care. Treatment costs increase exponentially as the need for the least restrictive LOC moves from *early intervention outpatient treatment* to *medically managed intensive inpatient treatment.* Outpatient services can be as low as $50 per day, while inpatient care will often top $1,000 per day.

Candidate for Early Intervention: Level 0.5

Mario is a 32-year-old Hispanic male who recently tested positive for marijuana on a random urine test on his job. He is a city park worker, employed for 8 years. He claims that he uses marijuana occasionally (approximately once monthly). He clearly states his intention to abstain completely from marijuana due to the importance of keeping his job. He claims he last used marijuana 3 weeks ago prior to getting drug screened. He denies regular use of alcohol and denies use of any other illicit substances.

The substance use assessment, which included the completion of a SASSI questionnaire (see screening instruments) and a toxicology screen, could not detect an SUD. His wife was also called as part of the evaluation, and she corroborated that Mario has not displayed any signs of Substance Abuse during their marriage.

Mario reports to be in good health, denies any family history of Substance Abuse or mental health disorders, and denies having any emotional conditions or complications. He is presently suspended from his job, pending the results from this evaluation. His wife appears supportive.

This potential patient is not at risk of withdrawal; displays no signs of any biomedical conditions or complications; exhibits no signs of emotional, behavioral, or cognitive conditions or complications; appears willing to explore how his marijuana use may affect his personal goals; and appears to be in need of some education and awareness-building to improve his chances of changing his drug-use pattern. He is a candidate for an early intervention LOC.

Outpatient Services: Level I

The term *least restrictive level of care* defines the LOC most appropriate, given all the diagnostic or assessment information available, for a given patient. Level I, outpatient treatment, is an LOC that provides the least amount of clinical supervision. Patients referred to this LOC are likely to be very motivated, are in safe living environments, and show a good deal of insight into their SUD. In other words, the need for a higher LOC has been ruled out. Theoretically, a person who has had no prior treatment would also qualify for this LOC I, and if they fail at this LOC, then they would be moved to the next least restrictive LOC, that is, LOC II. Although outpatient treatment (LOC I) is effective in treating

Selected Treatment Services

All Levels of Outpatient or Inpatient Care

Assessment and Treatment Planning

Motivational and Early Intervention Services

Detoxification

Early and Advanced Recovery

Adolescent Treatment

Dual Diagnosis Treatment

DWI/DWAI Programs

Drug and Alcohol Testing

Gay, Lesbian, Bisexual, and Transgender Programs

Psychiatric Services or Medication Management

Individual Counseling and Psychotherapy

Gender-Specific Counseling

Relapse Prevention

Drug and Alcohol Education

Family Program and Codependency Treatment

ACOA Services

12-Step Recovery Groups

Anger Management

Stress Reduction Program

Acupuncture

Yoga

motivated patients, it is more likely to serve as a "step down" as the patient requires less care, for example, from LOC II to LOC I.

Outpatient treatment programs are staffed with trained professionals working with addicted persons to achieve and maintain abstinence (and other agreed-upon goals) while continuing to live in their community. Community mental health centers, private clinics, and professional therapists in private practice are examples of settings in which outpatient treatment is offered. Outpatient treatment programs offer a range of services and treatment modalities, including pharmacotherapy, individual counseling, group therapy, psychoeducational sessions, and family counseling. Outpatient treatment allows individuals to live at home, continue working or attending school, and be involved in family and social activities while in treatment (Doweiko, 1990). The lowest outpatient LOC (LOC I) also serves as an assessment opportunity. A patient might be first referred to this LOC to determine whether an SUD exists and, if one does, what LOC and treatment services would be appropriate. Outpatient treatment might include individual counseling and some form of psychoeducational group work, one to three times per week. Involvement in a 12-step program is usually encouraged and, depending on biopsychosocial factors, other activities that might facilitate personal or vocational growth might also be encouraged. Treatment planning on this LOC is far more individualized and fine-tuned than on the

Candidate for Outpatient Treatment: Level I

Mary is a 51-year-old Caucasian female who was recently arrested for DWI. She flunked the field test, and her blood-alcohol content was .12. A DWI in almost all states is .08 or higher. Her court case is pending. Mary reports to previously drinking alcohol approximately three times weekly, consuming about three glasses of wine per evening. She claims last use of alcohol 2 weeks ago. Mary denies use of any other mood-altering substances. After a comprehensive substance abuse evaluation, Mary met the criteria for Alcohol Abuse.

Mary is recently divorced and has been dating. She has two grown daughters, 26 and 23 years old, who have both moved out and live independently. She claims both of her daughters would be willing to participate in her treatment if she asked.

Mary is not experiencing any signs of withdrawal. She does not report any biomedical conditions or complications except for high cholesterol. She claims one previous episode of psychotherapy during her separation from her husband. She claims periods of depression due to her loneliness and adjustment to being single. She does not meet the criteria for a Major Depressive Disorder.

Mary is employed as a pharmaceutical representative and loves her job. She claims no problems on her job.

It appears she is ready to pursue recovery and is motivated to follow treatment suggestions. She does need monitoring strategies and support in order to attain her recovery goals.

higher LOCs. Because the decision to treat at this LOC usually means the patient is functioning reasonably well in terms of occupational or academic standards, basic needs such as shelter, employment, and safety are not primary concerns. Level of care I usually involves less than 9 hours of treatment per week, and the duration of treatment is between 3 months and 2 years.

Excessive Treatment While it is important to determine the appropriate LOC and the services that the patient needs to ensure the best possible chance of recovery, overtreating can be as ineffective as undertreating. As discussed in Chapter 3, the appropriate LOC is determined through a process of elimination—or ruling out the need for specific services. A patient who has been in a 30-day rehabilitation program, for example, may gain little from a repeat of that experience. Outpatient services allow the patient to meet the challenges of life every day while having the support to manage his or her recovery. While inpatient care is an important LOC, outpatient treatment becomes the litmus test for success.

Opioid Maintenance Opioid maintenance is an important outpatient level of care that is discussed in Chapter 5 and in other sections of this book. These pharmacological approaches to treatment include the use of Methadone and, more recently, Buprenorphine.

Intensive Outpatient/Partial Hospitalization Treatment: Level II

Intensive outpatient services and partial hospitalization treatment—sometimes called *day hospital programs*—are similar in structure but different in intensity. Both allow the patient to receive the treatment he or she needs while living at home. But intensive outpatient services are intended for working clients, while partial hospitalization services are targeted to those who are not working or can get time off from work. A typical intensive outpatient service will run in the evening, three to four evenings per week, 3 to 4 hours per evening. Partial hospitalization services, however, are daytime programs and often require a commitment of 6 days per week, 5 to 6 hours per day.

Outpatient treatment on all LOCs is usually less expensive than residential treatment alternatives. It also allows for longer term support of the individual than is possible with inpatient programs. As discussed previously and in Chapter 3, the decision for any LOC is based on a thorough biopsychosocial assessment and on the patient's immediate or long-term treatment needs. Considerations for referring individuals to outpatient treatment programs include motivation for treatment, ability to discontinue use of alcohol or other drugs, social support system, medical condition, psychiatric status, and past treatment history.

Within LOCs, there are variations on the delivery of services, including modalities of care and services provided. There are also gradations of treatment. These gradations are sometimes referred to as *step-down programs*, that is, an opportunity for the patient to graduate from one LOC and go to the next-lowest re-

Candidate for Intensive Outpatient/
Partial Hospitalization Treatment: Level II

John is a 40-year-old Asian male referred to treatment by his job's employee assistance program (EAP) after allegations were made that he occasionally smelled of alcohol and for excessive absenteeism. John is in severe jeopardy of losing his job. He is currently on a medical leave from his job.

John admits to drinking alcohol regularly; approximately four or five times weekly. He claims he drinks beer, often consuming up to ten 12 ounce beers per occasion. He also admitted to using cocaine, intranasal, at least once weekly and sometimes more often, costing approximately $40 per occasion. His last use of alcohol was yesterday.

John is married and has three children, aged 10, 8, and 5. He admits his wife is angry over his drinking. He claims his wife is not aware of his cocaine use.

John made it very clear that he was not willing to go to an inpatient facility. He stated that he once tried going to an AA meeting at the urging of his wife and hated it.

John appears to display minimal risk of severe withdrawal. He does admit to having a history of hypertension, which is being monitored by a physician. He reports no history of emotional, behavioral, or cognitive conditions or complications. He seems to minimize the extent of his Substance Abuse and lacks awareness of its effect on his and his family's life. There is a high likelihood of continued use without close monitoring and support several times a week.

strictive LOC. For example, a patient may be admitted for inpatient detoxification (LOC IV), then move into inpatient rehabilitation (LOC III), then enter a day hospital program (LOC II), followed by intensive evening treatment (LOC II), and, finally, continuing care outpatient services (LOC I).

Residential/Inpatient Treatment: Level III

Because this LOC may incorporate an extensive array of clinical services, it can best be described by what it *cannot* provide, that is, the level of acute care expected and provided in hospitals. For example, a patient who requires acute or intensive care should be in a medical facility or a psychiatric facility—depending on whether the care needed is medical or psychiatric. For an individual who needs to be stabilized on psychotropic medications, or a medically complicated detoxification, or a patient whose diabetes is out of control, or a victim of an overdose of drugs, or a patient requiring dialysis, or a psychotic patient—a hospital facility will be necessary. All of these examples require a facility capable of services found in LOC IV. For most other cases requiring residential or inpatient care, LOC III will be the recommended and appropriate treatment.

If we use the criteria to determine LOC as discussed in Chapter 3, we can almost ensure that an effective LOC will be selected. But there are two important considerations: (1) the clinician who is assessing and determining the appropriate LOC needs to use all the information available to him or her to reach that decision, and (2) the gatekeepers (insurance companies and managed care organizations) need to be in agreement with the assessing clinician's findings. In other words, the clinician's decision must be trusted, or the final decision makers must be using the same standards and criteria to approve that particular LOC for a given patient. For example, most managed health care organizations' general rule for admission to an inpatient facility, LOC III, is that the patient must have previously tried and failed outpatient treatment, that is, LOC I or II. In other words, the thinking is that if the optimal LOC is the least restrictive LOC, then it would follow that LOC I or LOC II would have to be tried before introducing LOC III as the potentially most effective LOC. But general rules are not always good clinical practice. A case should be individually evaluated–using the criteria cited in Chapter 3–if an accurate treatment plan is to be expected. For example, a patient who is not physically or mentally stable, presents a high chance of relapse, is not very motivated, is potentially suicidal, or is living in an unsafe environment has little chance of success in an outpatient treatment program. Such a patient is a candidate for inpatient care–even without an earlier outpatient treatment failure. The patient can then be stepped down as stability is achieved.

Residential/Inpatient Treatment, LOC III, can best be divided into four broad program types:

1. Halfway House (Low Intensity)
2. Extended Care (Medium Intensity)
3. Therapeutic Community (High Intensity)
4. Rehabilitation/Minnesota Model (Medically Monitored)

Rehabilitation Programs and the Minnesota Model Alcohol has always been an integral part of American culture. Throughout the colonies, alcoholic beverages were considered necessary and beneficial. No serious attempt was made to restrict the normal use of fermented and distilled beverages. But there was an important distinction between drinking and drunkenness, succinctly expressed in a pronouncement attributed to Increase Mather, a prominent Puritan of the time: "The wine is from God, but the drunkard is from the Devil" (Mendelson & Mello, 1985, p.11).

Heavy drinking remained the social norm well into the twentieth century. Reaction to that norm led to the rise of politically charged temperance movements and, eventually, in 1920 to the passing of the 18th Amendment to the Constitution–Prohibition. That *noble experiment,* as it is sometimes referred to, ended in 1933 with the 21st Amendment–the repeal of Prohibition. The founding of AA would not be far behind. On June 10, 1935, William Griffith Wilson (Bill W.), a New York stockbroker, and Robert Holbrook Smith (Dr. Bob), a

Candidate for Clinically Managed
Low-Intensity Residential Treatment: Level III

Mark is a 38-year-old Caucasian male, who is voluntarily seeking help for his use of methamphetamine. Mark reports using methamphetamine on weekends with a gay lover. He claims that he cannot stop using methamphetamine once he starts. He last reports using it 5 days ago. In the past his methamphetamine use was recreational. It has now become an all-weekend-long binge once he gets started. He denies abuse of any other substance although occasionally drinks some alcohol and smokes some pot. Mark attempted outpatient treatment about 3 months ago but dropped out after realizing he could not stop while continuing the relationship with his lover who also abuses methamphetamine. His lover is not willing to stop using methamphetamine. He is now prepared to leave his lover but has no place to go. Mark's parents are both deceased, and he is estranged from his 32-year-old brother. Mark has begun attending Methamphetamine Anonymous (MA) meetings on his own but believes he needs additional support.

Mark does not display any acute intoxication or significant withdrawal potential. There are no medical conditions or complications noted in Mark's history. He has previously been in psychotherapy for depression but exhibits no signs of depression or other emotional conditions at this time. It doesn't appear Mark will succeed in discontinuing the use of methamphetamine while continuing to live with his actively using and unmotivated lover.

prominent Akron surgeon, launched, unwittingly, what would become the greatest resource for recovery imaginable. Alcoholics Anonymous—a simple idea of one person helping another person—gave new hope for the alcoholic. The concept would be a paradigm change in how we view otherwise incurable illnesses as well as our understanding of the power of people. Many different kinds of self-help programs would emerge in the twentieth century, based on the principles of this 12-step approach to recovery.

With this newfound hope for the alcoholic through AA, the foundation for the development of treatment programs had been laid. (Note that Alcoholics Anonymous, Narcotics Anonymous, Cocaine Anonymous, as well as the hundreds of self-help programs throughout the world are self-help programs, *not* treatment programs.) In 1948, Pioneer House was started by recovering alcoholic Patrick Cronin. It was soon followed by Hazelden in 1949 and then Willmar State Hospital in 1950, under the direction of Nelson Bradley, unlocking the doors of its treatment wards and separating alcoholics from mental patients. All three programs started with underpinnings in AA, eventually emerging its principles to include a multidisciplinary approach of modern clinical psychology, medical care, and spirituality (Spicer, 1993).

Jerry Spicer, former president of Hazelden, states, "There are still many ways to define the model. In fact, it may even be more accurate to speak of 'Minnesota

Models.'" Reducing them to their common denominators, they share these principles:

1. Treat people with chemical dependency instead of locking them up and ignoring them.

2. Treat them with dignity.

3. Help them recover physically, mentally, and spiritually (Spicer, 1993, p. 3).

As for the modern day rehabilitation programs, including the Minnesota models, the services provided may range from basic education about SUDs and recovery to acupuncture and hatha yoga. (See the "Selected Treatment Services" box.) The length of stay is between 2 weeks and 6 weeks. Traditionally, most are about 28 to 30 days.

Extended Care Extended care is a program designed to provide a safe environment for continuing recovery, growth, and development. Sometimes confused with continuing care, extended care programs are always inpatient, while continuing care is outpatient. Extended care programs support, solidify, and extend the recovery work done in prior treatment settings or LOCs. These programs facilitate a gradual reintegration back to family, social, cultural, educational, and employment systems that form the context of the patient's individual healing and growth. A patient entering an extended care facility is likely to have been referred there upon the completion of a rehabilitation program or Minnesota model program. Extended care will pick up where the rehabilitation program left off and continue modified treatment for an *additional* 2 weeks to 6 months. The objec-

---

Candidate for Clinically Managed
Medium-Intensity Residential Treatment: Level III

Larry is a 52-year-old African–American male who has been living in a homeless shelter for the past 2 months. Previously, Larry was living on the street for months after getting evicted from his deceased mother's apartment. Larry reports a history of heavy crack and alcohol use. He clearly meets the *DSM–IV-TR* criteria for Cocaine and Alcohol Dependence. He claims that he has been trying to discontinue the drug and alcohol use but is finding it very hard to do. He claims that having no money is helping him avoid getting high.

Larry was attending a therapeutic community type program 2 years ago but was involuntarily discharged for being "disruptive" and for displaying "mental health problems." A recent evaluation indicates that Larry has impaired cognitive functioning and possibly a Borderline Personality Disorder. He appears to be a good candidate for habilitation rather than rehabilitation.

Larry has hepatitis C and is a diabetic. He reports never being able to hold down a steady job and has only done menial work. He is a 10th grade dropout. Larry is an only child and has no family support.

tives of the extended care program are to reinforce progress that has been made in the rehabilitation program, promote self-motivation, and help the patient establish a strong support system for continuing recovery. The treatment plan is personalized, life skills training is offered, group therapy is emphasized, and continuing education in a variety of relevant subjects can be expected. There are also opportunities for family involvement, individual meetings with a counselor, relapse prevention workshops, and gender-specific issues might be addressed. Most extended care programs are also 12-step-oriented. While many of the services provided in extended care are similar to those found in inpatient rehabilitation, the emphasis is on the application of newly discovered recovery skills.

Halfway House The term *halfway house* describes any facility that provides housing and support as a continuation of, or introduction to, rehabilitation. While a halfway house is often a modality of care that follows the completion of rehabilitation or extended care, this is not always a perquisite for admission. But in order to ensure the safety and integrity of the facility, the prospective resident must be clean and sober. We should note that there are halfway houses that serve all types of populations, not just people with substance abuse disorders (PSUDs). Penal institutions often have halfway houses for the continuing rehabilitation of ex-offenders released from prison. There are halfway houses that provide shelter and help for victims of high-control religious organizations, helping them to heal from the emotional, psychological, and sociological effects of their trauma. There are even halfway houses for animals and mammals, including stray pets and injured manatees.

Whether the halfway house be for ex-offenders, domestic animals, wildlife critters, or individuals recovering from SUDs, the goal is the same—a safe environment while and before entering the challenging world of work, play, growth, and survival. For the PSUD, the supportive environment of a halfway house can be the bridge that spans the sometimes treacherous waters of ambivalence, denial, and relapse.

Because the objective of a halfway house is to facilitate responsible decision making and develop healthy relationships, the primary therapeutic activity is likely to be peer-group support. Some halfway houses might provide in-house 12-step meetings or psychoeducational activities facilitated by staff members; however, most encourage residents to attend both treatment and other growth activities outside the living facility. Tickets are often made available to attend musical events, theater, and even opera. Developing a clean and sober lifestyle is essential to continued recovery. The halfway house can facilitate this objective through the safety of a protective environment and the provision of opportunities to experience various social activities in the community. Halfway house administrators will often encourage involvement in activities by establishing a resident government, securing tickets to local events, and even starting up softball teams. In our halfway house, we had one resident, Frank, who remarked after viewing *Aida* at Lincoln Center that he would never have discovered this very different world of entertainment had a fellow resident not coaxed him: "Come on, let's go—maybe we'll meet some girls there," said the fellow resident. "Well, there were plenty of 'girls' there, for sure," Frank said. "But there were also young people, and older people, and a stage filled with beautiful priestesses, armored solders, and Egyptian kings. There was music and singing, goats, lambs, donkeys, and even an elephant. By the end of the show," Frank continued, "I knew I wanted to join the real world and enjoy the things I had never even known existed."

In terms of cost, halfway houses are less expensive levels of residential care because they are less labor intensive. There are less staff members present, and while personnel in halfway houses are experienced in working with such populations, they do not necessarily hold advanced degrees. Their presence is one of support, guidance, and facility management. In most facilities, the halfway house manager is likely to be a recovering person trained and experienced in facility management.

Therapeutic Community In 1958, Charles E. Dederich, a former AA member, established Synanon in California as a drug-free treatment center for drug addicts—primarily heroin and other opioids. The therapeutic community (TC) was an innovative approach, utilizing a powerful encounter component to treat the hardcore drug addict. Confrontation and encounter groups were the primary modalities, and weekend marathon encounter groups were not uncommon. The program was highly structured; the admission process was highly intimidating—prospective candidates for admission would be interviewed in a group environment of residents who had achieved some degree of status in the program.

Other TCs that followed the Synanon model, including Daytop, Phoenix House, Odyssey House, and Project R.E.T.U.R.N., were also structured on the Synanon model. All residents had job functions, and the jobs were assigned not by what you had experience in but rather by what you *didn't* have experience in. This idea provided both a learning experience for new residents and minimized resident complacency. A resident would likely spend some time in virtually every department, often starting in the kitchen. Resident status was not a function of the job you had but rather of time in the program and the resident management status you achieved. Respect was earned through promotions and ultimately reaching acting-staff level. A resident assigned to the kitchen could be promoted to a ramrod (a kind of foreman), then to department head, and eventually to acting staff. Acting staff was a clinical level, and residents on this level would corun encounter groups. Privileges, such as leaving the facility for a weekend, were earned. In the earliest programs, drinking alcoholic beverages when off-site was an earned privilege. The fact that alcohol was also a drug was not yet accepted by the TC, but as the model matured, so, too, did its clinical understanding. Alcoholic beverages also became a substance of abuse, and abstinence became the TC's goal.

With all the advances we have made in the treatment of addictions over the past 50 years, it is too easy to be critical of the early TC. But we should not forget that before Synanon there was little being done for the heroin or opioid addict, and the only treatment for most addicts of any type was jail. There were residential facilities throughout the country such as North Brothers Island in the East River of New York City, scatter beds in psychiatric facilities, and prison-based facilities like the hospital at the federal prison in Lexington, Kentucky. But treatment amounted to little more than peer groups, medications, and enforced abstinence. The Minnesota model previously discussed, because its treatment orientation was based on the 12 steps of AA, focused on helping the alcoholic. The later programs modified their treatment approach to meet the needs of the changing drug culture. Today there are a vast variety of such programs, providing a wide range of services.

The basic tenet of the original Synanon model TC was to separate the addict from the population at large. Synanon, in fact, was a self-contained community where the addict would never leave (Scanlon, 1991). Those who left Synanon were pejoratively referred to as *splitees*. That word carried over to the modified TCs that followed, describing residents that left treatment against medical advice (AMA).

Today's modified TC is a shadow of the original Synanon model. The emphasis of treatment remains long term, but most of these programs are now far more flexible in both length of stay and treatment philosophy. And the range of services provided are now not so different from those services found in Minnesota model rehabilitation facilities. (See the "Selected Treatment Services" box.) Most therapeutic communities are highly structured programs where positive peer interaction is emphasized. Separate and individualized programs are available for adolescents, adults, and all family members. Unlike the early TCs where program graduates often joined the program as staff members, today's TC staff consists of professionals in the fields of psychology, social work, medicine, and education. However, they have not totally abandoned the practice of former residents graduating to the level of treatment staff. But such candidates now go through intensive training and certification in counseling before they can qualify as potential treatment staff members.

Medically Managed Intensive Inpatient Treatment: Level IV

As discussed in Chapter 3, this is the most intensive LOC available. This LOC "involves a planned regimen of 24-hour medically-directed evaluation, care, and treatment of substance-related disorders in an acute inpatient setting" (ASAM, 2001, p. 107). Patients in this LOC have acute biomedical or psychiatric problems severe enough to require psychiatric, medical, or nursing services. Level of care IV can be provided in a general hospital or a psychiatric hospital or any facility meeting such criteria.

A LOC IV facility is expensive to operate and, therefore, treatment costs are also expensive. While Minnesota model treatment programs and other rehabilitation models can be found within hospital-based facilities, if there are no medi-

Candidate for Medically Managed
Intensive Inpatient Treatment: Level IV

Anne is a 45-year-old Caucasian female appearing much older than her stated age. She appears about 7 months pregnant due to her significantly distended abdomen. She claims she has been drinking about a quart of vodka daily. She reports this pattern of drinking to be continuing for several years. She begins drinking after work, alone at home, and often blacks out. Despite this pattern, she never misses work as a receptionist. A Breathalyzer reading indicates a blood-alcohol concentration of .12 ml despite not drinking for approximately 12 hours. She denies the use of any other mood-altering substances.

Anne has developed liver damage from her excessive drinking, causing a blockage of excretory functions and subsequently a build up in her abdomen, resulting in the appearance of being pregnant. She is very ill. She is also displaying a moderate-to-severe potential for withdrawal.

Anne has lived alone for many years. She has extreme difficulty with social interaction and appears to display evidence of either a personality disorder (e.g., Schizoid or Avoidant) or an anxiety disorder (e.g., Social Phobia).

cal or psychiatric reasons to use this LOC, then a free-standing LOC III facility should be used.

In discussing the early days of the Minnesota model, we said that Willmar State Hospital in 1950, under the direction of Nelson Bradley, unlocked the doors of its treatment wards, separating alcoholics from other mental health diagnoses (Spicer, 1993, p.3) This is a perfect example of a rehabilitation facility within a LOC IV. While patients treated for severe mental illnesses require high-cost maintenance, the treatment for garden variety alcoholics is low-tech. Willmar State Hospital was a full-service hospital, a facility that by today's standards would qualify as the most intensive LOC–LOC IV. Also by today's standards, because hospitals have a high overhead, treatment in such a facility is likely to be more costly than treatment in a free-standing LOC III rehabilitation facility.

While many PSUDs can be treated separately from those with other mental health disorders, there are also those patients who require treatment for both. A patient may have a diagnosis of Opioid Abuse, for example, and also be diagnosed with Schizophrenia, Paranoid Type. Or a cocaine dependent person might experience a Brief Psychotic Disorder. With such cases, LOC IV is likely to be the best LOC. If the SUD diagnosis is accompanied by a less severe psychiatric disturbance, however, such as a mild form of depression or a Social Phobia, an LOC III rehabilitation facility, or Level II IOP appropriately licensed and staffed, is expected to be the best choice. The staff will be clinically qualified to provide the appropriate and necessary services in such cases.

Hospital-based treatment facilities are also appropriate when there are medical problems that will require care. While this may include a complicated detoxification where medical staff and high-tech life-support equipment should be readily available, it will also include chronic and acute medical problems that require medical management. A diabetic whose insulin levels are dangerously abnormal or an older patient with chronically high blood pressure may need the highest LOC until stabilized.

Making It All Possible

The treatment of SUDs is an evolving profession. Its evolution is dependent on biological research, neurological exploration, and the thousands of behavioral laboratories called *treatment programs.* The progress made over the past century has not been by accident. It is the result of a partnership of many disciplines and organizations whose focus has centered on two objectives—to provide the best LOC where there are problems and to establish preventive measures where none yet exist. While the number of individuals that have made contributions to the art and science of addiction treatment over the centuries is immeasurable, their results are very visible through the millions of recovering people in societies and cultures throughout the world. Where would the treatment of addictions be today had it not been for the founding of AA in 1935? Although AA is not considered to be treatment itself, it proved that recovery is possible and laid the groundwork for much that followed. And the tools that take the guesswork out of treatment planning would not be available today had it not been for the efforts of other organizations, including, but not limited to, the American Psychiatric Association (APA), for *its Diagnostic and Statistical Manual of Mental Disorders;* the American Society of Addiction Medicine (ASAM), for its *Patient Placement Criteria for the Treatment of Substance-Related Disorders;* the American Medical Association (AMA), for its endorsement of SUDs as diseases; and the government agencies, including the U.S. Department of Health and Human Services, for their myriad research and development functions.

References

American Psychiatric Association. (2000). *Diagnostic and statistical manual of mental disorders* (4th ed.; Rev. ed.). Washington, DC: Author.

American Society of Addiction Medicine. (1996). *Patient placement criteria for the treatment of substance-related disorders* (2nd ed.). Chevy Chase, MD: Author.

Doweiko, H. E. (1990). *Concepts of chemical dependency.* Pacific Grove, CA: Brooks/Cole Publishing.

Fisher, G. L., & Harrison, T. C. (2005). *Substance abuse: Information for school counselors, social workers, therapists, and counselors.* New York: Pearson Education.

John, R., Knight, R. J., Wechsler, H., Meichun, K., Seibring, M., Weitzman, E. R., & Schuckit, M. A. (2002). Alcohol abuse and dependence among U.S. college students [Abstract]. *Journal of Studies on Alcohol,* 263–270. Available at http://alcoholstudies.rutgers.edu/journal/may02/abstract.shtml#article2

Mendelson, J. H., & Mello, N. K. (1985). *Alcohol: Use and abuse in America.* Boston: Little, Brown, & Company.

Office of Applied Studies. (2003). *Results from the 2002 National Survey on Drug Use and Health: Detailed tables.* Rockville, MD: Substance Abuse and Mental Health Services Administration.

Scanlon, W. F. (1991). *Alcoholism and drug abuse in the workplace: Managing care and costs through employee assistance programs.* New York: Greenwood.

Spicer, J. (1993). *The Minnesota model.* Center City, MN: Hazelden Educational Materials.

CHAPTER **5**

Acute Intoxication and Withdrawal Potential

This chapter will explore dependence on mood-altering substances and their potential for physical withdrawal symptoms. We will look at those factors responsible for physiological dependence, how to assess for withdrawal potential, and what treatments are appropriate. Current protocols for the detoxification of specific mood-altering substances as well as opioid maintenance therapies currently being used will also be reviewed.

Physiological dependence is usually characterized by the symptoms of *tolerance* and *withdrawal*. Tolerance is characterized by the following:

1. A need for markedly increased amounts of the substance to achieve intoxication or the desired effect.

2. Markedly diminished effect with continued use of the same amount of the substance (APA, 2000, p. 197).

Withdrawal is characterized by the following:

1. The development of a substance-specific syndrome due to the cessation of (or reduction in) substance use that has been heavy and prolonged.

2. The substance-specific syndrome causes clinically significant distress or impairment in social, occupational, or other important areas of functioning.

3. The symptoms are not due to a general medical condition and are not better accounted for by another mental disorder (APA, 2000, p. 202).

The symptoms of withdrawal are, minimally, physically and psychologically uncomfortable and, at worst, potentially life-threatening. *Physiological dependence is a medical condition with a clear biological basis.* Consequently, the assessment and treatment of withdrawal is medically based and may require either inpatient or outpatient detoxification in order to achieve stabilization. Clinicians in the field with little detoxification experience often view the process with trepidation. Hopefully, this chapter will ease the fear about the process of detoxification.

A Biological Understanding of Intoxication

To understand the process of intoxication, one must get a basic understanding of how drugs affect the brain. Much of this discussion is taken directly from the National Institute on Drug Abuse's (NIDA) slide presentation *Understanding Drug Abuse and Addiction: What Science Says* (NIDA, 2004).

Certain parts of the brain govern specific functions of the body. For example, the cerebellum is involved with coordination and the hippocampus with memory. Each section of the brain communicates with other sections, as well as with the rest of the body, through brain cells called *neurons*. The human brain consists of billions of these neurons. Neurons send and receive messages through a combination of electrical and chemical impulses. This process in the brain is known as *neurotransmission*. Neurotransmission involves chemical substances found in neurons called *neurotransmitters*. There are a variety of known neurotransmitters in the human brain. One neurotransmitter that appears to be particularly important during drug intoxication is *dopamine*. Dopamine will be used to explain the process of neurotransmission.

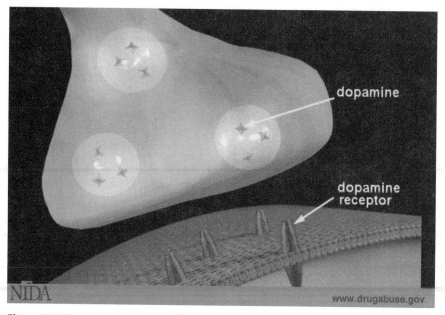

Figure 5.1 *The synapse and synaptic neurotransmission.*

Figure 5.2 *Dopamine neurotransmission and uptake pumps in the nucleus acumbens.*

In the normal communication process among neurons, an electrical impulse travels down a neuron and causes it to release dopamine from storage vessels, located inside the neuron, known as *vesicles*. The dopamine is released into a small gap between neurons called a *synapse*. The released dopamine binds with specialized proteins called *dopamine receptors* on a neighboring neuron, causing a new electrical impulse to occur. After the impulse occurs, the dopamine is released from the receptors and, within milliseconds, transported back to the storage site by the *dopamine transporter* (see Figures 5.1 and 5.2).

Drugs of abuse are able to interfere with this normal communication process in the brain by mimicking the neurotransmitters. Cocaine, for example, mimics dopamine. After cocaine is consumed, it blocks the dopamine transporters from working normally. This results in a buildup of dopamine in the synapse. In turn, this causes a continuous stimulation of the receiving neurons, causing the feelings of euphoria reported by cocaine users (see Figure 5.3).

Mood-altering substances appear to affect neurotransmission in a particular area of the brain known to be associated with feelings of reward or pleasure. (This area of the brain also appears to have the highest concentration of dopamine.) This reward area is also activated by other pleasurable activities, such as sex or eating. This section of the brain is actually a connected pathway (*reward pathway*) comprising three separate areas: the ventral tegmental area (VTA), the nucleus accumbens, and the prefrontal cortex. When activated by a rewarding stimulus (e.g., food, sex, or drugs), the information travels from the VTA to the nucleus accumbens and then up to the prefrontal cortex (see Figure 5.4).

Figure 5.3 *The action of cocaine; cocaine binding to dopamine receptors and uptake pumps.*

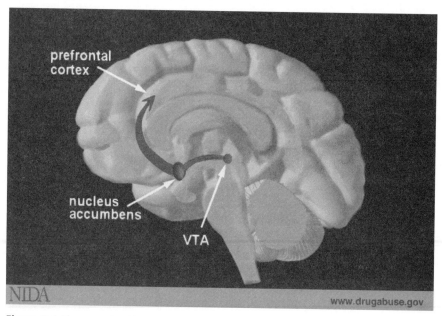

Figure 5.4 *The reward pathway.*

Homeostatis: How It Affects Tolerance and Withdrawal

Homeostasis is the body's way of achieving balance when altered by outside (environmental) influences. It is defined as "a tendency toward maintenance of a relatively stable internal environment in the bodies of higher animals through a series of interacting physiological processes" (Webster's, 2002). Homeostasis is the body's unique compensatory mechanism for maintaining equilibrium. When this process occurs in the brain, it is known as *neuroadaptation.*

The use of mood-altering substances may result in an abnormally elevated level of dopamine (as well as other neurotransmitters) in the brain. This abnormally high level causes the feeling state of euphoria. In order to return to a state of homeostasis, or balance, the body compensates by producing less dopamine in the brain. The process by which this occurs is still unclear and under investigation. It may be accomplished by reducing the number of receptors that bind with dopamine, by releasing less dopamine into the synapse, or by some other process.

Tolerance, needing more of the substance to get the same effect, also appears to be related to the process of homeostasis. The body compensates for repeated substance abuse by decreasing the amount of or sensitivity to dopamine. Consequently, the person using the mood-altering substance needs more of it to get the same effect.

When a person abusing a drug suddenly discontinues use, the body is unprepared. The brain, which had been producing either lower- or higher-than-usual levels of neurotransmitter activity because of continuous drug use, is unprepared for the sudden cessation. It continues the neuroadaptation process for days, weeks, or months after drug use is stopped. This is commonly known as the *withdrawal* or *abstinence syndrome.* For example, cocaine use (or the high release of dopamine) leads to a state of euphoria and a heightened sense of pleasure. Upon discontinuation of cocaine, the natural level of dopamine production, which was significantly curtailed through neuroadaptation, makes the person feel depressed and lacking pleasure. Opioid use (involving higher production and release of the neurochemicals called *endorphins*) leads to a decrease in sensation of pain, a state of euphoria, and a very relaxed state. Upon discontinuation of opioid use, endorphin levels, significantly decreased by neuroadaptation, create a heightened sense of pain sensitivity, overall discomfort, and agitation. In other words, *the state of withdrawal appears to be an overcompensation of the body to fight the elevated production of neurotransmitters released through drug abuse.* Withdrawal symptoms are the opposite effects, or the rebound effects, of those produced when the substance was taken. A person using stimulants, for example, might experience depression; if they were taking depressants or opioids, agitation might be the rebound effect.

Detoxification from Substances

Detoxification, also known as *detox,* is "the process through which a person who is physically dependent on alcohol, illegal drugs, prescription medications, or a combination of these drugs is withdrawn from the drug or drugs of dependence" (Center for Substance Abuse Treatment [CSAT], 1995a, p. 1); "The term detoxification implies a clearing of toxins" (Alling, 1992, p. 1); "Detoxification also includes the period of time during which the body's physiology is adjusting to the absence of drugs" (CSAT, 1995a, p. 1). Detoxification involves a variety of procedures used to eliminate the short-term symptoms of withdrawal from drug dependence. It also includes "a period of psychological readjustment designed to prepare the patient to take the next step in ongoing treatment" (Czechowicz, 1979, quoted from CSAT 1995a, p. 1).

Goals of Detoxification

The following goals of detoxification are cited from the American Society of Addiction Medicine's *Patient Placement Criteria for the Treatment of Substance-Related Disorders* (ASAM, 1996, p.12):

- Avoidance of the potentially hazardous consequences of discontinuation of alcohol and other drugs of dependence.

- Facilitation of the patient's completion of detoxification and linkages and timely entry into continued medical, addiction, or mental health treatment or self-help recovery as indicated.

- Promotion of patient dignity and easing of patient discomfort during the withdrawal process.

Principles of Detoxification

The following principles are cited from *Detoxification from Alcohol and Other Drugs* (CSAT, 1995a, p. 15):

- Detoxification *alone* is rarely adequate treatment for alcohol and other drug (AOD) dependencies.

- When using medication regimens or other detoxification procedures, only protocols of established safety and efficacy should be used in routine clinical practice.

- Providers must advise patients when procedures are used that have not been established as safe and effective.

- During detoxification, providers should control patients' access to medication to the greatest extent possible.

- Initiation of withdrawal should be individualized.

- Whenever possible, clinicians should substitute a long-acting medication for short-acting drugs of addiction.

- The intensity of withdrawal cannot always be predicted accurately.

- Every means possible should be used to ameliorate the patient's signs and symptoms of AOD withdrawal.

■ Patients should begin participating as soon as possible in follow-up support therapy, such as peer group therapy, family therapy, individual counseling or therapy, 12-step recovery meetings, and AOD recovery educational programs.

Detoxification Treatment Levels

The ASAM PPC-2R (2001) distinguishes four levels of detoxification services. Placement in any of these levels of care (LOC) depends upon the clinical severity of physical dependence to alcohol or other drugs. The following are the four LOCs for detoxification:

■ Level I-D: Ambulatory Detoxification without Extended On-Site Monitoring

■ Level II-D: Ambulatory Detoxification with Extended On-Site Monitoring

■ Level III-D: Residential/Inpatient Detoxification

■ Level IV-D: Medically Managed Intensive Inpatient Detoxification

Level I-D: Ambulatory Detoxification without Extended On-Site Monitoring

Level I-D is an organized outpatient service, which may be delivered in an office setting, health care or addiction treatment facility, or in a patient's home by trained clinicians who provide medically supervised evaluation, detoxification and referral services according to a predetermined schedule. (ASAM, 2001, p. 145)

This LOC is used for the patient experiencing mild signs and symptoms of withdrawal. The patient is assessed as having minimal risk of severe withdrawal and can be safely managed at this LOC. The patient at this LOC is assessed as being highly motivated to complete the detox process and continue follow-up support therapy. The patient is willing to accept recommendations for treatment and responds positively to emotional support and comfort. The patient is best served by having at least one supportive other who can ensure commitment and completion of the detox process and can monitor any medications given to the patient between treatment visits.

Physicians and nurses are essential to this LOC although they need not be present in the treatment setting at all times. Physician extenders (e.g., physician assistants or nurse practitioners), under the supervision of a physician, may perform the duties designated by the physician.

Level II-D: Ambulatory Detoxification with Extended On-Site Monitoring
This LOC is almost identical to the previous one with the exception of longer clinical monitoring during sessions. In Level I-D, after a comprehensive assessment, a patient is generally dispensed medications and seen only briefly, on a daily basis, for medical monitoring. In this level, medical personnel monitor the patient, over a period of several hours per day, to ensure safety and comfort around withdrawal. This usually includes serial nursing assessments, using appropriate measures of

withdrawal. The patient at this LOC may also be involved in other support services, including individual, group, and family therapy; acupuncture; and drug education. The setting for this LOC usually involves a general healthcare facility, such as a physician's office, an addiction or mental health treatment facility, or a hospital outpatient department. The medical personnel remain the same as Level I-D. The patient must display the same level of motivation and commitment as in Level I-D for completing ambulatory detox and following up with continued support therapy. The addition of at least one supportive other to ensure commitment and completion of the detox process is also encouraged.

At this LOC, the patient is assessed as being at moderate risk of severe withdrawal syndrome outside the program setting, free of severe physical and psychiatric complications, and able to respond safely to several hours of monitoring, medication, and treatment.

Level III-D: Residential/Inpatient Detoxification Level III-D is divided into two subcategories: Level III.2-D (Clinically Managed Residential Detoxification) and Level III.7-D (Medically Monitored Inpatient Detoxification). According to ASAM, "The difference between these two levels of detoxification is the intensity of clinical services, particularly as demonstrated by the degree of involvement of medical and nursing professionals" (ASAM PPC-2R, 2001, p. 146).

- Level III.2-D: Clinically Managed Residential Detoxification. Also known as *social setting detoxification,* this LOC provides 24-hour supervision, observation, and support for patients who are intoxicated or experiencing withdrawal. This LOC is characterized by its emphasis on peer and social support. While the patient requires 24-hour structure and support, ready on-site access to medical and nursing personnel is not necessary. The setting for this LOC may include a TC or other licensed residential addiction treatment facility.

The patient is assessed as not being at risk of severe withdrawal syndrome and having moderate withdrawal that can be safely managed at this LOC. The patient is assessed as not requiring medication but requires this LOC to complete detoxification and enter into continued treatment or self-help recovery because of inadequate home supervision or support structure. The patient's recovery environment may be assessed as being unsupportive toward detoxification and ongoing treatment, or the patient may lack adequate coping skills to deal with the unsupportive environment. The patient may have a history of not completing detox, of being noncompliant with treatment at less intensive levels, or failing to enter into continued treatment in the past.

- Level III.7-D: Medically Monitored Inpatient Detoxification. This LOC, delivered by medical and nursing professionals, provides 24-hour medically supervised evaluation and withdrawal management. *The withdrawal signs and symptoms are sufficiently severe to require 24-hour inpatient care.* The typical setting includes a freestanding detoxification center or other licensed health care or addiction treatment facility. Licensed and credentialed nurses are responsible for overseeing the monitoring of the patient's progress and administering medication as needed. A physician is available on a daily basis to monitor patient care and provide necessary evaluations. The physician is always available (24 hours a day) by telephone.

In order to obtain admission to this LOC, *the patient must be experiencing signs and symptoms of severe withdrawal, or there is evidence that a severe withdrawal syndrome is imminent.* The severe withdrawal syndrome is assessed as manageable at this LOC. There may be a strong likelihood that the patient will not complete detoxification or enter continued treatment at a lower LOC. The patient may have a coexisting physical or psychiatric condition that increases the severity of the withdrawal and complicates detoxification.

Level IV-D: Medically Managed Intensive Inpatient Detoxification This level is similar to Level III.7-D, with the addition of providing these services in an acute care setting. This setting may include an acute care general hospital, an acute care psychiatric hospital, or a chemical dependency specialty hospital with acute care medical and nursing staff and life-support equipment. *The patient, at this LOC, experiences severe withdrawal signs and symptoms, requiring primary medical and nursing care services.* The objective is to alleviate acute emotional, behavioral, or biomedical distress resulting from the patient's use of alcohol or other drugs. At this LOC, a physician is available 24 hours a day to medically manage the care of the patient. Nursing staff is available 24 hours a day for nursing care and observation. The detoxification regimen requires monitoring or intervention more frequently than hourly. Other factors for inclusion to this LOC include the following:

- A recent (within 24 hours) serious head trauma or loss of consciousness, with persistent mental status or neurological changes needing close observation.

- A drug overdose or intoxication that has compromised the patient's mental status, cardiac function, or other vital signs or functions.

- A significant acute biomedical disorder that poses substantial risk of serious or life-threatening consequences during withdrawal.

- A need for detoxification or stabilization while pregnant, until the patient can be safely treated in a less intensive LOC.

Treatment Protocols for Detoxification

This section will explore how to assess the potential of withdrawal severity, how to make LOC determinations based upon withdrawal potential, and pharmacologic treatment protocols for detoxification from substances known to cause physiological dependence. As discussed in Chapter 2, substances known to cause physiological dependence fall into two classes: *depressants* (e.g., alcohol, sedatives, and hypnotics) and *opiates* (e.g., heroin, Percodan, methadone, etc.). The treatment protocols to be reviewed are taken primarily from a manual published through a grant from the U.S. Department of Health and Human Services, *Detoxification from Alcohol and Other Drugs* (CSAT, 1995a). The manual is in the process of being revised at the time of this writing.

Assessing Withdrawal Potential for Alcohol

The signs and symptoms of alcohol withdrawal usually begin 6 to 24 hours after the last use of alcohol. The acute phase of the alcohol abstinence syndrome may begin when the patient still has significant blood-alcohol concentrations. Signs and symptoms may include the following:

- Restlessness, irritability, anxiety, agitation
- Anorexia, nausea, vomiting
- Tremor, elevated heart rate, increased blood pressure
- Insomnia, intense dreaming, nightmares
- Impaired concentration, memory, and judgment
- Increased sensitivity to sounds, alteration in tactile sensations
- Delirium (disorientation to time, place, or situation)
- Hallucinations (auditory, visual, or tactile)
- Delusions (usually paranoid)
- Grand mal seizures
- Elevated temperature

Symptoms do not always progress from mild to severe in a predictable fashion. In some patients, a grand mal seizure may be the first manifestation of acute alcohol abstinence syndrome (CSAT, 1995a).

Most patients can be detoxified from alcohol in 3 to 5 days. Providers should consider the withdrawal time frame in terms of when the patient will need the most support; for alcoholics, this occurs the second day after the last ingestion. Other factors that influence the length of the detoxification period include the severity of the dependency and the patient's overall health status. Patients who are medically debilitated should detoxify more slowly (CSAT, 1995a).

Hospitalization for alcohol detoxification (especially beyond a day or two) is generally not necessary except if accompanied by biomedical or psychiatric complications. Most alcohol-dependent patients can be detoxified in a modified medical setting, such as a nonhospital residential, partial day care, or ambulatory program as long as the assessment is comprehensive, medical backup is available, and staff knows when to obtain medical consultation.

Assessment Tools for Alcohol Withdrawal

One of the best-known, best-researched, and most commonly used instruments for assessing and monitoring alcohol withdrawal is known as the *Clinical Institute*

Withdrawal Assessment of Alcohol, revised (CIWA-Ar; Sullivan et al., 1989; Wiehl, Hayner, & Galloway, 1994). This quick and easy-to-use scale measures the signs and symptoms of 10 alcohol withdrawal factors. The assessment tool can be completed in about 2 to 5 minutes. The result of this assessment tool helps to determine LOC and is also useful for monitoring and managing the patient during withdrawal. Because the CIWA-Ar is not copyrighted, it may be used freely. You can find a copy as well as an interactive version at the following address: www .chce.research.med.va.gov/chce/presentations/PAWS/content/1CourseOv.htm

Symptoms of Alcohol Withdrawal Syndrome

Signs and symptoms of withdrawal from alcohol include two or more of the following, developing within several hours to a few days after cessation or reduction in heavy and prolonged use:

- Nausea and vomiting
- Increased hand tremor
- Paroxysmal sweats
- Anxiety
- Agitation and irritability
- Transient tactile disturbances and hallucinations (e.g., itching, pins-and-needles sensations, burning, or numbness)
- Transient auditory disturbances and hallucinations (e.g., very aware of sounds or hearing things that do not exist)
- Transient visual disturbances hallucinations or illusions (e.g., sensitivity to light or seeing things that do not exist)
- Headache and fullness of the head
- Orientation and clouding of sensorium (e.g., disorientation with date and place)
- Autonomic hyperactivity (e.g., diaphoresis—unusual heavy perspiration, tachycardia—a rapid heart beat, and elevated blood pressure)
- Insomnia
- Delirium tremens (DTs)
- Psychomotor agitation
- Grand mal seizures

The potential for alcohol withdrawal syndrome can be gauged only imprecisely by asking the patient the pattern, type, and quantity of recent and past alcohol use (such as screening with the AUDIT). Not all patients who are acutely intoxicated or physiologically dependent on alcohol will need pharmacological management of withdrawal symptoms.

The Clinical Institute Withdrawal Assessment of Alcohol Scale, Revised (CIWA-Ar) is the best-known and most extensively studied scale for quantifying alcohol withdrawal syndrome. It is a brief, empirically validated interview for assessing the severity of withdrawal risk.

The CIWA-Ar should be repeated at regular intervals (initially every 1 or 2 hours) to monitor patients' progress. Increasing scores on the CIWA-Ar signify the need for additional medication or a higher level of treatment; decreasing scores suggest therapeutic response to medication or treatment milieu. "Patients scoring less than 10 on the CIWA-Ar do not usually need additional medication for withdrawal" (Saitz et al., 1994; Sullivan et al., 1989; excerpted in CSAT, 1995a, p. 17).

Breathalyzer Readings

Another important tool for assessing the severity of acute intoxication or withdrawal potential is the use of a Breathalyzer. Most Breathalyzer readings use the unit "grams of alcohol per 100 milliliters of blood," abbreviated "gm%." Blood-alcohol concentration (BAC) levels can be gauged as follows (National Institute of Alcoholism and Alcohol Abuse [NIAAA], 1995):

- 0.00gm%—No alcohol is detected in the blood.

- 0.02–0.06gm%—This is the normal social drinking range. (Driving, even at these levels, is unsafe.)

- 0.08gm%—Memory, judgment, and perception are impaired. This is considered legally intoxicated in all states.

- 0.10gm%—Reaction time and coordination of movement are affected.

- 0.15gm%—Vomiting may occur in normal drinkers; balance is often impaired.

- 0.20gm%—Memory blackout may occur, causing loss of recall for events occurring while intoxicated.

- 0.30gm%—Unconsciousness in a normal person, though some remain conscious at levels in excess of 0.60gm% if tolerance is very high.

- 0.40–0.50gm%—Fatal dose for a normal person, though some survive higher levels if tolerance is very high.

A BAC greater than 0.3gm% indicates extremely high tolerance and usually warrants hospitalization. A BAC greater than 0.1gm% with accompanying withdrawal signs suggests the possibility of severe withdrawal and also warrants hospitalization (ASAM, 1991).

Serum Chemistry Profile

A serum chemistry profile, also known as a *liver function test,* is a blood test used to assess the health of the liver (NIAAA, 1995). It includes five serum assays that can be elevated by excessive drinking:

- AST (aspartate animotransferase)
- ALT (alanine transferase)
- GGTP (gamma glutamyl transpeptidase)
- Bilirubin
- Uric Acid

These assays should be examined as part of an overall alcohol severity assessment. Other important tools for assessing alcohol withdrawal severity include the measurement of vital signs, specifically pulse and blood pressure. A pulse reading greater than 110 or a blood pressure reading higher than 160/110 accompanied by a CIWA-Ar greater than 10 may suggest a severe withdrawal syndrome warranting hospitalization (ASAM, 1991). Other predictors of severe alcohol withdrawal potential include a past history of severe alcohol withdrawal, concurrent use of sedatives or hypnotics, and coexisting medical problems.

Assessing Alcohol Withdrawal and Determining Level of Care

Once we assess the severity of alcohol withdrawal, we can then determine the most appropriate (and least restrictive) LOC in which to treat the patient. After reading the following assessment, try to determine the appropriate LOC, utilizing information from the previous section, before reading our LOC recommendation. This will help test your understanding of alcohol withdrawal severity and LOC determination.

A Case Example

John is a 35-year-old male referred by his employee assistance program (EAP) after exhibiting a pattern of excessive absenteeism at work over the past 6 months. John is employed as a porter in a commercial office building. John admits that his absenteeism is the direct result of his alcohol use. John is accompanied by his wife of 12 years, who appears eager to get her husband the help he needs. (She denies any use of alcohol or drug use herself.) John also appears highly motivated to seek help for his drinking.

John meets the criteria for Alcohol Dependence. Upon administration of the Substance Use Disorders Diagnostic Schedule (SUDDS), John meets the criteria for all seven potential items of Alcohol Dependence (e.g., tolerance, withdrawal, drinking more than intended, inability to control use, preoccupation with use, sacrificing other activities due to drinking, and physical or psychological problems related to drinking).

John reports daily alcohol use for the past 6 months. He admits to drinking a pint of vodka daily and sometimes up to a quart of vodka on weekends. He reports his last use of alcohol yesterday (approximately 28 hours ago). His BAC is zero (0.00 %gm). John claims alcohol has been a problem for the past 10 years.

He denies any other use of illicit or prescribed medications. He denies any previous treatment for alcohol or other drug use.

John's vital signs (e.g., blood pressure, temperature, and pulse) are normal. A liver function test indicates a moderately elevated ALT score. A physical exam suggests John to be in relatively good health. He denies any history of delirium tremens, head trauma, loss of consciousness, or gastrointestinal disorders. He does admit to recent blackouts. On the CIWA-Ar, John scores an 11, indicating moderate withdrawal. He displays moderate anxiety, agitation, and tremor. Despite appearing anxious, John denies any history of psychiatric treatment or complications. His mental status exam does not indicate anything remarkable.

What is your recommended LOC for John?

LOC Determination John appears highly motivated for treatment and appears to have strong support from his wife. He clearly appears to have an Alcohol Dependence Disorder with alcohol withdrawal, as evidenced by the SUDDS, self-report, and the CIWA-Ar score. His alcohol withdrawal is not complicated by use of other addictive substances. His CIWA-Ar score of 11 indicates moderate withdrawal symptomology. He appears free from any severe physical or psychiatric complications other than some elevated liver enzymes and anxiety. He appears able to safely respond to several hours of daily monitoring, medication, and treatment. Consequently, our LOC recommendation would be a Level II-D: Ambulatory Detoxification with Extended On-Site Monitoring.

The Pharmacologic Treatment of Alcohol Withdrawal

The following section is taken directly from *Detoxification from Alcohol and Other Drugs* (CSAT, 1995a):

Benzodiazepines, such as chlordiazepoxide (Librium), clonazepam (Klonopin), chlorazepate (Tranxene), and diazepam (Valium), are considered effective tools in ameliorating signs and symptoms of alcohol withdrawal because they decrease the likelihood and number of withdrawal seizures and episodes of *delirium tremens.* Chlordiazepoxide is "currently the most commonly administered medication for alcohol withdrawal in the United States" (Saitz et al., 1994). Oxazepam (Serax) or lorazepam (Ativan) are sometimes used with patients who have severe liver disease because neither is metabolized by the liver.

There are several acceptable medication regimens for treating alcohol withdrawal:

- *Gradual, tapering doses.* Oral benzodiazepines are administered on a predetermined dosing schedule for several days and gradually discontinued. This regimen is the one most commonly used. Dosing protocols vary widely among treatment facilities.

- *Symptom-triggered therapy.* Using the CIWA-Ar, nurses are trained to recognize signs and symptoms of alcohol withdrawal and to give a benzodiazepine to their patients only when signs and symptoms of alcohol withdrawal appear.

- *Loading dose.* Staff administers a slowly metabolized benzodiazepine for only the first day of treatment. Patients in moderate-to-severe withdrawal receive 20 mg of diazepam (or 100 mg of chlordiazepoxide) every 1 to 2 hours until they show significant clinical improvement (such as a CIWA-Ar score of 10 or less) or become sedated.

According to a study, patients treated with symptom-triggered therapy completed their treatment courses sooner and required less medication than patients treated using the standard fixed-schedule approach (Saitz et al., 1994).

Sedative-Hypnotic Detoxification

Assessment Issues The other class of depressants, similar to ethyl alcohol that leads to physical dependency, is the group of substances known as sedative-hypnotics. Sedative-hypnotics, also known as *tranquilizers* and *sleeping pills,* include the benzodiazepines (e.g., Valium, Librium, and Xanax) and the barbiturates (e.g., Seconal, Tuinal, and Quaalude; see Chapter 2 for a more detailed discussion on these substances). The sedative-hypnotics are very similar in structure to alcohol. They have an addictive effect when combined with alcohol, have a similar intoxication pattern as alcohol, and have a similar potential for fatality during overdose and during withdrawal as alcohol. Assessing the severity of sedative-hypnotic withdrawal is not as easy as assessing the severity of alcohol withdrawal because there are no widely recognized assessment tools.

The following section is taken directly from *Detoxification from Alcohol and Other Drugs* (CSAT, 1995a):

> **Withdrawal from Benzodiazepines and Other Sedative-Hypnotics** For therapeutic use, barbiturates and the older sedative-hypnotics have been largely replaced by the benzodiazepines. The withdrawal syndromes from benzodiazepines and other sedative-hypnotics are similar, and the pharmacotherapy treatment strategies apply to both. This section focuses on the benzodiazepines and adds information about treatment of other types of sedative-hypnotic dependence when appropriate (Alling, 1992).
>
> Dependence on benzodiazepines and other sedative-hypnotics usually develops in the context of medical treatment. Benzodiazepines have many therapeutic uses: as therapy for some conditions, such as panic disorder, long-term treatment is appropriate medical practice. Physical dependency is sometimes unavoidable. Benzodiazepine dependency that develops during pharmacotherapy is not necessarily a substance use disorder (Alling, 1992). When the dependency results from patients taking the prescribed doses as directed by a physician, the term *therapeutic discontinuation* is preferable to the term *detoxification.*
>
> Use of either benzodiazepines or sedative-hypnotics at doses above the therapeutic range for a month or more produces physical dependence. Without appropriate medical treatment, withdrawal from benzodiazepines or other sedative-hypnotics can be severe and life-threatening. Withdrawal from benzodiazepines or

other sedative-hypnotics produces a similar withdrawal syndrome, described below under high-dose sedative-hypnotic withdrawal.

Some people will develop withdrawal symptoms after stopping therapeutic doses of benzodiazepines or other sedative-hypnotics after they have been used daily for 6 months or more. With "low-dose" withdrawal, the benzodiazepines and other sedative-hypnotics can produce qualitatively different withdrawal syndromes. These are described as *high-dose sedative-hypnotic withdrawal syndrome* and *low-dose benzodiazepine withdrawal syndrome.*

LOC Determinations for Sedative-Hypnotic Detoxification The following section is based upon the criteria developed in the ASAM PPC-2R (ASAM, 2001):

Level I-D: Ambulatory detoxification without extended on-site monitoring. In order to be treated for sedative-hypnotic detoxification at this LOC, there must be a reliable history that *the patient is withdrawing from therapeutic doses of sedative-hypnotics and no evidence of other alcohol or drug dependence.* The withdrawal symptoms have either responded to or are likely to respond to substitute doses of sedative-hypnotics in the therapeutic range within 2 hours.

Level II-D: Ambulatory detoxification with extended on-site monitoring. To be eligible for this LOC, *the patient has ingested sedative-hypnotics in excess of therapeutic levels daily for at least 4 weeks,* but the risk of seizures, hallucinations, dissociation, or severe affective disorder during unobserved periods outside the program is assessed as minimal. *There is no accompanying chronic mental or physical disorder* that poses a danger to the patient during withdrawal.

A second set of criteria for inclusion in this LOC is for the patient who has ingested *sedative-hypnotics (at not more than therapeutic levels) daily for at least 6 months, in combination with daily alcohol use or regular use of another mind-altering drug* known to have its own dangerous withdrawal syndrome. The risk of seizures, hallucinations, dissociation, or severe affective symptoms outside the program is assessed as minimal.

Level III.2-D: Clinically managed residential detoxification. This social setting program *does not include criteria for sedative-hypnotic detoxification.* This is likely due to the lack of medical staffing at this LOC. This LOC is not equipped to handle risky cases associated with sedative-hypnotic withdrawal.

Level III.7-D: Medically monitored inpatient detoxification. For inclusion to this LOC, the patient has ingested sedative-hypnotics at more than therapeutic levels daily for more than 4 weeks, in combination with daily alcohol use or regular use of another substance known to pose a severe risk of withdrawal. *The signs and symptoms of withdrawal are of moderate severity.* The patient may have been unable to be stabilized by the end of a period of ambulatory detoxification.

A second set of criteria for inclusion to this LOC involves the patient displaying marked lethargy or hypersomnolence (excessive sleep) due to intoxication with sedative-hypnotics, and a history of severe withdrawal syndrome, or the patient's altered level of consciousness has not stabilized by the end of a period of ambulatory detoxification.

Level IV-D: Medically managed intensive inpatient detoxification. To be eligible for this LOC, the patient

1. Must be experiencing seizures; delirium tremens; or severe, persistent hallucinations.

2. Must have ingested sedative-hypnotics at more than therapeutic levels daily for more than 4 weeks, with an accompanying acute mental or physical disorder complicating the withdrawal.

3. Must have ingested sedative-hypnotics for at least 6 months, in combination with daily alcohol use or other mood-altering drug known to pose a severe withdrawal syndrome, and accompanied by an acute mental or physical disorder that is complicating the withdrawal.

The Pharmacologic Treatment of Benzodiazepine Withdrawal Based on the *Detoxification from Alcohol and Other Drugs* (CSAT, 1995a), abrupt discontinuation of a sedative-hypnotic in patients who are severely physically dependent can result in serious medical complications and even death. For this reason, medical management is always needed, and treatment is best provided in a hospital setting. There are three general medication strategies for withdrawing patients from sedative-hypnotics, including benzodiazepines: (1) the use of decreasing doses of the agent of dependence; (2) the substitution of phenobarbital or another long-acting barbiturate for the addicting agent and the gradual withdrawal of the substitute medication (Smith & Wesson, 1970, 1971, 1983, 1985); and (3) the substitution of a long-acting benzodiazepine, such as chlordiazepoxide (Librium), which is tapered over 1 to 2 weeks. The method selected depends on the particular benzodiazepine, the involvement of other drugs of dependence, and the clinical setting in which detoxification takes place.

Opioid Detoxification and Maintenance Therapy

The class of opioids, also known as opiates, include all painkillers, such as the natural opioids (e.g., opium and morphine), the semisynthethic opioids (e.g., heroin and codeine), and the synthetic opioids (e.g., codeine, methadone, Vicodin, Percocet, and Percodan; For a more thorough review of opioids, see Chapter 2). This is the only other class of substances, besides the depressants, known to clearly produce physiological dependence (i.e., tolerance and withdrawal syndrome). All opioids produce similar withdrawal signs and symptoms. However, the time of onset and the duration of the abstinence syndrome may vary. The severity of the withdrawal syndrome depends on many factors, including the drug used (short versus Long acting), the total daily dose, how the drug was used (e.g., IV, oral, intranasal), the interval between doses, the duration of use, and the health and personality of the addict. While opioid withdrawal can be extremely uncomfortable and painful, it is not generally life-threatening, contrary to popular opinion.

There are two general methods for treating opioid dependence. These two methods have contrasting objectives. The objective of the first method is to get the patient drug-free by initiating a detoxification protocol, as discussed for the depressants in the previous section, followed by addiction counseling to repair the consequences of the addiction and to prevent relapse. The objective of the second method is not a drug-free state, but rather a *maintained* state on an opioid compound such as methadone or buprenorphine. Through opiate maintenance therapy, the patient is regularly maintained on an opioid compound to avoid withdrawal symptoms, drug cravings, and intoxication. Thus, the patient is expected to lead a more productive life without the pressure and consequences of compulsive opioid-seeking, opioid-taking, and withdrawal sickness. We will begin with a discussion of the factors involved in opioid detoxification followed by a discussion of opioid maintenance therapy.

The Signs and Symptoms of Opioid Withdrawal Severity The signs and symptoms of withdrawal from heroin or morphine begin 8 to 12 hours following the patient's last dose. *The peak intensity occurs at about 36 to 72 hours following the last dose.* They subside over a period of 5 to 7 days, with some lingering effects, such as insomnia, lasting longer.

Signs and symptoms of withdrawal from methadone begin 12 hours after the patient's last dose. The peak intensity occurs on the third day of abstinence or later. Symptoms gradually subside, but may continue for 3 weeks or longer. Methadone abstinence syndrome develops more slowly and is more prolonged but usually less intense than other opioid abstinence syndromes.

There are no standardized assessment devices currently being used to determine severity of opioid withdrawal, comparable to the CIWA-Ar for alcohol. A valid and reliable opioid withdrawal scale would be an important addition to our field. The scale that we currently rely upon to determine opioid severity is called the Narcotic Withdrawal Scale (Fultz and Senay, 1975; in ASAM, 1991). This scale divides opioid withdrawal signs and symptoms into four distinct stages of severity, with Grade 1 being "mild withdrawal" and Grade 4 being "severe withdrawal":

Grade 1: Lacrimation (tearing or crying), rhinorrhea (runny nose), diaphoresis (sweating), yawning, restlessness, and insomnia

Grade 2: Dilated pupils, piloerection (goosebumps), muscle twitching, myalgia (muscle pain), arthralgia (joint pain), and abdominal pain

Grade 3: Tachycardia (increased heart rate), hypertension, tachypnea (rapid breathing), fever, anorexia, nausea, and extreme restlessness

Grade 4: Diarrhea, vomiting, dehydration, hyperglycemia, hypotension, and curled-up (fetal) position

LOC Determinations for Opioid Detoxification Determining the appropriate LOC for opioid detoxification is not as precise as that found in the ASAM PPC-2R (ASAM, 2001) for the depressants (e.g., alcohol and the sedative-hypnotics). One approach is the Narcotic Withdrawal Scale previously presented to determine LOC. For example, a patient exhibiting Grade 1 symptoms on the withdrawal scale could be managed in a Level I-D ambulatory setting or in a Level III.2-D social setting detox program. Grade 2 symptoms would best be managed in a Level II-D setting (ambulatory detox with extended care). Grade 3 symptoms may be managed in a Level III.7-D setting (medically monitored inpatient detoxification setting). Last, Grade 4 symptoms are best treated in a Level IV-D setting (medically managed intensive inpatient detoxification setting).

The ASAM PPC-2R (ASAM, 2001) suggests the following guidelines for determining treatment levels for opiate detoxification:

Level I-D: Ambulatory detoxification without extended on-site monitoring. Injectable opiates have not been daily for more than 2 weeks preceding admission or the use of opiates is near the therapeutically recommended level. *The patient is exhibiting only mild withdrawal symptoms.*

Level II-D: Ambulatory detoxification with extended on-site monitoring. The abstinence syndrome (as indicated by vital signs and evidence of physical discomfort or craving) can be stabilized by the end of each day's monitoring and managed at home with appropriate supervision. *The withdrawal signs and symptoms are of such severity or instability that extended monitoring is required to determine appropriate dosage.*

Level III.2-D: Clinically managed residential detoxification. There are no criteria listed for opiate detoxification at this LOC.

Level III.7-D: Medically monitored inpatient detoxification. Injectable opiates have been daily for more than 2 weeks, and the patient has a history of inability to complete withdrawal as an outpatient or without medication in a Level III.2-D residential detoxification setting. Antagonist medication (e.g., naltrexone and naloxone) is to be used in a brief, but intensive, detoxification. (We will discuss the terms *antagonist* and *agonist* shortly.)

Level IV-D: Medically managed intensive inpatient detoxification. The patient is experiencing a severe opioid withdrawal syndrome that has not been stabilized or managed at a less intensive LOC. Antagonist medication is to be used in rapid withdrawal (i.e., induction of naloxone over 6 hours).

Opioid Detoxification

Withdrawal from opiates is generally not life-threatening, but it is often unpleasant and painful. Some characterize it as similar to the symptoms of a bad flu. Opioid detoxification usually involves some form of pharmacologic treatment to alleviate the discomfort associated with the withdrawal syndrome. The following section is primarily taken from *Detoxification from Alcohol and Other Drugs* (CSAT, 1995a):

Pharmacological Treatments for Opioid Withdrawal Pharmacological treatments are as follows:

- *Clonidine (Catapres)*. Clonidine, a medication marketed for the treatment of hypertension, has been used for treatment of the symptoms of opioid withdrawal since 1978 (Gold, Redmond, & Kleber, 1978). Although clonidine has not been approved by the FDA for the treatment of opioid withdrawal, its use has become standard clinical practice (Alling, 1992). Clonidine has some practical advantages over methadone for treating narcotic withdrawal, particularly in drug-free programs (Clark & Longmuir, 1986). These advantages include the following:
  - It is not a scheduled medication.
  - The use of opiates can be discontinued immediately in preparation for naltrexone induction or admission to a drug-free treatment program.
  - It does not produce opiate euphoria, and patients' need for drugs is therefore reduced. Clonidine is most effective when used for detoxification in an inpatient setting, as side effects can be monitored more closely.
- *Methadone in a Detoxification Protocol*. As stated earlier, methadone can be used for either opioid maintenance therapy or as part of a detoxification protocol. This section will focus on methadone as a detoxification protocol.

Programs Licensed for Methadone Detoxification

Inpatient Treatment Programs A starting dose of 30 to 40 mg per day of oral methadone is adequate to prevent severe withdrawal symptoms in most opiate-dependent patients. The methadone is administered four times daily, beginning with 10 mg doses, and the patient is observed for 2 hours following each dose. If the patient is sleepy, the next dose is decreased to 5 mg. If the patient shows *objective* signs of opioid withdrawal, the dose is increased to 15 mg. After 24 hours, the methadone is withdrawn by 5 mg per day; thus, most patients are withdrawn over 8 days.

Outpatient Methadone Detoxification Clinics In an outpatient clinic, treatment staff usually administers medication no more than twice a day. Thus 20 mg of methadone, given orally twice daily, is a good starting point. To prevent an unacceptable level of withdrawal symptoms, some outpatients may need up to 60 mg of methadone per day administered in divided doses. After a second day, the methadone is tapered by 2.5 mg per day.

Federal Regulations Governing Methadone Detoxification As of 1989, federal regulations allow short-term methadone detoxification of 30 days and long-term detoxification of 180 days.

Short-Term Detoxification In a short-term detoxification regimen, patients are not allowed to take their methadone home. A patient is required to wait at least 7 days between concluding a short-term detoxification treatment episode and beginning another. Before a short-term detoxification attempt is repeated, the program physician must document in the patient's record that the patient continues to be or is again physiologically dependent on narcotics. These requirements apply to both inpatient and outpatient short-term detoxification treatment.

Long-Term Detoxification Federal methadone treatment guidelines define long-term detoxification treatment as longer than 30 days but not in excess of 180 days. For long-term detoxification, the opioid must be administered by the program physician or by an authorized agent who is supervised by and under the orders of the physician. The drug must be administered on a regimen designed to help the patient reach a drug-free state and to make progress in rehabilitation in 180 days or fewer.

Opioid Maintenance Therapy

Opioid maintenance therapy, also known as *opioid substitution therapy,*

> encompasses a variety of pharmacologic and nonpharmacologic treatment modalities, including the therapeutic use of specialized opioid compounds such as methadone and LAAM (levo-alpha-acetylmethadol) to psychopharmacologically occupy opiate receptors in the brain, extinguish drug craving and thus establish a maintenance state. The result is a continuously maintained state of drug tolerance in which the therapeutic OMT agent does not produce euphoria, intoxication or withdrawal symptoms. (ASAM, 2001, p. 137). [It should be noted that LAAM is no longer used for maintenance therapy.]

Methadone Maintenance Opioid maintenance therapy is commonly provided in an ambulatory (Level I) setting with daily medication administration, urine monitoring, and regularly scheduled psychosocial treatment sessions. Lengths of service in this setting can vary from a few months to many years. In order to be accepted into this LOC, a physician determines that the patient is physiologically dependent upon an opiate drug and became physiologically dependent at least one year before admission. For more detailed information on this treatment approach, readers are encouraged to read the TAPS 7, *Treatment of Opiate Addiction with Methadone: A Counselor Manual,* available from SAMHSA's national clearinghouse, online (SAMHSA Publications).

Opiod maintenance therapy is controversial in the addiction treatment community. The predominant objective in the field is for addicted patients to eventually lead a drug-free lifestyle. Commonly, patients on an opioid maintenance compound are perceived as second-class citizens in the recovering community. These patients often choose to hide the fact that they are on an opioid maintenance compound (e.g., methadone) for fear that they will be judged. There continues to exist 12-step support groups that deny participants the right to speak at a meeting if they are on an opioid maintenance substance.

There are several reasons for prejudice against opioid maintenance substances such as methadone. First, it is commonly said that methadone leads to an intoxicated state. Consequently, patients on methadone are considered to be high. This may be partially true. To understand this from a more scientific perspective, we will soon discuss the terms *agonist* and *antagonist*. Second, methadone has been claimed to be even more difficult to detoxify from than a substance like heroin. While methadone detox is usually more prolonged than a heroin detox, it is usually less intense. Third, many people believe substituting one addictive substance for another cannot be considered successful treatment. However, much data has shown that opioid maintenance therapy is a viable alternative to drug-free treatment. Many opioid dependent patients have repeatedly failed at drug-free treatment and found OMT to be their best option for leading a more normal and productive lifestyle.

Agonists and Antagonists

Before discussing the next medication, buprenorphine, it is helpful to define the medical terms *agonist* and *antagonist*. An *agonist* is a drug that stimulates the receptors of a brain cell, causing psychoactive effects. Heroin is considered a *full agonist*, which means it fully stimulates brain receptors and produces the psychoactive effects of pain relief and intoxication. The more fully a drug stimulates the brain receptors, the more powerful its effects will be. A *partial agonist* only partially stimulates the brain receptors, producing less powerful physiologic effects. Buprenorphine, which will be discussed shortly, is a partial agonist. It produces more moderate psychoactive effects than full agonist drugs such as heroin, methadone, or LAAM. Consequently, buprenorphine would produce psychoactive effects similar to heroin, but less powerfully.

An *antagonist* is a drug that binds to the receptor of a cell, blocking the action of another drug without producing any psychoactive effect itself. Naltrexone and naloxone are examples of antagonist medications. If a person were physically dependent on heroin and administered either naltrexone or naloxone, that person would immediately go into a state of withdrawal. The antagonist medication, which has a stronger binding property or affinity for the brain receptor, pushes the agonist drug off the receptor and replaces it.

Naltrexone, brand name ReVia, is an opioid antagonist used to assist opiate dependent individuals maintain freedom from the psychoactive effects of opiates. Because naltrexone binds strongly with opioid receptors, the use of any other opiate has no effect. The naltrexone binds with the receptors, preventing other opiates from binding. It does not have any abuse potential itself. Naltrexone is also used in alcohol abuse treatment to reduce the cravings for alcohol. We will discuss naltrexone further in the next chapter.

Buprenorphine is the newest medication to come on to the scene for the treatment of opioid dependence. It was approved for prescription and sale by the Food and Drug Administration (FDA) in October, 2002. It is the first opioid treatment approved for use by physicians in their own offices. Buprenorphine is a partial opiate agonist. It is safer and more convenient to use than other opioid maintenance therapies (e.g., methadone and LAAM). It has a ceiling effect, which means that above a certain dosage level, additional dosing has no effect. This reduces its abuse potential as well as the risk of fatal overdose. Second, buprenorphine, known on the street as *bup*, has a longer duration than methadone. It can be administered about every 2 or 3 days, compared to daily dosing of methadone. Third, it is more convenient to use than methadone. The patient can be seen in the less stringent confines of a physician's office rather than in a structured clinic. Finally, the level of physical dependence caused by buprenorphine is significantly less than methadone or heroin. Most patients find buprenorphine easier to discontinue than methadone, with fewer withdrawal signs and symptoms.

It is available by prescription in two forms: a buprenorphine hydrochloride (HCl) tablet (Subutex) and a combination tablet (Suboxone) containing buprenorphine HCl and naloxone. Suboxone was developed to reduce the potential for abuse. If a person attempted to inject Suboxone, the naloxone, an antagonist added to the buprenorphine, would precipitate an opioid withdrawal syndrome (Jones, 2004). Both medications come in tablet form available by prescription at the local pharmacy. It is administered sublingually (under the tongue) to dissolve. If it is swallowed, it is not absorbed and therefore becomes ineffective.

Dr. Hendrée Jones perfectly sums up the importance of Buprenorphine for the treatment of opioid dependence. "Given buprenorphine's (particularly Suboxone's) lower potential for abuse and strong safety profile—its plateau of subjective effects with increasing doses and the fact that it causes little respiratory depression—it is considered a first-line medication option for beginning opioid-dependence treatment (Fudula et al., 2003; Ling and Compton, 1997)" (Jones, 2004, p. 7).

Buprenorphine treatment is well suited for patients who do not have extremely high levels of opiate addiction (i.e., those on very high doses of methadone). Because buprenorphine is a partial agonist and has less powerful psychoactive effects than a full agonist, it may not offer enough bang for those who are severely addicted. Buprenorphine is also well suited for younger individuals who have a shorter history of use and may be using smaller amounts of opiates (Mann, 2004).

The following co-occurring medical conditions can be contraindicated for buprenorphine use:

- Difficult breathing or lung problems
- Kidney or gallbladder problems

- Head injury
- Severe mental disorders
- Adrenal or thyroid dysfunction
- Urination problems or enlarged prostate
- Pregnancy

Patients with liver dysfunction, such as hepatitis, should be monitored regularly while on buprenorphine. Buprenorphine has been found to be effective for opioid maintenance therapy as well as for opiate detoxification. The optimal maintenance dose varies from patient to patient. It should be the lowest possible dose to suppress withdrawal signs and symptoms. A dose of between 4 and 24 mg per day has been suggested as likely to be efficacious for many patients, although doses of 32 mg and higher are being used (Jones, 2004; Strain, 2001). Once a stable dose is achieved, buprenorphine can be administered every other day or, in some cases, three times weekly (Johnson et al., 2000; Jones, 2004; Mattick et al., 2003). A sustained-release buprenorphine injection is currently being successfully studied that may be effective for up to 6 weeks (Sobel et al., 2004).

For additional information on buprenorphine, readers are encouraged to order a copy of the Substance Abuse and Mental Health Services Administration (SAMHSA) guide, "Clinical Guidelines for the Use of Buprenorphine in the Treatment of Opioid Addiction," Treatment Improvement Protocol (TIP) number 40. This can be ordered by telephone through SAMHSA's clearinghouse at 1-800-729-6686.

As mentioned earlier, LAAM (levo-alpha-acetylmethadol) is a long-acting drug, previously approved by the FDA as a maintenance medication for opioid dependence. At the time of this writing, it appears that LAAM is being discontinued by the manufacturer because of safety concerns (FDA, 2003).

Nonpharmacological Behavioral Therapies

Besides the pharmacologically based treatments for opiate detoxification, the use of other therapies can provide significant benefit and should not be overlooked. *Group therapy,* as part of an inpatient or outpatient detoxification setting, can be extremely useful for the patient. It can provide a foundation of positive social supports with peers, education concerning the process of addiction and recovery, a forum to express long-held emotions and ideas, a challenge to the belief that one's situation is unique, and an introduction to the group process. *Individual therapy* can also be very useful for motivating the patient to ongoing treatment beyond detoxification, for imparting useful information, for dealing with suppressed feelings, and for improving coping skills. *Educational classes* on drug use, health, and nutrition can also be beneficial. These seminars provide the patient with useful information about the recovery process, the consequences of continued drug abuse, coping skills, prevention of contagious diseases associated with drug use, treating coexisting medical and psychiatric problems, and gaining useful information about nutrition and other health-related matters. *Family or significant other involvement* can be another crucial element for success. The earlier the significant others are involved in the patient's treatment, the greater the chance for long-term success. Providing *family or couples therapy* during the detoxification process allows them to begin to work through obstacles toward successful recovery. Providing these family members education about addiction and recovery can increase their support and participation in the recovery process. *Acupuncture* has also been found to be a useful adjunct to treatment, decreasing drug cravings and overall stress.

As a whole, these services provide the patient with the impression that they are cared for and are important. The more attention they and their families receive, the greater the probability that they will continue the recovery process following detoxification.

Outpatient versus Inpatient Detoxification

There has been a lot of controversy surrounding the use of ambulatory detoxification. Because detoxification was previously administered only in an inpatient facility, many clinicians are reluctant to accept the feasibility of ambulatory protocols. The primary argument is that ambulatory detoxification is not as effective as inpatient detoxification. Many clinicians believe patients need to be in a protective environment in order to detox successfully. Others argue that it is unsafe to detox patients on an ambulatory basis. The fear is that medical complications cannot be monitored effectively on an outpatient basis. It is also assumed that patients, experiencing withdrawal on an ambulatory basis, will self-medicate using street drugs in combination with their prescribed medications. We believe that ambulatory detox, for appropriate patients, can be a safe and effective means for treating physiological dependence leading to a withdrawal syndrome.

Patients appropriate for ambulatory detoxification include the following:

- Those who have minimal risk of a complicated withdrawal (lack medical/psychiatric complications)
- Those who are highly motivated (likely to complete detoxification and enter ongoing treatment)
- Those who respond positively to emotional support and treatment
- Those who comply with medical direction and suggestions
- Those who live in a supportive environment with other sober adults willing to help

Patients accepting ambulatory detoxification must agree to the following rules:

- No alcohol or nonprescribed drug use during the detoxification process
- Urine toxicology screens to be taken upon demand
- No missed appointments accepted during the detoxification process

- No driving or other hazardous activity during the detoxification process

- Use of an emergency number if there are any complications

- Agree to accept inpatient treatment if deemed necessary

- Understand that noncompliance with any of these rules warrants termination of ambulatory detoxification

As discussed earlier, detoxification is only the first step in the treatment process—sometimes referred to as an *introduction to treatment*. It is often done out of medical necessity and does not necessarily reflect the patient's desire for continued treatment. Nevertheless, it is an opportunity for the program to engage the patient and move him or her to the next LOC. It provides a window of opportunity that, through counseling and education, can present the patient new lifestyle options. Whether medical detoxification is conducted inpatient or outpatient, there should always be a behavioral treatment component to motivate the patient toward long-term recovery.

References

Alling, F. A. (1992). Detoxification and treatment of acute sequelae. In J. H. Lowinson, P. Ruiz, & R. B. Millman (Eds.), *Substance abuse: A comprehensive textbook* (pp. 402–415). Baltimore: Williams and Wilkins.

American Psychiatric Association. (1994). *Diagnostic and statistical manual of mental disorders* (4th ed.). Washington, DC: Author.

American Psychiatric Association. (2000). *Diagnostic and statistical manual of mental disorders* (4th ed. Rev. ed.). Washington, DC: Author.

American Psychiatric Association, Task Force on Benzodiazepine Dependency. (1994). *Benzodiazepine dependence, toxicity, and abuse.* Washington, DC: Author.

American Society of Addiction Medicine. (1991). *Patient placement criteria for the treatment of substance-related disorders.* Chevy Chase, MD: Author.

American Society of Addiction Medicine. (1996). *Patient placement criteria for the treatment of substance-related disorders* (2nd ed.). Chevy Chase, MD: Author.

Center for Substance Abuse Treatment. (1995a). *Detoxification from alcohol and other drugs* (DHHS Publication No. SMA 95-3046). Rockville, MD: U.S. Department of Health and Human Services.

Center for Substance Abuse Treatment. (1995b). *LAAM in the treatment of opioid addiction* (DHHS publication No. SMA 95-3052). Rockville, MD: U.S. Department of Health and Human Services.

Center for Substance Abuse Treatment. (1995c). *Matching treatment to patient needs in opioid substitution therapy* (DHHS Publication No. SMA 95-3049). Rockville, MD: U.S. Department of Health and Human Services.

Center for Substance Abuse Treatment. (2004). *Clinical guidelines for the use of buprenorphine in the treatment of opioid addiction.* (DHHS Publication SMA 04-3939.) Rockville, MD: U.S. Department of Health and Human Services.

Chiang, C. N., & Hawks, R. L. (2003). Pharmacokinetics of the combination tablet of buprenorphine and naloxone. *Drug and Alcohol Dependence, 70* (Suppl.), 39–47.

Clark, H. W., & Longmuir, N. (1986). Clonidine transdermal patches: A recovery-oriented treatment of opiate withdrawal. *California Society for the Treatment of Alcoholism and Other Drug Dependencies News, 13,* 1–2.

Czechowicz, D. (1979). *Detoxification treatment manual.* National Institute on Drug Abuse Treatment Program Monograph Series No. 6. Rockville, MD: National Institute on Drug Abuse.

Devenyi, P., & Harrison, M. L. (1985). Prevention of alcohol withdrawal seizures with oral diazepam loading. *Canadian Medical Association Journal, 132,* 798–800.

Fudala, P. J., Bridge, T. P., Herbert, S., Williford, W., Chiang, C. N., & Jones, K., et al. (2003). Office-based treatment of opiate addiction with a sublingual-tablet formulation of buprenorphine and naloxone. *New England Journal of Medicine, 349,* 949–958.

Fultz, J. M., & Senay, E. C. (1975). Guidelines for the management of hospitalized narcotic addicts. *Annals of Internal Medicine, 82,* 815–818.

Geller, A. (1991). Protracted abstinence. In N. S. Miller (Ed.), *Comprehensive handbook of drug and alcohol addiction* (pp. 905–913). New York: Marcel Dekker.

Gold, M. S., Redmond, D. E., & Kleber, H. D. (1978). Clonidine blocks acute opiate-withdrawal symptoms. *Lancet, 2,* 599–602.

Johnson, R. E., Cone, E. J., Henningfield, J. E., & Fudala, P. J., et al. (1989). Use of buprenorphine in the treatment of opiate addiction. 1. Physiologic and behavioral effects during a rapid dose induction. *Clinical Pharmacology and Therapeutics, 46*(3), 335–343.

Johnson, R. E., Chutuape, M. A., Strain, E. C., Walsh, S. L., Stitzer, M. L., & Bigelow, G. E., et al. (2000). A comparison of levomethadyl acetate, buprenorphine, and methadone for opioid dependence. *New England Journal of Medicine, 343*(18), 290–297.

Johnson, R. E., Strain, E. C., & Amass, L. (2003). Buprenorphine: How to use it right. *Drug and Alcohol Dependence, 70*(Suppl. 2), 59–77.

Jones, H. E. (2004). Practical considerations for the use of buprenorphine. *Science and Practice Perspectives, 2*(2), 4–20.

Kuhlman, J. J., Jr., Levine, B., Johnson, R. E., Fudala, P. J., & Cone, E. J. (1998). Relationship of plasma buprenorphine and norbuprenorphine to withdrawal symptoms during dose induction, maintenance, and withdrawal from sublingual buprenorphine. *Addiction, 93*(4), 549–559.

Ling, W., & Compton, P. (1997). Opiate maintenance therapy with LAAM. In S. M. Stine & T. R. Kosten (Eds.), *New treatments for opiate dependence* (pp. 231–253). New York: Guilford.

Ling, W., Charuvastra, C., Collins, J. T., Batki, S., Brown, L. S., Jr., and Kintaudi, P., et al. (1998). Buprenorphine maintenance treatment of opiate dependence: A multicenter, randomized clinical trial. *Addiction, 93*(4), 475–486.

Ling, W., & Smith, D. (2002). Buprenorphine: Blending practice and research. *Journal of Substance Abuse Treatment, 23*(2), 87–92.

Lintzeris, N., Clark, N., Muhleisen, P., Ritter, A., et al. (2001). *National clinical guidelines and procedures for the use of buprenorphine in the treatment of heroin dependence.* Canberra, Australia: Department of Health and Aged Care.

Mann, A. (2004). Successful trial caps 25-Year buprenorphine development effort. *NIDA Notes, 19*(3), 7–9.

Mattick, R. P., Ali, R., White, J. M., O'Brien, S., Wolk, S., & Danz, C., et al. (2003). Buprenorphine versus methadone maintenance therapy: A randomized double-blind trial with 405 opioid-dependent patients. *Addiction, 98*(4), 441–452.

McCann, M. J., Rawson, R. A., Obert, J. J., & Hasson, A. J. (1994). *Treatment of opiate addiction with methadone: A counselor manual.* Center for Substance Abuse Treatment Technical Assistance Publication Series 7. Rockville, MD: U.S. Department of Health and Human Services (Substance Abuse and Mental Health Services Administration).

Mee-Lee, D., Shulman, G. D., Fishman, M., Gastfriend, D. R., & Griffith, J. H. (Eds.). (2001). *ASAM patient placement criteria for the treatment of substance-related disorders* (2nd ed. rev.). Chevy Chase, MD: ASAM.

Miller, W. R., Zweben, A., DiClemente, C. C., & Rychatrik, R. G. (1994). Motivational enhancement therapy manual: A clinical research guide for therapists treating individuals with alcohol abuse and dependence. Project MATCH monograph series, vol. 2 DHHS Publication No. 94-3723. Rockville, MD: NIAAA.

National Institute on Drug Abuse. (2004). Understanding drug abuse and addiction: What science says. http://www.drugabuse.gov/pubs/teaching/Teaching3/teaching.html

Petitjean, S., Stohler, R., Dellon, J., Liveti, S., Waldvogel, D., & Uehlinger, C., et al. (2001). Double-blind randomized trial of buprenorphine and methadone in opiate dependence. *Drug and Alcohol Dependence, 62*(1), 97–104.

Rickels, K., Schweizer, E., Case, W. G., & Greenblatt, D. J. (1990). Long-term therapeutic use of benzodiazepines: I. effects of abrupt discontinuation. *Archives of General Psychiatry, 47,* 899–907.

Saitz, R., Mayo-Smith, M. F., Roberts, M. S., Redmond, H. A., Bernard, D. R., & Calkins, D. R., et al. (1994). Individualized treatment for alcohol withdrawal: A randomized double-blind controlled trial. *Journal of the American Medical Association, 272,* 519–523.

SAMHSA Publications. SAMHSA National Clearing House. Technical Assistance Publications (TAPS). Retrieved from http://store.health.org/catalog/results.aspx?h=drugs&topic=102

Sellers, E. M., Naranjo, C. A., Harrison, M., Devenyo, P. Roach, C., & Sykora, K., et al. (1983). Diazepam loading: Simplified treatment of alcohol withdrawal. *Clinical Pharmacology Therapy, 34,* 822–826.

Smith, D. E., & Wesson, D. R. (1970). A new method for treatment of barbiturate dependence. *Journal of the American Medical Association, 213,* 294–295.

Smith, D. E., & Wesson, D. R. (1971). A phenobarbital technique for withdrawal of barbiturate abuse. *Archives of General Psychiatry, 24,* 56–60.

Smith, D. E., & Wesson, D. R. (1983). Benzodiazepine dependency syndromes. *Journal of Psychoactive Drugs, 15,* 85–95.

Smith, D. E., & Wesson, D. R. (1985). Benzodiazepine dependency syndromes. In D. E. Smith & D. R. Wesson (Eds.), *The benzodiazepines: Current standards for medical practice* (pp. 235–248). Hingham, MA: MTP Press.

Sobel, B. F., Sigmon, S. C., Walsh, S. L., Johnson, R. E., Liebson, I. A., & Nuwayser, E. S., et al. (2004). Open-label trial of an injection depot formulation of buprenorphine in opioid detoxification. *Drug and Alcohol Dependence, 73*(1),11–22.

Strain, E. C. (Ed.). (2001). Use of buprenorphine in the pharmacological management of opioid dependence: A curriculum for physicians. Retrieved January 30, 2003, from http://buprenorphine.samhsa.gov

Sullivan, J. J., Sykora, K., Schneidermann, J., Naranjo, C. A., & Sellers, E. M. (1989). Assessment of alcohol withdrawal: The Revised Clinical Institute Withdrawal Assessment for Alcohol Scale. (CIWA-Ar). *British Journal of Addiction, 84,* 1353–1357.

U.S. Food and Drug Administration. (2002). *Federal Register* (21 CFR Part 291). Washington, DC: Department of Health and Human Services.

U.S. Food and Drug Administration. (2003). Product discontinuation notice: ORLAAM. http://www.fda.gov/cder/drug/shortages/orlaam.htm

Wartenberg, A. A., Nirenberg, T. D., Liepman, M. R., et al. (1990). Detoxification of alcoholics: Improving care by symptom-triggered sedation. *Alcoholism: Clinical and Experimental Research, 14,* 71–75.

Webster's third new international dictionary. (2002). Springfield, MA: Merriam-Webster.

Wiehl, W. O., Hayner, G., & Galloway, G. (1994). Haight Ashbury Free Clinic's drug detoxification protocols, part 4: Alcohol. *Journal of Psychoactive Drugs, 26,* 57–59.

CHAPTER 6

Biomedical Conditions, Medications, and Genetic Factors

This chapter will discuss biomedical conditions and their association with Substance Use Disorders (SUDs). It will also review medications used in the treatment of SUDs and explore genetic factors in understanding family vulnerability. For our purposes, biomedical conditions and related complications will encompass all physical illnesses caused by or exacerbated by the chronic use of psychoactive substances. Withdrawal and detoxification for mood-altering substances will not be covered in this chapter as they were already covered in Chapter 5.

First, it might be important to understand the word *biomedical*. *Bio* is short for biological (as opposed to biographical) and covers that relating to biology or to life and living processes, including the study of genetic (family history) relationships. *Medical*, on the other hand, relates to medicine and the provision of medical treatment. So, in simple terms, biological refers to the body, and medical refers to its treatment. The words *biomedical* and *medical* will be used interchangeably in this chapter. Examples of SUD-related biomedical and medical conditions include, but are not limited to, liver disease, pulmonary and respiratory disorders, cardiovascular disorders, and infectious diseases (e.g., HIV/AIDS, hepatitis, and tuberculosis).

In our earlier discussion on the ASAM's *Patient Placement Criteria*, we discussed the six problem areas or dimensions that need to be assessed for severity. Dimension 2 was *Biomedical Conditions and Complications*. The greater the severity of biomedical conditions and complications, the higher the level of care (LOC) needed to treat the patient. For example, a patient with mild hypertension is not likely to need inpatient, 24-hour medical monitoring for his or her condition. On the other hand, a person with liver failure may need 24-hour monitoring of the condition to ensure the best possible chance of recovery. This patient may either need medically monitored (Level III) or medically managed (Level IV) care to successfully resolve the medical condition.

This chapter will expand our discussion beyond the physical health conditions associated with SUDs and also include a discussion on the developing pharmacological treatments for SUDs (other than detoxification protocols and opioid maintenance medications covered in Chapter 5). We will also explore the current research on the role of genetic factors involved in predisposing individuals to SUDs.

The Medical Consequences of Substance Abuse

Our nation pays dearly for the abuse of mood-altering substances in terms of medical expenses. The costs are associated with substance-related illnesses and injuries such as visits to physicians' offices, hospitals, and emergency rooms. Let's not forget other people affected by the use of substance abuse through accidental injury, crime, or violence. Drug users visit emergency rooms more than 527,000 times each year. Healthcare costs associated with Substance Abuse was estimated to be over $114 billion (Robert Wood Foundation, 2001), and that figure continues to grow.

During an initial assessment, it is incumbent upon the SUD treatment professional or other qualified healthcare professionals to be aware of signs of existing or incipient biomedical conditions that could complicate treatment. It is always prudent to do a thorough medical screening and physical examination to determine the appropriate LOC for patients seeking substance abuse treatment. This will facilitate treatment planning and ensure the appropriate LOC and treatment services when related biomedical conditions are discovered. It is good medical practice, in fact, to quarantine newly admitted inpatients until the critical lab results, such as chest x-rays, are reviewed. (This will also serve to protect the general patient population from contracting certain nosocomial infections— diseases acquired by patients during hospital visits.) It is vital, in fact, that the entire medical community (i.e., general practitioners, emergency room doctors, dentists, emergency medical technicians, pediatricians, psychotherapists, and psychiatrists) be aware of the diagnostic signs of an SUD . By detecting symptoms early on in its progression, potential medical consequences may be averted and successful treatment outcomes more likely.

While there are many ways to assess the impact of SUDs on society, here are some statistics involving their medical consequences. Over 100,000 people die every year in the United States from substance-related causes. Forty percent of all general hospital admissions in the United States are related to SUDs. Substance-related health problems are estimated to cost our society more than $33 billion

Consequences of Drug Use

Condition	Associated Drug(s)
Cardiovascular	Tobacco, alcohol, marijuana, cocaine, amphetamines, anabolic steroids, ecstasy, and inhalants
Liver Disease	Alcohol, IV drug use (heroin, cocaine, etc.), inhalants
HIV/HCV/AIDS	IV drug use, risky behavior facilitated through drug use
Pulmonary/Respiratory	Tobacco, marijuana, combining alcohol and depressants
Accidents/Violence	Alcohol, heroin, cocaine, amphetamines, anabolic steroids, and various designer drugs

a year in lost productivity (NIDA, 2000a). Let's look at some of the more common biomedical conditions caused or exacerbated by SUDs.

Cardiovascular Diseases

Cardiovascular diseases pertain to conditions and complications negatively affecting the heart and blood vessels. These diseases include heart attacks, hypertension, cardiac arrhythmias, strokes, and so on. Cardiovascular conditions and complications are associated with the use of tobacco, alcohol, marijuana, cocaine, amphetamines, anabolic steroids, ecstasy, and inhalants.

The use of stimulants (e.g., cocaine, methamphetamine, amphetamine, nicotine) increases the heart rate, placing an extra strain on the heart muscle and, consequently, increasing the chance of myocardial infarction (heart attack) or other heart complications such as dysrhythmias, cardiomyopathies, aortic dissection, and endocarditis. Myocardial infarctions and dysrhythmias may be the major causes of sudden death related to cocaine use (Brick, 2004). Stimulants are also related to narrowing of the blood vessels. An increase in the heart rate combined with a narrowing of the blood vessels has the effect of increasing blood pressure with the potential for hypertension (high blood pressure) and stroke. These cardiovascular consequences can occur even in those who are not found to be at high risk for these problems (i.e., healthy athletes). A recent hypothesis is that the combination of cocaine use with the use of anabolic steroids may produce much greater cardiovascular problems in athletes who use both substances. A recent study has identified changes in blood components after use of cocaine that may play a role in initiating heart attack and stroke (NIDA, 2002b).

Tobacco Cigarette smoking significantly increases the risk of heart disease, including stroke, heart attack, vascular disease, and aneurysm. Approximately 20 percent of all deaths from heart disease are attributed to smoking ("Medical

Consequences," 2004). The largest risk for sudden cardiac death is cigarette smoking. The risk of heart attack in a cigarette smoker is more than twice that of non-smokers ("Cardiovascular Disease," 2004). Passive or secondary smoke is believed to contribute to as many as 40,000 deaths per year from cardiovascular disease ("Medical Consequences," 2004).

Alcohol Chronic heavy use of alcohol has also been associated with negative effects to the cardiovascular system. Alcoholics have an increased propensity for hypertension, strokes, and cardiomyopathy. Alcoholic cardiomyopathy (a deterioration of the heart muscle) is the most common cause of cardiomyopathy in Western societies and a major source of heart failure and death (NIAAA, 2000). Women may be more susceptible to such illnesses even though they typically drink less than men (Fernandez-Sola et al., 1997; Urbano-Marquez et al., 1995).

The irony is that in low to moderate doses (i.e., one to two drinks per day), alcohol consumption actually lowers the risk of coronary heart disease. Possible explanations of this include the belief that alcohol may prevent the constriction of coronary arteries, inhibit clot formation, and enhance recovery following a heart attack (NIAAA, 1999). The potential problem in promoting this therapeutic use of alcohol is that the incipient alcoholic or the alcoholic who has stopped drinking might rationalize this to be a worthwhile tradeoff. He or she might delude him- or herself into believing that if one or two drinks is good for him or her, what harm could three or four drinks do? The physician who recommends this prophylactic use of alcohol should not do so without a profile of the patient's drinking history.

Heavy alcohol use is also associated with hypertension (high blood pressure; York & Hirsch, 1997; Campbell, Ashley, Carrurhers, Lacourciere, & McKay, 1999). "It is estimated that one drink per day can chronically increase blood pressure one millimeter of mercury in middle-aged individuals, and even more in the elderly and people with preexisting hypertension" (Beilin, Puddey, & Burke, 1996). Hypertension due to alcohol consumption may also increase the possibility of stroke. "Among young people, long-term heavy alcohol consumption has been identified as an important risk factor for stroke." (You et al., 1997 as cited in Brick, 2004, p. 30).

Ecstasy A recent study found that ecstasy (methylenedioxymethamphetamine, or MDMA) use may increase a type of valvular heart disease whereby heart valves becomes ineffective, causing the heart to become enlarged with blood, rendering it ineffective in sending blood throughout the body (NIDA, 2004b).

Inhalants The popular use of inhaling volatile hydrocarbons in the late 1950s and 1960s caused deaths of teenagers and led to the term *sudden sniffing death* (SSD). These deaths, caused by the abuse of inhalants, were found to be the result of lethal cardiac arrhythmias (Bass, 1970). Inhalants believed to be associated with cardiac arrhythmias and SSD include Freon; bromochlorodifluoromethane (great word for Scrabble); butane; propane; 1,1,1-trichloroethane; gasoline; and

Long-Term Effects of Inhalant Abuse

Solvents are easily absorbed from the blood into lipid-rich tissues. Chronic inhalant abuse can damage the brain, heart, lungs, kidney, liver, and peripheral nerves. Continued chronic inhalant abuse has been associated with neurological damage. People who abuse inhalants chronically have demonstrated a range of mental dysfunction, from mild to severe cognitive impairment (e.g., lack of concentration or attention, poor memory, and poor learning skills). In some instances, these effects are permanent, while in others they resolve after a long period of abstinence. Personality Disorders, particularly Antisocial Personality Disorder, violent behavior, and depression, have been associated with inhalant abuse.

trichloroethylene (Bass, 1978; Brady, Stremski, Eljaiek, & Aufderheide, 1994; Heath, 1986; King, Smialek, & Troutman, 1985; Morita, Miki, Kazama, & Sakata, 1977; Siegel & Wason, 1990; Smeeton & Clark, 1985).

Liver Disease

Normal liver functioning is crucial for life. It is responsible for producing energy and filters and neutralizes impurities and poisons in your bloodstream (NIAAA, 1995). Chronic and heavy alcohol use appears to be the most potentially damaging substance to the liver. It is a major cause of illness and death in the United States. Approximately 10 to 35 percent of heavy drinkers develop alcoholic hepatitis, and 10 to 20 percent develop cirrhosis (NIAAA, 1998).

Alcohol-Induced Liver Disease The symptoms of alcohol-induced liver disease (ALD) range from fatty liver (reversible with abstinence) to alcoholic hepatitis (characterized by persistent inflammation of the liver) to cirrhosis (characterized by progressive scarring of the liver tissue). Alcohol use begins to damage the liver by altering normal metabolism and causing fat to accumulate in the liver (fatty liver). Eventually, this abnormal metabolism may begin to destroy healthy liver cells. In turn, the death of liver cells may cause inflammation of the liver, further destroying healthy liver tissue (alcoholic hepatitis). The inflammation of the liver and tissue damage may eventually result in irreversible scarring (cirrhosis) of the liver and cell death.

When the liver becomes damaged, it begins to leak enzymes into the blood stream, and it becomes less efficient in its functioning (NIAAA, 1995). The testing of liver enzymes in the blood can be an effective marker for detecting alcohol problems. While it is advised that medical professionals should be responsible for reading the results of liver enzyme tests, it would be helpful for all substance treatment professionals to gain an understanding as to what the liver enzyme elevations seem to suggest. There are a variety of medical conditions that can cause elevations in liver enzymes, but it is important to rule out the cause being alcohol use.

Aspartate aminotransferase (AST), previously known as *serum glutamic oxalcetic transaminase* (SGOT), and *alanine transferase* (ALT), previously known as *serum glutamic pyruvate transaminase* (SGPT), are enzymes that reflect the liver's overall health. Abnormal elevations in these enzymes seem to suggest some form of liver damage.

Liver enzyme elevations can occur for reasons other than heavy drinking. However, any elevations of these enzymes should be a red flag to the reader of the possibility of heavy drinking. The good news is that through abstinence, these elevated enzymes often show improvement and return to normal. Continued, heavy drinking can cause these elevations to be irreversible. It is also worth noting that some studies seem to suggest that just having a physician explain these results to a patient may significantly reduce the patient's level of drinking (Chick, Lloyd, & Crombie, 1985; Elvy, Wells, & Baird, 1988; Kristenson, Ohlin, Hulten-Nosslin, Trell, & Hood, 1983).

Susceptibility to ALD varies considerably among alcohol users despite similar drinking patterns. It is believed that genetic factors, dietary factors, and gender may play a role in the susceptibility to ALD. Women have a higher incidence of alcoholic hepatitis and a higher rate of death from cirrhosis than men even though, as stated previously, women, as a rule, drink less than men (Hall, 1995). Also, having the hepatitis C virus may increase the susceptibility for ALD and increase the severity of alcoholic cirrhosis. It's a disturbing sight to see women with distended abdomens appearing pregnant, only to discover that it is due to cirrhosis. Heavy drinking increases the severity of hepatitis C, which further complicates its treatment (NIAAA, 1998).

The most effective way of treating ALD is through abstinence from alcohol. Fatty liver and alcoholic hepatitis are frequently reversible through abstinence. Survival is also enhanced, in those with cirrhosis, through abstinence. Liver transplantation is an effective treatment for those who are terminally ill due to cirrhosis. Unfortunately, the potentially long wait for a liver donor can be life threatening.

Blood-Borne Diseases

Blood-borne diseases are those that are transmitted from one individual to another through the exchange of infected blood, most commonly through the sharing of syringes to inject drugs. Blood-borne diseases can also be transmitted through other means such as in traumatic sexual activity where blood vessels may be broken, such as anal sex, and through blood transfusions that, due to more effective screening procedures, is less common since around 1992. In speaking about blood-borne diseases, we will be focusing particularly on the transmission of the hepatitis virus and the human immunodeficiency virus (HIV) virus.

Viral Hepatitis

Hepatitis literally means "inflammation of the liver" and has a number of causes, including viral infection and alcohol abuse. Viral hepatitis infects the cells of the

Common Risk Factors for Hepatitis C

- Blood transfusion(s) or a solid organ transplant (e.g., kidney, liver, or heart) before July 1992
- Blood-clotting problems with a blood product made before 1987
- Long-term kidney dialysis
- Exposure to blood products from medical procedures (e.g., patients with hemophilia, solid organ transplants, chronic renal failure, or who are undergoing chemotherapy)
- Contact with blood in the workplace (e.g., healthcare workers, police personnel, and firefighters)
- Use of recreational drugs that are injected with a needle (e.g., heroin or cocaine), even once many years ago, or shared straws while inhaling cocaine
- Engaging in sexual behaviors that are considered high-risk, such as anal sex, having had multiple partners, or having ever had a sexually transmitted disease (STD)
- Tattoos or body piercing
- Living with a person who is infected with HCV and having shared items such as nail clippers, razors, or toothbrushes, which might have had blood on them

Source. http://www.pegasys.com/default.asp

---

liver. The most common types of viral hepatitis are hepatitis A, hepatitis B, and hepatitis C. Out of these three, hepatitis C is currently the most cause for concern. (There are currently vaccines available for hepatitis A and B, but not for hepatitis C.)

Hepatitis C Approximately 4 million Americans are infected with the HCV. It occurs when the blood (and, less commonly, other body fluids such as semen and vaginal fluid) of an infected person enters the body of an uninfected person (CDC, 2001). It is the most common blood-borne infection in the United States. With 35,000 new cases of HCV found each year in the United States, it is one of our most serious health problems. The hepatitis C virus can lead to cirrhosis (liver scarring) and liver cancer (hepatocellular carcinoma). It is the leading cause of liver cancer and results in more liver transplants than any other disease. Approximately 8,000 to 10,000 deaths per year in the United States are attributed to HCV (NIDA, 2000b).

Injection drug use (IDU) is the leading cause for the transmission of HCV. This results from the sharing of syringes and other paraphernalia. Presently, IDU accounts for at least 60 percent of HCV transmission in the United States. It can also be spread through sexual contact, but the risk is low. (Sexual transmission accounts for less than 20 percent of HCV transmission. The highest risks for sexual transmission are due to having multiple sex partners and participating in traumatic sex [NIDA, 2005c]). Drugs associated with high-risk sexual behavior include alcohol, crack cocaine, and methamphetamine.

Sixty-five percent of injection drug users are infected within 1 year of injecting. Within 6 years, over 76 percent are infected (NIDA, 2000b). The highest rate of new HCV infection is found in young people aged 20 to 39. Other potential risks for HCV transmission include the sharing of blood-contaminated straws during intranasal (snorting) use of drugs and the sharing of contaminated razors and toothbrushes (NIDA, 2005c).

Symptoms of HCV are rare and appear to be flu-like (i.e., fatigue, nausea, abdominal pain) and sometimes jaundice (the yellowing of skin). Usually, the only way to detect it is through a blood test for antibodies to the virus. For many infected individuals, they don't become aware of the infection until their liver is affected. This can occur 10 to 20 years after contracting the infection. Cirrhosis occurs in 10 to 20 percent of those with chronic infection. One to five percent develops primary liver cancer (NIDA, 2005c). Alcohol consumption may increase the risk of progression and should be avoided.

There is no vaccine available to immunize people against HCV. The only treatment currently available is the use of an antiviral medication, *interferon*, used alone or in conjunction with another antiviral medication, *ribavirin*. The combination of these two drugs is found to be effective in about 30 to 40 percent of those treated (NIDA, 2005c).

It is common for injection drug users who are infected with HCV to also be infected with hepatitis A, hepatitis B, or HIV. Consequently, injection drug users should be screened for all of these infections and immunized whenever possible.

Hepatitis B The hepatitis B virus (HBV) can also be transmitted through infected blood or body fluids, making injection drug users and those prone to high-risk sexual activity (unprotected sex with multiple partners) very susceptible to this infection. It is a less common infection than hepatitis C, affecting approximately 5 percent of the U.S. population. Approximately 1.25 million people have chronic HBV infection (CDC, 2002). Unlike hepatitis C, this viral infection can be prevented through immunization.

Hepatitis A According to the CDC, "Hepatitis A virus (HAV) is primarily transmitted through the fecal-oral route, when a person puts something in his or her mouth (such as food or a beverage) that has been contaminated with feces of a person infected with HAV" (CDC, 2002, p. 2). Consequently, HAV is not directly associated with substance abusers.

HIV/AIDS

The abbreviation HIV stands for the human immunodeficiency virus, which causes acquired immunodeficiency syndrome (AIDS). "AIDS is a condition characterized by a defect in the body's natural immunity to diseases, and individuals who suffer from it are at risk for severe illnesses that are otherwise not a threat to anyone whose immune system is working properly. Although many individuals who have AIDS or carry HIV may live for many years with treatment, there is no known cure or vaccine" (NIDA, 2005b). While progress is being made, there are still far too many new cases each year. "By the end of 2000, an estimated 900,000 Americans were living with HIV. Approximately 40,000 new cases of active AIDS disease are diagnosed annually" (NIAAA, 2002). African Americans and Hispanics account for approximately 70 percent of all new AIDS cases (CDC, 2001; Karon, Fleming, Steketee, & DeCock, 2001).

Behavior associated with drug abuse is the single largest factor in the spread of HIV/AIDS in the United States. "Drug abuse and HIV are truly interlinked epidemics," says former NIDA director, Dr. Alan I. Leshner (NIDA, 1997, p. 1). The common modes of transmitting viral hepatitis are similarly found in the transmission of HIV, namely IDU and high-risk sexual activity. It is estimated that between 30 and 40 percent of all new HIV infections results from injection drug use. Twenty-seven percent of all injection drug users are HIV-infected (Holmberg, 1996). The overall number of AIDS cases through December 31, 2002, was 859,000. Approximately 25 percent of those are directly related to IDU or sexual contact with an injection drug user (CDC, 2001). Surprisingly, the greatest predictor of HIV infection for injection drug users (both male and female) is not in the sharing of needles, but through high-risk sexual behavior (Strathdee, 2001). Among injecting drug users, "high-risk homosexual activity was the most important factor in HIV transmission for men; high-risk heterosexual activity was the most significant for women" (NIDA, 2003a, p. 5).

Injecting drugs is especially dangerous in that it potentiates the spread of bloodborne viruses. Whatever the route of administration, however, drug use can

---

HIV SYMPTOMS

The first symptoms of HIV infection can resemble symptoms of common cold or flu viruses. The symptoms of early infection can also be similar to the symptoms of other STDs and other infections such as mononucleosis or hepatitis, which are much more commonly and more easily transmitted. Stress and anxiety can also produce symptoms in some people, even though they do not have HIV. Some people who contract HIV experience very strong symptoms, but others experience none at all. Those who do have symptoms generally experience fever, fatigue, and, often, rash. Other common symptoms can include headache, swollen lymph nodes, and sore throat. These symptoms can occur within days or weeks of the initial exposure to the virus during a period called *primary* or *acute HIV infection*.

Note. Because of the nonspecific symptoms associated with primary or acute HIV infection, symptoms are not a reliable way to diagnose HIV infection.
Source. http://hivinsite.ucsf.edu/hiv?page=basics-00-02

increase the chances of getting infected with HIV. Young inner-city crack smokers are three times more likely to become infected with HIV than non-crack using youths. Risk-taking behavior begets risk-taking behavior. Noninjecting drug users, for example, who trade sex for drugs or who engage in unprotected sex with multiple partners are, predictably, more likely to contract the virus (NIDA, 1999b).

Those with Alcohol Use Disorders are also more likely than the general population to get infected with HIV. This is due to alcohol's association with high-risk sexual behavior and IDU. Alcohol use increases one's susceptibility to some infections associated with AIDS complications, such as tuberculosis, pneumonia, and hepatitis C (a leading cause of death among those with HIV). Alcohol also increases the severity of AIDS-related brain damage. Last, heavy alcohol use has been found to decrease medication compliance and leads to a poorer response to HIV therapy in general (NIAAA, 2002).

Pulmonary and Respiratory Diseases

Tobacco Pulmonary and respiratory diseases affect the lungs and breathing. This includes such disorders as bronchitis, emphysema, and lung cancer. Cigarette smoking has been associated with approximately 90 percent of all lung cancer cases. Even the regular inhalation of secondary smoke is estimated to cause about 3,000 lung cancer deaths per year in the United States. Tobacco smoking is a primary cause of chronic bronchitis and emphysema. It also has been found to exacerbate asthma symptoms in adults and children ("Medical Consequences," 2004).

Marijuana Marijuana smoking and, to a lesser extent, crack cocaine smoking also have negative consequences on one's pulmonary and respiratory functioning. "Marijuana smoke contains up to 50 percent more carcinogens than filtered tobacco cigarettes and results in substantially greater tar deposits in the lungs. Such increased affects likely occur because marijuana users smoke unfiltered material, inhale the smoke more deeply, and hold the smoke longer in their lungs than tobacco smokers (Hoffman, Brunnemann, Gori, & Wynder, 1975; Institute of Medicine, 1982; Roth et al., 1998; Tashkin et al., 1987, 1991; Wu, Tashkin, Djahed, & Rose, 1988)" (Brick, 2004, p. 173).

Chronic smoking of marijuana increases the likelihood of respiratory illness and leads to symptoms of bronchitis similar to tobacco smoking (Bloom, Kaltenborn, Paoletti, Camilli, & Lebowitz, 1987; Polen, Sidney, Tekawa, Sadler, & Friedman, 1993; Tashkin et al., 1987; Taylor, Poulton, Moffitt, Ramankutty, & Sears, 2000). The chronic use of both marijuana and tobacco smoking is likely to increase the adverse effects on the respiratory system (Barsky, Roth, Kleerup, Simmons, & Tashkin, 1998; Roth et al., 1998).

Depressants The combining of depressants, such as mixing alcohol with barbiturates or benzodiazepines (e.g., Xanax, Valium, and Ativan), can lead to respiratory depression and possibly death. Another potentially harmful combination that can cause respiratory depression and death is combining alcohol and heroin.

This is a synergistic effect—the whole is greater than the sum of its individual parts.

Route of Administration The route of administration of stimulants such as cocaine and methamphetamine can result in pulmonary and respiratory problems. The potential problems of smoking cocaine in the form of crack or freebase or smoking methamphetamine include acute respiratory infection; an exacerbation of the symptoms of asthma, pulmonary edema, lung disease, barotraumas (middle ear/sinus infection), pulmonary hypertension; and a persistent gas-exchange abnormality (Brick, 2004). The chronic intranasal use of cocaine and other stimulants may also negatively irritate the nasal passageways or cause nasal ulcers leading to breathing difficulties. The pulmonary effects from inhalant abuse, while rare, include oxygen displacement, hypoxia, asphyxiation, and suffocation (Linden, 1990).

Tuberculosis

Beside the blood-borne infectious diseases just discussed, there are also other infectious diseases associated with drug abuse that are transmitted by means other than the blood. These may include sexually transmitted diseases (STDs) such as syphilis, chlamydia, trichomoniasis, gonorrhea, and genital herpes, as well as the highly contagious disease known as tuberculosis (TB).

Tuberculosis is a chronic and infectious lung disease. It is transmitted through an infected person's cough, causing the release of airborne bacteria. It results in either a latent (dormant) infection or in an active disease for the recipient. The

Tuberculosis (TB) Symptoms

Symptoms of TB depend on where in the body the TB bacteria are growing. TB bacteria usually grow in the lungs. Tuberculosis in the lungs may cause the following:

- A bad cough that lasts longer than 2 weeks
- Pain in the chest
- Coughing up blood or sputum (phlegm from deep inside the lungs)

Other symptoms of TB disease include the following:

- Weakness or fatigue
- Weight loss
- No appetite
- Chills
- Fever
- Sweating at night

latent type may develop into an active type if the person does not receive preventive therapy. Tuberculosis is most prevalent in crowded, low-income areas with substandard health conditions. Injection drug use and the onset of the HIV/AIDS epidemic in the 1980s contributed to its resurgence (NIDA, 1998). "Drug users are from two to six times more likely to contract TB than nonusers. Compared to others with TB, IDUs are more likely to develop the disease in multiple organs and sites, rather than only in the lungs" (NIDA, 1999). The good news is that TB is a treatable disease. Since 1992, new cases of TB have been on the decline.

Cancer

Substance abuse is usually not directly related to cancer, with the exception of nicotine and alcohol. Nicotine, one of the most heavily used addictive substances in the United States, is linked to one-third of all cancers (*Nicotine Index*, 2005). The most prevalent cancer killer is lung cancer, which is directly linked to tobacco smoking. In fact, cigarette smoking has been associated with about 90 percent of all lung cancer cases (*Nicotine Index*, 2005). Heavy alcohol use is associated with various cancers of the gastrointestinal system, including esophageal cancer (Brick, 2004) and colorectal cancer (alcoholism.about.com). There has also been some research suggesting that marijuana is associated with the risk of cancers to the lung, head, and neck (NIDA, 2004a).

Renal Damage

The term *renal* pertains to the kidneys. The substances often associated with kidney damage include the opiates, ecstasy, and the inhalants. Some adulterants in street opiates have been linked to kidney damage (Brick, 2004). Heroin has also been known to cause the life-threatening kidney condition called *glomerulosclerosis*.

Chronic Pain and the Addicted Patient

Before leaving this section on the medical consequences of SUDs, it is worth noting the dilemma in treating chronic pain patients who have a co-occurring SUD. A recent study of three methadone maintenance programs reported a 61 percent prevalence rate for chronic pain (New York State Office of Alcohol and Substance Abuse Services [OASAS], 2002). The most frequent pains cited were headaches and back pain. In general, patients with chronic pain reported more chronic illness and psychiatric symptoms.

Because moderate to severe pain is often treated with addictive, opiate-based medications (e.g., codeine, oxycodone, oxycontin, morphine, dilaudid, etc.), physicians may be reluctant to prescribe these medications to individuals with a history of an SUD, especially those with a prior history of opiate dependence. There is controversy over this. Some addiction specialists believe that prescribing an opiate to a recovering addict would reignite the addictive disorder and lead to relapse. There are many stories to back this up. Others believe that those suffering from legitimate pain would only get the analgesic properties of the medication without the euphoric effects. There may be some truth in each of these notions, but if the medication is managed effectively, a relapse is less likely, and the idea that many patients do not experience euphoric effects is not consistent with the properties of the drugs just cited. After all, in addition to their analgesic properties, opioids also have mood-altering properties. More research is needed to end this controversy, and more research is needed to find alternatives for effectively treating pain in this undertreated population.

Addiction Medications

In Chapter 5, we discussed medications used for the treatment of the withdrawal syndrome through detoxification. This section will explore the most commonly used medications for treating SUDs other than for detoxification. We will also review the current research on potential medications for treating SUDs. The research to discover new medications for treating addictive disorders is moving at such a rapid pace that, by the time you read this, many more will be researched, and several of the ones you will read here will most likely be abandoned.

Presently, a primary strategy being used by researchers is to see if currently available medications approved for use in treating other disorders can also be effective in treating SUDs. The rationale for this strategy involves considerations of cost and time. If medications that are currently approved by the U.S. Food and Drug Administration (FDA) for other disorders can aid in the treatment of SUDs, then a great deal of time and money could be saved—time and money studying both the potential side effects of new medications as well as the often protracted process of obtaining FDA approval. (It currently takes about 9 years to get approval from the FDA for a new medication.)

It is important to note that all of the medications to be discussed, while potentially helpful in the treatment of SUDs, should be combined with addiction counseling. None of the medications discussed should be initiated without consultation with an experienced physician trained in addiction medicine.

Opiates

In Chapter 5, we discussed several medications used for opiate withdrawal and opioid maintenance, including clonidine, methadone, LAAM, and buprenorphine. This section will discuss the use of *naltrexone* as an adjunct to an opioid-free lifestyle. Naltrexone, often called by its product name ReVia, is an opiate antagonist. In other words, it completely blocks the effects of opiates for a period of 24 to 72 hours. Anyone regularly taking naltrexone would not experience the euphoric effects of opiates such as heroin. If someone takes naltrexone while physically dependent on an opiate, he or she would immediately go into a state of withdrawal. Consequently, patients using naltrexone to ensure abstinence from opiates are usually detoxified from opiates prior to initiating naltrexone. It is a nonaddictive and safe medication.

Patients are usually administered naltrexone three times weekly. In order for naltrexone to be successful, someone other than the patient must take responsibility to monitor and ensure that the patient is taking the medication as prescribed. Patients self-administering naltrexone may conveniently forget to take or refill their medication prior to a relapse. With a monitor, the patient has little choice but to take the medication. Monitors are trained to call the treating clinician if the patient fails or refuses to take the medication. Researchers are now testing a long-lasting formulation of naltrexone that is injected and slowly released over the course of several weeks (Comer, 2002).

Cocaine and the Stimulants

There are over 20 medications currently being researched for the treatment of Cocaine Dependence. One is called *propranolol,* used for treating high blood pressure. Patients who experience severe withdrawal symptoms (e.g., anxiety and craving) when discontinuing cocaine use stay in treatment longer and use less cocaine when treated with propranolol (Kampman et al., 2001). Another medication is called *amantadine,* used for Parkinson's disease. This medication seems to slightly increase the release of dopamine, causing a decrease in the dysphoria (the opposite of euphoria) often felt during cocaine withdrawal. So far, patients treated with amantadine appear to use less cocaine and are more likely to remain cocaine abstinent (Kampman et al., 2001; Shoptaw, Kintaudi, Charuvastra, & Ling, 2002). *Baclofen,* a muscle relaxer, has also shown promise in reducing cocaine use (Shoptaw et al., 2002). In one study, baclofen was found to be more effective with females than with males (Campbell, Morgan, & Carroll, 2002). *Vigabatrin* (GVG), used to treat epilepsy outside of the United States, appears to show evidence in blocking the addictive effects of all stimulants (Brodie, Figueroa, & Dewey, 2003; Schiffer, Marsteller, & Dewey, 2003).

There are also other medications showing some promise for treating Cocaine Dependence. These include Ritalin, a stimulant-acting medication used for treating Attention-Deficit/Hyperactivity Disorder (ADHD); inderal (a blood-pressure medication); and the SSRI antidepressant medications, such as Prozac, Effexor, and Lexapro. Last, there's research currently being initiated to develop a cocaine vaccine.

Alcohol

Antabuse (disulfiram) has been around since the 1940s and used as a form of aversion therapy or deterrent for those attempting to abstain from alcohol. A person taking Antabuse would develop a strong, physiologic reaction if combined with the consumption of alcohol. This reaction may be as mild as a flush and throbbing in the head and neck to nausea, vomiting, breathing difficulty, chest pain, heart failure, and even, in rare circumstances, death. Antabuse is an antagonist that reduces ethanol metabolism, allowing a toxic metabolite, acetaldehyde, to build up in the blood (McNeece & DiNitto, 2005, p. 52; see Breakdown of Alcohol box). As with naltrexone, discussed previously, compliance with the taking of Antabuse must be monitored daily. Monitored administration of Antabuse has been found to be more effective than taking it unmonitored (Meyers & Smith, 1995). As with naltrexone, monitors are trained to call the treating clinician if the patient fails or refuses to take the medication. Patients are also given a contract to sign, indicating their agreement to take Antabuse and to be monitored. The contract also lists things to avoid while taking Antabuse that may include alcohol (e.g., mouthwashes, colognes, etc.). Patients are made aware of the dangers of consuming alcohol while on Antabuse. Patients with a history of diabetes, seizures, or liver disease should take Antabuse only under the supervision of a physician.

Antabuse has recently shown some unexpected promise in treating Cocaine Dependence (NIDA, 2005a). While it's unclear how it reduces cocaine use, it is hypothesized that Antabuse hinders the normal breakdown of cocaine in the body, increases dopamine levels, and decreases norepinephrine, another neurotransmitter in the brain. The result is to reduce withdrawal symptoms leading to cravings ("Addiction Treatment," 2004).

Breakdown of Alcohol

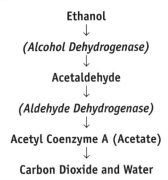

Ethanol
↓
(Alcohol Dehydrogenase)
↓
Acetaldehyde
↓
(Aldehyde Dehydrogenase)
↓
Acetyl Coenzyme A (Acetate)
↓
Carbon Dioxide and Water

Alcohol is changed (oxidized) in the liver by the enzyme *alcohol dehydrogenase*, which changes alcohol to its primary metabolite, acetaldehyde. Acetaldehyde (very toxic) is transformed by another enzyme, *Aldehyde dehydrogenase*, to acetyl coenzyme A, which is eventually broken down to carbon dioxide and water and excreted.

Note. Italics refer to enzymes.
Source. Brick and Erickson (1999).

ReVia (naltrexone), the opiate blocker discussed in the section on opiate medications, has also been found to help block the pleasurable effects of alcohol and reduce cravings. It doesn't make users of the medication sick like Antabuse; it just makes drinking less pleasurable. According to the OASAS, naltrexone has been shown to double the rate of alcohol abstention in placebo-controlled trials (OASAS, 2000). It was approved for the treatment of alcoholism in 1994. It is a nonaddictive and safe medication.

Acamprosate, trade name *Campral,* is used in Europe to maintain abstinence in alcohol-dependent patients by decreasing the craving for alcohol. Some European studies seem to indicate good results with this medication, even better than when compared to subjects on ReVia. It was FDA approved in 2005.

Topiramate is another potential medication that may be useful for treating Alcohol Dependence. As with ReVia and Campral, this medication doesn't prevent drinking but reduces consumption and the cravings to drink in those still drinking. The side effects of topiramate seem to be more severe than those found when taking ReVia and Campral, such as dizziness, tingling under the skin, psychomotor slowing, word-naming difficulties, and weight loss. It also appears to be helpful in reducing alcohol withdrawal symptoms (Johnson, 2004). This medication is not yet FDA approved.

Nicotine

There's a concerted effort at present in our country to curtail the use of nicotine products, especially cigarette smoking. The number of deaths attributed to nicotine use from a variety of diseases is approximately 430,000 per year in the United States. Some commonly known tools for treating Nicotine Dependence include the use of replacement therapies such as the skin (transdermal) patch, nicotine gum, aerosol sprays, and inhalers that provide a gradual reduction in the intake of nicotine to avoid the discomfort of withdrawal. Women, for some unexplained reason, seem less successful than men with nicotine replacement therapy (NIDA, 2000c).

The antidepressant bupropion (commonly known by its product names *Zyban* or *Wellbutrin*) has also been shown to be effective in decreasing the craving for nicotine. Other medications being used for nicotine treatment include *clonidine* (also used for opiate detoxification), *buspirone,* and *mecamylamine.* Studies on mecamylamine have also indicated that it may be helpful for reducing cravings for cocaine (Reid, Mickalian, Delucchi, & Berger, 1999).

Some exciting research is currently being performed to develop a nicotine vaccine. The vaccine currently being studied is called NicVAX, manufactured by Nabi. This vaccine, supported by a grant from NIDA, is in clinical trials for the next few years. So far, the results with rats have proven effective. The vaccine may be useful for enhancing treatment by helping smokers decrease their cravings for nicotine. The vaccine may also be useful in preventing new smokers by eliminating the pleasurable effects of nicotine use.

The Genetic Factors of SUDS

Why do some people abuse substances while others do not? Are there biological determinants for drug abuse? If so, what are they? Are addicts biologically or neurologically different from nonaddicts? If so, are these differences found prior to drug abuse or as a result of drug abuse? What are the factors that make one person more vulnerable for substance abuse than another? Is this vulnerability associated with one, several, or all substances? What contributes more to SUDs, environmental or genetic factors?

These are some of the questions we will attempt to explore in this section. It's been stated throughout this book that the causes and manifestations of SUDs are usually a mixture of biological, psychological, social, environmental, and spiritual factors. This section will review the recent research on the genetic and biochemical factors involved in SUDs.

Family, Adoption, and Twin Studies

It has long been believed that genes or inherited traits play a significant role in the development of SUDs. Alcohol and drug abuse appear to be more prevalent in families of alcoholics and drug abusers than in families without these disorders (Cloninger, 1987; Goodwin, 1981; Stabenau, 1990). A recent family study found that relatives of drug abusers are eight times more likely to abuse drugs than relatives of people who are not drug abusers (NIDA, 1999).

It's not always easy, however, to determine whether this higher incidence rate is due to learned behavior or caused by genetic factors. Is the higher prevalence rate of SUDs in families of substance abusing parents due to learned behavior or due to genetic influences? Researchers have attempted to separate environmental from genetic factors involving SUDs through the use of adoption,

---

Alcoholism and Genetics

Since ancient times, observers have noted that alcoholism is passed from one generation to the next. More recently, family studies have shown that first-degree relatives of alcoholics are *three to four times* more likely to have alcoholism than first-degree relatives of nonalcoholics. An estimated 20 to 25 percent of sons and brothers of alcoholics become alcoholic, and 5 percent of the daughters and sisters. These observations raise the issue of nature versus nurture in the development of alcoholism. Does the higher risk of alcohol problems in relatives of alcoholics result from a common environment or from shared genes? Most researchers believe the influences of both genes and environment combine to determine alcoholism risk.

Source. http://www.familystudies.org/alcoholism&genetics.htm

---

family, and twin studies. For example, if children of alcoholics or drug addicts are adopted and raised away from the influence of biological parents, we cannot credit the influence of the parents' modeling behavior for the children's subsequent alcohol or drug behavior. A study at the University of Iowa found male adoptees, whose parents were substance abusers, were more likely to abuse drugs than adoptees whose biological parents were not substance abusers (NIDA, 1999).

Another useful method for determining the influence of genetic factors on drug abuse patterns is to compare the rates of drug abuse between identical and fraternal twins. Identical twins have the same genetic make-up—as opposed to fraternal twins. Thus, any differences in drug abuse patterns between the two groups living in the same environment may be attributed to genetic factors. A recent study, funded by NIDA, compared the extent of drug use, abuse, and dependence in identical and fraternal twins. "The researchers found that genetic influences played a greater role in clinically diagnosed drug abuse and dependence, while environmental factors played a greater role in occasional drug use" (NIDA, 1999, p. 4). In another NIDA-supported study, identical and fraternal female twins were compared on patterns of marijuana and cocaine use. It determined that genetic factors play a major role in the progression from use of cocaine or marijuana to abuse and dependence. The study claimed that genetic factors accounted for approximately 60 to 80 percent of the differences in abuse and dependence between fraternal and identical twins (NIDA, 1999).

While it appears evident that genetic factors contribute, to some extent, to the development of subsequent SUDs, it is not clear what factors may cause this vulnerability. The accomplishment of mapping the entire human genetic code in recent years will, no doubt, advance our understanding of the genetic influence. (Recently, NIDA granted $7 million to identify genes that make people vulnerable to addiction. This grant is called the Vulnerability to Addiction Initiative.) What does appear clear is that there are no unique genes responsible for SUDs. Rather, genetic factors seem to be a contributing factor in making individuals more vulnerable or predisposed to the influence of SUDs. It's believed that the more severe the Substance Abuse, the greater the role of genetic influences (Comings, 1996). What's our current understanding on what vulnerability factors may be inherited? We will divide these vulnerability factors into 3 classes:

1. Neurochemical
2. Psychophysiological
3. Electrophysiological

Neurochemical

In Chapter 5, the process of intoxication and neurotransmission were discussed. It is commonly understood that getting high involves brain chemicals known as *neurochemicals* or *neurotransmitters*. The exact process by which these neurochemicals interact to produce intoxication is still being uncovered. A primary difficulty in understanding this process has been the inability to directly observe and measure the process of neurotransmission in humans. Although recent brain imaging techniques (e.g., positron emission tomography [PET] scan and magnetic resonance imaging [MRI]) and other neurochemical assay techniques (e.g., plasma and cerebrospinal fluid levels) have improved our understanding of these processes, it's far from clear. Presently, our understanding about the process of neurotransmission remains inconclusive.

What we know is that different mood-altering substances seem to have greater effects on different neurochemicals. For instance, cocaine seems to specifically target the neurochemical, dopamine; LSD and mescaline seem to target serotonin; amphetamine affects dopamine, serotonin, and norepinephrine; heroin targets the opiate peptides, also known as *endorphins;* nicotine is associated with acetylcholine; and marijuana targets anandamide. Knowing that specific drugs affect specific neurotransmitters has led to the self-medication hypothesis (Khantzian, 1997). This theory suggests that some individuals have inherent imbalances or deficiencies in specific neurotransmitters, leading to susceptibilities for specific drugs of abuse. For instance, when a person with abnormal levels of dopamine tries cocaine, he or she may feel a greater affinity for cocaine than a person with normal levels of dopamine. The person with abnormally low levels of opiate peptides may be particularly susceptible to heroin and other opiates. Inherently low levels (or high levels) of specific neurochemicals may make individuals susceptible to particular drugs of abuse. The cause of these neurochemical imbalances may be due to genetic factors or to some other factors.

Another popular theory is that neurochemical factors may affect particular personality traits and behaviors, making a person more susceptible to SUDs (Gordon & Glantz, 1996). Genes may modify neurochemical balances in the brain, causing mental and addictive disorders (Comings, 1996). These theories will be discussed in more detail shortly.

Dopamine Dopamine has been the neurotransmitter most associated with the sensation of pleasure. Most pleasurable activities, such as having sex, eating a good meal, or getting high, seem to be associated with large releases of dopamine in the brain. Dopamine is found in various parts of the brain. Dopamine most closely associated with pleasure is found in the reward circuit of the brain, especially in the area known as the *nucleus acumbens.* (The brain or reward circuit was presented in Chapter 5). In fact, it's believed that all addictive substances enhance, either directly or indirectly, the dopamine reward system in the nucleus acumbens (Gardner, 1999). Cocaine use, in particular, seems related to dopamine levels. "G. DiChiara has found that pharmacological as well as biochemical studies performed with the brain microdialysis in freely moving rats suggest that many drugs of abuse mimic the incentive properties of natural rewards. That is, they raise dopamine in the nucleus accumbens" (Ruden, 2000, p. 173).

Neurotransmitter Functions

Dopamine	Motor systems, pleasure or rewards, mental illness, craving
Norepinephrine	Arousal, stress, mental illness, learning, sleep
Epinephrine	Sympathetic arousal
Serotonin	Sleep, dreaming, mental illness, craving, eating
Glutamate	Alcohol or drug intoxication
Aspartate	Alcohol effects
Substance P	Pain responses
Acetylcholine	Motor systems, learning
Opioid Peptides	Pain responses, learning, eating, addiction
Gamma-Aminobutyric Acid GABA	Relaxation or anxiety, alcohol intoxication

Could defects in the dopamine reward system lead some individuals to be more prone to using drugs initially or lead to a greater vulnerability of abuse (Gordon & Glantz, 1996)? The answer to this question is being extensively researched at present. However, there are several difficulties to proving this hypothesis. First, it's very difficult to directly assess dopamine activity in human brains. And second, it is difficult to determine the exact process by which dopamine may affect vulnerability.

If vulnerability to drug abuse is caused by having lower levels of dopamine in the reward system, what causes the lower levels? Do some individuals have a genetic defect in the ability to produce or metabolize dopamine? If so, which genes are involved? Are dopamine defects inherited, caused by drug use, or caused by other illnesses? Is the defect associated with having fewer dopamine receptors? Is it related to a defect in the dopamine reuptake process? These are just a few of the more interesting questions being researched about dopamine's relation to drug abuse. It's believed that the answers to these questions may, one day, cure or prevent SUDs.

Serotonin *Serotonin* is another neurotransmitter often implicated in studies on substance abuse. Serotonin has been implicated in a wide variety of psychiatric disorders, including alcoholism, drug addiction, depression, suicide, aggressive behaviors, antisocial and borderline personality disorders, phobias, panic attacks, Eating Disorders, ADHD, and Tourette's Disorder (Brown & van Praag, 1990; Comings, 1990; Murphy, 1991; Whitaker-Azmitia & Peroutka, 1990). Decreased serotonin activity has been correlated with aggression and impulsivity (Coccaro, 1992). The interactions between levels of dopamine and serotonin have been implicated in the overall effects of cocaine (Sora et al., 1998).

Other Neurotransmitters Several other neurotransmitters have been implicated in the process of intoxication, including norepinephrine, the opiate peptides, acetylcholine, and anandamide. However, these neurotransmitters have been studied less extensively than dopamine and serotonin. Further research may discover more neurotransmitters involved in the process of intoxication. We may even discover distinctions within classes of neurotransmitters. For example, it may be revealed that there are several different types of dopamine or serotonin found within the human brain.

Psychophysiological Factors

Certain personality traits and behaviors seem to predispose individuals to SUDs (Tsuang & Lyons, 1996). These traits and behaviors include impulsivity, hyperactivity, Conduct Disorder, Mood Disorders, and Anxiety Disorders (Comings, 1996; Iacono, Lykken, & McGue, 1996; Tsuang & Lyons, 1996). These traits and behaviors also seem to be more prevalent in certain families, suggesting that they may be inherited. There is now a growing belief that our genes may play a significant role in modifying the neurotransmitter balance of our brains, resulting in impulsive, compulsive, addictive, affective, and anxiety disorders (Comings, 1996). In other words, genetically inherited neurochemical imbalances may lead to specific personality characteristics and disposition, thus making some individuals more susceptible to SUDs. The specific genes involved in this process are still undiscovered.

This is not to say that every person with an SUD has a psychiatric condition or neurochemical imbalance. However, having specific genetic abnormalities, leading to neurotransmitter imbalances, may make a person more susceptible to substance abusing behavior.

Electrophysiological Factors

Electroencephalogram (EEG) Measurements An EEG measures the amount of electrical activity in the brain. Greater electrical activity of the brain suggests greater cerebral arousal. The EEG activity is measured by placing electrodes on the scalp of the person through a painless procedure. Studies have shown that identical twins have very similar EEG profiles under similar conditions, suggesting a genetic influence (Lykken, Tellegen, & Iacono, 1982; Lykken, Tellegen, & Thorkelson, 1974; Stassen, Bomben, & Propping, 1987; Stassen, Lykken, Propping, & Bauben, 1988). The EEG profiles have also been associated with criminality and alcoholism (Gabrielli et al., 1982; Propping, Kruger, & Mark, 1981; Raine, Venables, & Williams, 1990). Is it then possible to suggest that particular EEG patterns may be associated with a predisposition for SUDs? The literature seems to support this notion (Iacono, Lykken, & McGue, 1996). More research is needed to understand the significance of similar EEG profiles and their relation to SUDs.

P3 Wave Deficiencies A specific alteration in EEG activity occurs when the brain reacts to changes in stimuli, such as changes in sights or sounds. These changes are known as event-related potentials (ERPs). Event-related potentials are believed to be genetically determined, as evidenced through identical twin studies (Buchsbaum, 1974; Dustman & Beck, 1965; Lewis, Dustman, & Beck, 1972; Osborne, 1970; Restak, 1988; Rust, 1975; Surwillo, 1980). ERPs were studied in alcoholics. These studies seemed to suggest that ERPs, specifically P3 or P300 (because it is the third ERP wave producing a positive voltage deviation and lasts about 300 milliseconds) may be biological markers for alcoholism. Begleiter, Porjesz, Bihari, and Kissin (1984) discovered that sons of alcoholics produced smaller P3 amplitudes than sons of nonalcoholics. The reason for this discrepancy remains unclear.

Begleiter et al. (1984) believed genetics played a stronger role for type 2 alcoholics in predisposing them to alcoholism than type 1 alcoholics. "In type 1 alcoholics, one parent—either the mother or the father—is alcoholic, alcohol-related difficulties begin after age twenty-five, and there is no history of antisocial or criminal behavior. In type 2 alcoholics, the father and not the mother is alcoholic, problems begin in the teen years and, typically, are accompanied by antisocial experiences such as fighting, arrests, and criminality" (Restak, 1988, p. 122). Begleiter et al. were able to identify, through P3 waves, 89 percent of individuals whose fathers were type 2 alcoholics.

Further research has indicated that P3 deficiencies seem to disappear as the sons of alcoholics matured (Iacono et al., 1996). Children of alcoholics, aged 7 to 15, showed diminished P3 amplitude. However, children of alcoholics, aged 18 years old or older, had mixed results. This suggests that P3 deficiencies may be indicative of a developmental delay that may be overcome as individuals mature (Iacono et al., 1996).

Electrodermal Reactivity One's response to electrical stimulation of the skin also seems to have a strong genetic influence (Iacono et al., 1996). Studies have shown electrodermal deviations in alcoholics as well as in their children (Finn & Pihl, 1987; Finn, Zeitouni, & Pihl, 1990; Pihl, Finn, & Peterson, 1989). Studies have shown relatives of alcohol-dependent men to have electrodermal deviations characterized by either overarousal or underarousal (Finn et al., 1990; Pihl et al., 1989). The hypothesis around electrodermal overarousal is that these individuals may find a depressant drug like alcohol reinforcing "because it reduces their exaggerated responding, thus increasing their propensity for substance abuse" (Iacono et al., 1996, p.137). The hypothesis around underarousal is that these individuals "may be at increased risk for substance abuse because they are insensitive to the negative, punishing consequences of their behavior" (Iacono et al., 1996, p.138).

Physiological deviations, especially in the brain, possibly caused by genetic influences, may predispose some individuals to SUDs. The extent to which these physiological deviations contribute to SUDs has not yet been clearly ascertained. This is just the beginning of our understanding of the biological influences on

SUDs. The next decade, involving genetic mapping, improved brain imaging techniques, and a greater knowledge of neurological processes, will greatly improve our overall understanding of the etiology of SUDs. If we consider the potential inter- and intrarelationships of biomedical conditions, addictions' medications, and genetics, the comprehension and treatment of SUDs is only in its infancy. The HCV, for example, was isolated less than 2 decades ago; Prozac and other important advances in the treatment of SUDs is even more recent; and the developing science of the human genome is so new that it still seems like science fiction. Clearly, while behavioral treatment approaches in the treatment of SUDs are likely to always be what ultimately gets the client clean and sober, the science of addiction and its developing advances are certain to make the treatment professional's job both more challenging and more rewarding.

References

American Society of Addiction Medicine. (2001). *Patient placement criteria for the treatment of substance-related disorders* (2nd ed.; Rev. ed.). Chevy Chase, MD: Author.

Barsky, S. F., Roth, M. D., Kleerup, E. C., Simmons, M., & Tashkin, D. P. (1998). Histopathologic and molecular alterations in bronchial epithelium in habitual smokers of marijuana, cocaine, and/or tobacco. *Journal of the National Cancer Institute, 90,* 1198–1205.

Bass, M. (1970). Sudden sniffing death. *Journal of the American Medical Association, 12,* 2075–2079.

Bass, M. (1978). Death from sniffing gasoline [Letter]. *New England Journal of Medicine, 299,* 203.

Begleiter, H., Porjesz, B., Bihari, B., & Kissin, B. (1984). Event-related brain potentials in boys at risk for alcoholism. *Science. 225,* 1493–1496.

Beilin, L. J., Puddey, I. B., & Burke, V. (1996). Alcohol and hypertension—Kill or cure? [Review]. *Journal of Human Hypertension, 10*(suppl. 2), 1–5.

Bloom, J. W., Kaltenborn, W. T., Paoletti, P., Camilli, A., & Lebowitz, M. D. (1987). Respiratory effects of non-tobacco cigarettes. *British Medical Journal, 295,* 1516–1518.

Brady, W. J., Stremski, E., Eljaiek, L., & Aufderheide, T. P. (1994). Freon inhalational abuse presenting with ventricular fibrillation. *American Journal of Emergency Medicine, 12,* 533–536.

Brick, J. (2004). *Handbook of the medical consequences of alcohol.* New York: Haworth.

Brick, J., & Erickson, C. K. (1999). *Drugs, the brain, and behavior.* New York: Haworth.

Brodie, J. D., Figueroa, E., & Dewey, S. L. (2003). Treating cocaine addiction: From preclinical to clinical trial experience with y-vinyl GABA. *Synapse, 50*(3), 261–265.

Brown, S.-L., & van Praag, H. M. (1990). *The role of serotonin in psychiatric disorders.* New York: Brunner/Mazel.

Buchsbaum, M. S. (1974). Average evoked response and stimulus intensity in identical and fraternal twins. *Physiological Psychology, 2,* 365–370.

Cable News Network. (2004). Addiction treatment might be old drugs. http://www.cnn .com/2004/HEALTH/conditions/08/30/treating.addiction.ap/index.html

Campbell, N. R., Ashley, M. J., Carrurhers, S. G., Lacourciere, Y., & McKay, D.W. (1999).

Lifestyle modifications to prevent and control hypertension. 3. Recommendations on alcohol consumption. *Canadian Medical Association Journal, 160*(suppl. 9), 513–520.

Campbell, U. C., Morgan, A. D., & Carroll, M. E. (2002). Sex differences in the effects of Baclofen on the acquisition of intravenous cocaine self-administration in rats. *Drug and Alcohol Dependence, 66,* 61–69.

Cardiovascular disease risk factors. (2004). Yale New Haven Hospital web site. http://www.ynhh.org/cardiac/risk

Centers for Disease Control, National Center for HIV, STD, and TB Prevention, Divisions of HIV/AIDS Prevention. (2001). *HIV/AIDS Surveillance Report: Year-End 2001 Edition.* http://www.cdc.gov/hiv/stats/hasrlink.htm

Centers for Disease Control, National Center for HIV, STD, and TB Prevention, Divisions of HIV/AIDS Prevention. (2002). *Viral Hepatitis and Injection Drug Users.* http://www.cdc.gov/idu/hepatitis/viral _hep_drug_use.htm

Chick, J., Lloyd, G., & Crombie, E. (1985). Counselling problem drinkers in medical wards: A controlled study. *British Medical Journal, 290,* 965–967.

Cloninger, C. R. (1987). Recent advances in family studies of alcoholism. *Progress in Clinical and Biological Research, 241,* 47–60.

Coccaro, E. F. (1992). Impulsive aggression and central serotonergic system function in humans: An example of a dimensional brain-behavioral relationship. *International Journal of Clinical Psychopharmacology, 7,* 3–12.

Comer, S. D., Collins, E. D., Kleber, H. D., Nuwayser, E. S., Kerrigan, J. H., & Fischman, M. W., et al. (2002). Depot naltrexone: Long-lasting antagonism of the effects of heroin in humans. *Psychopharmacology, 159,* 351–360.

Comings, D. E. (1990). *Tourette syndrome and human behavior.* Duarte, CA: Hope Press.

Comings, D. E. (1996). Genetic factors in drug abuse and dependence. *NIDA Monograph Series, 159,* 16–38.

DeBakey, S. F., Stinson, F. S., Grant, B. F., & Dufour, M. C. (1996). *Liver cirrhosis mortality in the United States, 1970–93.* Surveillance Report No. 41. Bethesda, MD: National Institute on Alcohol Abuse and Alcoholism.

Dufour, M. C., Stinson, F. S., & Caces, M. F. (1993). Trends in cirrhosis morbidity and mortality: United States, 1979–1988. *Seminars in Liver Disease, 13*(2), 109–125.

Dustman, R. E., & Beck, E. C. (1965). The visually evoked potential in twins. *Electroencephalograms in Clinical Neurophysiology, 19,* 570–575.

Elvy, G. A., Wells, J. E., & Baird, K. A. (1988). Attempted referral as intervention for problem drinking in the general hospital. *British Journal of Addiction, 83,* 83–89.

Fernandez-Sola, J., Estruch, R., Nicolas, J. M., Parr, J. C., Sacanella, E., & Antunez, E., et al. (1997). A comparison of alcohol cardiomyopathy in women versus men. *American Journal of Cardiology, 80*(4), 481–485.

Finn, P. R., & Pihl, R. O. (1987). Men at risk for alcoholism: The effect of alcohol on cardiovascular response to unavoidable shock. *Journal of Abnormal Psychology, 96,* 230–236.

Finn, P. R., Zeitouni, N., & Pihl, R. O. (1990). Effects of alcohol on psycho-physiological hyperreactivity to nonaversive and aversive stimuli in men at high risk for alcoholism. *Journal of Abnormal Psychology, 99,* 79–83.

Fox, B. S. (1996). Development of a therapeutic vaccine for the treatment of cocaine addiction. *Drug and Alcohol Dependence, 48,* 153–158.

Gabrielli, S. G., Mednick, S. A., Volavka, J., Pollock, V. E., Schulsinger, F., & Itil, T. M., et al. (1982). Electroencephalograms in children of alcoholic fathers. *Psychophysiology, 19*(4), 404–407.

Gardner, E. L. (1999, April). The biology of reward mechanisms. Presented at the Drug Addiction Treatment: New Research Findings conference, New York.

Goodwin, D. W. (1981). Genetic component of alcoholism. *Annual Review of Medicine, 32,* 93–99.

Gordon, H. W., & Glantz, M. D. (1996). Individual differences in the biobehavioral etiology of drug abuse. *National Institute on Drug Abuse Monograph Series 159,* 1–15.

Hall, P. (1995). Factors influencing individual susceptibility to alcoholic liver disease. In P. Hall (Ed.), *Alcoholic liver disease: Pathology and pathogenesis* (2nd ed.; pp. 299–316). London: Edward Arnold.

Heath, M. J. (1986). Solvent abuse using bromochlorodifluoromethane from a fire extinguisher. *Medical Science Law, 26*(1), 33–34.

Hoffmann, D., Brunnemann, K. D., Gori, G. B., & Wynder, E. L. (1975). On the carcinogenicity of marijuana smoke. In V. C. Runeckles (Ed.), *Recent advances in phytochemistry* (pp. 63–81). New York: Plenum.

Holmberg, S. D. (1996). The estimated prevalence and incidence of HIV in 96 large U.S. metropolitan areas. *American Journal of Public Health, 86*(5), 642–654.

Iacono, W. G., Lykken, D. T., & McGue, M. (1996). Psychophysiological prediction of substance abuse. *National Institute on Drug Abuse Monograph Series, 159,* 129–149.

Institute of Medicine. (1982). *Marijuana and health.* Washington, DC: Author.

Johnson, B. A. (2004). Progress in the development of topiramate for treating alcohol dependence: From a hypothesis to a proof-of-concept study. *Alcoholism: Clinical & Experimental Research, 28*(8), 1137–1144.

Kampman, K. M., Volpicelli, J. R., Mulvaney, F., Alterman, A. I., Cornish, J., & Gariti, P., et al. (2001). Effectiveness of propranolol for cocaine dependence treatment may depend on cocaine withdrawal symptom severity. *Drug and Alcohol Dependence, 63*(1), 69–78.

Karon, J. M., Fleming, P. L., Steketee, R. W., & DeCock, K. M. (2001). HIV in the United States at the turn of the century: An epidemic in transition. *American Journal of Public Health, 91*(7), 1060–1068.

Khantzian, E. J. (1997). The self-medication hypothesis of substance use disorders: A reconsideration and recent applications. *Harvard Review of Psychiatry, 4*(5), 231–244.

King, G. S., Smialek, J. E., & Troutman, W. G. (1985). Sudden death in adolescents resulting from the inhalation of typewriter correction fluid. *Journal of the American Medical Association, 253*(11), 1604–1606.

Kristenson, H., Ohlin, H., Hulten-Nosslin, M. B., Trell, E., & Hood, B. (1983). Identification and intervention of heavy drinking in middle-aged men: Results and follow-up of 24–60 months of long-term study with randomized controls. *Alcoholism: Clinical and Experimental Research, 7,* 203–209.

Lewis, E. G., Dustman, R. E., & Beck, E. C. (1972). Evoked response similarity in monozygotic, dizygotic and unrelated individuals: A comprehensive study. *Electroencephalography and Clinical Neurophysiology, 23,* 309–316.

Linden, C. H. (1990). Volatile substances of abuse. *Emergency Medicine Clinics of North America, 8(3),* 517–566.

Lykken, D. T., Tellegen, A., & Thorkelson, K. A. (1974) Genetic determination of EEG frequency spectra. *Biological Psychology, 1,* 245–259.

Lykken, D. T., Tellegen, A., & Iacono, W. G. (1982). EEG spectra in twins: Evidence for a neglected mechanism of genetic determination. *Physiological Psychology, 10,* 60–65.

McNeece, C. A., & DiNitto, D. M. (2005). *Chemical dependency: A systems approach* (3rd ed.). Boston: Pearson Education.

Medical consequences of nicotine use. (2004). ImentalHealth web site. http://imentalhealth.com/nicotine

Mee-Lee, D., Shulman, G. D., Fishman, M., Gastfriend, D. R., & Griffith, J. H. (Eds.). (2001). *Patient placement criteria for the treatment of substance-related disorders* (2nd ed.; Rev. ed.). Chevy Chase, MD: American Society of Addiction Medicine.

Meyers, R. J., & Smith, J. E. (1995). *Clinical guide to alcohol treatment: The community reinforcement approach.* New York: Guilford.

Miller, W. R., Zweben, A., DiClimente, C. C., & Rychtarik, R. G. (1994). Motivational enhancement therapy manual: A clinical research guide for therapists treating individuals with alcohol abuse and dependence. Project MATCH Monograph Series, Vol 2. DHHS Publication #94-3723. Rockville, MD: NIAAA.

Morita, M., Miki, A., Kazama, H., & Sakata, M. (1977). Case report of deaths caused by freon gas. *Forensic Science, 10,* 253–260.

Murphy, D. L. (1991). Neuropsychiatric disorders and the multiple human brain serotonin receptor subtypes and subsystems. *Neuropsychopharmacology, 3,* 457–471.

National Institute on Alcohol Abuse and Alcoholism. (1998). *Alcohol Alert No. 42: Alcohol and the Liver: Research Update.* Rockville, MD: Author.

National Institute on Alcohol Abuse and Alcoholism. (1999). *Alcohol Alert No. 45: Alcohol and Coronary Heart Disease.* Rockville, MD: Author.

National Institute on Alcohol Abuse and Alcoholism. (2000). *Tenth special report to the U.S. Congress on alcohol and health.* Washington, DC: U.S. Department of Health and Human Services.

National Institute on Alcohol Abuse and Alcoholism. (2002). *Alcohol Alert No. 57: Alcohol and HIV/AIDS.* Rockville, MD: Author.

National Institute on Drug Abuse. (1997). CDC report highlights link between drug abuse and spread of HIV. *NIDA Notes 12*(2), 1.

National Institute on Drug Abuse. (1998). The rise and fall of TB in the United States. *NIDA Notes, 13*(3). Retrieved July, 1998, from http://www.drugabuse.gov/NIDA_Notes/NNVol13N3/USTB.html

National Institute on Drug Abuse. (1999). Infectious diseases and drug abuse. *NIDA Notes, 14*(2), 15.

National Institute on Drug Abuse. (1999). Institute will expand research into the interaction of genetics and environment in vulnerability to drug abuse and addiction. *NIDA Notes, 13*(6), 4.

National Institute on Drug Abuse. (2000a). Addressing the medical consequences of drug abuse. *NIDA Notes, 15*(1), 3–4.

National Institute on Drug Abuse. (2000b). Facts about drug abuse and hepatitis C. *NIDA Notes, 15*(1), 15.

National Institute on Drug Abuse. (2000c). Update on nicotine addiction and tobacco research. *NIDA Notes, 15*(5), 15.

National Institute on Drug Abuse. (2002). High-risk sex is main factor in HIV infection for men and women who inject drugs. *NIDA Notes, 17*(2), 5–10.

National Institute on Drug Abuse. (2003a). Cocaine's effect on blood components may be linked to heart attack and stroke. *NIDA Notes, 17*(6), 5–10.

National Institute on Drug Abuse. (2003b). Medication for multiple sclerosis may help in treating cocaine addiction. NIDA Newsroom. http://www.drugabuse.gov/newsroom/04/NS-04.html

National Institute on Drug Abuse. (2004a). Beyond the brain: The medical consequences of abuse and addiction. *NIDA Notes, 18*(6), 3–4.

National Institute on Drug Abuse. (2004b). MDMA use may increase risk for cardiac valve disease. *NIDA Notes, 18*(6), 7–10.

National Institute on Drug Abuse. (2005a). Developing effective addiction treatments. *NIDA Notes, 19*(1).

National Institute on Drug Abuse. (2005b). Drug abuse and AIDS. http://www.drugabuse.gov/Infofax/DrugAbuse.html

National Institute on Drug Abuse. (2005c). NIDA community drug alert bulletin–Hepatitis. http://165.112.78.61/HepatitisAlert/HepatitisAlert.html

New York State Office of Alcoholism and Substance Abuse Services. (2005). ReVia fact sheet. Available at http://www.oasas.state.ny.us/admed/meds.fyi-revia.htm

New York State Office of Alcoholism and Substance Abuse Services. (2005). Pain and the addicted patient. Available at http://www.oasas.state.ny.us/admed/pubs/fyipain.htm

New York State Office of Alcoholism and Substance Abuse Services. (2005). Integrating addiction medicine into addiction treatment. http://www.oasas.state.ny.us

Nicotine index. (2005). MedicineNet web site. http://www.medicinenet.com

Osborne, R.T. (1970). Heritability estimates for the visual evoked response. *Life Science, 9*, 481–490.

Pihl, R. O., Finn, P., & Peterson, J. (1989). Autonomic hyperreactivity and risk for alcoholism. *Progress in Neuropsychopharmacology Biological Psychiatry, 13*, 489–496.

Polen, M. R., Sidney, S., Tekawa, I. S., Sadler, M., & Friedman, G. D. (1993). Health care use by frequent marijuana smokers who do not smoke tobacco. *Western Journal of Medicine, 158*, 596–601.

Propping, P., Kruger, J., & Mark, N. (1981). Genetic disposition of alcoholism: An EEG study in alcoholics and their relatives. *Human Genetics, 59*, 50–51.

Raine, A., Venables, P. H., & Williams, M. A. (1990). Relationships between central and autonomic measures of arousal at age 15 years and criminality at age 24 years. *Archives of General Psychiatry, 47*, 1003–1007.

Reid, M. S., Mickalian, J. D., Delucchi, K. L., & Berger, S. P. (1999). A nicotine antagonist, mecamylamine reduces cue-induced craving in cocaine-dependent subjects. *Neuropsychopharmacology, 20*(3), 297–307.

Restak, R. M. (1988). *The mind*. New York: Bantam Books.

Robert Wood Foundation. (2001). Substance abuse: The nation's number one health problem. [Substance Abuse chartbook]. http://www.sachartbook@rwsf.org

Roth, M. D., Arora, A., Barsky, S. H., Klrerup, E. C., Simmons, M., & Tashkin, D. P., et al. (1998). Airway inflammation in young marijuana and tobacco smokers. *American Journal of Respiratory Critical Care Medicine, 157*, 928–937.

Ruden, R. A. (2000). *The craving brain*. New York: HarperCollins.

Rust, J. (1975). Genetic effects in the cortical auditory evoked potential: A twin study. *Electroencephalography and Clinical Neurophysiology, 39*, 321–327.

Schiffer, W. K., Marsteller, D., & Dewey, S. L. (2003). Sub-chronic low dose y-vinyl GABA (vigabatrin) inhibits cocaine-induced increase in nucleus acumbens dopamine. *Psychopharmacology, 168*(3), 339–343.

Shoptaw, S., Kintaudi, P. C., Charuvastra, C., & Ling, W. (2002). A screening trial of amantadine as a medication for cocaine dependence. *Drug Alcohol Dependence, 66*(3), 217–224.

Siegel, E., & Wason, S. (1990). Sudden death caused by inhalation of butane and propane. *New England Journal of Medicine, 323*(23), 1638.

Smeeton, W. M. I., & Clark, M. S. (1985). Sudden death resulting from inhalation of fire extinguishers containing bromochlorodifluoromethane. *Medical Science Law, 25*(4), 258–262.

Sora, I., Wichems, C., Takahashi, N., Li, X. F., Zeng, Z., & Revay, R., et al. (1998). Cocaine reward models: Conditioned place preference can be established in dopamine- and in serotonin-transporter knockout mice. *Proceedings of the National Academy of Sciences USA, 95*(13), 7699–7704.

Stabenau, J. R. (1990). Addictive independent factors that predict risk for alcoholism. *Journal of Studies in Alcoholism, 51*, 164–174.

Stassen, H. H., Bomben, G., & Propping, P. (1987). Genetic aspects of the EEG: An investigation into the within-pair similarity of monozygotic and dizygotic twins with a new method of analysis. *Electroencephalography and Clinical Neurophysiology, 66*, 489–501.

Stassen, H. H., Lykken, D. T., Propping, P., & Bauben, G. (1988). Genetic determination of the human EEG. *Human Genetics, 80*, 165–176.

Strathdee, S. A., Galai, N., Safaican, M., Celentano, D. D., Johnson, L., & Nelson, K. F., et al. (2001). Sex differences in risk factors for HIV seroconversion among injection drug users. *Archives of Internal Medicine, 161*, 1281–1288.

Surwillo, W. W. (1980). Cortical evoked potentials in monozygotic twins and unrelated subjects: Comparisons of exogenous and endogenous components. *Behavioral Genetics, 10*, 201–209.

Tashkin, D. P., Coulson, A. H., Clark, V. A., Simmons, M., Bourque, L. B., & Duann, S., et al. (1987). Respiratory symptoms and lung function in habitual heavy smokers of marijuana alone, smokers of marijuana and tobacco, smokers of tobacco alone, and nonsmokers. *American Review of Respiratory Disease, 135*, 209–216.

Taylor, D. R., Poulton, R., Moffitt, T. E., Ramankutty, P., & Sears, M. R. (2000). The respiratory effects of cannabis dependence in young adults. *Addiction, 95*, 1669–1677.

Tsuang, M. T., & Lyons, M. J. (1996). An identical twin high-risk study of biobehavioral vulnerability. *NIDA Monograph Series, 159*, 81–112.

Urbano-Marquez, A., Estruck, R., Fernandez-Sola, J., Nicolas, J. M., Parr, J. C., & Rubin, E., et al. (1995). The greater risk of alcoholic cardiomyopathy and myopathy in women compared with men. *JAMA, 274*(2), 149–154.

Whitaker-Azmitia, P. M., & Peroutka, S. J. (1990). *The neuropharmacology of serotonin.* New York: New York Academy of Sciences.

Wu, T. C., Tashkin, D. P., Djahed, B., and Rose, J. E. (1988). Pulmonary hazards of smoking marijuana as compared with tobacco. *New England Journal of Medicine, 318,* 347–351.

York, J. L., & Hirsch, J. A. (1997). Association between blood pressure and lifetime drinking patterns in moderate drinkers. *Journal of Studies in Alcohol, 58*(5), 480–485.

You, R. X., et al. (1997). Risk factors for stroke due to cerebral infarction in young adults. *Stroke, 28*(10), 1913–1918.

CHAPTER 7

Coexisting Mental Disorders

As stated throughout this book, an accurate assessment is the key to effective treatment. A crucial component of the assessment process is the identification of coexisting mental conditions or complications. Assessing for psychiatric conditions or complications is covered under Dimension 3 of the American Society of Addiction Medicine's *Patient Placement Criteria for the Treatment of Substance-Related Disorders* (Mee-Lee, Shulman, Fishman, Gastfriend, & Griffith, 2001).

Let's begin with the bad news. Science has not made much progress in understanding mental illness. The study of the brain and mind is extremely complex and unpredictable. Despite our improved clarity in detailing the symptoms of particular mental disorders, we know little about their cause and progression. Currently, we are attempting to treat mental disorders, often through trial and error, with little understanding of them. This can be frustrating for the clinician but not as frustrating as it is for the patient.

The good news is that in this new century, science will make great strides in understanding, preventing, and even curing many of the mental disorders seen today. While it would be overly optimistic to ever expect a cure for most mental health and Substance Use Disorders, through our growing knowledge of brain chemistry, brain imaging, and gene mapping, we will be able to greatly expand our understanding of these disorders. Until that time, we must provide the best possible care currently available, despite its limited success. This chapter will provide an overview of mental disorders commonly associated with SUDs.

Mental Illness Common in Substance Use Disorders

According to the widely referenced study, *The Comorbidity of Mental Disorders with Alcohol and Other Drug Abuse*, which interviewed over 20,000 U.S. residents, an estimated 37 percent of individuals with Alcohol Use Disorders have a coexisting mental disorder at some point in their lifetime. This study also estimated that a coexisting mental disorder occurs in 53 percent of individuals with drug use disorders (other than alcohol; Regier et al., 1990).

Despite these high prevalence rates among people with Substance Use Disorders (PSUDs), there is too little emphasis on developing good diagnostic and treatment skills for mental disorders in the addiction field. For example, in New York, the test for credentialing substance abuse counselors barely touches on knowledge of mental disorders. It is no wonder that patients with SUDs and those with coexisting mental disorders are perceived as enigmas and often referred out for treatment. It is essential for substance abuse counselors to develop the skills for diagnosing and treating mental disorders.

The reason for such a high prevalence of mental disorders with alcohol or drug abuse is as yet unclear. There are biological, psychological, and social theories to account for the connection between mental disorders and substance abuse. There is growing evidence that addiction disorders and mental disorders may affect similarly acting brain chemicals, such as serotonin or dopamine. Another theory suggests that substance abusers may be self-medicating for an underlying mental disorder or for painful emotional states (Khantzian, 1985). As stated previously, the growing sophistication of brain imaging techniques, knowledge of brain chemistry, and genetic mapping may, eventually, prove or disprove these theories.

One psychological theory suggests that drugs of abuse may be used as a compensatory mechanism for poor coping skills (Monti, Abrams, Kadden, & Cooney, 1989). Because individuals with a great deal of psychopathology often have poor coping skills, it is assumed that they find comfort in using drugs and alcohol to deal with uncomfortable situations.

Another theory, more social in nature, assumes individuals with mental disorders have poor social skills, leading to isolation. Consequently, the only social group willing to accept them is the underclass of substance abusers. This eventually leads to an increase in the individual's own use of drugs.

People with SUDs and coexisting mental disorders have been labeled with a variety of names and acronyms, including *dual diagnosis, dual focus, mentally ill chemical abuser (MICA), and chemically abusing mentally ill (CAMI)*, to name a few. Rather than helping, these labels seem to add to the confusion of treating this

Lexicography of Terms

Helping or Hindering Progress?

- *Dual Diagnosis:* A clinical finding of two or more diagnoses
- *Dual Focus:* A treatment focus on both (all) presenting disorders
- *MICA:* The mentally ill chemical abuser with focus on the mental illness
- *CAMI:* The chemical abusing mentally ill with focus on the chemical abuse

population and may lead to further stigmatization. Dual diagnosis and dual focus are terms that can technically be used when diagnosing anyone with two diagnostic categories (e.g., Alzheimer's disease and AIDS). The terms MICA and CAMI have been used to identify which disorder is more severe. If the mental illness is more severe, the term MICA has been used. If the mental illness is only the result of a brief, substance-induced psychiatric disorder, then CAMI is used (Sciacca, 1991). But is the field enhanced by these distinctions? We don't believe so. The overabundance of names for the same disorder and the use of different names to discriminate the disorders only make things more confusing. For purposes of this book, we will use the term *SUDs and coexisting mental disorders*.

Treatment Implications

Substance abuse counselors, with little training about mental disorders, tend to avoid addressing these disorders when seen. At worst, these clinicians may be causing more harm than helping. This chapter intends to demystify mental illnesses and enable substance abuse clinicians to feel more comfortable in treating them.

Problem Types

There are several problems worth mentioning that are specifically inherent in working with this population. Once we become aware of these problems, we can adjust our expectations about the outcome.

Dual Denial First is the issue of *dual denial*. People with SUDs and coexisting mental disorders may have difficulty admitting to having an SUD as well as to having a mental disorder. Our experience has shown that many individuals with both disorders are more likely to admit to having an SUD as opposed to admitting to having a mental disorder. There seems to be more of a stigma attached to a mental disorder.

SUD Denial *SUD denial* is another issue. Conversely, many other individuals will embrace the mental illness diagnosis and deny the SUD. The rationale is a simple one: Admitting to the SUD is also admitting that something must be done about it, such as practicing abstinence. This is an alternative very difficult to accept given that the patient views alcohol and other drugs not as the problem but as a solution to the problem. In other words, "I'd rather be mentally ill than alcoholic because if I'm alcoholic, I have to stop drinking, but if I'm mentally ill, I do not. Alcohol [or other drugs] helps me feel good."

Double Resistance Another related issue is *double resistance*. Not only may the patient resist treatment for the SUD (e.g., not attending 12-step meetings), but he or she may also resist treatment for the mental disorder (e.g., noncompliance with medication). Because the patient has two disorders, there is also an *increased risk of relapse*. The patient may relapse back to substance use or may have reoccurring symptoms of a mental disorder, each increasing the risk for relapse of the other disorder.

Mental Disorder Specific Problems

Several problems are specifically related to those with mental disorders. These are important considerations in both the diagnosing of and the treatment of such disorders.

Lack of Social Support *A lack of social support* is a common problem among this population. These individuals have difficulty developing adequate social skills to make friends. Additionally, due to the high incidence of relapse, many family members have become discouraged and discontinue assisting these individuals.

Twelve-Step Meetings Related to this problem is the *difficulty in 12-step meetings*. Because of their lack of adequate social skills, social withdrawal, and mistrust of others (which includes paranoia in extreme cases), the mentally ill are very uncomfortable in group settings.

Good Drugs versus Bad Drugs Another problem is the *good drugs versus bad drugs dilemma*. Mental health professionals usually discourage the use of illicit drugs (bad drugs) among this population, even though those drugs may have pleasant effects for the patient. Instead, we encourage the use of prescribed, psychotropic medications (good drugs) that may have unpleasant side effects. This may lead to patient mistrust, noncompliance with medication, and resistance.

Risk of Suicide *A higher risk of suicide* is another serious problem when working with this population. The higher rates of suicide may be related to extreme despair, especially among the depressed, or may be due to greater impulsivity in this population.

Risk of Developing an SUD Last, individuals with mental disorders have *a higher rate of developing an SUD* (often 3 times more likely) than those without a mental disorder (Regier et al., 1990).

Assessing for Mental Health Disorders

Mental disorders most commonly associated with coexisting SUDs fall into four main categories: *Psychotic Disorders, Mood Disorders, Anxiety Disorders,* and *Personality Disorders*. There are also a few specific disorders worth mentioning due to their close association with SUDs. These include adult Attention-Deficit/Hyperactivity Disorder and Intermittent Explosive Disorder. The mental disorders to be discussed are taken directly from the *Diagnostic and Statistical Manual, 4th edition, Text Revision (DSM-IV-TR;* APA, 2000a). We believe the *DSM-IV-TR* to be one of the most important reference manuals to be used by clinicians. The more time you spend in reviewing the *DSM-IV-TR,* the sharper your diagnostic skills will become for mental disorders, and, as we keep reiterating, accurate assessment and diagnosis are the keys to effective treatment.

The Multiaxial Evaluation

Before starting a discussion on the specific mental disorders, it is important to review the *Multiaxial Evaluation Report Form* found in the *DSM-IV-TR* (APA, 2000a). This evaluation report is a significant blueprint of a patient's biopsychosocial profile. Although typically completed by a psychiatrist, this evaluation report should be understood by all clinicians treating patients with mental disorders. The function of the mutiaxial report is to communicate a brief and concise overview of a patient's mental disorders, medical conditions, psychosocial or environmental stressors, and level of overall psychological functioning. The report avoids narration. When completed properly, the report conveys a great deal of clinical information using very few words; it's a form of clinical poetry.

The Multiaxial Evaluation Report Form consists of five categories called *Axes* and is divided into Axis I through Axis V (see box Multiaxial Evaluation Report Form on page 154).

Axis I Axis I lists any and all clinical disorders or other conditions that may be a focus of clinical attention, with the exception of Personality Disorders and Mental Retardation. Substance-Use Disorders, Psychotic Disorders, Mood Disorders, Anxiety Disorders, and all other *DSM-IV-TR* clinical disorders would be listed on Axis I. These disorders are usually listed in order of priority from the top down. You may list as many clinical disorders or other conditions as determined in your assessment. Keep in mind that the purpose of the multiaxial report is to convey as much information as necessary. Include as much information and as many disorders as you deem necessary to give a clear picture of the patient. Sometimes a patient may exhibit signs of a disorder, but not enough to accurately conclude that the disorder exists. When uncertain about a diagnosis, list the disorder as a rule-out abbreviated *R/O*. For example, you may write R/O Cocaine Dependence, R/O Major Depressive Disorder, or R/O Schizophrenia.

Axis II Axis II lists all of the Personality Disorders as well as Mental Retardation. (We will be discussing the eleven Personality Disorders later in this chapter.) When a patient exhibits less than the full criteria for a personality disorder, we may list this as *features* rather than a disorder. For example, a patient displaying less than the full criteria for Borderline Personality Disorder may be listed as having *borderline features*.

More than one personality disorder may be listed on Axis II. If there is more than one personality disorder present, list the Personality Disorders in order of priority. If there are no disorders present on Axis II, state this with the word *None*. Axis II also lists disorders of intellectual functioning, such as Mental Retardation or Borderline Intellectual Functioning.

Multiaxial Evaluation Report Form

Axis I: Clinical Disorders and/or other conditions that may be a focus of clinical attention

Diagnostic code   DSM-IV name

___ ___ ___.___ ___   _____

___ ___ ___.___ ___   _____

___ ___ ___.___ ___   _____

Axis II: Personality Disorders and/or Mental Retardation

Diagnostic code   DSM-IV name

___ ___ ___.___ ___   _____

___ ___ ___.___ ___   _____

Axis III: General Medical Conditions

ICD-9-CM code   ICD-9-CM name

___ ___ ___.___ ___   _____

___ ___ ___.___ ___   _____

Axis IV: Psychosocial and Environmental Problems

Check:

___ Problems with primary support group *Specify:* _____

___ Problems related to the social environment *Specify:* _____

___ Educational problems *Specify:* _____

___ Occupational problems *Specify:* _____

___ Housing problems *Specify:* _____

___ Economic problems *Specify:* _____

___ Problems with access to health care services *Specify:* _____

___ Problems related to interaction with the legal system/crime *Specify:* _____

___ Other psychosocial and environmental problems *Specify:* _____

AXIS V: Global Assessment of Functioning (GAF) Scale

Score: _____ Time frame: _____

Source. Reprinted with permission from the *DSM-IV-TR* (APA, 2000, p. 36)

Sample Multiaxial Evaluation Report Form—Completed

Axis I:

303.90   Alcohol Dependence

296.32   Major Depressive Disorder, Recurrent, Moderate

Axis II:

301.7   Antisocial Personality Disorder

Axis III:

                          Hypertension

Axis IV:

Check:

___X___   Problems with primary support group *Specify:* Marital
                          Discord

___X___   Problems related to interaction with the legal system/
                          crime *Specify:* On Probation

AXIS V:

Score: 60   Time frame: Current

Note. In summary, when reviewing the Multiaxial Evaluation Report, the reader should be able to quickly obtain an overall understanding of the patient's biopsychosocial profile, a sort of blueprint of the patient's life.

Axis III Axis III lists all of the general medical conditions that may cause or be affected by the patient's mental condition. These may include conditions such as hypothyroidism, hepatitis C, AIDS, and cirrhosis of the liver. Axis III also includes medical conditions not related to the mental disorder, but significant enough to be monitored, such as diabetes mellitus. If there are no conditions on Axis III, state this with the word *None*.

Axis IV Axis IV lists all of the psychosocial and environmental problems negatively affecting the patient. These problems are categorized into subtypes. For example, "Problems with primary support group" includes problems related to the family, such as death, illness, divorce, and sexual or physical abuse. "Problems related to the social environment" includes problems related to friends, lack of social supports, and loneliness. "Educational problems" includes lack of proper education

---

DSM-IV-TR Axis V

Global assessment of functioning is reported on Axis V:

- Range 1–20 represents the persistently or sometimes dangerous.

- Range 21–40 represents the patient whose reality testing is severely impaired by delusions or hallucinations or shows major impairment in several areas.

- Range 41–60 represents a patient who has serious, nonpsychotic symptoms that interfere with his time management, such as obsessional rituals.

- Range 61–80 represents a patient who has some mild (61–70) or transient symptoms (71–80), which cause difficulties in social, occupational, or school functioning.

- Range 81–100 represents a person who shows good functioning in all areas with a wide range of interests and activities and level of social effectiveness.

- This scale provides a convenient way to communicate the patient's psychosocial competence and rounds off the diagnostic assessment.

Source. DSM-IV-TR (APA, 2000a).

---

or academic problems. "Occupational problems" includes unemployment, job jeopardy, and job dissatisfaction. "Housing problems" includes homelessness, poor housing, and an unsafe neighborhood. "Economic problems" includes poverty and severe financial debt. "Problems with access to health care services" include inadequate health care and inadequate health insurance. "Problems related to interaction with the legal system/crime" includes arrest, criminal charges pending, and being a victim of a crime. "Other psychosocial and environmental problems" includes exposure to a disaster or other hostilities (APA, 2000a).

Axis V Axis V lists the clinician's subjective perception of the patient's overall level of functioning. This is called the Global Assessment of Functioning (GAF) Scale. The GAF lists the patient's overall functioning on a scale from 1 to 100 (see *DSM-IV-TR* Axis V box). A score of 1 indicates "persistent danger of severely hurting self or others" *or* "persistent inability to maintain minimal personal hygiene" *or* "serious suicidal act with clear expectation of death." A score of 100 is considered "superior functioning" with "no symptoms". Most patients seeking mental health treatment typically have a GAF score at or below 60. The GAF is usually scored for current functioning. Sometimes a GAF score is requested for the highest level of functioning over the past year as a comparison to current functioning.

The Funnel-Down Approach

There are four classes of psychiatric disorders commonly associated with SUDs: Psychotic Disorders, Mood Disorders, Anxiety Disorders, and Personality Disorders. When attempting to diagnose a patient for a mental disorder, we use what we call the *funnel-down approach*. We begin with an impression that the patient may have a mental disorder and then ask ourselves, "Does the patient have a psychotic disorder, mood disorder, anxiety disorder or personality disorder?" In the majority of SUD cases, the patient fits into one of these general classes of mental health disorders. We begin the funnel-down approach by ruling out different classes of disorders rather than ruling them in. Does the patient display a psychotic disorder? If the patient does not appear to have a psychotic disorder, we move on to the next major class of disorders and ask, "Does the patient have a mood disorder?" We first attempt to diagnose by the way we feel during the assessment interview. (This strategy is employed with each of the four classes of disorders). A helpful question to ask yourself during the assessment in order to rule out a psychotic disorder is "Did I have an unusually difficult time in completing the assessment because of the patient's trouble in directly answering my questions?" This may suggest a thought disorder. If you determine that the patient does seem to have a psychotic disorder, you would then funnel-down to the subcategories within psychotic disorders to determine which disorder is most likely. (These will be reviewed shortly.)

Next, try to identify your own mood at the end of a patient assessment. Ask yourself, "How do I feel? Am I feeling depressed? Do I feel manic?" If you feel a dramatic change of mood following the assessment, consider the possibility that this patient may have a mood disorder. If there does not appear to be a mood disorder, move on to the next major diagnostic category—Anxiety Disorders.

In ruling out an anxiety disorder ask yourself, "Do I feel anxious at the end of the assessment?" If you answer "yes," this could suggest that the patient may have an anxiety disorder. If you believe the patient displays an anxiety disorder, funnel-down to the subcategories of Anxiety Disorders.

Next, ask yourself if you found the patient to be odd, peculiar, or unlikable. If so, consider the possibility of a personality disorder. Then, funnel-down the list of Personality Disorders to determine which one best seems to fit the patient.

This systematic process of elimination can be an effective method for diagnosis. As we narrow down the diagnostic possibilities, we then use the *DSM-IV-TR* as a reference to determine the most accurate diagnosis. This is known, technically, as the process of *differential diagnosis*.

Psychotic Disorders

Symptoms of Psychotic Disorders

Psychotic Disorders, the prime example being Schizophrenia, are usually characterized by disordered thinking patterns, delusions, hallucinations, and disorganized behavior. Thought disorders make the psychotic patient's conversation confusing at best and unintelligible at worst. Individuals with Psychotic Disorders have difficulty organizing their thinking so that ideas and speech can flow

Schizophrenia and Substance Use Disorders

John is a 38-year-old male living alone, who is unemployed and supporting himself through Social Security Disability income and financial assistance from his sister. He spends most of his days lying on the couch watching television. Periodically, he will have acquaintances come to his apartment to get high on an assortment of drugs. John has been diagnosed with Schizophrenia since the age of 20. He has been hospitalized for his mental illness on numerous occasions since 20 years old. He has reported episodes of having a dialogue with his deceased parents who speak to him about the condition of his life. He appears odd and speaks in a very disorganized style and has little to say. Sometimes he seems to appear preoccupied and laughs to himself in an inappropriate manner. His appearance is disheveled. He has been prescribed several antipsychotic medications, which he takes inconsistently due to their uncomfortable side effects. His sister has given him an ultimatum to attend an outpatient program for his mental illness and Substance Abuse in order for her to continue providing financial support. He has no desire to stop getting high, claiming this is his only social outlet.

in an organized manner. Speaking with individuals experiencing psychotic symptoms can be very frustrating because of their difficulty in organizing thoughts and ideas.

Loosening of Associations Sometimes a psychotic person will answer a question with a response completely unrelated or barely related to the initial question. This is known as *loosening of associations*. Oftentimes the person with a psychotic disorder will answer a question by going off into many tedious details. This is called *circumstantiality*. Or, the psychotic will answer questions with little more than a "yes" or "no" response known as *poverty of speech*. Whenever we are struggling to collect information during an assessment, we need to consider the possibility that the individual may be exhibiting a thought disorder. Thought disorders run on a continuum from mild to severe.

Delusional Thinking A second common symptom of a psychotic disturbance is *delusional thinking*. A delusion is defined as "a false belief based on incorrect inference about external reality that is firmly sustained despite what almost everyone else believes and despite what constitutes incontrovertible and obvious proof or evidence to the contrary" (APA, 2000a, p. 821). For example, the belief that a particular ethnic group is out to destroy one's family, based upon very illogical evidence, is known as a *persecutory delusion*. The belief that a famous person is in love with you with no credible evidence is called an *erotomanic delusion*. Other delusions include the *grandiose* type, with the false belief of having great talents, insights, or connections to celebrities, or, the *jealous* type, with the false belief that a loved one is unfaithful. It is important to be cautious in assessing for delusions for two reasons. First, we need to be certain that the individual's belief is not based upon any credible evidence or logical reasoning. If there is some type of evidence that may suggest the stated belief, then we cannot assume a delusion. Second, we must take into account cultural differences affecting beliefs. For example, some Hispanic cultures believe in spirits. Before we determine that a person is exhibiting delusions about spirits, we must understand how the belief may fit into his or her cultural background.

Delusions are further divided into two categories: *bizarre* and *nonbizarre delusions*. Bizarre delusions are delusions that have no logical merit. Two examples of bizarre delusions include the belief that someone is implanting thoughts into one's mind (thought insertion) and the belief that others can hear one's thoughts (thought broadcasting). A person exhibiting a bizarre delusion needs no other symptoms of a psychotic disorder to be diagnosed as psychotic; one bizarre delusion is enough to warrant the diagnosis.

Hallucinations A third common symptom of a psychotic disorder is a *hallucination*. A hallucination is defined as "a sensory perception that has the compelling sense of reality of a true perception but that occurs without external stimulation of the relevant sensory organ" (APA, 2000, p. 823). Hallucinations are divided

---

Selected Terminology

Psychotic Disorders

Loosening of Associations: Nonrelated responses or ideas

Circumstantiality: Overly detailed responses

Poverty of Speech: Yes and no answers

Delusional Thinking: False beliefs about reality

Persecutory Delusion: Irrational persecutory beliefs

Erotomanic Delusion: Irrational belief of another's love

Grandiose Type: False belief of great personal talents, and so on

Jealous Type: Irrational belief that someone is unfaithful

Visual Hallucinations: Seeing something that does not exist

Auditory Hallucinations: Hearing something that does not exist

Olfactory Hallucinations: Smelling something that does not exist

Tactile Hallucinations: Feeling something that does not exist, such as a bug

Somatic Hallucinations: Experiencing physical sensations within the body, like electricity

Gustatory Hallucinations: Tasting something that does not exist

Disorganized Behavior: Laughing at an inappropriate time

Catatonic Behavior: Immobility or excessive, purposeless motor activity

into *visual hallucinations* (seeing something that does not exist, such as people or flashes of light); *auditory hallucinations* (hearing something that does not exist, such as voices); *olfactory hallucinations* (smelling something that does not exist, such as an odor); *tactile hallucinations* (feeling something that does not exist, such as bugs crawling on or under one's skin); *somatic hallucinations* (experiencing physical sensations within the body, such as feeling electricity in the body); and *gustatory hallucinations* (tasting something that does not exist).

It is important not to confuse an illusion with a hallucination. An illusion is a sensory perception that is misperceived or misinterpreted. For example, incorrectly believing you have seen the figure of a person in a forest that turns out to be a tree would be an example of an illusion rather than a hallucination.

Disorganized Behavior A fourth common symptom of a psychotic disorder is known as *disorganized behavior.* Disorganized behavior may be exhibited by inappropriate affect, such as laughter during a serious conversation; a lack of adequate hygiene; inappropriate dress; and peculiar mannerisms, such as an unusual gait, body movements, or tics. An associated symptom is *catatonic* behavior, exhibited by motor abnormalities such as immobility or excessive, purposeless motor activity.

Psychotic Disorders are divided into nine subtypes as follows:

1. Schizophrenia

2. Schizophreniform Disorder

3. Brief Psychotic Disorder

4. Schizoaffective Disorder

5. Delusional Disorder

6. Shared Psychotic Disorder

7. Psychotic Disorder Due to a General Medical Condition

8. Substance-Induced Psychotic Disorder

9. Psychotic Disorder Not Otherwise Specified

Schizophrenia

Schizophrenia is the classic example of a psychotic disorder. Its onset occurs in the early to mid-20s for men and the late 20s for women. The disorder may occur earlier or later in life. There is no known, definitive cause for Schizophrenia. It is more commonly believed to be a brain disorder rather than being caused by some psychological disturbance. There are many theories as to the cause of this disorder. A popular belief is that it may be caused by some congenital, viral infection that lay dormant until later in life. There also seems to be evidence of genetic influences involved in Schizophrenia; there is a higher rate of Schizophrenia among biological relatives than in the general population (APA, 2000a).

Forty-seven percent of schizophrenics have an SUD (Regier et al., 1990). The reason for such a high prevalence of SUDs among this population is unknown. Theories include poor coping skills, loneliness and boredom, self-medication, or being accepted only by the deviant subculture of substance abusers.

Active or Acute Phase Schizophrenia is divided into two phases, the *active or acute phase* and the *residual or stable phase.* The active phase symptoms, also known as *positive symptoms,* listed previously (disorganized speech, delusions, hallucinations, and grossly disorganized or catatonic behavior), must last at least 1 month. The person must display at least two of these four symptoms to be diagnosed with Schizophrenia. There are two exceptions to this rule: If the delusion is a bizarre delusion (a totally implausible belief) or if the hallucination involves two or more voices speaking to each other, no other symptoms are necessary. The active phase is typically brief and acute. The antipsychotic medications currently on the market are very effective in reducing these active phase or positive symptoms.

Residual or Stable Phase It is more difficult diagnosing Schizophrenia in the residual phase. In this phase the schizophrenic is not displaying active phase symptoms, such as delusions, hallucinations, incoherence of speech, or disorganized behavior. Rather, the individual is displaying behaviors labeled as *negative symptoms.* These symptoms appear odd, but they do not clearly indicate a psychotic disturbance. Negative symptoms include *affective flattening,* defined as the "absence or near absence of any signs of" emotional expression (APA, 2000a, p. 819).

Schizophrenia

Cannabis as a Risk Factor

"There is a small but significant minority of people who have a predisposition to psychosis and who would be well advised to steer clear of cannabis," said Jim van Os, a Dutch researcher (Stuff, 2005).

Based on a research study of New Zealand teenagers, Dr van Os, a psychiatrist at the University of Maastricht, claims that marijuana is responsible for up to 13 percent of Schizophrenia cases in the Netherlands. He said the figure will only increase because cannabis use among teenagers was increasing in many countries, the age at first use was falling, and the strength of cannabis was rising.

After carefully controlling for self-medication and other confounding factors, researchers found that those who had smoked cannabis three times or more before the age of 15 were much more likely to suffer symptoms of Schizophrenia by the time they were 26—they had a 10 percent chance compared with 3 percent for the general population.

The team concluded that there was a vulnerable minority of teenagers for whom cannabis is harmful.

Source. http://www.stuff.co.nz/

The schizophrenic may not laugh at a seemingly funny situation or discussion, or they may not exhibit sadness during a moment when almost everyone else is showing sadness. Another negative symptom is called *alogia,* defined as "an impoverishment in thinking that is inferred from observing speech and language behavior" (APA, 2000a, p. 820). Examples of this include brief and restricted responses to questions or speech that conveys minimal information. Dustin Hoffman portrayed this symptom well in the movie *Rainman.* A third negative symptom is called *avolition,* the lack of motivation "to initiate and persist in goal-directed activities" (APA, 2000a, p. 820). Many schizophrenics will spend the entire day in front of a television set, lacking any desire to seek employment or other positive activities. It is also worth noting that schizophrenics usually exhibit deterioration in functioning (e.g., work, school, self-care, and relationships) at the time of onset of the disorder.

The stable or residual phase of Schizophrenia, technically known as Schizophrenia, Residual Type, is usually the predominant phase. This phase could conceivably last a lifetime. Periodically, the schizophrenic may fall back into the active phase; however, this is becoming less common given the effectiveness of antipsychotic medications. Most of the time when we meet a patient with Schizophrenia, he or she will be in the residual phase of the disorder.

In addition to having two phases, Schizophrenia is further broken down into five subtypes: Paranoid Type, Disorganized Type, Catatonic Type, Undifferentiated Type, and Residual Type. The predominant symptom in the *Paranoid Type* is one or more delusions or frequent auditory hallucinations. The essential features of the *Disorganized Type* are disorganized speech and behavior and flat or inappropriate affect. In the *Catatonic Type,* the predominant feature is marked psychomotor disturbance, such as immobility or excessive motor activity. The *Undifferentiated Type* does not easily fall into any of the other categories. The *Residual Type* exhibits no positive or active-phase symptoms, only the negative symptoms usually seen in the residual phase of the disorder.

In order to be diagnosed with Schizophrenia, the patient must display a minimum of 1 month of active phase symptoms plus a minimum of 6 months of residual phase symptoms. For those of you interested in learning more about the different subtypes of Psychotic Disorders, you are encouraged to read the *DSM-IV-TR* to gain a more thorough understanding of these disorders.

Treating Psychotic Disorders

Forty-seven percent of all persons with Schizophrenia have an SUD (Regier et. al., 1990). Given this high frequency, it is important to assess for SUDs among all psychotic patients. It is helpful to gain an understanding of the perceived benefits that the patient gets from the continued use of the substance or substances.

Some writers have suggested treating the SUD separately from the psychotic disorder, with more emphasis on one disorder before treating the other. We dis-

Treatment Approaches

Sequential
The patient participates in one system, then the other.

Parallel
The patient participates in two systems simultaneously.

Integrated
The patient participates in a single unified and comprehensive treatment program for dual disorders.

Note. The integrated treatment approach is the most effective model. This gives both the mental health disorder and the Substance Use Disorder equal importance, providing a clear message to both the qualified health professional and the patient that one problem is not secondary to the other.

agree. Treating a psychotic disorder while ignoring the SUD would be counterproductive as would treating the SUD while ignoring the psychotic disorder. Both disorders must be treated simultaneously (see Treatment Approaches)

Treating Psychotic Disorders usually includes some form of an antipsychotic medication in conjunction with some psychosocial intervention. The medications used to treat Psychotic Disorders are rapidly changing and evolving. What is being used today may be outdated by the time this publication is in print. The newer medications (second-generation medications) currently on the market include Clozaril (clozapine), Risperdol (resperidone), Zyprexa (olanzapine), Seroquel (quetiapine), Geodon (ziprasidone), and Abilify (aripiprazole). These newer medications are effective in reducing the symptoms of Psychotic Disorders and appear to be better tolerated by patients. They also seem to have fewer side effects and easier dosing schedules than the older antipsychotic medications (e.g., Thorazine, prolixin, mellaril, haldol), which results in better compliance. Some side effects from these medications can include neurological side effects, sedation, cardiovascular effects, weight gain, effects on sexual functioning, and peripheral effects such as dry mouth, blurred vision, and constipation (APA, 2004).

In addition to antipsychotic medication, some type of psychosocial intervention is recommended. Supportive psychotherapy is preferable over a more insight-oriented approach. Patients with a psychotic disorder usually do not feel at ease discussing in-depth, psychodynamic issues involving childhood, past trauma, familial patterns, and the like. It is advisable to stick to more concrete, here-and-now issues, such as medication compliance, drug or alcohol abstinence, leisure time activities, and social skills building. Although confrontation is an essential component of substance abuse counseling, it is advised to avoid any aggressive confrontation with this population. Aggressive confrontation may lead a psychotic patient to decompensate and revert back to the more disabling symptoms of psychosis, such as delusions or hallucinations.

For the psychotic patient, monitoring overall functioning is crucial, and monitoring medication compliance is essential. If you are treating these patients on an outpatient basis, continual assessment for hospitalization is also essential. Monitoring for significant side effects of the medication is also important. Monitoring one's activities of daily living (ADL) skills (e.g., grooming, eating habits, sleeping patterns, finances, etc.) is also advised. Some clinicians effectively recommend group therapy for selected hospital patients, but it may be counterproductive for patients displaying active-phase psychosis. Similarly, we would not push a patient with active-phase symptoms to attend 12-step meetings. Individual therapy seems to be the recommended modality for this patient. Dismissing a patient's delusions or hallucinations can also be counterproductive and detrimental to building rapport with the patient. The priority for a patient with an increase in acute-phase symptoms is stabilization. This patient is more likely to increase the use of illicit drugs as a means of coping with the intensifying disorder.

The residual phase of psychosis is less complicated to treat than the active phase. It is much easier to hold a conversation because the symptoms are less acute and the patient more rational. A greater focus on treating the SUD can occur with this patient, as his or her thinking has become more rational. The psychotic patient with residual-phase symptoms continues to need monitoring of functioning in all areas of life. Monitoring is needed in such areas as medication compliance, signs of decompensation, sobriety, and ADL functioning. These patients also benefit from structure. They are usually socially isolated and would benefit from a full-day program (partial hospitalization) that includes a daily program of structured activities and socialization.

Counseling should continue to be more supportive than psychodynamic in its approach. Schizophrenics tend to have difficulty maintaining long social encounters. Try to keep sessions brief with this population, usually lasting no more than 30 minutes. Although sessions with schizophrenics tend to be briefer, they need long-term support and would not benefit as much from brief therapy models. Social skills training and cognitive-behavioral–coping skills training can also be very helpful for this population. Training may include such areas as conversation skills, recreation and leisure activities, handling negative emotions, and problem-solving skills. Vocational rehabilitation and supported employment services may be helpful for this population, as this could lead to permanent employment and, ultimately, improved self-esteem, financial independence, improved social contact and social status, and a structured daily routine. Last, family participation in treatment in order to gain needed information for the patient's treatment as well as for imparting information for the family to cope with the disorder has been clearly found to be effective.

For those interested in more information on treating Schizophrenia, we recommend reading the practice guideline for the treatment of Schizophrenia in the *Practice Guidelines for the Treatment of Psychiatric Disorders* (APA, 2004).

Mood Disorders

The prominent feature involved in a mood disorder is a disturbance of mood leading toward impairment socially, occupationally, or personally. According to the comorbidity study cited earlier, 8.3 percent of U.S. residents will develop a mood disorder at some point in their life. Thirty-two percent of these individuals will have a coexisting SUD.

Mood Disorders are divided into episodes and disorders. Episodes are the building blocks for developing a diagnosis of a mood disorder. In order to have mood disorder, one must have the presence or absence of particular Mood Episodes. These episodes will be explained further during the discussion of the Mood Disorders.

Mood Disorders are divided into eight subtypes as follows:

1. Major Depressive Disorder

2. Dysthymic Disorder

3. Bipolar I Disorder

4. Bipolar II Disorder

5. Cyclothymic Disorder

6. Due to a General Medical Condition

7. Substance-Induced

8. Not Otherwise Specified

Major Depressive Disorder

In order to have a Major Depressive Disorder, a person must have at least one Major Depressive Episode. A Major Depressive Episode includes five or more of the following symptoms for at least 2 consecutive weeks. It *must* include either depressed mood most of the day, nearly every day (symptom 1) or diminished pleasure or interest in almost all activities (symptom 2):

1. Depressed mood most of the day, nearly every day

2. Diminished pleasure or interest in almost all activities

3. Significant weight loss or gain

4. Insomnia or hypersomnia (too much sleep)

5. Psychomotor agitation or retardation

6. Fatigue or loss of energy

7. Feelings of worthlessness or guilt

8. Difficulty thinking or concentrating or indecisiveness

9. Recurrent thoughts of death or suicide (APA, 2000a)

A Major Depressive Disorder includes one or more Major Depressive Episodes. If this is a person's first and only Major Depressive Episode, the person is technically diagnosed with Major Depressive Disorder, Single Episode. If the person has had two or more Major Depressive Episodes, then the diagnosis is Major Depressive Disorder, Recurrent. Approximately 50 to 85 percent of patients with a single episode of major depression will have another episode (APA, 2004). It is more common to have multiple episodes of major depression than a single episode. Eighty percent of patients experience a recurrence of major depression within 3 years (APA, 1996).

There is no known cause for Major Depressive Disorder. However, there appears to be clear evidence of a genetic predisposition toward this disorder (APA, 2000b). Severe psychosocial or environmental stressors can also cause a sudden onset of Major Depressive Disorder.

Many people develop Major Depressive Episodes following heavy use of mood-altering substances, especially cocaine and other stimulants. Because drug intoxication or withdrawal can mimic a Major Depressive Disorder, it is advised, whenever possible, that a diagnosis for Major Depressive Disorder be delayed for up to 4 weeks following the last heavy intoxication. During this time, we often see a cessation of the symptoms of a Major Depressive Disorder. Patients with a history of Major Depressive Disorder and a coexisting SUD are more likely to need hospitalization, more prone to suicidality, and less likely to comply with treatment than those without an SUD (APA, 2004).

It is interesting to note that many people with Major Depressive Disorders choose depressants (e.g., alcohol, sedatives, and hypnotics) as their drug(s) of choice. The reason for this has not yet been adequately explained. One would expect a depressed person to choose a stimulant as his or her drug of choice rather than a depressant.

Major Depressive Disorder with Substance Use Disorder

Beth is a 48-year-old Caucasian female who reports recent episodes of missing work due to her inability to get out of bed because of feeling depressed. She also admits to almost daily use of alcohol. Her symptoms, which are reported to be occurring for about 3 months, include insomnia, loss of appetite, suicidal thoughts (without a plan), fatigue, a general state of despair, and feelings of worthlessness. She lives alone and drinks alone. Her symptoms have begun to affect her work performance, and she is fearful of losing her job. It is unclear whether her symptoms are due to a Major Depressive Disorder or due to Alcohol Dependence.

Patients with depression are at risk for suicide and should be assessed routinely. Major Depressive Episodes may be acute or chronic. The episodes may develop quickly and intensely and end just as quickly, or the episodes may be prolonged for extended periods of time. An episode of depression typically lasts at least 6 months but can be as short as 2 weeks (APA, 2000b). The lifetime prevalence rate for Major Depressive Disorder is 26 percent for women and 12 percent for men (APA, 2004).

Some types of Depressive Disorders can be attributed to significant life stressors, bereavement, postpartum depression, and changes in the season (e.g., seasonal affective disorder).

Dysthymic Disorder

Related to Major Depressive Disorder is Dysthymic Disorder. The two disorders have similar symptoms, with Dysthymic Disorder being less severe but more chronic (longer lasting) than Major Depressive Disorder. It seems that a more appropriate name for this disorder should be *hypodepressive disorder.* The word *hypo* suggests "less than," so hypodepressive suggests less than a Major Depressive Disorder. In Dysthymic Disorder, the individual must have a depressed mood most of the time *for at least 2 years,* whereas Major Depressive Disorder has symptoms lasting only 2 weeks or longer.

Some people have both disorders known as *double major depressive disorder.* These individuals regularly function with low-grade depression and, at times, develop more severe signs of depression. It is not hard to understand why these individuals choose to self-medicate their mood states.

Treating Depressive Disorders

The treatment of Depressive Disorders, including Major Depressive Disorder and Dysthymic Disorder, usually involves psychosocial interventions, pharmacotherapy, or some combination of the two. Less frequently, treatment may include electroconvulsive therapy (ECT) or light therapy (APA, 2000b).

Psychosocial interventions are usually the first line of treatment considered, especially for mild forms of Depressive Disorders such as Dysthymic Disorder and mild cases of Major Depressive Disorder. These types of interventions may include psychotherapy, combination therapy (psychotherapy and medication), or other adjunctive approaches, such as psychoeducation, bibliotherapy (reading material), and videotherapy (educational videos). There are many forms of psychotherapy that may be utilized, including cognitive therapy, interpersonal therapy, brief dynamic therapy, and behavior therapy (APA, 2000b).

Cognitive and Interpersonal Therapies Cognitive therapy is a very effective psychotherapeutic intervention for Depressive Disorders. It is based upon the premise that one's thoughts and beliefs affect one's feelings. In other words, if a person believes he or she is useless and incompetent (beliefs), then that person will develop negative emotions, such as depression (feelings). Cognitive therapy attempts to challenge irrational thinking patterns, which negatively affect feeling states. Interpersonal therapy focuses on present-day issues that negatively affect relationships and self-concept. These issues may include grief, role transition, interpersonal disputes, and interpersonal deficits. Brief dynamic therapy utilizes the exploration of childhood experiences, significant developmental events, and psychoanalytic techniques to understand present-day behavior. It should also be noted, says Irving B. Weiner, that "psychodynamic psychology can, and often does, focus on current rather than past events in an effort to foster self-understanding." In such cases, Weiner adds, "self-understanding is the vehicle, not the end goal," which in the case of a depressed person, "would be aimed at understanding and helping to resolve underlying concerns." Such concerns, unless addressed, are likely to continue to foster and contribute to the depression (I. B. Weiner, personal communication, 2005).

Behavior therapy focuses specifically on changing behavior patterns that, ultimately, change thoughts and feelings. Although all psychotherapeutic interventions have been shown to be helpful in treating Depressive Disorders, cognitive therapy and interpersonal therapy have the strongest empirical support for treating patients in the acute phase of Major Depressive Disorder (APA, 2004).

Pharmacotherapy Pharmacotherapy is the use of medications to foster relief from mental illness such as depression. Antidepressant medications are placed into four categories: selective serotonin reuptake inhibitors (SSRIs), tricyclic antidepressants (TCAs), atypical antidepressants, and monoamine oxidase inhibitors (MAOIs). Antidepressant medications are usually considered, in conjunction with psychotherapy, when there is a moderate-to-severe form of depression.

Selective serotonin reuptake inhibitors are the most commonly prescribed antidepressant medications currently on the market. They are better tolerated, have less dramatic side effects, and are safer in overdose than older medications (APA, 2000b). The most commonly prescribed SSRIs include Prozac (fluoxetine), Luvox (fluvoxamine), Paxil (paroxetine), and Zoloft (sertraline).

Tricyclic antidepressants have generally been replaced by the SSRIs primarily due to their potential for fatality with overdose. These medications include Aventyl, Pamelor (nortriptyline), Norpramine, Pertofrane (desipramine), Trazadone (Desyrel), and Tofranil (imipramine).

Atypical antidepressants are used as an alternative to the SSRIs. These include Wellbutrin, Zyban (buproprion), Serzone (nefazadone), Remeron (mirtazapine), and Effexor (venlafaxine).

Monoamine oxidase inhibitors are generally no longer considered for use due to their dangerous side effects and difficulty of administration. These medications include Marplan (isocarboxazid), Nardil (phenelzine), and Parnate (trancyclopromine; APA, 2000b).

Electroconvulsive Therapy Electroconvulsive therapy (ECT) "is the use of electrically induced repetitive firings of the neurons in the central nervous system in order to bring about improvements in depression" (APA, 2000b, p. 13). It is usually not a first line of treatment. Electroconvulsive therapy is recommended when the depressive symptoms are severe; when there are psychotic features due to depression, as a rapid response to strong suicidal potential, during a deteriorating physical condition; or when there is intolerable suffering. It may also be used when alternative therapies are riskier, such as intolerable side effects to medications, or when antidepressant medications prove to be unhelpful (APA, 2000b).

Light Therapy Light therapy is used to treat a depressive condition known as seasonal affective disorder (SAD). Seasonal affective disorder involves a pattern of Major Depressive Episodes at specific times of the year, most commonly in fall or winter. Light therapy "is controlled exposure to specific levels of light in order to create relief from an evident seasonal pattern of depression" (APA, 2000b, p. 15). It involves lamps with specific light frequencies designed to treat the condition effectively.

It is important to monitor for signs of a deteriorating condition throughout treatment, suggesting the need for hospitalization. Signs may include a high potential for suicide, severe psychotic features, inability to eat or sleep for long periods, or posing a threat to others.

For more information on treating Major Depressive Disorder, the reader is encouraged to read the practice guideline for the treatment of Major Depressive Disorder in the *Practice Guidelines for the Treatment of Psychiatric Disorders* (APA, 2004).

Bipolar I Disorder

On the other end of the mood spectrum are *Manic Episodes* and *Mixed Episodes*. Manic episodes are abnormally elevated or expansive mood states. They may also be manifested as a predominately irritable mood state. We have met patients who have become so irritable in manic episodes that they have gotten into altercations leading to arrests. Manic episodes must last *at least 1 week*, as opposed to depressive episodes that must last at least 2 weeks.

Manic Episode *Manic episodes* are characterized by *3 or more* of the following symptoms:

1. Inflated self-esteem or grandiosity
2. Decreased need for sleep (often 3 hours or less nightly)
3. More talkative or developing pressured speech
4. Racing thoughts
5. Easily distracted

6. Psychomotor agitation

7. Excessive involvement in activities that may be harmful (e.g., sex, drug use, spending sprees; APA, 2000a)

A primary criterion for a Manic Episode is that the episode leads to impairment either socially or occupationally. The episode may cause a psychotic disturbance or the need for hospitalization. Manic episodes are usually acute in nature, leading to intense but short-lived changes in mood.

Mixed Episode A *Mixed Episode* is a mood state that alternates between manic episodes and major depressive episodes for 1 week or longer. One can't imagine the discomfort of being on this sort of emotional roller coaster.

Bipolar I Bipolar I Disorder involves having one or more manic or mixed episodes and, often, one or more major depressive episodes (APA, 2000b). This disorder was previously known as Manic-Depressive Disorder. This disorder needs only one Manic Episode to meet the criteria for Bipolar I Disorder. It is more severe than Bipolar II Disorder and often leads to hospitalization. There is also evidence that bipolar disorder may be an inherited illness (APA, 2004).

Sixty percent of individuals with Bipolar I Disorder have a coexisting SUD (Regier et al., 1990). Substance abuse may precipitate mood episodes or mask the symptoms of these episodes.

Bipolar II Disorder (Hypomanic Episodes)

A Hypomanic Episode is very similar to a Manic Episode except for a few subtle distinctions: the duration can be less than 1 week (at least 4 days), and the episode is *not* severe enough to cause impairment in social or occupational functioning

---

Manic Episode

Rule-Out SUD

Mary is a wealthy 55-year-old African American female who has been brought into the hospital's emergency room by her husband. Her husband reports that Mary, who has been in recovery from Alcohol Dependence and attending an outpatient program for the past 5 months, has been acting very odd over the past few days and getting worse. He is not sure whether she has relapsed and is intoxicated or mentally ill. Mary claims she has been getting treatment for depression with medication since entering her outpatient recovery program. She claims her medication was recently changed. She speaks in a loud, rapid manner, which makes it difficult to interrupt in order to ask questions. Her thoughts seem to be racing. She appears elated and grandiose. She claims she recently had a revelation to purchase an alcohol treatment center. She reports that her new mission has caused sleeplessness and an all-consuming quality. A blood test could not detect alcohol or illicit drug use. Her recent change in medication appears to have precipitated a manic episode.

---

or the need for hospitalization. Furthermore, there are no psychotic features present. Bipolar II Disorder contains one or more hypomanic episodes and one or more major depressive episodes. There are no manic episodes in this disorder. It is not an easy task to differentiate a Bipolar I Disorder from a Bipolar II Disorder.

Cyclothymic Disorder

To further complicate Mood Disorders, we also have Cyclothymic Disorder. A Cyclothymic Disorder involves numerous periods of hypomanic and depressive symptoms that do not meet the criteria for either a Major Depressive Episode or a Manic Episode. These symptoms must last for at least 2 years (APA, 2000b). This is a chronic condition consisting of low-grade depressive and manic states that are not severe enough to be considered major depressive or manic episodes.

Treating Bipolar Disorders

The specific goals of treatment are to decrease the frequency, severity, and psychosocial consequences of episodes and to improve psychosocial functioning between episodes (APA, 2004). Usually, the first line of defense in treating Bipolar Disorders is pharmacological treatment (medication). Lithium (Lithobid, Lithonate, Cibalith-S, and Eskalith) is considered the primary medication for treating bipolar disorder. Lithium is a first-line pharmacological treatment and prevention for Bipolar Disorders. A majority of patients are expected to have some beneficial response to lithium (APA, 2004). However, due to possible toxic effects, patients being treated with lithium must provide periodic blood samples to monitor serum levels. Up to 75 percent of patients treated with lithium experience some side effects, which can be minor, reduced, or eliminated by lowering the dose or changing the dosage schedule (APA, 2004). Side effects may include polyuria, polydypsia, weight gain, cognitive problems, tremor, sedation or lethargy, impaired coordination, gastrointestinal distress, hair loss, benign leukocytosis, acne, edema, hypothyroidism, and kidney damage (APA, 2004).

While Depakote (Valproate or valproic acid) and Tegretol (carbamazepine) are primarily anticonvulsant medications, they are also used in the treatment of Bipolar Disorders. Both of these medications exhibit effectiveness in the treatment of acute manic episodes. However, these medications also have potentially unpleasant dose-related side effects. The choice of medication depends on an assessment of each patient's risks and benefits of and preferences for each of these three mood stabilizers (APA, 2004).

Sometimes these medications can be combined. Certain patients who are resistant to the antimanic effects of a single mood stabilizer may benefit from the combination of any of the three mood stabilizers discussed.

Several other medications are worth mentioning, although at the time of this writing, the FDA has not approved them for the treatment of Bipolar Disorders. These include Lamictal (lamotrigine) and Neurontin (gabapentin), which exhibit fewer side effects than lithium or Depakote. Others include Topamax (topiramate), ABS-103, Zyprexa (olanzapine), and Seroquel (quetiapine fumarate).

Mood stabilizers usually take between 2 and 3 weeks to become effective. This can be problematic for a patient suffering from an acute Depressive Episode or Manic Episode wanting immediate relief.

Another effective treatment for Bipolar Disorders is ECT. However, ECT is usually implemented after mood stabilizers have proven ineffective. Electroconvulsive therapy should be considered as a first-line treatment in the presence of pregnancy, neuroleptic malignant syndrome, catatonia, and general medical conditions that preclude the use of standard pharmacological treatments (APA, 2004).

Psychotherapeutic treatments are also very beneficial in decreasing the psychosocial consequences of episodes, improving the patient's psychosocial functioning between episodes, and for the prevention of future episodes of Bipolar Disorders. These psychotherapeutic treatments can be implemented in a variety of settings, including hospitals, day programs, intensive outpatient programs, outpatient programs, and private therapy offices (APA, 2004).

There is no one specific psychotherapeutic treatment that appears more effective than others. However, we have found supportive psychotherapy and cognitive-behavioral therapy to be more helpful in treating this disorder than psychodynamic psychotherapy and psychoanalytic treatments. Both group therapy and individual therapy appear to be helpful for treating bipolar patients in the maintenance (nonacute) phase of the disorder. However, a patient in an acute Manic Episode may be too disruptive for group therapy and would benefit from more intensive, individualized attention. The APA recommends setting clear limits for the manic patient in a firm and unprovocative manner (APA, 2004).

Specific self-help support groups for patients with Mood Disorders can also be helpful (e.g., the National Depressive and Manic-Depressive Association). These groups can provide useful information in a supportive and nonjudgmental atmosphere.

For more information on treating Bipolar Disorders, the reader is recommended to read the practice guideline for the treatment of Bipolar Disorders in *Practice Guidelines for the Treatment of Psychiatric Disorders* (APA, 2004).

Anxiety Disorders

The predominant feature of an anxiety disorder is anxiety or the avoidance of anxiety. Interacting with a person with an anxiety disorder usually leads to anxiety in the other person as well. According to the comorbidity study, the lifetime prevalence rate for developing an anxiety disorder is 14.6 percent (Regier et al., 1990). Additionally, 23.7 percent of individuals with an anxiety disorder also have a coexisting SUD.

Anxiety and Substance Use Disorder

Fred is a 38-year-old Caucasian male employed as a doorman. He is referred to an outpatient treatment program after several reports of tenants smelling alcohol on his breath. Fred appears very anxious in the first assessment interview. He reports to be prescribed Xanax due to his anxiety and takes it as prescribed. He admits to frequent use of alcohol to alleviate his anxiety. He reports several recent episodes of going to the emergency room due to feeling as if he were suffocating. The doctors could not detect any medical complications causing these symptoms and suggested they were psychologically based panic attacks. Fred reports persistent and excessive worry about many different areas of his life. He also reports repetitive acts of calling his boss many times a day to be assured that everything is okay with his job performance.

The following is a list of the 11 subtypes of Anxiety Disorders:

1. Panic Disorder with or without Agoraphobia
2. Agoraphobia without History of Panic Disorder
3. Specific Phobia
4. Social Phobia
5. Obsessive-Compulsive Disorder
6. Posttraumatic Stress Disorder
7. Acute Stress Disorder
8. Generalized Anxiety Disorder
9. Due to a General Medical Condition
10. Substance-Induced
11. Not Otherwise Specified (APA, 2000a)

Panic Disorder

Panic Disorder is based upon recurrent panic attacks. A panic attack is a period of intense fear or discomfort. The symptoms of a panic attack develop abruptly and usually peak within 10 minutes. A panic attack must include four or more of the following symptoms:

1. Palpitations, pounding heart, or accelerated heart rate
2. Sweating
3. Trembling or shaking
4. Shortness of breath or smothering
5. Choking

6. Chest pain or discomfort

7. Nausea or abdominal distress

8. Dizzy, unsteady, lightheaded, or faint

9. Derealization (feelings of unreality) or depersonalization (being detached from oneself)

10. Fear of losing control or going crazy

11. Fear of dying

12. Paresthesias (numbness or tingling sensations)

13. Chills or hot flushes (APA, 2000a)

A Panic Disorder includes recurrent and unexpected panic attacks followed by either concern about having more attacks, worry about the consequences of an attack, or a change in behavior related to the attacks. Panic Disorder appears to be highly familial, suggesting a genetic component to the disorder (APA, 2004). According to the comorbidity study, 35.8 percent of individuals with a Panic Disorder have an accompanying SUD (Regier et al., 1990).

Panic Disorder without Agoraphobia A Panic Disorder without Agoraphobia includes recurrent panic attacks in the absence of Agoraphobia. A Panic Disorder with Agoraphobia includes recurrent panic attacks with the presence of Agoraphobia. One-third to one-half of individuals diagnosed with Panic Disorder also have Agoraphobia (Weissman et al., 1997).

Agoraphobia Agoraphobia is a disorder involving anxiety about being in places or situations from which escape might be difficult or embarrassing, or in which help may not be available in the event of panic-like symptoms. Examples of this may include difficulty leaving home alone; being in a crowd; standing in lines; being on a bridge; or traveling in a bus, car, or train. These situations are either avoided or endured with significant distress. Often, the person with Agoraphobia requires a companion to accompany him or her when leaving the home.

Individuals who have developed the presence of Agoraphobia but lack the criteria for a Panic Disorder are diagnosed as having *Agoraphobia without History of Panic Disorder.*

Treating patients with Agoraphobia on an outpatient basis may be difficult due to their reluctance to travel to the treatment office. Any patient exhibiting signs of extreme anxiety associated with traveling should be considered for a diagnosis of Agoraphobia.

Specific Phobia

A Specific Phobia is a marked and persistent fear that is considered excessive or unreasonable. The presence or anticipation of a specific object or situation (e.g., flying, animals, or heights) cues it. Exposure to the feared object provokes an anxiety response or possible panic attack. Phobic situations are avoided or endured with intense anxiety. The avoidance or distress of the phobic stimulus interferes with one's normal routine, occupational functioning, or social functioning (APA, 2000a). This disorder is not commonly a focus of treatment in substance abuse programs.

Social Phobia

A Social Phobia is a marked or persistent fear of one or more social or performance situations. Examples include public speaking and meeting strangers at a social gathering. The fear is centered on the possibility of acting in a humiliating or embarrassing way around others. The person recognizes this fear as excessive or unreasonable.

Exposure to a social or performance situation leads to anxiety. Consequently, the situation or situations are avoided or endured with intense anxiety. This avoidance or distress interferes with one's normal routine, occupational functioning, or social activities (APA, 2000a). As you will see in the next section on Personality Disorders, Social Phobia is very similar to a specific personality disorder called an Avoidant Personality Disorder.

Obsessive-Compulsive Disorder (OCD)

Obsessive-Compulsive Disorder (OCD) is often referred to as a biologically based disorder involving obsessions, compulsions, or both. It should be noted, however, that familial, psychosocial, and environmental influences are believed to be contributing causative factors. It is estimated that OCD affects 2 to 3 percent of the U.S. population. The onset of OCD usually occurs by 15 to 17 years old. The cause of OCD is not yet understood but appears to be related to a chemical imbalance in the brain. Scientists have located sites in the brain affected by this disorder (National Alliance for the Mentally Ill, 2005). Stress seems to exacerbate this condition.

Obsessions are defined by the following:

- Recurrent or persistent thoughts, impulses, or images experienced as intrusive or inappropriate and causing anxiety or distress

- Thoughts, impulses, or images are not excessive worries about real-life problems

- Attempts are made to ignore or suppress the thoughts, impulses, or images

- Thoughts, impulses, or images are perceived as a product of one's own mind

Compulsions are defined by the following:

- Repetitive behaviors or mental acts driven to be performed in response to an obsession

- The behaviors or mental acts are aimed at preventing or reducing distress (APA, 2000a)

The obsessions or compulsions cause significant distress, are time consuming, or interfere with one's life functioning. Thirty-three percent of individuals with OCD have a coexisting SUD sometime in their lives (Regier et al., 1990). There appears to be a strong genetic component to this disorder. In the next section on Personality Disorders, we will present a similarly named but separate disorder called an *Obsessive-Compulsive Personality Disorder.*

Posttraumatic Stress Disorder

Posttraumatic Stress Disorder (PTSD) occurs following exposure to a traumatic event involving actual or threatened death or serious injury to self or others. These events include severe physical or sexual abuse, being in war, or witnessing the death of someone else.

The symptoms of PTSD include (1) recurrent reexperiencing of the traumatic event (i.e., recollections of the event, dreams, flashbacks, etc.), (2) avoiding stimuli associated with the trauma (i.e., thoughts, feelings, activities, places, people associated with the event), and (3) increased arousal symptoms (i.e., difficulty sleeping, concentrating, controlling anger, hypervigilance, and an exaggerated startle response; APA, 2000).

The symptoms of PTSD must cause significant distress or impairment in one's life functioning. Also, the symptoms must continue for at least 1 month. If the duration of the symptoms is less than 3 months, it is specified as Acute; if more than 3 months, it is specified as Chronic. If the symptoms begin at least 6 months after the stressful event, it is specified as with Delayed Onset. We have found many substance abusing patients to have a coexisting diagnosis of PTSD. It is very likely that these patients are coping with their stress through self-medication.

Acute Stress Disorder

Acute Stress Disorder is almost identical to PTSD except that the disturbance only lasts from 2 days to 4 weeks (unlike PTSD, which must last at least 1 month). Also, the symptoms of Acute Stress Disorder must develop within 4 weeks of the stressful event (APA, 2000a).

Generalized Anxiety Disorder

A Generalized Anxiety Disorder is characterized by excessive worry about many events or activities. The person usually reports difficulty controlling the worry. It is associated with restlessness, fatigue, difficulty concentrating, irritability, muscle tension, and sleep problems. The symptoms must cause impairment in one's life functioning. The disorder must last for 6 months or longer.

The Treatment of Anxiety Disorders

Since Anxiety Disorders frequently have a medical cause or component, it is advised that individuals receive a thorough medical check-up prior to initiating psychological or psychiatric care. The treatment of Anxiety Disorders commonly includes both pharmacological and psychotherapeutic approaches.

Benzodiazepines Historically, Anxiety Disorders were treated with a class of antianxiety agents known as the benzodiazepines. The benzodiazepines include such medications as Valium, Xanax, Ativan, and Librium. However, due to their highly addictive nature, benzodiazepines are usually avoided for patients with a history of SUDs. The class of substances known as depressants (e.g., alcohol, sedatives, and hypnotics) is very effective medication for anxiety. It is no wonder that individuals with Anxiety Disorders often use alcohol and sedatives to self-medicate. It is advisable that patients with a history of substance abuse *not be* prescribed these medications. It is a concern to hear about physicians prescribing these medications without getting their patient's substance use history. It is our responsibility to question any physician prescribing benzodiazepines to someone under our care for an SUD.

Antidepressants Antidepressant medications have also been found effective in treating Anxiety Disorders. These include the SSRIs, the TCAs, and the MAOIs.

Specific Serotonin Reuptake Inhibitors The SSRIs, which consist of such medications as Prozac (fluoxetine), Paxil (paroxetine), Zoloft (sertraline), and Luvox (fluvoxamine), are generally considered to be the safest. The TCAs and the MAOIs often have more serious side effects and the potential of overdose. The decision of which medication to use should be left to the physician in collaboration with the patient.

The most effective psychotherapeutic treatments for Anxiety Disorders include cognitive and behavioral treatments. Psychodynamic psychotherapy has not been found to be as effective for this class of disorders.

Cognitive-Behavioral Therapy Cognitive-behavioral therapy (CBT) has been shown to be a particularly effective psychotherapy for treating Panic Disorder. "CBT encompasses a range of treatments, each consisting of several elements, including psychoeducation, continuous panic monitoring, development of anxiety management skills, cognitive restructuring, and in vivo exposure" (APA, 2004, p. 620).

Behavioral therapies attempt to correct painful and intrusive patterns of behavior through such techniques as relaxation, breathing exercises, and desensitization or exposure therapy. Behavioral therapies have been particularly effective for the treatment of Agoraphobia and other phobias, OCD, PTSD, and Generalized Anxiety Disorder.

Eye Movement Desensitization and Reprocessing A fairly new treatment showing promise for PTSD patients is called *eye movement desensitization and reprocessing (EMDR)*. This technique utilizes a patient's eye movements to unblock painful emotional experiences of the past. The developer of this approach, Francine Shapiro, PhD, discovered that moving one's eyes while remembering painful events could permanently reduce the intensity of emotional responses to the past event. There have been numerous studies citing the efficacy of this approach (Shapiro, 1995).

Self-Help Self-help groups, for individuals suffering with Anxiety Disorders, provide support and education and should be encouraged whenever possible. Generally, patients with Anxiety Disorders prefer individual therapy to group therapy. This is acceptable. Never force a patient with an anxiety disorder to participate in group therapy. However, encourage participation in group therapy whenever possible. The benefits of group therapy for socialization, as well as its power to modify behavior, are well established.

Personality Disorders

A personality disorder is a pattern of behavior that deviates markedly from the expectations of the person's culture. The individual exhibits deviations in cognition, such as perceiving or interpreting situations markedly different from others. The individual exhibits deviations in affectivity (mood states), such as regularly displaying emotions with extreme intensity or quickly changing mood from one moment to the next (lability). The individual's social functioning may be markedly impaired, causing people to avoid dealing with him or her whenever

Personality and Substance Use Disorders

Belinda is a 28-year-old African American female referred to an outpatient drug treatment program after giving birth to a child born with a positive toxicology for cocaine. She has two other children, aged 9 and 5. The children are from three separate fathers. Belinda admits to having a 2-year dependence on crack and cocaine. She claims no use of any mood-altering substances since the birth of her third child 3 months ago. Belinda reports feelings of depression and anxiety. However, she does not meet the criteria for either a depressive disorder or for an anxiety disorder. She admits to having a great deal of emotional volatility throughout her life. Belinda admits to having anger management problems and reports several incidents of domestic violence in which she has physically attacked different boyfriends. She has very little trust in men, beginning with her father who abandoned the family. Belinda claims no man is able to put up with her for any considerable period of time. She is currently on public assistance for financial support. She has a 10th grade education. When asked what she makes of her life, she replies that society is filled with prejudice toward Black people, especially female Blacks. She claims she uses crack because society has practically forced her into using it. Belinda believes that her calling in life is to fight for the rights of all Black female Americans. This is despite the fact that she has never participated in any civic demonstrations or political activities associated with this cause. She is not very likable and appears highly guarded and defensive.

possible. The individual's impulse control may show significant deficits, leading to inappropriate behavior or speech (APA, 2000a).

Personality Disorders are inflexible and pervasive. They are rigidly followed in most areas of the person's life (i.e., work, school, or home). They are chronic conditions that usually begin in adolescence or early adult life and continue, to some degree, throughout one's life. The cause of Personality Disorders is unknown and theoretical at best. There are currently no effective medications to treat these disorders. Personality Disorders are listed on Axis II of the Multiaxial Evaluation.

While reviewing Personality Disorders, it is common for readers to believe they fit the criteria for one or more of the following disorders. Although many of us display the *features* of these disorders, most of us do not have Personality Disorders. In order to have a personality disorder, the disorder must lead to significant impairment in one's life functioning, such as work, social functioning, or personal distress. There are currently 11 distinct Personality Disorders:

1. Paranoid
2. Schizoid
3. Schizotypal
4. Antisocial
5. Borderline
6. Histrionic
7. Narcissistic
8. Avoidant
9. Dependent
10. Obsessive-Compulsive
11. Not Otherwise Specified

Paranoid Personality Disorder

People with a Paranoid Personality Disorder have a pervasive pattern of distrust and suspiciousness, but not to the degree of delusional thinking patterns. They often interpret others' motives as malicious. They tend to perceive others as exploitative, disloyal, and unfaithful (APA, 2000). They often bear grudges and perceive benign remarks as threatening. They appear to be very defensive. An individual with a Paranoid Personality Disorder does not display paranoid delusions (e.g., "The FBI is after me.") as found in Schizophrenia and the Psychotic Disorders.

Others tend to avoid dealing with the person possessing this disorder. This only intensifies his or her distrust and contempt for others. If a person with this disorder is fortunate enough to have an intimate relationship with another, the relationship is usually fraught with suspicion of infidelity and distrust.

Treating people with a Paranoid Personality Disorder is understandably difficult. They are not very likable. Given their high levels of distrust and suspiciousness, it is generally not advisable to place them in group therapy. It is difficult enough for them to develop a trusting relationship with one person, the therapist. Begin the treatment with individual therapy if possible. Remain honest with them at all times. Catching you in a lie will only reinforce their distrust. Attempt to develop rapport with them by being personable. Avoid confrontation until rapport is solidly developed. Avoid overuse of humor. They may easily misinterpret the meaning of your humor. Keep your motives clear with them at all times. Fully explain why you have done or not done something involving them.

Schizoid Personality Disorder

The Schizoid Personality Disorder is characterized by a pervasive pattern of detachment from others (APA, 2000a). They prefer being alone. They lack close friends, usually have few sexual experiences, and appear emotionally distant. They tend to find minimal pleasure in most activities and display a restricted range of emotion. Many of the features of Schizoid Personality Disorder have similarities to major depressive episodes (i.e., appearing depressed, lacking pleasure in activities, withdrawn).

You may question why preferring to be alone is a disorder. The point of all the Personality Disorders is that it must cause impairment in one's life. The schizoid patient is probably not concerned about social impairment but may be concerned about his disorder negatively affecting his occupational performance. A Schizoid Personality Disorder may impair work functioning by creating accusations of not being a team player or by having poor communication on the job.

As with the Paranoid Personality Disorder, it is best to begin working with this population individually rather than in group therapy. Because they have difficulty developing relationships, it is best to begin developing a relationship with the counselor. Like the Paranoid Personality Disorder, these individuals are not very likable and are difficult to engage.

Building rapport with them is not an easy task. When treating them, attempt to find common interests. Keep sessions low-key at first, with little confrontation. They usually do not initiate treatment freely, but are rather coerced into treatment by someone else (e.g., employer, courts, etc.). Our experience is that individuals with this disorder seem to prefer the depressants (e.g., alcohol, sedatives, and hypnotics) as their drug of choice.

Schizotypal Personality Disorder

An individual with a Schizotypal Personality Disorder appears very odd and eccentric. The person with Schizotypal Personality Disorder may display cognitive or perceptual distortions. This may take the form of odd beliefs, magical thinking, belief in clairvoyance, or bizarre fantasies (APA, 2000a). They may display odd thinking and speech that resemble a thought disorder in Schizophrenia. They may be overly suspicious and paranoid. They display constricted affect and difficulty developing relationships with others. They often tend to dress oddly and are perceived as strange or even bizarre.

Schizotypal Personality Disorder may actually be a form of Schizophrenia. We think this disorder should have been the one called Borderline Personality Disorder because it can best be described as the border between normalcy and a psychotic disturbance.

This is a difficult disorder to treat. The long-term prognosis for improvement is not good. It is possible that antipsychotic medications may be somewhat helpful, but this disorder is typically treated through psychotherapy. We would recommend utilizing a more cognitive style of psychotherapy than psychodynamic psychotherapy. The goal of treatment would be to challenge the patient's irrational thoughts and perceptions through cognitive therapy. These individuals may do well in either group or individual therapy.

Antisocial Personality Disorder

Individuals with an Antisocial Personality Disorder have a disregard for and often violate the rights of others. They have difficulty conforming to social norms, rules, and laws (APA, 2000a). They are regularly involved in criminal behavior, possibly with aggressive or violent acts. They can be deceitful, irresponsible, without remorse, and impulsive. They are not always intimidating. Sometimes they can con someone with their wonderful charm. Eighty-four percent of them have an accompanying SUD (Regier et al., 1990).

This diagnosis cannot be made before the age of 18. Prior to 18, the diagnosis is called Conduct Disorder (a disorder usually first diagnosed in childhood or adolescence). Individuals with an Antisocial Personality Disorder seem to respond well to the old-school TC confrontational approach, which includes a highly structured environment and strict punishment for those failing to conform to the rules of the milieu setting. Antisocial Personality Disorder was most likely the prevalent disorder among heroin addicts treated in the early TCs. This confrontational approach seems to mimic a behavioral therapy approach, in which negative behavior is punished and positive and conforming behavior is rewarded. Group therapy seems to be more effective than individual therapy for this disorder. The power of the group seems more influential than the power of the individual counselor.

Borderline Personality Disorder

Our favorite way of describing the individuals with Borderline Personality Disorder is that they are "consistently inconsistent." They exhibit a pattern of unstable relationships, mood, and self-image (APA, 2000a). They can love you one minute, believing you are the greatest person, and hate you the next, believing you are the worst person. Their mood can change rapidly in any direction. They often display inappropriate and intense anger and, at times, may have difficulty controlling their anger. Their self-image may include frequently changing goals, values, and vocational aspirations, as well as confusion about sexual identity.

They exhibit a great deal of impulsivity and impatience. They often expect immediate gratification and may display intense anger when their needs are not immediately met. They exhibit impulsivity in many areas, including spending, sexual activity, and gambling, to the point that it may be self-damaging. Substance abuse is very common with borderline patients. Their impulsivity can lead to frequent suicidal threats and gestures as well as self-mutilative acts, which may include cutting oneself with razors or other sharp objects and burning oneself with cigarettes.

Individuals with Borderline Personality Disorder often report feelings of emptiness and low self-esteem. They also report fear of being abandoned by others. They are full of insecurity. They often display poor coping skills. Under significant stress, they can display paranoid ideation and dissociative symptoms like feeling one is in a dream. Borderlines are crisis-prone and report a myriad of symptoms (i.e., polysymptomatic).

It is no wonder that many clinicians are reluctant to work with these individuals. They are possibly the most demanding patients. However, they can also be very rewarding to work with. We have seen borderline patients make significant progress. They often realize how difficult they can be and truly appreciate the therapist's commitment to them. Because of their fear of being abandoned, they often test the therapist's willingness to stick with them by exhibiting even more difficult behavior. Once the therapist passes these tests of loyalty, the relationship may become stronger and more stable.

The cause of Borderline Personality Disorder is uncertain. It usually begins by adolescence or early adulthood and appears to be commonly passed on in certain families. It is more commonly diagnosed in females than males with a gender ratio of 3:1 (APA, 2004). We believe it is an overly misused diagnosis. Patients difficult to diagnose are often lumped into the category of borderline. The disorder is commonly misdiagnosed as bipolar disorder due to the intensity of emotions in each of these disorders. Judith Herman, in her classic book *Trauma and Recovery* (1997), believes that there is no such disorder as Borderline Personality Disorder. Rather, it is an array of symptoms caused by Posttraumatic Stress Disorder.

The primary strategy in working with these patients is to maintain stability in all areas of your work with them. For instance, maintain consistent appointment times and punctuality, especially early in the relationship. The therapist must also maintain stability in mood. You may verbalize your anger and frustration with them, but do not lose control over your own emotions. They rely on our stability to provide them with stability. If we seem unstable, they will panic and react negatively.

Despite your need to personally show consistency while working with them, you must simultaneously allow them flexibility. For example, expect frequent cancellations. They have difficulty maintaining consistent appointments and punctuality. Expect inconsistencies in mood and behavior. Do not take their remarks and behavior personally. Keep in mind that these individuals are in deep emotional pain. Expect to be tested regularly.

Develop rapport before confronting their behavior. Prematurely focusing on their negative attributes can lead to early termination of treatment. Individual therapy is an important component of their treatment. They may benefit from group therapy as well, but they should not be forced into it. They can become very disruptive in group therapy, dominating it with one crisis after another, or they can display fits of intense anger toward other members of the group, causing further problems.

Limit setting is a necessary component of treatment with borderlines. Despite the importance of flexibility with these patients, they also need structure. For example, set limits in terms of punctuality. Do not allow them to be seen after a specific time. Also, set limits on how loud they are permitted to scream in session. They need to learn limitations on their behavior.

A recently popularized treatment approach that has shown efficacy in treating the borderline patient is dialectical behavior therapy (DBT), developed by Marsha Linehan (1993). This manually guided approach teaches skills such as mindfulness and emotional regulation.

Coping skills therapy is also a useful component of treatment with borderlines. This may include such skills as anger management training, problem-solving skills, and dealing with criticism. Working with the borderline patient is challenging but can be extremely rewarding. Once you become aware of what to expect with this population, working with them becomes easier.

Histrionic Personality Disorder

Individuals with Histrionic Personality Disorder exhibit a pervasive pattern of excessive emotionality and attention-seeking behavior. They appear very theatrical and melodramatic, often exaggerating feelings involving events or situations. For example, they may cry uncontrollably over a relatively minor event.

They are usually uncomfortable when not the center of attention. They may use their physical appearance to draw attention to themselves. They may dress seductively and act in a flirtatious manner. They frequently exaggerate the intimacy of relationships. Often, they use provocative behavior to bring attention to themselves (APA, 2000a).

Histrionics use excessively impressionistic speech, but with a lack of detail. For instance, they may strongly state a preference for a political candidate, but provide little reason why. They are suggestible and easily influenced by others.

The preferred method of treatment for the Histrionic Personality Disorder is a combination of group and individual therapy. The goal of group therapy is to have the individual's peers confront the attention-seeking behavior, ultimately making the patient reluctant to continue that behavior in the group. The negative reinforcement received in the group is eventually generalized to situations outside of the group. Individual therapy is used to support the patient while he or she experiments with new behavior and also provides another forum for confronting inappropriate behavior.

Narcissistic Personality Disorder

Narcissistic Personality Disorder is a pervasive pattern of grandiosity, need for admiration, and lack of empathy for others. These individuals believe they are special and unique and can only be understood by other special people. They require excessive admiration and display arrogant, haughty behaviors and attitudes. They typically display a sense of entitlement and can be exploitative, using others for their own benefit. They are often envious of others or believe others are envious of them. They typically fantasize about unlimited success, power, brilliance, beauty, or ideal love. They are often described as being emotionally cold (APA, 2000a).

This disorder is more commonly diagnosed in males. Their drug of choice seems to be cocaine. The reason for this is unclear. Narcissistic Personality Disorder is frequently confused with Bipolar Disorders involving either manic or hypomanic episodes, because both disorders involve grandiosity. However, the grandiosity in bipolar disorder is usually transient, whereas the grandiosity in Narcissistic Personality Disorder is chronic.

Individuals with Narcissistic Personality Disorder usually resist group therapy because they feel superior to others and prefer the complete attention of the therapist. However, persuading them to maintain attendance in group therapy may be very beneficial. As with the Histrionic Personality Disorder, having one's behavior confronted by a group of peers can lead to significant behavioral change. Also, gaining insight into the value of others regardless of social class, educational level, or race can result in tremendous growth for the narcissist.

If you are only able to treat them through individual therapy, it is useful to explore their grandiosity as a possible overcompensation (defense mechanism) for low self-esteem. Treat them with sensitivity. They have a strong sense of entitlement and expect special treatment. Do not keep them waiting long for appointments. They are usually very impatient. However, do set reasonable limits with them or else they will eventually attempt to control the sessions.

Avoidant Personality Disorder

Avoidant Personality Disorder is a pervasive pattern of social inhibition, feelings of inadequacy, and hypersensitivity to negative evaluation. Individuals with Avoidant Personality Disorder avoid people unless certain of being liked. They are preoccupied with being criticized or rejected. They view themselves as being socially inept, personally unappealing, or inferior to others (APA, 2000a). They are on the opposite pole from those with a Narcissistic Personality Disorder.

These individuals are reluctant to try new activities or to take risks for fear of being embarrassed. They avoid occupational activities that involve significant interpersonal contact because of fears of criticism, disapproval, or rejection. They are restrained in intimate relationships for fear of being shamed or ridiculed.

Avoidant Personality Disorder is commonly confused with several other disorders. First and foremost is the overlap with Social Phobia (discussed in the section on Anxiety Disorders). As with Social Phobia, both disorders involve fear of scrutiny by others. These disorders may very well be elements of the same condition. Another similar condition is Schizoid Personality Disorder. The difference is that the schizoid prefers social isolation, whereas the avoidant desires relationships with others but avoids them out of fear. Another disorder commonly confused with Avoidant Personality Disorder is Major Depressive Disorder. Both of these disorders involve social withdrawal and feelings of inadequacy. It is often difficult to differentiate the two disorders.

Individuals with Avoidant Personality Disorder commonly choose depressants as their drug of choice, such as alcohol. The reason for choosing depressants may lie in the disinhibitory effects of the depressants. The depressants permit them to socialize without their usual anxiety.

These individuals typically resist group therapy for obvious reasons. However, getting them to join a group can have tremendous benefit. For instance, gaining acceptance by other group members can be very rewarding. Group therapy frees the patient to try new social skills in a safe environment. On the other hand, it is inadvisable to force these patients into group therapy.

Individual therapy is also very helpful for these patients. It allows the development of a positive relationship with the therapist, which may be the first intimate relationship in a long time. Cognitive therapy is a valuable approach for this disorder. Cognitive therapy challenges the patient's irrational and negative beliefs about self. Homework assignments involving social skills tasks can also be helpful for patients with this disorder.

Dependent Personality Disorder

Dependent Personality Disorder "is a pervasive and excessive need to be taken care of that leads to submissive and clinging behavior and fears of separation" (APA, 2000a, p. 721). Individuals with this disorder have difficulty doing things independently. They feel helpless when left alone. They need others to assume most responsibilities. They have difficulty making decisions, including those of everyday situations.

They are people pleasers and self-sacrificers, who say "yes" to unpleasant things in order to gain acceptance. They are preoccupied with fears of being left to take care of themselves. When a close relationship ends, they quickly seek a replacement.

Dependent Personality Disorder is often used interchangeably with the term *codependency*. Both disorders suggest individuals who focus on others to the exclusion of themselves. This disorder is more commonly diagnosed in females.

This disorder can be difficult to distinguish from Avoidant Personality Disorder due to both disorders sharing feelings of inadequacy.

Patients with Dependent Personality Disorder often do well in group therapy where they receive the support and nurturance to focus on their own needs. Codependency Anonymous (CODA) meetings, which are self-help groups for codependents, can be a very helpful addition for these patients.

Obsessive-Compulsive Personality Disorder

Obsessive-Compulsive Personality Disorder is a pervasive pattern of "preoccupation with orderliness, perfectionism, and mental and interpersonal control, at the expense of flexibility, openness, and efficiency" (APA, 2000a, p. 725). Individuals with this disorder are preoccupied with details, rules, lists, order, organization, or schedules to the extent that the point of the activity is lost. The perfectionism interferes with the completion of the task.

These individuals are often rigid and stubborn. They have a need for control over all tasks. They are often inflexible about matters of morality, ethics, and values. They can be so devoted to work that they neglect leisure activities. These individuals tend to be miserly and regularly hoard worthless objects.

This disorder is often confused with the anxiety disorder of a similar name, Obsessive-Compulsive Disorder (OCD). Unlike OCD, Obsessive-Compulsive Personality Disorder does not involve true obsessions and compulsions. This disorder is more commonly diagnosed in males. As with OCD, this disorder may be best treated using some form of behavior modification.

Personality Disorder Not Otherwise Specified

This diagnosis is given when an individual does not meet the criteria for any particular personality disorder but has features of several Personality Disorders leading to some impairment in life functioning. It is also known as a *mixed personality disorder* (APA, 2000a).

Because this diagnosis fails to convey much information about the patient, we rarely use it. Instead, we prefer to list each of the specific personality features that the patient exhibits on Axis II. For example, we will list a patient's histrionic features, narcissistic features, and borderline features on Axis II. This conveys more useful information than a diagnosis of Not Otherwise Specified.

If an individual does not meet the criteria for any specific personality disorder, but has distinct features of a personality disorder, you may still list the personality features on Axis II. Remember that the multiaxial evaluation is a means of conveying valuable information about a patient's mental state.

Other Disorders

Before closing this chapter, there are two other disorders commonly associated with SUDs that are worth mentioning: Attention-Deficit/Hyperactivity Disorder and Intermittent Explosive Disorder. Neither of these disorders fit neatly into a major diagnostic category.

Attention-Deficit/Hyperactivity Disorder

Attention-Deficit/Hyperactivity Disorder (ADHD) is listed in the *DSM-IV-TR* in the section on Disorders Usually First Diagnosed in Infancy, Childhood, or Adolescence. Because this disorder is usually considered to be a childhood disorder, it is often overlooked in adults. However, we have found this disorder to be common among adult substance abusers, especially cocaine abusers. Researchers have estimated that 30 to 50 percent of individuals with this disorder will self-medicate with drugs (Richardson, 1999). There appears to be a biological basis for this disorder.

Attention-Deficit/Hyperactivity Disorder involves a "persistent pattern of inattention and/or hyperactivity-impulsivity that is more frequently displayed and more severe than is typically observed in individuals at a comparable level of development" (APA, 2000a, p. 85). Inattention is exhibited by failing to give close attention to details, difficulty organizing tasks, frequent careless mistakes at work, difficulty completing projects, difficulty sustaining attention in conversation or in leisure activities, and by being easily distracted and forgetful.

Hyperactivity involves excessive fidgeting, difficulty sitting still, difficulty engaging in leisure activities quietly, excessive talking, and difficulty with relaxing. Impulsivity involves difficulty waiting one's turn, often interrupting or intruding on others, and blurting out answers before questions have been completed.

These symptoms usually are present before the age of 7 and lead to impairment in school, work, or home. It is more commonly diagnosed in males. It is believed that only a minority of individuals fully experience ADHD symptoms in adulthood. Attention-Deficit/Hyperactivity Disorder is further subtyped into three categories, where the predominant symptoms are either inattention, hyperactivity-impulsivity, or a combined type including inattention and hyperactivity-impulsivity.

Although this disorder is believed to be rare among adults, we have experienced a significant portion of substance abusers, usually abusing a stimulant such as cocaine, who appear to meet the criteria for ADHD.

The medication Ritalin (methylphenidate), a stimulant, is the common treatment for childhood ADHD. Other stimulant medications used for treating ADHD include Cylert (pemoline), Dexedrine, Adderall, and Desoxyn. Paradoxically, the use of stimulants actually calms ADHD patients down rather than exciting them further as would be expected from a stimulant. It is possible that this paradoxical effect is also occurring in adult ADHD patients. The use of stimulants such as cocaine, amphetamine, methamphetamine, caffeine, and nicotine may actually be calming these individuals.

There has been controversy about whether prescribing stimulant medications to children is associated with later Substance Abuse. A recent study of youths treated for ADHD concluded that those treated with stimulant therapy actually had a reduced risk of subsequent alcohol and drug use disorders (Wilens, Faraone, Biederman, & Gunawardene, 2003).

Intermittent Explosive Disorder

Intermittent Explosive Disorder is a disorder that is listed in the *DSM-IV-TR* in the category Impulse-Control Disorders Not Elsewhere Classified. It is similar to ADHD in that they both involve difficulty with impulsivity.

Intermittent Explosive Disorder is characterized by "the occurrence of discrete episodes of failure to resist aggressive impulses that result in serious assaultive acts or destruction of property" (APA, 2000a, p. 664). The extent of the aggressiveness is considered out of proportion with the extenuating circumstances.

Although this disorder is considered rare, we have experienced a significant population of substance abusers that appear to meet the criteria for this disorder. It is possible that their inability to control one set of impulses (aggression) may be associated with their inability to control another set of impulses (substance use).

In closing, let us again reiterate the helpfulness of using the funnel-down approach when obtaining a differential diagnosis. Begin with the four most common mental health categories associated with SUDs: Psychotic Disorders, Mood Disorders, Anxiety Disorders, and Personality Disorders. Begin eliminating categories by asking yourself questions such as, "Does this person display a thought disorder, delusions, or hallucinations? Does this person seem to display the residual (negative) symptoms of Schizophrenia? Did I have difficulty following this person's train of thought? Does this person predominantly show signs of a mood disturbance? Does this person display signs of depressive or manic episodes? Did I leave the session feeling depressed? Does this person predominantly appear anxious? Did I leave the session feeling anxious?" Once you have ruled out Psychotic Disorders, Mood Disorders, and Anxiety Disorders, consider the Personality Disorders. Does this person predominantly exhibit suspiciousness, isolation, odd or bizarre behavior, criminal behavior, or inconsistencies in mood and behavior? Is this person melodramatic, grandiose, fearful of others, overly dependent, or overly detailed? If not, then the person may not have a mental disorder, or you may have to begin ruling out other *DSM-IV-TR* categories such as Cognitive Disorders, Somatoform Disorders, Dissociative Disorders, and Adjustment Disorders.

This chapter has attempted to review the disorders commonly associated with SUDs. We have discussed the criteria for diagnosing each of these disorders and some strategies for treating each of them. There is no mystery in working with patients suffering from both an SUD and a coexisting psychiatric disorder. Once the clinician develops an accurate assessment of the patient's mental health problem, successful treatment has already begun.

References

American Psychiatric Association. (1996). Major Depressive Disorder in adults. In American Psychiatric Association (Eds.), *Practice Guidelines* (pp. 79–134). Washington, DC: Author.

American Psychiatric Association. (2000a). *Diagnostic and statistical manual of mental disorders* (4th ed.; Rev. ed.). Washington, DC: Author.

American Psychiatric Association. (2000b). *Practice guidelines for the treatment of patients with Major Depression* (2nd ed.). Arlington, VA: Author.

American Psychiatric Association. (2004). *Practice guidelines for the treatment of psychiatric disorders: Compendium 2004.* Arlington, VA: Author.

Herman, J. (1997). *Trauma and recovery.* New York: Basic.

Khantzian, E. J. (1985). The self-medication hypothesis of addictive disorders: Focus on heroin and cocaine dependence. *American Journal of Psychiatry, 142*(11), 1259–1264.

Linehan, M. M. (1993). *Cognitive-behavioral treatment of Borderline Personality Disorder.* New York: Guilford.

Mee-Lee, D., Shulman, G. D., Fishman, M., Gastfriend, D. R., & Griffith, J. H. (Eds.). (2001). *Patient placement criteria for the treatment of substance-related disorders* (2nd ed.; Rev.ed.). Chevy Chase, MD: American Society of Addiction Medicine.

Monti, P. M., Abrams, D. B., Kadden, R. M., and Cooney, N. L. (2002). *Treating alcohol dependence: A coping skills training guide.* (2nd ed.). New York: Guilford.

National Alliance for the Mentally Ill. (2005). National Alliance for the Mentally Ill web site. http://www.nami.org

Regier, D. A., Farmer, M. E., Rae, D. S., Locke, B. Z., Keith, S. J., & Judd, L. L., et al. (1990). Comorbidity of mental disorders with alcohol and other drug abuse. *Journal of the American Medical Association, 264*(19), 2511–2518.

Richardson, W. (1999). The link between ADHD and addiction. *Professional Counselor, April,* 30–32.

Sciacca, K. (1991). An integrated treatment approach for severely mentally ill individuals with substance disorders. *New Directions for Mental Health Services, 50,* 69–84.

Shapiro, F. (1995). *Eye movement desensitization and reprocessing: Basic principles, protocols, and procedures.* New York: Guilford.

Weissman, M. M., Bland, R. C., Camino, S. J., Faravelli, C., Greenwald, S., & Hwu, H. G., et. al. (1997). The cross-national epidemiology of panic disorder. *Archives of General Psychiatry, 54,* 305–309.

Wilens, T. E., Faraone, S. V., Biederman, J., & Gunawardene, S. (2003). Does stimulant therapy of Attention-Deficit/Hyperactivity Disorder beget later substance abuse? A meta-analytic review of the literature. *Pediatrics, 111*(1), 179–185.

CHAPTER 8

Recovery and the Living Environment

Throughout this book Substance Use Disorders (SUDs) are often referred to as *family problems* or *family illnesses*. If we review the literature on alcohol and drug addiction, it is not difficult to see why this is so: Genetic predisposition and family environment are frequently part of the discussion on alcoholism and on other drugs of abuse. It has long been established that heredity or milieu or both contribute to the development of an SUD in an individual. It is not uncommon to uncover a history of SUDs and enabling behaviors through several generations. Enabling behaviors are not limited to immediate family members; such behaviors can also be exhibited by friends, relatives, colleagues, coworkers, and even helping professionals. The person with the Substance Use Disorder (PSUD) impacts those around him or her, while those around him or her also impact the person.

Although the recovering individual is ultimately responsible for the decisions he or she makes, family, workplace, and social environments impact such decisions. While these influences can often be positive, at their worst they can also undermine treatment and inhibit, if not preclude, recovery. The treatment professional whose case management does not include current and ongoing assessment of the recovery environment is likely to compromise the chance of a successful outcome. And while this may be a no-brainer for most professionals, its practice and application might not always be easy. Although the patient's living environment is a consideration when choosing the appropriate level of care (see six dimensions, Chapter 4), ongoing monitoring throughout continuing care is often overlooked. It's not that the subject is *not* discussed if and when introduced by the patient. In all likelihood it is. But family, social, and workplace environments are dynamic issues that need ongoing attention even if the patient does *not* introduce them. This is especially vital during early recovery. Counting

Enabling Defined

Enabling refers to any behavior, direct or indirect, no matter how well meaning, that allows the alcoholic or addict to continue drinking or using (Mooney et al., 1992, p. 576).

Why do people enable? Not, oddly enough, for the benefit of the sick person—enabling harms the alcoholic or addict. They enable in order to meet their own needs. It's an attempt to restabilize the relationship, to counter growing alienation, or to lure the alcoholic or addict back into the relationship by providing a counterforce to the alcohol and drugs that seem to be tugging the other person away. It allows the disease to progress to a more serious stage and worsens the prognosis for a good recovery (Mooney et al., 1992, p. 501).

days of abstinence is an important measure of success in treatment, but measuring changes in family, social, and workplace activities are equally important. A relapse will often start as a dysfunction in one of these environments.

Environmental Impact on Recovery

The living environment is an important consideration in assessing treatment needs because without a safe and supportive environment, recovery is difficult. In combination with the other five dimensions discussed in Chapter 3, environment is a factor in planning and achieving both short- and long-term recovery goals. If the patient's living environment is not one that reinforces recovery and growth, then the treatment plan has to include strategies that will address such concerns and encourage appropriate actions. In fact, all the client's recovery environments—*family, social, and workplace*—require ongoing monitoring if success is to be expected.

Family Environment

The family is an important consideration in both treatment and ongoing recovery. It can be a supportive or discouraging influence—or both. Most often it will be a complex of mixed messages, some enabling and shaming, some compassionate and reinforcing. Financial problems, legal concerns, unresolved household matters, or another family member's drinking or drug use are important factors in early recovery. The person in treatment is not likely to do well if the environment that enabled his or her addiction remains unchanged in recovery. The immediate environment—the family—can be critical to the outcome of treatment efforts and cannot be ignored or viewed as an inconvenience. Removing the family from the recovering person's life is not an option, but engaging the family in treatment is. Every effort should be made to ensure the family's involvement in the treatment process.

Healthy Family Traits

Ranked in Order of Importance

1. Communicates and listens.
2. Affirms and supports one another.
3. Teaches respect for others.
4. Develops trust.
5. Has a sense of play and humor.
6. Exhibits a sense of shared responsibility.
7. Teaches a sense of right and wrong.
8. Has a strong sense of family values.
9. Has a balance of interaction among members.
10. Has a shared religious core.
11. Respects the privacy of one another.
12. Values service to one another.
13. Fosters family table time and conversation.
14. Shares leisure time.
15. Admits problems and is willing to seek help.

White: Invitational model

Family History

Taking a family history starts with gathering information on current family behavior. What are the drinking and drug use habits of the PSUD's family? The family includes anyone presently living in the home of the client and anyone in the family who might influence the client's behavior. Are there members of the client's family of origin who should participate in treatment? In order for the treatment professional to effectively help the client identify possible triggers, an understanding of family attitudes toward drinking and other drug use is important. The client is not likely to understand the power of such attitudes and may need some help in identifying them. Substance Use Disorders are diseases of secrets. There may have been psychological or physical abuse within the family or against the client that need to be assessed. If a safer living environment is one of the goals of treatment, then whatever in the environment is perceived to be a threat should be known. The quality of all the relationships that the client currently has should be supportive in nature; any relationships that are not supportive are likely to be destructive.

Family History Impacts Recovery

- What are the drinking and drug use habits of members of the client's family of origin (mother, father, grandparents, siblings, aunts, uncles, etc.)?

- Are there persons in the client's family of origin who have alcohol or other drug problems?

- What were the attitudes toward drinking alcohol and other drug use in the client's family of origin?

- How does the client describe his or her relationship with family-of-origin members?

- Was there a history of psychological or physical (including sexual) abuse in the family?

- What is the client's current relationship with family members? (McNeece & DiNitto, 2005, p. 109).

The Family Dynamics

Families are described as dynamic systems influenced by changes that occur both within and outside of the family system (Fisher & Harrison, 2000, p. 173). The term *family homeostasis* is used to describe the natural tendency of families to behave in such a manner as to maintain a sense of balance, structure, and stability in the face of change (Jackson, 1957). In other words, if one of the family members changes his or her behavior, the entire family will be affected and have to make an adjustment. A family member with an SUD who gets clean and sober is just such a change. But family adjustment is not easy, and resistance is likely. For the recovering PSUD, this resistance will have a negative impact on potential success. While it may appear that the family is pleased with the identified patient's decision to work toward recovery, incorporating such a change into the family's collective functioning means all family members, in some way, will also have to change. Roles, rules, boundaries, and values are challenged, and something has to give. The family's dysfunctional behaviors are no longer effective, and the existing homeostasis must redefine itself if recovery is to continue and the family is to survive. It should be noted that the dysfunctional family does not view itself as dysfunctional until it is challenged by change. The recovering family member is that kind of challenge. With recovery comes responsibility; in reassuming responsibilities neglected in the past, other family members may feel threatened by this shift in roles. Managing finances might be one such responsibility. The husband and father who had been too impaired to manage the finances suddenly feels the need to take on the checkbook. How would this impact on the wife and mother who for the past 10 years managed the finances for the entire family, including school tuition, utilities, savings, food, mortgage, and insurance premiums? It is not likely that such responsibility—and control—would be surrendered without resistance. Might she sabotage her husband's recovery—consciously or unconsciously—to maintain this base of power and control?

While some families may have the internal resources to manage such changes without treatment, that would be the exception. And while the recovering family member may have the tools and support to deal with these challenges, engaging the family in the treatment process will improve chances for a successful outcome. The provision of family therapy services is beyond the scope of this book, but there are two concepts that are necessary to understand if treatment of the recovering person is to be successful: *childhood roles* and *family rules*.

Childhood Roles

Black, as cited in Fisher and Harrison, 2005, describes the roles adopted by children of alcoholic homes as based upon their perceptions of what they need to do to survive and bring stability to their lives (Fisher & Harrison, 2005, p. 194). Wegscheider, as cited in Fisher and Harrison, identifies the dysfunctional family roles of children as *hero, scapegoat, lost child,* and *mascot.* Along with the *enabler,* these roles could probably apply to adult children or even adults. She goes on to say the roles assumed by children in homes where alcohol and other drugs are present tend to be fixed and rigid, resulting in family dysfunction. They are survival roles in families and are viewed as dysfunctional and maladaptive (ibid., p. 195).

Given this hypothetical construct, it is not difficult to imagine the challenge of a family in adjusting to a now substance-free mother or father. Place Wegscheider's *childhood roles* (below) within the context of the *family rules* and you have a complex of rigidity and inflexibility that, if not addressed, is certain to drive the recovering family member back to alcohol or other drugs. Add to that family a parent just discharged from a rehabilitation program after spending 60 days submerged in intensive care, including education groups, psychotherapy, peer support, individual counseling, a healthy diet, and a total treatment experience with little about anything other than recovery, relapse prevention, and spirituality. This

---

Wegscheider's Children's Roles

Hero/Heroine: High achiever who defocuses attention from alcoholism in the family system

Scapegoat: Acts out the family problem through defiance and irresponsibility

Lost Child: Shy, withdrawn, and requires little attention

Mascot: Funny and mischievous and defuses tension inherent in alcoholic families and the classroom clown

Source. (Wegscheider, 1981).

---

will not be the same person that the family knew just a couple of months ago. And needless to say, without help, the family will not know how to respond to such a dramatic change.

Family Rules

All families have overt and covert contracts between their members that operate as rules governing family interactions (Fisher & Harrison, 2005, p. 195). According to Bernard, as cited in Fisher and Harrison, 2005, these governing rules are divided into six subgroups:

1. What, when, and how family members can communicate their experiences about what they see, hear, feel, and think.
2. Who has permission to speak to whom about what.
3. The extent and manner in which a family member can be different.
4. The manner in which sexuality can be expressed.
5. What it means to be male or female.
6. How family members acquire self-worth and how much self-worth a member can experience.

Although culturally and ethnically diverse families are also governed by such rules, the differences between groups might be in the punishment for violations, for example, shaming, restrictions, or physical discipline. Black, as cited in Fisher and Harrison, 2005, states that the three rules that govern *alcoholic* families are don't talk; don't trust; don't feel (p. 196). It would be safe to conclude that such dysfunctional rules apply whatever the drug of choice might be. Typical statements heard in families with SUDs might include the following:

Rule 1: Do not believe that your mother uses amphetamines!

Rule 2: This is family business, and it should stay here!

Rule 3: Your brother was never a problem!

Rule 4: You know your father does not like how you look in tank tops!

Rule 5: I don't care what your brother said; girls don't use that kind of language!

Rule 6: You're getting a little big for your britches, aren't you!

Recovery Without the Family

With the importance of family involvement in the treatment of SUDs notwithstanding, recovery is also possible *without* family involvement. And while one is tempted to add a caveat—"but more difficult,"—that is often not the case. On the contrary, individual treatment without family involvement is sometimes clinically appropriate. It may be advisable, in fact, for the individual to focus on personal recovery and build the contingencies necessary to facilitate that goal. The family is the basic unit of society, and homeostasis, as defined by Jackson is the "natural tendency of families to behave in such a manner as to maintain a sense of balance" (1957, pp. 31, 79–90). Wegscheider, in Fisher and Harrison, adds that "If drinking is removed from the family system, the family can be thrown into chaos" (2005, p. 192). Implicit in homeostasis is the importance of family roles, which is defined by Shertzer & Stone, cited in Fisher and Harrison, as individual behaviors: "One's own actions as well as the actions with whom one is involved" (2005, p. 193).

Based on all of the preceding, and reinforced by countless scholars who have written on the subject, the implication is that the family needs to be in treatment if the family member with the SUD is to be successful in recovery. Well, is that really implied or is that what the reader often infers? Actually, what most of these authors say is not that the family needs to be in treatment but rather that the family needs to change. Wegscheider, cited in Fisher and Harrison, takes this one step further with "Unless the family can adjust adequately, drinking may be initiated again to reestablish balance" (2005, p. 192).

While Wegscheider is wise in alerting the therapist to the potential peril of an inflexible family environment, it is important to note that she said drinking *may be*, not *will be*, initiated again. This distinction is a small but important one in that it does not mandate family adjustment as a prerequisite to recovery. Equally important, while successful family treatment is likely to facilitate positive change, it is not wise to view family treatment as a condition for individual recovery. It's not.

Where does all this leave the recovering family member? Well, that all depends on the discipline that you ask. The family therapist would feel that the objective of treatment is to help the family heal and grow. The SUD specialist might see this as a noble goal, but only if it does not compromise the potential recovery of the individual. Here is where a good clinical assessment goes beyond LOCs discussed in Chapter 4, and to the balancing of individual recovery treatment choices. This does not mean that the recovering person should walk away from family members and their difficulties, but rather that their dysfunction should not become his or her problem. If this begins to happen, the chance of maintaining sobriety is dangerously compromised. While family involvement in the individual's recovery should always be explored, the term identified patient should not be ignored—other family members may actually be far less healthy than the recovering person.

Bruce Cotter, interventionist and author of *When They Won't Quit: A Call to Action for Families, Friends, and Employers of Alcohol and Drug-Addicted People*, believes the family is important to initiating the intervention process. Part of that process is to understand the family's involvement in the identified patient's dependence or abuse and to formulate a provisional plan based on that information and on the identified patient's history. A former competitor in sports, Cotter views every case as the "seventh game of the World Series" and he doesn't start the game without a game plan. Family involvement and other collateral information are critical to this plan, but in Cotter's model, that is were the family involvement ends. While the family may eventually get into treatment down the road, his intervention strategy is to meet one-on-one with the identified patient. He states that this spares the family the stress of confrontation and ensures that he, not they, is managing the process. Recognizing the power of the family, Cotter said, "A family can undo three months of progress in five minutes" (personal communication).

While much of the literature on treatment leans toward family involvement, this is not to the exclusion of alternatives. Engaging the family in treatment is a clinical decision and involves the ability to recognize the pros and cons of such a decision. Much of the discussion in this section involved individuals with families—the merits of their involvement. In reality, many individuals who get to treatment do not have families, or their families are not accessible. Our job as treatment professionals is to work with whatever we have and develop a treatment plan that meets the needs of the client. Such a plan should reflect alternatives that make up for whatever might be missing. If the family is missing or too toxic to be engaged, then the engagement of a different kind of family should be considered. A 12-step recovery program is a good place to start.

Social Environment

Family, social, and *workplace* environments impact each other. They exist in one form or another in the patient's total recovery environment. Relapse triggers are certain to be present in each of the three recovery environments, and identifying such triggers is the essence of relapse prevention. In order for the recovering PSUD to successfully negotiate life's challenges and the potential threat of relapse, two factors must be managed: individual change and environmental change. The recovering person needs to learn how to change or modify both personal behaviors and recovery environment, whenever necessary. The mantra of AA—to be aware of "people, places, and things"—underscores the importance of vigilance in recovery.

If a patient is in an inpatient treatment program, whether it be a 28-day rehabilitation facility, a TC, or an extended-care facility, the environment is protected. It provides an opportunity to address potential relapse triggers likely to be encountered after discharge. The focus of inpatient treatment is on self-awareness, relapse prevention, building therapeutic alliances, and short-term recovery planning. This experience is often an important one, generating motivation and providing the necessary tools to help better negotiate life's challenges and effectively manage early recovery. Residential treatment might be likened to the running start that a pole-vaulter needs to clear the bar. Without such a start, the pole-vault would not be successful.

While inpatient treatment may not always be necessary, for those who qualify for this LOC, it can reduce the chance of relapse after discharge. A seamless transition from inpatient to outpatient provides a running start—an opportunity to begin to apply all that has been learned in a relatively short period of time.

Ideally, a typical day in one's life is divided into family involvement, social life, work activities, and sleep. While both work and family environments may present countless relapse triggers for the person in early recovery, social activities often revolve totally around drug use. Were it not for the pursuit and pleasure of getting high, there would be no social life for the substance-dependent individual. Even going to the movies, visiting friends, seeing a football game, or attending a concert is likely to involve mood-altering substances before, during, and after the event. The expression *recreational drug use* underscores the relationship of substances with fun. And when the PSUD is not actually using substances, he or she is likely to be thinking about them.

Recovery Defined

Recovery is described as the ongoing process of overcoming physical and psychological dependence on mood-altering substances (including alcohol) and learning to live in a state of total abstinence, without the need or desire for those substances. In recovery, one's physical and mental states are modified so that chemical substances are unnecessary for happiness and fulfillment (Mooney,

---

Four Dimensions of Recovery

Physical recovery is the least complex of the four, even though it is often the most immediate. Physical recovery happens primarily as the result of abstinence alone. The body has an amazing ability to repair itself, especially when combined with medical attention.

Mental recovery is more complex because it includes not only issues associated with brain function and brain chemistry but also with issues of attitudes, belief systems, and rational, abstract thought.

Emotional recovery is more complex yet. It involves not only attitudes, belief systems, and rational thought, but also thought's first cousin—feelings. Emotional recovery involves learning to deal with feelings openly, honestly, and responsibly. It includes learning to express and resolve feelings in appropriate and effective ways. For most people in recovery, emotional recovery takes years.

Spiritual recovery is the most complex of all because it involves all of the following:

- It incorporates aspects of the other three life areas.
- It occurs on a deeper human level than the others.
- It takes a lifetime and is never completed.
- It is rather abstract and illusive in nature (Roper, 2005).

Eisenberg, & Eisenberg, 1992, p. 577). It should be added that, in addition to those dependent on mood-altering substances, this definition of recovery also applies to abusers of mood-altering substances. Another perspective on recovery is that it consists of four dimensions—physical, emotional, mental, and spiritual—and that for recovery to be long lasting it should occur on all levels of the recovering person's life (Roper, 2005).

Moderation Management

Moderation management or moderated drinking is a treatment model that eschews the quest for total abstinence. Although this is not a new idea, advocates for moderation rather than abstinence have formalized models that help alcohol abusers adopt more moderate drinking practices rather than give up alcohol totally. Proponents of this model cite the limited success of abstinence-based models and the success of moderated drinking approaches to engage those who might not otherwise get help. One such proponent, G. L. Connors, as cited in McNeece

---

Moderation Management

Moderation Management (MM) is a behavioral change program and national support-group network for people concerned about their drinking and who desire to make positive lifestyle changes. Moderation Management empowers individuals to accept personal responsibility for choosing and maintaining their own path, whether moderation or abstinence. Moderation Management promotes early self-recognition of risky drinking behavior, when moderate drinking is a more easily achievable goal.

Assumptions of MM

- Problem drinkers should be offered a choice of behavioral change goals.
- Harmful drinking habits should be addressed at a very early stage, before problems become severe.
- Problem drinkers can make informed choices about moderation or abstinence goals based upon educational information and the experiences shared at self-help groups.
- Harm reduction is a worthwhile goal, especially when the total elimination of harm or risk is not a realistic option.
- People should not be forced to change in ways they do not choose willingly.
- Moderation is a natural part of the process from harmful drinking, whether moderation or abstinence becomes the final goal. Most individuals who are able to maintain total abstinence first attempted to reduce their drinking, unsuccessfully. Moderation programs shorten the process of discovering if moderation is a workable solution by providing concrete guidelines about the limits of moderate alcohol consumption (www.moderation.org).

---

and DiNitto, states that moderate drinking techniques are a viable treatment approach for some alcohol abusers. The author adds, however, that while such an approach may be effective with low to moderate alcohol abusers, "good outcomes are less likely with severely dependent alcoholics" (McNeece & DiNitto, 2005, p. 177).

The concept of a program that helps the alcohol abuser control or manage his drinking is likely to prompt a spirited debate among any group of treatment professionals. Such models, under any other name, challenge the very foundation of the abstinence-based model and may even pose a threat to those who are in early recovery and ambivalent about their decision. It challenges the belief that one drink will inevitably lead to another and that the only goal for an SUD diagnosis is total abstinence. Yet we cannot deny that if we are to broaden our patient base—to reach greater numbers of individuals who have SUDs—new ideas are necessary. We need to develop treatment models that will reach those who would not otherwise be accessible to treatment. In order to improve our success rates, we need to improve treatment options. If we are not totally successful with what we have, it's time to figure out what else we need. The "my way or the highway" approach will work for many—now we need to find options that might work for the rest.

We appear to be moving in that direction. Alternative treatment approaches that were thought to be radical and even dangerous 20 years ago are now becoming mainstream. The notions that yoga, acupuncture, meditation, antidepressants, and other medication would become important functions of treatment would have been viewed as irresponsible not too long ago. Needle exchange programs, as controversial as they may be today, would not have been considered a decade or two ago. While abstinence remains the ultimate treatment goal, harm reduction is now a viable alternative. The logic here is a simple one: If we cannot get the addict clean and sober today, let's minimize health and safety risks until we can. Successful research studies and responsible treatment trials have opened the door to creative treatment applications that provide hope for even the most difficult cases. While abstinence may be the ideal recovery, recovery can also be on a continuum with success measured in increments.

A Drug-Free Social Environment

With evolving new ideas in treatment notwithstanding, a drug-free social environment is far easier to manage than one where the rules are clouded with harm-reduction and moderation-management treatment goals. This is not to say that it cannot or should not be done—it should. But if moderation management is the treatment plan of choice, such a plan should be managed only by a skilled clinician who has both training and experience in this approach. Such treatment is a slippery slope, and an error in clinical judgment can be disastrous.

Abstinence, however, is far easier to manage than moderation. When abstinence is the goal, the discussion on consumption ends, and the focus on life begins. Rather than hoping for moderation to improve the recovering person's quality of life, the abstinence model focuses on quality of life itself. Sobriety is a dynamic state, and its success is closely tied to personal growth—whatever that might mean for the individual. Success is measured in terms of life itself. If alcohol is no longer an option in the recovering person's life, then treatment is focused on addressing those issues that made sobriety such an elusive commodity in the first place. It tackles relapse prevention strategies, social enhancement ideas, relationship building, self-esteem, anger management, self-confidence, and other areas of personal growth. Even the 12 steps of AA have only one step that mentions the word *alcohol*—the first step. The remaining steps are dedicated to personal growth.

For many who are in recovery, recovery is more than a change in behavior. It is a passionate movement with implications that go far beyond the decision to drink or not to drink, to get high or not to get high. For such individuals, recovery is also the beginning of a social life. Bowling, softball games, New Year's Eve dances, recovery vacations, sailing events, sober cruises, fun runs, book clubs, and virtually any social activity found in society at large will also be found in recovery. While such activities are not functions of 12-step programs such as AA, NA, or CA, when organized by a recovering person, its participants will almost always be recovering persons and family members. Such activities serve an important purpose for all in recovery but especially for those in early recovery. Contrary to what many may believe, the recovering individual is not doomed to a lifetime of meetings in dark, dank, dingy church basements with a single dim lightbulb swinging overhead. In fact, meeting places are as grungy-chic as an east Greenwich Village clubhouse or as upscale as the boardroom of a major financial organization.

People in recovery are joining together in groups and organizations to advocate for treatment, to combat stigma, and to share the miracle of recovery with those who are still suffering from addiction, their family members, policy makers, and entire communities (Fisher & Harrison, 2005, p. 172). As a result, the stigma associated with SUDs is diminishing—even among high profile personalities, young people, and those in the entertainment industries. Actors Robert Downey Jr., Charlie Sheen, Drew Barrymore, and Robert Lowe are a few of the more recent recovering people helping eradicate the stigma attached to SUDs. Earlier generations of recovering persons include Kitty Dukakis, Kelsey Grammer, and Bonnie Raitt, who have all gone public with their stories, setting the stage for the many that followed. And, of course, there is Betty Ford, former first lady, who took her recovery so seriously that she opened the now world-known Betty Ford Clinic.

Faces and Voices of Recovery (facesandvoicesofrecovery.org) is a national recovery movement where you can find information about recovery organizations in your area (Fisher & Harrison, 2005, p. 172). This is a well-organized grassroots national nonprofit organization with a steering committee of 13 members from across the country. The organization describes itself as a "national campaign, a working alliance of scores of individuals and organizations across the country committed to the rights of people with addictions and united for more effective advocacy."

The Culture of Addiction

In order to effectively facilitate recovery, the treatment provider should first understand the world of addiction. He or she should understand the unique universe supporting the PSUD's survival—that exclusive culture that becomes a momentous power in maintaining his addiction. W.L. White (1996, p. 4) identifies this as the "culture of addiction." The author states that drug users seek out and build relationships with other people whose drug use mirrors their own, that they "create small groups within which they can nurture the rituals of drug use." He goes on to say that such groups form "loosely constructed tribes" bound by "geography, ethnicity, and drug choice." A simple typology is used to divide the culture of addiction into three different groups: The Acultural Addict; The Culturally Enmeshed Addict; and The Bicultural Addict (White, 1996, pp. 10–16).

While there remains a lingering belief among addictions counselors that an "addict is an addict is an addict," enlightened treatment approaches are putting this myth to rest. Perpetuated by the cocaine epidemic of the 1980s, this erroneous mantra was the response by many existing alcoholism treatment facilities when asked the question, "But what do you know about treating other drug dependencies?" And although many individuals successfully completed treatment

---

The Cultures of Addiction Defined

The Acultural Addict is a person who has initiated and sustained addiction in isolation from other addicts, for example, physician addicted to Demerol; addiction following painful trauma; or closeted alcoholic or Valium addict.

Culturally Enmeshed Addicts have increasingly lost touch with, or have never been a participant in, a social world where abstinence and moderation are governing values for psychoactive drug consumption. They are members of a deviant subculture, addicted to drugs and a way of life that ensures their membership, for example, born into a culture of addiction or poverty; or born of wealth, discovering heroin or crack, and totally submerging oneself into the drug culture.

The Bicultural Addict lives simultaneously in the mainstream culture and in the culture of addiction. Such addicts have two identities, operating in two worlds, each serving to meet certain needs—neither world commanding total loyalty, for example, lawyer addicted to heroin; addict in Vietnam smoking heroin with no previous drug history (White, 1996, pp. 10–16).

---

at such facilities, there is no telling how many more would have been helped sooner had we better understood both the addict and his culture of addiction. There are many similarities in the treatment approaches for heroin, cocaine, methamphetamine, marijuana, and alcohol, but if their respective cultures are not understood, the treatment professional's credibility and treatment ability are compromised. This understanding does not mean the treatment professional should have experienced the addict's experience. But the treatment professional needs to have a basic sociological framework of the addict's culture of addiction. The notion that all addicts are the same, no matter what their differences may be, is naïve at best and arrogant at worst.

As the Cultures of Addiction Defined box shows, a culture is not necessarily defined by the drug of choice but by the behavior necessary to sustain the addiction. An opioid user might be a person living in two worlds (Bicultural), or totally involved in living in a single world of drug use (Culturally Enmeshed), or living with his addiction in total isolation from other addicts (Acultural). Conversely, an alcoholic can be found in any one of the three cultures: a closet drinker (Acultural); a homeless person, sometimes living in shelters (Enmeshed); or business man by day and frequenter of biker watering holes at night (Bicultural).

Whatever the drug of choice might be and whatever the culture of addiction might be, the recovering individual will be making a major transition if he or she is to successfully maintain recovery. Managing recovery is managing triggers that threaten it. This does not necessarily mean all triggers need to be removed from the recovering person's life; this is neither possible nor even desirable. But triggers are flags that identify potential problems, not excuses to rationalize or justify self-destructive behavior.

The Workplace Environment

In Western culture, the most important goal for a person who is not employed is to get a job. For those who already have a job, it is often to get a better job. And for the student, the dream is to one day have a good job. Whether the recovering alcoholic be employed, unemployed, or a student, the goal remains the same—a good job. Sometimes, however, the drive to secure employment is met with ambivalence—particularly for those who have not had any good past working experiences. Nevertheless, the Protestant ethic prevails, driven by sociocultural dreams of personal success. To paraphrase the words of an anonymous lyricist, "The only thing worse than working is being unemployed." A job provides the means with which to have things in life that only money can secure. While there are other ways to get money, working is the most common—and the most predictable.

A simple definition of *work* is the provision of services in exchange for currency or goods. An employer has a problem or a need that can be solved by an

Clinical Questions

Employment and the Recovery Environment

- What is the client's current job or school environment, and are there threats to recovery in this environment? What other jobs has the client held?

- How often has the client changed jobs? Why?

- What is the client's favorite type of work? Is this a high drinking or drug-using environment?

- Has the client experienced job difficulties, and what seems to be the cause of these problems? Is the client currently experiencing such difficulties?

- If the client is not working, is financial support being obtained from other sources? What are these sources? Does this support involve behavior that is not supportive of early recovery?

employee, so he or she hires one. The problem may be as simple as capping bottles in a factory or as complicated as running a multinational corporation. Whatever the function may be, the exchange should be favorable to both parties. The employer gets the job done, and the employee is financially rewarded.

Gainful employment, however, is more than a means to securing income. It is also an opportunity to demonstrate skills, broaden social activities, and secure acceptance in society. It identifies one's station in life and projects an immediate image for all to see. For most individuals, the job one holds is also a reflection of how he perceives himself. And, fair or not, how others perceive him. As much as we try to separate our work from the rest of our life, it remains an integral part of it. In an environment where we are likely to spend half of our waking day, the workplace is likely to become more than just a place we go to earn a living. It is also an environment that makes demands above and beyond the job function—social and intellectual demands that, on a good day, are often as important as the remuneration enjoyed at the end of a day's work.

For the PSUD, however, not all days are good days. And for the person in early recovery, every day is likely to be a challenge. This is a particularly important treatment implication when we consider the availability of drugs in both schools and workplaces. This means that the person in early recovery needs not only to get or have a job to provide a means of support and reinforce personal growth, he or she must also contend with the availability of substances in his work or school environment. This is especially true if work or school were his primary sources for social or substance-using activity. When we consider that 10.9 percent of the females and 12.3 percent of the males between the ages of 12 and 17 are currently using drugs, it is not difficult to understand the temptation for the young person attempting to stay clean or not use in the first place (*Behavioral Health Care Tomorrow*, 2004). As for the workplace, the Drug-Free Workplace Act of 1988 (DFWA) was created for a reason. The statute and its subsequent regulations, which were published in the *Federal Register* in 1990, were a much needed response to the epidemic escalation of drug use throughout the 1970s and 1980s (Scanlon, 1991, p. 28). Cocaine and, later, crack-cocaine were turning workplaces in drug dens, creating environments that were hazardous for nonusers and disastrous for the recovering person. (It might be important to note here the difference between a *statute* and a *regulation*. With the implementation of laws such as the DFWA, some aspects are enforceable by statute and some by regulation. A statute is the public law itself (Title V, Subtitle D of P.L, 100-690). A regulation is that which has been written by a regulatory agency, usually the Office of Management and Budget, which further defines and clarifies the statute. A regulation, however, cannot rewrite the law [Scanlon, 1991, pp. 28, 29]).

The DFWA did not eliminate drug use in the workplace, but it created a safer environment for those work organizations that are required to comply with the provisions of such laws as well as those that voluntarily adopted such regulations as the standard for their organization.

Recovery in Summary

As stated previously, recovery is a dynamic, ever-changing environment where family issues, workplace challenges, and social stressors both test and reinforce sobriety. Not only is the world of the recovering person in a constant state of change, but the individual in recovery is also in a constant state of change. As the PSUD moves through stages of recovery and develops the tools to take on greater and greater responsibility, his perspective on life changes. The first and most dramatic change is that the recovering person no longer drinks or uses other drugs. While this may seem like a relief and joy for the family, and it is on one level, it also means that the family will endure some changes. The awkwardness of family social drinking, lingering pessimism on the prospect of continuing recovery, and children's problems that didn't seem important before suddenly become important. Financial, behavioral, and other responsibilities that were not priorities in the past take on new importance. The emergence of new friends in recovery—male and female—that had not existed before, and an ever-increasing amount of time away from home to attend these so-called meetings present a whole new, yet very different, set of problems for the family. Suspicion of infidelity may even arise. Feelings that some things seemed better before recovery, implied if not stated, are not uncommon.

When a family member—recovering or not—has an alcohol or drug problem, the entire family will be affected. Substance use disorders identified as family disorders have long been documented. The start of Al-Anon for spouses and other adult loved ones in 1954 and Alateen for children in 1975 underscore the need for family help when an individual within the family has a substance problem (Fisher & Harrison, 2005, p. 190). Recovery is a transition, and this transition needs to be managed. Case management is not just the clinical management of the individual in treatment; it's the management of his environment as well. The family is the basic unit of society. If individual treatment is to be successful, the family unit needs to share the responsibility for the family's recovery. The recovery activities of the family are at least as important as the activities of the individual in treatment.

Social life, initially, is not likely to feel very social for the recovering person. Friends of the past may no longer be significant to his new life. Values that seemed so important to his or her survival are now threats to his or her survival. The former addict who may have needed his or her particular culture of addiction to exist is now attempting to get comfortable in a culture in which he or she had been an outcast. The drinking buddies who the alcoholic would have sought out in the past are now triggers that need to be avoided. The drug connection who was critical to an addict's existence is now the pariah that needs to be shunned. Change is the cornerstone of recovery. The recovering person may need to change the route he or she used to take to go home; may need to establish relationships with new and different types of people, remembering that, no matter what else happens, taking a drink, smoking a joint, or using any other drug will immediately halt that life-changing process called recovery. As much as a relapse is a function of recovery, it is also a setback that needs to be taken seriously.

As for the workplace, it serves several purposes in recovery, including the most fundamental—a means of support. And it also shapes one's identity. Whatever that person's workplace may be—the school campus or a place of employment, success or failure in it is usually easily measurable. On the job, the measure of success is earnings, promotions, and favorable reviews. As a student, it will be grades, extracurricular activities, and acceptance by others, both fellow students and faculty.

Within both workplace and school environments, there are certain to be triggers that threaten sobriety. "People, places, and things" not conducive to sobriety will set the stage for relapse and diminish the importance of recovery. And their emergence is not predictable—they are sure to appear on good days as well as bad days. While a slip may be just that and end in one episode, it may also lead to a full relapse and quickly transport the individual from the culture of recovery to his respective culture of addiction.

Work and school environments often serve as both starting places and continuing sources for drugs. The degree to which this is so depends on the individual and his workplace relationships as well as the toxicity of the environment. Whatever the threat level might be, the treatment plan should reflect actions necessary to minimize the potential for relapse. While a change in environment may sometimes be the best option, the consequences of such an action must be carefully weighed. A new job might not be easy to come by. But a newly recovering alcoholic working in a bar or an abuser of pharmacological substances stocking shelves at a pharmacy might best consider changing careers. On the other hand, a stockbroker at the exchange who works around cocaine-using employees may need to seek out local support such as recovery meetings or other recovering persons. Wherever there is a drug-using environment, there will also be a recovery environment. Another recovering person is never more than a telephone call away. If one looks hard enough, drugs can be found. The objective of treatment, however, is to instead help the recovering person seek out and discover avenues of support. To do this effectively, the counselor needs to monitor the client's environment through discussion and ongoing assessment. While it's not necessarily the function of the counselor to tell the client what to do or what not to do, it is his job to assist the client in making decisions. Problems within the family environment, social environment, and workplace environment are difficult for the recovering person to see. Metaphorically put, "The tongue cannot taste itself." Helping to sort out such problems is an essential clinical function, and facilitating the decision-making process, when necessary, is nothing less than good treatment.

References

Behavioral Healthcare Tomorrow. (2004). Almanac for Mental Health and Addiction Professionals CD-ROM. Compliments of *Addiction Professional.* Providence, RI: Manisses Communications Group.

Drug Free Workplace Act (DFWA) (1988). 49 USC Sections 702 et seq.

Fisher, G. L., & Harrison, T. C. (2005). *Substance abuse: Information for school counselors, social workers, therapists, and counselors* (3rd ed.). New York: Pearson Education.

Jackson, D. D. (1957). The question of family homeostasis. *Psychiatric Quarterly Supplement, 31,* 79–90.

Moderation management. http://www.moderation.org

Mooney, A. J., Eisenberg, A., & Eisenberg, H. (1992). *The recovery book.* New York: Workman Publishing.

Roper, C. N., High bottom drunk. http://www.highbottomdrunk.com/index.html

Scanlon, W. F. (1991). *Alcoholism and drug abuse in the workplace.* New York: Praeger/Greenwood Press.

White, W. L. (1996). *Pathways from the culture of addiction to the culture of recovery.* Center City, MN: Hazelden.

CHAPTER 9

Spirituality: The Neglected Dimension

Mario was a 45-year-old Caucasian male in outpatient treatment for Alcohol Dependence. He had been sober for several months. He had also been diagnosed with Dysthymic Disorder, a low-grade, chronic depression. Mario felt empty for many years. He found it difficult to feel joy. He had been placed on a variety of antidepressant medications with minimal success. Raised a Catholic, educated in Catholic elementary and high schools, Mario rebelled against what he believed to be the hypocritical and dogmatic views of Catholicism and religion in general. He was lost. He felt no connection to the universe. He considered himself an atheist. Through readings of nonreligious spiritual books and attendance at AA meetings, he rediscovered his connection to the universe. He regained his grounding. He found a place for himself in the universe, a cause for his life, and he eventually found *joy*.

Of all the chapters in this book, this one was the most enjoyable to write and, in some ways, the most challenging. Creating the other chapters was primarily a function of the intellect, involving left-brain tasks such as logic, analysis, and objectivity. This chapter, although also engaging these tasks, drew heavily on the right brain—intuitive, holistic, and subjective functions. Simply put, it is a product of the mind but created from the soul.

In recent times, a different perspective has evolved in the treatment of SUDs and other mental health disorders. While most such disorders and their related problems can be identified and explained in psychological terms, it has become more apparent that many of them suffer from a spiritual deficit as well. This spiritual deficit can manifest itself through depression, SUDs, and interpersonal problems as well as somatic concerns including insomnia, chronic body pain, chronic fatigue, and so on. At the core of the problem we will often discover

Voice of the Soul

> Once a week, people in the thousands show up for their regular appointment with a therapist. Whatever the (therapeutic) approach, the aim will be health or happiness achieved by the removal of these (presented) central problems. Care of the soul is a fundamentally different way of regarding daily life and the quest for happiness. The emphasis may not be on problems at all. One person might care for the soul by buying or renting a good piece of land, another by painting his house or his bedroom. Care of the soul is a continuous process that concerns itself not so much with fixing a central flaw as with attending to the small details of everyday life, as well as to major decisions and changes (Moore, 1992, pp. 3–4).

the lack of a spiritual connection and an absence of purpose in life. The universe becomes a vague and nebulous entity of which the individual is not a part. Some might describe this as a state of spiritual bankruptcy.

Many people in our society have unknowingly lost that connection. They feel alone in the universe, which can be very frightening. There is a profound sense of purposelessness, and life has little meaning. Life becomes one of boredom and emptiness—a chronic fear envelops their spirit. Some people deal with this chronic fear and boredom through behaviors that provide comfort and distraction, such as the use of mood-altering substances, eating, spending, sex, working, and exercising. Our society spends a great deal of time in behaviors meant to comfort. These pleasing and enjoyable behaviors may comfort us temporarily, but the comfort is not likely to last. For the otherwise healthy individuals who indulge themselves in such escapism, the moment of comfort discovered is likely to give way to the reality and responsibilities of life. They are not prone to follow a path of self-destruction. But for others, their discovery of such distractions will preclude self-discovery and problem solving. What they may consider to be depression and unhappiness may actually be an unrealized or lost connection with their spiritual core. The adaptation of comfort-seeking behaviors might be a substitute search for a spiritual connection. And while comfort may be found in such short-term solutions, such solutions are likely to lead to a need for treatment for what started out as a solution to their problems. It might be said that bars and treatment facilities are filled with people who take life too seriously or not seriously enough. By finding purpose and meaning in one's life, the need for deviant behaviors meant to comfort and distract may be significantly reduced.

The popularity of 12-step meetings such as AA is evidence of the desire of many to find that spiritual connection. The intention of this chapter is to discuss some of the basic spiritual principles that are important to share with our patients as well as to learn for ourselves. The following are some spiritual principles that have been picked up along our spiritual journey. We hope they will assist you along yours.

What Is Spirituality?

Spirituality is a level of consciousness beyond our intellect, beyond our emotions, and beyond our thoughts. It is truth in its purest form. Have you ever heard something and just knew deep down that it was the truth? Many memorable books and films have conveyed these truths, sometimes directly and sometimes in symbolic form. People love stories associated with them but are unaware as to why they enjoy these books and films so much. For some reason beyond the scope of this chapter, we have lost touch with many of these truths. When we hear them, we are reminded of them. Rediscovering them brings comfort. This is spirituality. It is getting in touch with a higher form of consciousness. Some call it *intuition.* Some call it *enlightenment.* Some call it *a higher power.* Some call it *God.*

Unfortunately, the word *God,* over thousands of years, has taken on many connotations. People fight over it, abuse others over it, and kill over it. For many, the word *God,* has taken on negative and hypocritical associations. Religions have "so overlaid with extraneous matter" (Tolle, 1999, p. 6) that the true meaning of what the spiritual leaders attempted to convey has been lost. Consequently, some people have become resentful of God and its associated religions. Many people have become atheists and agnostics. As Tolle wrote, "God is being itself, not a 'Being'" (Tolle, 1999, p. 187).

To be spiritual is to be present. It is being connected to all that is without judgment. It is allowing all that is to be. To some, it is called *Being.* "Being is the eternal, ever-present, One Life beyond the myriad forms of life that are subject to birth and death. . . . Your own deepest self, your true nature" (Tolle, 1999, p.10). Being "is your very essence . . . the feeling of your own presence" (Tolle, 1999, p.11). To be aware of Being is to be in a state of enlightenment.

One must find peace and serenity through one's association with this being rather than seeking it through material means. Some believe that we are evolving as a species toward becoming higher forms of consciousness—that we are spiritually evolving. Some people are already believed to be more spiritually evolved then others. The great spiritual leaders in history have come closer to this spiritual

Spirituality as a Way of Life

Spirituality is, above all, a way of life. We don't just think about it or feel it or sense it around us—we live it. Spirituality permeates to the very core of our human being, affecting the way we perceive the world around us, the way we feel about that world, and the choices we make based on our perceptions and sensations. In the experience of spirituality, three essential elements are always at play: what we see; how we feel; and why we choose (Kurtz & Ketcham, 1992, p. 68).

World Health Organization Defines Health

A definition of health by the World Health Organization is that man should be healthy physically, mentally, emotionally, socially, and spiritually, only then is he considered healthy. Spirituality is the resolute pursuit of cosmic consciousness. It aims at enabling man to manifest in all his fullness the divine cosmic consciousness that is present within and outside him. A healthy mind has a happy body (Ghooi, 1981).

evolution than the rest of us and have, consequently, been revered by some and despised by others. They include such avatars as Jesus, Buddha, Muhammad, and other enlightened souls such as Mahatma Gandhi and Martin Luther King, Jr.

Spirituality is the realization that everything in the universe is connected to this Being— this form that is more powerful than anyone or anything. To be truly spiritual is to be totally fearless. It is having the belief that a power greater than ourselves will never let us down despite the hardships and travails we experience. It's the faith that we are not alone, but rather connected to a divine source of power assisting our evolving spirit. To be spiritual is to be unafraid of death. The truly spiritual person is connected to an inner truth that life as we know it is only one brief episode of our true nature. Our true being will not perish, but rather transform. Spirituality originates from beyond the physical body. It originates in the soul. The *soul* is difficult to describe because it is nonphysical. "Your soul is that part of you that is immortal" (Zukav, 1989, p. 30). It's the part of you, unlike your physical body and personality, that will live on for eternity.

Spirituality is difficult to measure. It is not scientifically based. Spirituality is an enlightened state of mind. Enlightenment

is simply your natural state of *felt* oneness with Being. It is a state of connectedness with something immeasurable and indestructible, something that, almost paradoxically, is essentially you and yet is much greater than you. It is finding your true nature beyond name and form. The inability to feel this connectedness gives rise to the illusion of separation, from yourself and from the world around you. You then perceive yourself, consciously or unconsciously, as an isolated fragment. Fear arises and conflict within and without becomes the norm. (Tolle, 1999, p. 10)

Dimensions of Life

Physical, Mental, and Spiritual Dimensions

There are three basic dimensions that can be experienced in our lives: the physical dimension, the mental dimension, and the spiritual dimension. All of these dimensions are interconnected. The condition of any dimension can either negatively or positively affect the others. The physical dimension involves the condition of our body. It is the most primitive dimension in the sense that it was the dimension first used for power and control over others. The mental dimension involves our emotional state and our cognitions (our thoughts and reasoning). It developed later in our evolution and is considered the dimension of our ego. The use of our mental dimension for power and control over others has been gradually replacing the physical dimension. The spiritual dimension is the most powerful dimension of all, but the least used at this stage in our evolution. It is the dimension of absolute power and control, but still not acknowledged by most people. The great individuals that we most revere have often accessed this dimension. While we may have revered these leaders, we have not all been cognizant of why. For many, all they know is that they are attracted to their wisdom, conviction, and exemplary lifestyle. Many have strived to grasp this dimension through religion, but failed because of obstacles put in their way by their mental dimension, for example, ego.

The spiritual dimension is our connection to all that was and all that will be. It is the unifying force that is the source of all that has been created. It has all the answers if we put our faith in its power. It is the Higher Power, the Source, the Being, the God, and the Soul. It is a power that will continue long after our physical and mental dimensions, as we know them, are gone.

Somehow, we, as a species, have lost our connection to this power and are trying to reconnect. Why we lost our connection to this dimension is not clearly understood. In its place we trusted the physical dimension and, eventually, our mental dimension for all power and control. We believed these two dimensions were all we had. Unfortunately, these dimensions made us feel apart, disconnected, and scared. We developed the need for security– the need to protect ourselves from others. Instead of trusting, we developed distrust. Instead of feeling secure, we developed mass insecurity. The result has been thousands of years of wars and killing and fear of our own demise.

Those truly fortunate enough to grasp the spiritual dimension do not live in fear and distrust, but understand that they are connected to a power far beyond the human experience that has larger intentions for us then we can fully realize. These fortunate people do not have to attain power and wealth to feel secure. The security comes from a much more profound place. How many great tales have we read about people who were not afraid to die for what they believed to be right? These people knew they were protected by a power much greater than their own bodies and minds. These are the people we praise throughout history. They are what we all strive to be–free of fear and full of serenity.

Ego versus Humility

There is a saying in AA meetings that *ego* stands for "Easing God Out." In other words, the ego is the mental dimension perceiving us as separate and, consequently, needing self-defense. Because the ego perceives itself as separate, it has no role for God (the spiritual dimension). Gary Zukav discusses the difference

Ego

When the Ego takes flight
And sours to dizzy heights
On Science's flimsy wings
Read a page or two
From some wondrous book
To realise [sic] there is more
Between "heaven" and "earth"
Than man will ever know.

(Pillay, 1997, p. 77)

between a five-sensory human and the multisensory human in his classic book, *The Seat of the Soul* (Zukav, 1989). He claims the five-sensory human is one who only perceives the world through his or her five senses. This person is limited to perceiving only the physical world reached through sight, sound, smell, taste, and touch. Having this point of view, physical survival is the primary goal—security the utmost objective. This ego-driven human is out to protect him- or herself at all costs. Any potential threat to his or her safety or happiness must be eliminated.

Zukav discusses how the human race is evolving toward multisensory beings. These beings are striving to achieve *authentic power* as opposed to external power. Authentic power is realizing your connection to the universe—realizing your own immortality. It is realizing that our body and personality are just a piece of who we are. It is the realization that our personality is not who we are, but only a vehicle to serve the energy of the soul. "Easing God out" (ego) is at the root of our fear, boredom, and confusion. We must learn to ease God, also known as *spirituality,* back in and accept the help of our Source. We must accept that we are not alone and are part of a greater plan. We must find our faith and let go of external power in order to achieve authentic power—a power that loves life in every form that it appears; a power that does not judge what it encounters; a power that perceives meaningfulness and purpose in the smallest details upon the Earth. This is authentic power. When we align our thoughts, emotions, and actions with the highest part of ourselves, we are filled with enthusiasm, purpose, and meaning. Life is rich and full. We have no thoughts of bitterness. We have no memory of fear. We are joyously and intimately engaged with our world. This is the experience of authentic power (Zukav, 1989).

We often enjoy the company of those who are "great for our ego." Examples include the attractive person of the opposite sex, or of the same sex, who gives us lots of attention, or the friend who constantly compliments our achieve-

Ego: The "Optical Delusion"

A human being is part of the whole, called by us "Universe"; a part limited in time and space. He experiences himself, his thoughts and feelings as something separated from the rest: a kind of optical delusion of his consciousness. This delusion is a kind of prison for us, restricting us to our personal desires and affection for a few persons nearest us. Our task must be to free ourselves from this prison by widening our circle of compassion to embrace all living creatures and the whole nature in its beauty. Nobody is able to achieve this completely but striving for such achievement is, in itself, a part of the liberation and a foundation for inner security. (Albert Einstein)

ments, or the patients who sing our praise. While these ego-driven situations feel good (and, as a result, can potentially be addictive), they also lead us away from humility. Without humility, we are driven by our egos. What becomes important is how much pleasure we can attain, how much better we perceive ourselves to be over others, and how much more success and wealth we can accumulate. We become separate from others and, therefore, competitive. To live a humble life means removing our ego-driven behaviors as much as possible. To practice humility is to perceive our connection to humanity and to the world rather than claiming our separateness. To practice humility is to ask how one can help life rather than how one can help oneself. One may ask, "What's the benefit of distancing from the pleasures of the ego and living with humility?" The answer is joy rather than pleasure.

Pleasure versus Joy

What is it that a person wants when he uses mood-altering substances? Essentially, he or she wants to feel good. Humans have always strived to feel good. In the preceding section, we discussed the idea that people invest time in behaviors that comfort and distract from feelings of aloneness, boredom, and disconnection. These behaviors include the use of mood-altering substances. These behaviors take us out of ourselves for a brief time, allowing a temporary distraction from our routine lives. The more unhappiness we perceive in our lives, the greater the impetus to involve ourselves in these activities. These activities are perceived as pleasurable. They provide a temporary sense of respite, reward, and happiness. They gratify our senses and mood. We come to depend upon these behaviors as our primary means of comfort. We begin to perceive a life devoid of these behaviors as unpleasant and maybe even downright intolerable.

The behaviors being discussed are behaviors that provide pleasure. Pleasure is always temporary. Pleasing activities are not meant to last. They are meant to provide transitory relief from our physical being—the part of us that perceives the world only from our five senses and what Zukav describes as the five-sensory human (Zukav, 1989).

Drugs may provide a feeling of euphoria, a feeling of being on top of the world. They may provide a state of confidence to speak in public, to sell, to perform sexually. They may give a feeling of physical strength and invincibility.

Everyday Life Is All We've Got

The deep, wonderful secrets of life, the mysterious presence of the Divine, the joy of cherishing each other, the beauty of nature, the satisfaction of helping out, our journey into the Ageless Wisdom—all exist *only* in our everyday life. There is no bigger ball field on which to find meaning. It's either right here, today, or it's nowhere. (Lozoff, 1999, p. 63)

Letting Go

The phrase "letting go" has to be high in the running for New Age cliché of the century. It is overused, abused daily. Yet it is such a powerful inward maneuver that it merits looking into, cliché or no. There is something vitally important to be learned from the practice of letting go. Letting go means just what it says. It's an invitation to cease clinging to anything—whether it be an idea, a thing, an event, a particular time, or view, or desire. It is a conscious decision to release with full acceptance into the stream of present moments as they are unfolding. To let go means to give up coercing, resisting, or struggling, in exchange for something more powerful and wholesome which comes out of allowing things to be as they are without getting caught up in your attraction to or rejection of them, in the intrinsic stickiness of wanting, of liking and disliking. It's akin to letting your palm open to unhand something you have been holding on to. (Kabat-Zinn, 1994, p. 53)

They may enhance our sensory perception, allowing us to perceive things more vividly. But a reliance on pleasurable activities for lasting happiness ultimately leads to disappointment. Eventually, individuals come to the conclusion that these behaviors do not lead to happiness. This causes a state of great distress. "If I can't find lasting happiness through these activities, what's left?" We have met many wealthy people in our work who have achieved perceived power in their careers and enough money to buy all the pleasing activities that money could buy and still lacked joy in their lives. Why? Because the only path to true happiness is finding joy. Where pleasurable activities provide temporary relief and comfort, joy provides lasting happiness and peace. Where pleasurable activities comfort our five senses, joy comes from a deeper, more profound place. It comforts the soul.

So how do we find this joy? First, we find it by not seeking it in the physical world, through money, relationships, power, and mood-altering chemicals. It is an inside job. Joy comes from within. It comes from profound satisfaction. It comes from appreciation for what is, not for what will be. It comes from living life according to your own values, fully and completely. It comes from living in the moment, not dwelling on the past or anticipating the future. It comes from having gratitude for what is rather than from what should be.

Very few people ever experience complete and lasting joy, not because of the present events of one's life, but because of a life pattern of regretting past events or worrying over future ones. As Tolle discusses in his acclaimed book, *The Power of Now,* "As soon as you honor the present moment, all unhappiness and struggle dissolve, and life begins to flow with joy and ease" (1999, p. 56).

To live a joyful life takes faith and practice—faith in the ability to bring joy by living a life in the present. If one's life is consistently unhappy, what would be the downside of trying another path? As in most areas of life, to get proficient at things takes practice. To live a life of staying in the now, of letting go of regrets and resentments, and of letting go of expectations and anticipations takes continual work. In order to do the work, one must have the faith that it is worth it. Very few have become masters of faith-based living. That is because few have continually practiced living a faith-based lifestyle. Those who do are the individuals we revere.

Acceptance versus Resistance

Many of us walk around in a state of despair, worrying about some situation that must be handled or regretting or resenting something that has occurred. We carry these situations around throughout our day, allowing them to negatively impact all of our affairs. Tolle writes that resistance to what is leads to all of our suffering. Our inability to accept all that is and all that will be leads to our despair. We regularly work with individuals who present with depression and anxiety. These individuals are often abusing mood-altering substances to alleviate their pain. However, we find that these chemicals only provide short-term relief. Diagnoses such as Major Depressive Disorder or Generalized Anxiety Disorder are often offered to explain their symptoms. They are frequently prescribed antidepressant or antianxiety medications but find minimal relief. The reason drugs do not help many is because their pain and suffering is not due to a biochemical imbalance or a neurotransmitter reuptake dysfunction or other mental health abnormalities, but rather because of a spiritual disconnection. It might be viewed as an unwillingness to accept life on its own terms.

Acceptance is the act of letting go of control. It is having faith that a power greater than ourselves is in control. It is practicing humility by accepting that which we cannot control. The idea of *letting go* is very frightening for us. The idea of surrendering our will to a power that we cannot tangibly see takes faith. However, once we do let go and witness the positive results, we gain more faith in its power. As our faith grows, so does our willingness to accept more of all that is. We begin to fear less and less. We replace that fear with confidence—a confidence that we are not alone and that all will be okay as long as we keep our ego in check.

In the book *If Life is a Game, These are the Rules*, Carter-Scott states "Acceptance is the act of embracing what life presents to you with a good attitude" (Carter-Scott, 1998, p. 9). We see people fighting what is all of the time. If they could only realize that it takes less energy to accept things than to fight them. You may be wondering, "If I accepted everything, then others would take advantage of me." The basis of non-acceptance is fear. Fear is based on lacking faith that a power greater than ourselves is there to protect us. We are afraid to let go and allow our higher power to take control. We are fearful of the journey, with its unknowns, that is ahead of us.

Acceptance is a choice. You can choose to accept things or not. The serenity prayer that is regularly recited in 12-step support groups goes, "God, grant me the serenity to accept the things I cannot change, the courage to change the things I can, and the wisdom to know the difference." This prayer conveys the message that we have two choices in life. We can either accept things as they are or have the courage to change them. Both choices, to some extent, rely on faith to help us get through them. But before we can make the correct choice, we must also have the wisdom to make the right choice. Where does that wisdom come from? It comes from within us. "Wisdom is not a state to be achieved, but rather a state to be recalled" (Carter-Scott, 1998, p. 129). Wisdom is our innate intuition passed down from generation to generation. It is that voice within, beyond our fear, which gives us the correct answer. Zukav wrote in *The Seat of the Soul*, "[I]nsights, intuitions, hunches and inspirations are messages from the soul, or from advanced intelligences that assist the soul on its evolutionary journey" (Zukav, 1989, p. 80). Many times we ignore those insights, hunches, and inspirations. Why? Out of fear. We allow our fear to make the choice for us. Our fear-based choices often lead to even more pain and suffering.

Our two choices are either acceptance or change. If we, through our wisdom, accept our powerlessness over a situation, we choose acceptance. If we cannot accept a situation because it hinders our growth or goes against our values and we see other options, we must choose to change the situation. For many of us, our common reaction toward needing change is to simply leave the situation— leave our jobs, leave our families, or leave our errors behind. However, this isn't always the best solution for change. The more difficult but wiser solution for change would be to attempt to change the situation through dialogue rather than simply discarding the unacceptable situation. Many of us believe we have made the effort to change the situation through discussion but are really deluding ourselves. We have difficulty being direct and assertive about our needs, wants, and dislikes. We believe we are direct, but often, we discover that our needs were not communicated clearly. Having the courage to change situations we cannot accept takes great effort, more effort than just walking away and giving up. By putting in this effort we grow. We also help others to grow and often are given appreciation for helping others to grow through our courage. Simply walking away from an unacceptable situation should be the last resort to change, not the first.

Serenity is achieved through accepting what is or accepting that one must change the situation. Serenity is not achieved by complaining, fighting, or medicating what is. We must accept what is or change what is. If we do not have the courage to change what is, then we have no other choice but to accept it. Substance abuse is prevalent in poverty-stricken neighborhoods. Why? Possibly because many who live in poverty have not been able to accept their situation nor have they been able to find the courage to change it. They are stuck. They cannot find the serenity within themselves. Consequently, they medicate their state of despair. Conversely, being affluent does not preclude despair or the attempt to numb it with mood-altering substances or with other distractive behaviors. A sense of hopelessness can also be found among the rich. Some of our most challenging clients are those we call trust-fund recipients. All their material wants can often be satisfied with a signature on a check, yet happiness remains elusive. They, too, may medicate their state of desolation.

Serenity is having faith that a power greater than ourselves is seeking to assist us in all of our affairs. By accepting what life offers us, we also exhibit the willingness to accept the lessons that our higher power has put in front of us. Life is a set of challenges, lessons, and tests to grow through. As M. Scott Peck said in his classic book *The Road Less Traveled,* "Life is difficult" (Peck, 2003, p. 15). Once we accept that life is difficult, it is no longer difficult. Life is a set of lessons, said Carter-Scott. These lessons "will be repeated until learned" (Carter-Scott, 1998, p. 52).

The opposite of acceptance is *resistance.* Resistance is an effort to fight what is. It is a state of nonacceptance. As will be discussed in Chapter 11, resistance to change is a state we must de-escalate in our work with patients. Resistance is not pretty to observe. War is resistance, hatred is resistance, and illness in all its forms may be examples of resistance. To resist takes a great deal of energy. Many people live their lives engulfed in resistance. They are often very unhappy people. Others tend to avoid being around them if possible. They resist accepting the authority of a work supervisor, their work conditions, and their salary, but do nothing to change the situation. They resist accepting the behaviors of their spouse or children, but do very little to change the situation. They resist accepting their living environment, but display inactivity in changing the situation. Such individuals often put their energy into complaining instead of taking actions to change the situation. When you offer resistant individuals solutions, they come up with myriad reasons why those solutions would not work for them. They are stuck in their resistance to change or accept what is.

Discipline versus Irresponsibility

We were not sure if a discussion on discipline and irresponsibility belonged here or elsewhere. It is as much a part of psychology and behavior as it is of spirituality and spiritual growth. We decided to include it here, however, because discipline and responsibility are principles that, when practiced, can improve spiritual evolution.

Many people in our society view substance abuse problems as caused by a lack of discipline or willpower. This often leads to arguments between those who perceive it as a disease and those who view it as a state of irresponsibility. Those who view it as a state of irresponsibility believe substance abusers are lacking discipline and responsibility. This view led to treating substance abusers through the Synanon model developed in the 1960s. The Synanon model was a therapeutic community model, discussed in greater detail in Chapter 4, of teaching addicts a new set of values through discipline and behavioral conditioning. Behaviors considered positive were rewarded through increased privileges, and behaviors deemed negative were punished by taking away privileges. This treatment approach is still rather prevalent in the field of addiction treatment, albeit modified to a great extent.

For some individuals SUDs may be disease based, while for others a lack of discipline may be the culprit. The diagnosis of Substance *Abuse,* for example, may include a lack of discipline as an etiological factor, but this is less of a factor in a diagnosis of Substance *Dependence.* Substance Dependence better fits the disease model as its criteria includes more biological properties as described in that model (see Chapter 6).

M. Scott Peck wrote a powerful section in *The Road Less Traveled* on the importance of discipline (2003, p. 15). He spoke about discipline being "the basic set of tools we require to solve life's problems." He believes that the challenge of solving life's problems is what allows us to grow spiritually and mentally. However, many of us avoid or resist dealing with problems, thereby missing the opportunity to grow through their resolution. To face our problems is uncomfortable or downright painful. Many of us shun confronting them or procrastinate in the hope that they will magically disappear. Others run away from their problems through mood-altering substances or find other distracting behaviors. Whatever distraction or avoidance behaviors are employed, the result is stagnation and an absence of spiritual growth. Peck believes we must teach ourselves and our children to value the necessity of suffering or, "the need to face problems directly and to experience the pain involved" (Peck, 2003, p. 17). To accomplish this, we need the basic tools of discipline. These tools include delaying gratification, accepting responsibility, dedication to truth, and balancing.

Delaying Gratification

"Delaying gratification is a process of scheduling the pain and pleasure of life in such a way as to enhance the pleasure by meeting and experiencing the pain first and getting it over with" (Peck, 2003, p. 19). It is based upon the old adage, "Work before play." Peck explains that we must find the discipline to delay gratification. By dealing with the arduous tasks first, we will actually enhance our pleasure later by feeling rewarded for our earlier efforts and also for avoiding any guilt and shame attached to neglecting our necessary tasks. It takes discipline to do our homework before play, to do our bills before going out, or to exercise before eating large meals.

Peck discusses the pain of confronting problems: "To willingly confront a problem early, before we are forced to confront it by circumstances, means to put aside something pleasant or less painful for something more painful. It is choosing to suffer now in the hope of future gratification rather than choosing to continue present gratification in the hope that future suffering will not be necessary" (Peck, 2003, p. 31).

Accepting Responsibility

The second basic tool of discipline is accepting responsibility. We must first accept responsibility for our problems before we can solve them. All too often we blame others for our problems and don't take ownership over having to solve them. Regardless of how the problem developed, we are still responsible for solving it. It takes discipline to accept responsibility for our problems and go about the task of solving them expeditiously.

Dedication to the Truth

The third tool of discipline is through dedication to the truth. Often, to tell the truth is painful. We avoid telling the truth because we don't want to deal with another person's reaction to the truth. Instead, we lie or avoid the truth. Telling the truth takes the discipline to face and accept the consequences of our actions. In the book *The Four Agreements*, Don Miguel Ruiz discusses ancient Toltec wisdom stating that the first rule or code of conduct is to "Be impeccable with your word" (1997, p. 25). Ruiz claims this is the most important and most difficult agreement to honor. He claims it is the most difficult because we have learned to lie "as a habit of our communication with others and more importantly with ourselves" (p. 33).

Peck tells us to never speak falsehood and that withholding the truth is a heavy moral decision that should never be taken lightly. He tells us that "the energy required for the self-discipline of honesty is far less than the energy required for secretiveness," and that "The more honest one is, the easier it is to continue being honest" (Peck, 2003, p. 63). Finally, Ruiz tells us that "when you are impeccable with your word, you feel good; you feel happy and at peace" (Ruiz, 1997, p. 44).

Balancing

The last tool of discipline discussed by Peck is what he calls *balancing*. This is the opposite of gluttony. Rather than abusing that which makes us feel good, we learn to moderate all activities, thoughts, and emotions. By balancing we keep our lives orderly—not too much play, work, eating, sleeping, pondering, or even feeling. We avoid having things get out of control. Peck tells us that the act of giving up something that is pleasurable or beneficial is, in some way, painful, thereby requiring discipline. Not having balance leads to chaotic and out-of-control lifestyles. Our lives become unmanageable. The discipline of finding balance in all that we do and the ability to say "no" when we want to say "yes" brings feelings of self-accomplishment, pride, and joyfulness—far more gratifying than the temporary relief sought through overconsumption.

Commitment takes discipline. To commit to doing something such as abstaining from mood-altering substances is very difficult. To continue living a life of self-indulgence and irresponsibility is much simpler than the effort it takes to commit to a higher standard of life—a lifestyle achieved through discipline, commitment, and self-love.

Living in the Moment

The title idea for this section comes from the short novel written by Spencer Johnson called *The Precious Present* (1984). The story, recited by an old, wise man, is about a young boy who was told about the greatest gift of all called *the precious present.* The old man explains that anyone who receives this gift is happy forever. However, the old man never tells him what the precious present is. He only provides hints to what it is. The old man, throughout the years, hints that the precious present has nothing to do with wishing; when you have it, you are perfectly content to be where you are; the wealth of it only comes from itself, and we already know what it is, but have forgotten. The boy grows up frustrated at never discovering what the precious present is. Then, as an old man himself, he suddenly figures out what the precious present is: the present! "Not the past; and not the future, but 'The Precious Present'" (Johnson, 1984, p. 38). Whenever he returns to the precious present, he is happy. He learns to treat each precious moment as a gift and, consequently, lives a life of full contentment.

Many of us have tremendous difficulty living in the moment, also known as *living in the now.* We are much more comfortable living in the past with all our regrets or anxiously contemplating the future over which we have no absolute control. However, the only thing we truly have control over is the present moment, yet we spend the least amount of time experiencing it. Our habitual obsession with the past and future actually deprives us from experiencing life. Whenever we are focused on the past or the future, we are missing out on the present. To be truly present and to be truly in life means to be present in the now. You could try it right now. Put down this book and get into the now. Look around. Take in the sights. Smell the air. Become aware of your breathing. How long can you stay in the now before reverting back to the past or thinking about something in the future? Five seconds? Thirty seconds? One minute? Spiritual people practice this regularly. Some can remain in the now for hours at a time. Tolle, in *The Power of Now,* offers a technique for distracting ourselves from our obsessive thinking and forcing us into the now. He suggests closing your eyes and saying to yourself, "I wonder what my next thought is going to be" (1999, p. 77). Most people get stuck trying to answer this because there is no way to predict our next thought. The question forces you to focus on the now.

Tolle explains that our identification with the mind afflicts us with incessant thinking and emotional turmoil. He calls this mind identification the *ego.* "To the ego, the present moment hardly exists. Only the past and future are considered important" (Tolle, 1999, p. 18). He states that our identification with our ego makes us feel alone and vulnerable. As long as we are identified with the ego, pain is inevitable. This is not to say we should never think. Our mind is a wonderful tool to solve problems. However, identifying yourself with the ego rather than perceiving it only as a useful tool inevitably leads to pain and suffering. The ego is there to protect itself. Consequently, it forces you to focus on all the powers trying to destroy it, for example, other people—which is further identified as trying to destroy you. Consider what Tolle said about our need to escape from our own minds:

> Already for most humans, the only respite they find from their own minds is to occasionally revert to a level of consciousness below thought. Everyone does that

every night during sleep. But this also happens to some extent through sex, alcohol, and other drugs that suppress excessive mind activity. If it weren't for alcohol, tranquilizers, antidepressants, as well as the illegal drugs, which are all consumed in vast quantities, the insanity of the human mind would become even more glaringly obvious than it is already. I believe that, if deprived of their drugs, a large part of our population would become a danger to themselves and others. These drugs, of course, simply keep you stuck in dysfunction. Their widespread use only delays the breakdown of the old mind structures and the emergence of higher consciousness. While individual users may get some relief from the daily torture inflicted on them by their minds, they are prevented from generating enough conscious presence to rise above thought and so find true liberation (Tolle, 1999, pp. 84–85).

Tolle suggests that rather than participating with the ego, we become an observer of the ego, what he calls, "watching the thinker" (p. 14). We have also heard it defined as "witness consciousness" or learning to disidentify with the mind (Janis, 2000, p. 249). The moment we become conscious of our thinking we become free of its bondage, we become enlightened, and we gain a higher level of consciousness. We must discipline ourselves (there's that word again) to separate from our mind rather than to allow our mind to control us. This is the key to serenity, peacefulness, and enlightenment—to separate thinking from being. This is the ultimate purpose of meditation.

Love

A chapter on spirituality would not be complete without discussing love. As the Beatles wrote and sang in their classic hit, "All You Need Is Love," love is the fuel and source of our spiritual growth. "The essence of love is what makes life worth living" (Janis, 2000, p. 319). Scott Peck defined love as, "The will to extend one's self for the purpose of nurturing one's own or another's spiritual growth" (Peck, 2003, p. 81). Peck wrote that love is an action rather than a feeling state. What most consider being love is really infatuation (i.e., falling in love), a deep, romantic attraction that has an obsessive quality to it. Infatuation feels great and, in fact, is great. However, it is also potentially addictive. Also, it is not necessarily long lasting. Romantic love can evolve into true love, but it is not truly love as defined in this section. "Love is not an emotion; it is your natural state of being" (Tolle, 1999, p. 23).

How Do We Cultivate Love?

To grow flowers, we must first clear a plot of ground. To grow love, we must clear the weeds of attachment and greed from our hearts. Soil must be watered and fertilized. The heart must be prepared by learning compassion for all. When the tender shoots of service and devotion sprout, they must be kept free of the insects of egoism. (Roof, 1994, p. 140)

Let's look at Peck's definition of love, "The will to extend one's self for the purpose of nurturing one's own or another's spiritual growth." First, he defines love as a conscious choice. We must exhibit "the will to extend one's self." This implies a choice. It implies willingness—an intention to expend the energy of love for ourself or for another. "Genuine love is volitional rather than emotional. The person who truly loves does so because he or she made a decision to love. This person has made a commitment to love whether or not the feeling of love is present" (Peck, 2003, p. 119).

To love, according to this definition, takes effort. To impart love takes energy, for love is the strongest energy field possible. In the book *The Celestine Prophecy*, Redfield writes about how the physical world is a vast system of energy and that energy flows within each of us. He writes that humans have been unconsciously competing for that energy among each other. He claims that when we dominate another person, we take energy from them unwillingly. When we love another, we impart our energy in order to strengthen them (Redfield, 1993). It takes a lot of effort to love. Many times when someone needs our help, we don't want to be bothered. It just takes too much effort. Peck says that "the more and longer we extend ourselves, the more we love, the more blurred the distinction between self and the world" (Peck, 2003, p. 95).

Peck's definition of love states that the purpose of love is to nurture "one's own or another's spiritual growth." This implies that the road to spiritual growth is driven by love. Without love, spiritual growth could not occur. "The only true end of love is spiritual growth or human evolution" (Peck, 2003, p. 106).

Peck writes that

> [T]he principal form the work of love takes is attention. When we love another we give him or her our attention; we attend to that person's growth. When we love ourselves we attend to our growth. When we attend to someone, we are caring for that person. The act of attending requires that we make the effort to set aside our existing preoccupations and actively shift our consciousness. (Peck, 2003, p. 120)

He writes that the most important way of exercising attention is through listening. He claims that the act of listening takes a great deal of effort and, therefore, is avoided by the majority of us. When we discuss reflective listening in Chapter 11, we will see how demanding this skill is to master. Reflective listening demands attention. Consequently, we may claim that reflective listening is an act of love.

> True listening, total concentration on the other, is always a manifestation of love. An essential part of true listening is the discipline of bracketing, the temporary giving up or setting aside of one's own prejudices, frames of reference and desires so as to experience as far as possible the speaker's world from the inside, stepping inside his or her shoes. This unification of speaker and listener is actually an extension and enlargement of ourselves, and true knowledge is always gained from this. (Peck, 2003, p. 127)

Peck goes on to say how important the act of attention is in child rearing and in successful marriages.

Love takes risks. If you risk loving another person, they may hurt you. "If you move out to another human being, there is always the risk that that person will move away from you, leaving you more painfully alone than you were before" (Peck, 2003, p. 133). The self-loving act of growing up, leaving childhood, and becoming independent takes courage and risk. "It is only when one has taken the leap into the unknown of total selfhood, psychological independence and unique individuality that one is free to proceed along still higher paths of spiritual growth and free to manifest love in its greatest dimensions" (Peck, 2003, p. 139).

The act of a loving confrontation takes risk. "To fail to confront when confrontation is required for the nurture of spiritual growth represents a failure to love equally as does thoughtless criticism or condemnation and other forms of active deprivation of caring" (Peck, 2003, p. 153). This applies as well to the clinician who may feel uncomfortable confronting a patient as it does to the patient. Peck explains that there are two ways to confront; the first way is with arrogance, unquestionably believing one is right; the second way is with humility, questioning the veracity of one's belief. Confrontation can lead to exhibitions of resistance in the person being confronted if not handled properly. This will be explored clinically in the next chapter. "If we want to be heard we must speak in a language the listener can understand and on a level at which the listener is capable of operating. If we are to love we must extend ourselves to adjust our communication to the capacities of our beloved" (Peck, 2003, p. 154).

The motivation or will to be self-disciplined comes from the power of self-love. Without self-love, one would not exert the effort needed to be disciplined and to grow spiritually. Love is at the core of our spiritual growth. It is what drives it. Without love, we become spiritually stagnant. We lack interest in improving ourselves. Without self-love, we only wish to survive with the least discomfort and effort possible. Without self-love, we can never give love to others.

Love is separateness. "A major characteristic of genuine love is that the distinction between oneself and the other is always maintained and preserved" (Peck, 2003, p. 160). Peck goes on to say that, "Genuine love not only respects the individuality of the other but actually seeks to cultivate it, even at the risk of separation or loss" (2003, p. 168). Love is not possessive. Love is not selfish. It is selfless. As Sting wrote in one of his hit songs, "If you love somebody set them free" (Sting, 1985). "If in your relationships you experience both 'love' and the opposite of love—attack, emotional violence, and so on—then it is likely that you are confusing ego attachment and addictive clinging with love. You cannot love your partner one moment and attack him or her the next. True love has no opposite" (Tolle, 1999, p. 126).

Peck goes on to say, "When I genuinely love I am extending myself, and when I am extending myself I am growing. The more I love, the longer I love, the larger I become. Genuine love is self-replenishing. The more I nurture the spiritual growth of others, the more my own spiritual growth is nurtured" (Peck, 2003, pp. 159–160).

Forgiveness

One of the greatest acts of love is forgiveness. We have seen many patients who are full of pain and despair because of their unwillingness to let go of resentments and to forgive. They medicate their resentments through drugs and alcohol to mask their hurt. They are people stuck in the past. They are incapable of completely enjoying the *precious present* because they are still fixated on the past. But who are they hurting in their unwillingness to forgive? The answer is most likely themselves. Their pattern of holding on to resentments probably means they have lost many friends and family members. These unforgiving people walk around with negative feeling states of anger, hurt, tension, and pain (both physically and emotionally). People who interact with them often feel their negative Karma and choose to keep a protective distance. We began this piece by saying forgiveness is one of the greatest acts of love, not only toward another, but also toward yourself. As the Reverend Dr. Martin Luther King, Jr., said, "We must develop and maintain the capacity to forgive. He who is devoid of the power to forgive is devoid of the power to love" (Janis, 2000, p. 237).

Forgiving is freeing yourself from self-inflicted bondage. "Harboring resentments consumes a lot of energy" (Carter-Scott, 1998, pp. 42–43). Carter-Scott discussed four types of forgiveness: beginning forgiveness of yourself, beginning forgiveness of another, advanced forgiveness of yourself, and advanced forgiveness of another. Beginning forgiveness of yourself is forgiving yourself for mild to moderate transgressions, such as being late for an appointment. Beginning forgiveness for another is forgiving another for mild to moderate transgressions, such as someone being late for an appointment with you. A third kind of forgiveness is advanced forgiveness of yourself. These are serious transgressions that have caused you chronic feelings of guilt and shame. Finally, there is the advanced forgiveness of another. This may be the most difficult act of forgiveness to attempt. There is something soothing about holding on to resentments toward those who have wronged us. Maybe it makes us feel superior or more righteous. However, it is the act of forgiveness that truly shows our growth and maturity.

The greater the transgression against us that we allow forgiveness, the more respect we gain from ourselves as well as from others. As Tolle said, "Forgiveness is to offer no resistance to life. . . . the alternatives are pain and suffering, a greatly restricted flow of life energy, and in many cases physical disease" (Tolle, 1999, p. 100).

Conclusion

Spirituality transcends religion—they are not synonymous. A person may be religious and also be spiritual, or he may be spiritual and not be religious. But being spiritual does not require following the teaching or dogma of any particular religion. Religion is a personal set or institutionalized system of religious attitudes, beliefs, and practices—a commitment or devotion to religious faith or observance. It is simply a set of rules, while spirituality is, hopefully, the goal. Identifying oneself as religious does not necessarily ensure the achievement of that goal. As previously discussed, the belief in God is frequently exploited to justify self-serving causes, and religion is often the vehicle used to defend and rationalize otherwise indefensible behavior. In most cases it is not the religion that is to blame, it is its interpretation. And even where a religion's teachings appear to have taken a detour into an abyss hardly tantamount to spiritualism, individual interpretation, not dogma, is likely to blame. Spirituality is a set of values incorporated into daily living practices—qualitative values, not quantitative values. The frequency with which one attends services, follows religious traditions, or makes financial donations to the church, mosque, or temple of their choosing can be measured. They are quantitative. But spirituality is far more difficult to measure, yet it serves as a prerequisite for all values that are measurable. Robert Maynard Hutchins (1899–1977), chairman of the board of editors of *Encyclopedia Britannica*, cofounder of the Committee to Frame a World Constitution, and dean of Yale Law School, viewed spirituality as an essential human quality: "Equality and justice," he said, "the two great distinguishing characteristics of democracy, follow inevitably from the conception of men, *all men* [emphasis added], as rational and spiritual beings" (Bartlett, 1980, p. 845).

As a growth objective, the value and power of spirituality cannot be denied. There is no body—individual or organizational—that cannot reap the benefits of the spiritual dimension. The quest for good physical health and good mental health in life are a given—they are two sides of the same coin. Spirituality, however, is an intangible that seldom gets the attention it deserves. Yet it is the balancing factor that determines purpose and joy. Mario, in the opening section, after much suffering, finally found a place for himself in the universe. He didn't find religion—he had that earlier on, and it did not work for him. He discovered spirituality, and it did.

References

Bartlett, J. (1980). *Bartlett's familiar quotations.* Boston: Little, Brown, & Company.

Carter-Scott, C. (1998). *If life is a game, these are the rules.* New York: Bantam Doubleday Dell.

Ghooi, C. (1981) *Spirituality and health.* Andhra Pradesh, India: Sri Sathya Sai Books.

Janis, S. (2000). *Spirituality for dummies.* New York: Hungry Minds.

Johnson, S. (1984). *The precious present.* New York: Doubleday.

Kabat-Zinn, J. (1994). *Wherever you go, there you are.* New York: Hyperion.

Lozoff, B. (1999), *Deep & simple: A spiritual path for modern times.* Durham, NC: Human Kindness Foundation.

Moore, T. (1992). *Care of the soul.* New York: HarperCollins.

Peck, M. S. (2003). *The road less traveled: 25th anniversary edition.* New York: Touchstone.

Pillay, V. K. (1997). *Quest for divinity.* Chennai, India: Author.

Redfield, J. (1993). *The celestine prophecy.* New York: Warner Books.

Roof, J. (1994). *Pathways to God.* Faber, VA: Leela.

Ruiz, D. M. (1997). *The four agreements: A practical guide to personal freedom.* San Rafael, CA: Amber-Allen.

Sting. (1985). "If you love somebody set them free." On *The dream of the blue turtles* [album]. London: A & M Records.

Tolle, E. (1999). *The power of now: A guide to spiritual enlightenment.* Novato, CA: New World Library.

Zukav, G. (1989). *The seat of the soul.* New York: Simon & Shuster.

Treatment

THE WILEY
CONCISE GUIDES
TO MENTAL HEALTH

Substance
Use
Disorders

CHAPTER 10

Initiating Commitment: Structured Intervention Strategies

The Myth of Hitting Bottom

The focus of this book is treatment for individuals and families with Substance Use Disorders (SUDs). Our objective is to provide the reader with an understanding of alcohol and other drug problems, including treatment options once the problem is identified. But before we can identify the problem and provide treatment, we need a patient for whom to provide treatment. Some will find their way to treatment or to a 12-step program without much prompting. Others might even experience a spontaneous remission—problem recognition and resolution without formal treatment. Family members, friends, and employers are often instrumental in such instances. Still others will believe that hitting bottom is necessary—that people with Substance Use Disorders (PSUDs) cannot be helped until they are ready to be helped. In one way they are right—awareness of the problem is necessary before treatment is considered. But there is little reason to wait for the person to hit bottom—or for them to recognize that they have *already* hit bottom. The illness can be interrupted anywhere along its progression, and effective treatment can begin. In effect, the bottom can be presented to them before they are capable of seeing it. This often takes the form of an intervention— an intervention involving family, friends, employers, or significant others who are concerned about the identified patient's (IP) substance use. Often called the *structured intervention,* this can be a critical step in both getting the individual the help he or she needs and the family the help it needs. Denial, resistance, and ambivalence are typical features of SUDs. This chapter will examine the structured intervention—family and workplace models.

Alcohol Abuse

A Family Tragedy

> There's a letter from Dad. He's coming home two days before Christmas. He says everything will be different, he's a new man, he hopes we're good boys, obeying our mother, attending to our religious duties, and bringing us something for Christmas. . . . There is no sign of my father. Mam says he might be asleep in one of the carriages but we know he hardly sleeps even in his own bed. She says the boat from Holyhead might have been late and that would make him miss the train. The Irish Sea is desperate at this time of the year. "He's not coming, Mam," I say. "He doesn't care about us. He's just drunk over there in England." Next day Dad walks in the door. His top teeth are missing and there's a bruise under his left eye. He says the Irish Sea was rough and when he leaned over the side his teeth dropped out. Mam says, "It wouldn't be the drink, would it? It wouldn't be a fight?" (McCourt, *Angela's Ashes*, 1996, pp. 268–269)

Resistance and Ambivalence

Substance Use Disorders were designated illnesses by the American Medical Association in 1987, but they are often different from other medical problems in two important ways: resistance and denial. The patient denies the problem because he or she does not have the objectivity to recognize it and resists treatment because it is a threat to his or her drinking or drug use. In fact, the very thing that we view as the problem, the individual sees, not as the problem, but rather as the solution to the problem. Even with progressively deteriorating job performance, escalation of family concerns, or emerging medical and health issues, the destructive behavior continues. The impaired individual does not see the cause and effect relationship; in fact, the mood-altering substance is used to avoid such problems. For the PSUD, the substance is not the problem, it is the *solution* to the problem. The problems get worse, the substance use progresses, and the level of denial often escalates. Even if the IP recognizes his or her increasing alcohol or other drug use, serious contemplation of positive change is wrought with ambivalence and fear. A structured intervention is a powerful tool that can lessen ambivalence and increase motivation. It is a pretreatment strategy that helps the IP make the connection between substance use and substance-related problems.

A Brief History on Intervention

Intervention is a powerful word—a word often used in politics, warfare, criminal justice, medical care, and behavioral health services. Whatever the discipline may be, the word is usually used to mean to "come in or between by way of hindrance or modification" or "to interfere with the outcome or course, especially of a condition or process, as to prevent harm or improve functioning" (*Merriam-Webster's*, 2003). From the Latin word *intervenire*, intervention is a word that denotes action. The kind of intervention discussed in this chapter is behavioral, targeted to an existing condition with an objective to prevent harm and improve functioning. It is an action initiated by an individual, a group, an employer, a family, or a friend that will, hopefully, end or contain a self-destructive condition. While the IP could be presenting any behavioral problem (spending, gambling, eating disorders, etc.), we will focus exclusively on SUDs in this chapter.

The First Structured Intervention

The use of structured intervention in the treatment of behavioral health problems is not a new idea. It was first developed by Vernon E. Johnson, who founded the not-for-profit Johnson Institute in 1966. The Institute's two objectives were to design specific programs for alcoholics through applied research and to educate the public in methods of intervention. Johnson concluded that the secretive nature of the problem inhibited the opportunity for treatment. Rather than seeing the problem as a family problem, it was generally viewed as an individual problem. Johnson's book *I'll Quit Tomorrow* (1973) began to change that. This work was instrumental in getting the treatment community to recognize the importance of family in the treatment of the individual. The fundamental premise of the Johnson Institute model of intervention was that the chemically dependent person can accept reality if it is presented to him or her in a receivable way.

Structured Intervention

The Johnson Institute Model

1. Meaningful persons must present the facts or data.
2. The data presented should be specific and descriptive of events that have happened or conditions that exist.
3. The tone of the confrontation should not be judgmental. The data should show concern.
4. The chief evidence should be tied directly into drinking wherever possible.
5. The evidence of behavior should be presented in some detail to give the sick person a panoramic view of himself during a given period of time.
6. The goal of the intervention, through the presentation of this material, is to have him see and accept enough reality so that, however grudgingly, he can accept in turn his need for help.
7. At this point, the available choices for treatment may be offered (Johnson, 1973, pp. 49–51).

The Intervention Idea Was Empirically Based

According to Johnson (1973), the idea for intervention as a strategy to get alcoholics into treatment was the conclusion of a study of 200 patients that the Johnson Institute conducted. The study reaffirmed that alcoholics did not seek help until a serious crisis, or collective crises, brought them to treatment. Only when their impenetrable defenses (denial system) collapsed under the weight of their alcohol-related problems did they seek treatment. The very crises that the enabling family and friends often tried to help the alcoholic *avoid* were what ultimately motivated him or her to seek treatment (Scanlon, 2003). These findings became the underpinnings for the structured intervention. But two things had to happen. First, family, friends, colleagues, and employers had to learn that keeping the problem a secret exacerbated the illness, and second, in order to get the PSUD into treatment before hitting his or her bottom, a crisis had to be precipitated. In other words, the alcoholic's so-called bottom had to be raised so that he or she could see it. "Unlike hitting bottom, structured intervention provides a safe way for the denial to be broken" (Wheeler, 2001, p. 31).

The Johnson Institute web site cites *Motivational Interviewing* as a "landmark technology in addiction treatment" (Johson Institute, 2005) and, according to Miller and Rollnick, authors of the now widely acclaimed book of the same name, the relationship between this work and Johnson's earlier insights are evident: "Johnson explicitly emphasized the importance of empathic listening, and described a form of counseling that is more compassionate than aggressive" (1991, p. 9).

While the Johnson Institute no longer provides intervention services, it "still strongly believes that professional interventions are an integral early step in helping addicted people, and their families, begin the recovery process" (http://www.johnsoninstitute.org).

Founding of the Betty Ford Clinic

Since the early days of the Johnson Institute, the structured family intervention has become an important function in the continuum of care—not just for SUDs,

---

Best Sites for the Intervention

- **The office of the interventionist:** This might be best but sometimes inconvenient for the participants.
- **Place of business:** This is a particularly good place, especially if the employer or employees are involved.
- **Home of a relative or friend:** Such a location will usually be comfortable for all participants, including the IP.
- **Home of the IP:** This is *not* a good place. The IP would become the host, and that would affect the dynamics.

---

but for other behavioral health problems as well. It is a pretreatment process whereby the most resistant substance abuser, even when in the precontemplation phase of addiction—before the individual considers treatment—could be successfully moved toward treatment (Miller & Rollnick, 1991, p. 15). Individuals from all strata of society, including many public personalities, owe their recovery to an intervention. One of the better known celebrated examples is the former First Lady, Betty Ford. She and Ambassador Leonard K. Firestone later cofounded the now world-renowned Betty Ford Center at Eisenhower in Ranch Mirage, California—a tribute to both the family intervention and to her continuing recovery (Scanlon, 2003).

Researching the Structured Intervention

While there are many success stories found in existing literature, few formal statistical studies have been done. And while such stories are likely to be true, they lack the credibility of reports based on actual research. There are few, if any, comprehensive studies of statistical significance. Published rates of success can sometimes be found, but such findings are almost always anecdotal, narrow in focus, outdated, and without clinical detail. There is little, if any, primary research available on intervention outcomes based on actual cases. Much of the existing information is a rehash of the old literature, promoting the value of the family intervention without defining the meaning of success.

A statistical analysis of 33 structured family interventions was conducted and reported in *Addiction Professional* (Scanlon, 2003). As Figures 10.1, 10.2, 10.3, and 10.4 show, the report discussed preintervention treatment experience, age breakdowns of the IPs, primary drugs of abuse, gender differences, and intervention success rates. Fifty-eight percent of the subjects in this study were men, and 42 percent were women. The study showed that interventions really reach those who do not know they need help. Sixty-seven percent of the IPs in this study had no prior treatment experience (see Figure 10.1).

Only 33 percent of IPs in this study had any prior treatment experience—18 percent inpatient and 15 percent outpatient. This comparison is significant. It demonstrated that structured intervention reaches substance abusers that might not otherwise get help.

Success in getting the IP to treatment is where recovery must start. In this study, 82 percent were referred to treatment. Of this 82 percent, 49 percent went to inpatient treatment programs, and 33 percent agreed to outpatient. Eighteen percent declined treatment, but most stated they would resume involvement in a 12-step program. It should be noted that *treatment*

Family Intervention Defined

Family intervention is a process that allows family members to focus on their own internal value system, share this value system, and encourage a journey together whereby each family member gets help.

means clinical treatment managed by a qualified health care professional, not self-help programs such as AA or NA. In most cases, however, such programs were included as provisions of the treatment plans. All admissions to treatment programs following the intervention were verified by the interventionist (Scanlon, 2003).

Selected Intervention Models

The Ten-Hour Model

The success of an intervention is in its preparation. There are many details that must be addressed, and every one of them is important. The process examined here is based on a modification of the Johnston Institute model and is called the *Ten-Hour model,* which reflects the approximate amount of time that the interventionist spends in session with the participants and the IP. Additional time is spent interacting with the participants prior to the intervention and with the IP after. This includes telephone contacts, e-mails, and faxes with participants, managed-care companies, and treatment providers.

The Ten-Hour model is completed in four group sessions within a 2-week period of time: (1) information and education; (2) preparation and rehearsal; (3) intervention; and (4) postintervention. In this model, the identified patient is not present until the third session—the intervention. While the four sessions are task-driven, not time-driven, the first session usually takes approximately 4 hours. Each of the three subsequent sessions is 3 hours, 2 hours, and 1 hour, respectively. As for the participants, they are usually those who are concerned about the IP's behavior. These may include family members, colleagues, friends, and possibly employers—and the person who initiates the intervention might be someone from any of these subgroups. While the group size might be as few as 2 or as many as 15, the optimal number of participants is somewhere in between. As stated earlier, the objectives of the intervention are twofold: to get the identified patient the help he or she needs and to get the family the help it needs.

Session One of Four It is not uncommon for some of the participants *not* to know each other. The uniqueness of this event may bring together family members, fellow employees, and friends that may not otherwise cross paths. Facilitated by the interventionist, his or her first task is to ensure that everyone meets everyone else and that a pleasant environment is established. The room should be comfortable, and refreshments might even be served.

■ In a timely fashion, the interventionist congratulates the group in its decision to address the problem of a loved one that probably has been going on for far too long. A major decision has been made, and it is important to acknowledge it. The uniqueness of this event should also be acknowledged—unique in that it is far more common to ignore such matters than to invest the time and resolve to do something about them.

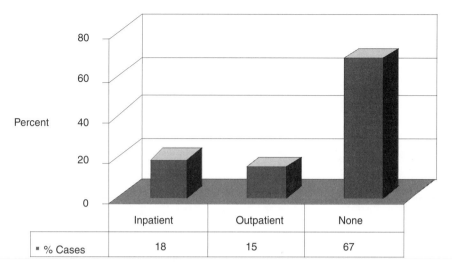

Figure 10.1 *Preintervention treatment: Level of care.*
Note. The figure shows that 67 percent of the IPs studied had no previous treatment experience. The conclusion is that interventions interrupt the progression of addiction (Scanlon, 2000).

■ The session changes gears at this point, and the interventionist turns to one of the participants and asks that he or she share with the group his or her relationship with the IP. (Remember, the IP is not present until the third session.) With appropriate coaching and support, the participants are encouraged to talk in turn about good times as well as bad. Everyone in the room shares the relationship each has with the IP. This is likely to be the first time the relationship was thought about, no less verbalized. As a result, this experience is often emotional and stress reducing—a collective bond has been established, and the intervention process is ready to move forward.

■ After this important breakthrough, the interventionist takes this opportunity to educate the group both about SUDs and the power of the intervention. This information should be basic but interesting for the participants. The nature of this discussion serves to clarify what an SUD is and reinforces the need for and objective of an intervention. The knowledge and skill of the interventionist should shine here—his or her knowledge, skill, and confidence are reassuring to the participants.

■ At this point, the participants are fully engaged and are now ready to share what they might like to say to the IP if he or she were here. In the same order that they were asked to talk about their relationships with the IP, they are asked to take this dynamic to the next level, that is, digging a bit deeper and expressing their genuine concern (whatever form that may take) in preparation for session three—

Double Trouble

Attempting to conduct the intervention at the IP's home and using a surprise party strategy are double trouble. Surprising the IP rather than inviting him or her to join the family begins the intervention on a dishonest note. While there may be an exception to this rule, it is discouraged. Dropping in on the IP in his or her home is begging for a disaster. In one such case, the IP expressed his anger by going to the refrigerator, pulling out a bottle of beer, picking up the telephone, and announcing: "If you all don't get the hell out of here right now, I'm calling the cops."

the intervention. There are several objectives achieved here. One is to allow the participant to take this step without (perceived) retaliation. Another is to give the participants the opportunity to find the appropriate words to express themselves. A third reason is its immediate therapeutic effect. Throughout the entire intervention process, the interventionist addresses each participant with warm, empathic encouragement. It is important to remember that the participants are the clients at this point. They have come to the interventionist to help them with a problem *they* are having. That problem is that someone close to them has an SUD, and they need to help this person.

■ This is usually the best time to discuss other important matters, including where the intervention will be held (to insure the availability of the IP, a differ-

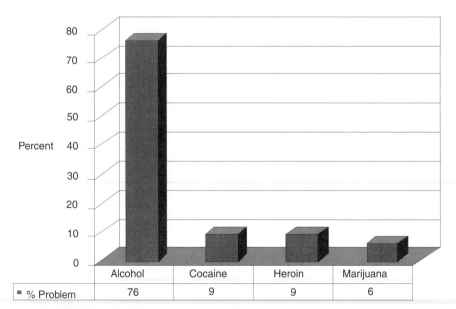

	Alcohol	Cocaine	Heroin	Marijuana
■ % Problem	76	9	9	6

Figure 10.2 *Presenting problem.*
Note. Most IPs presented alcohol as the primary problem. Given that alcohol is the number one drug problem in the United States, this is not surprising (Scanlon, 2001).

ent location from the present location may be advisable). Also covered will be possible letters (statements) provided by other loved ones who could not be present but are important to the IP, level of care (LOC) necessary for the IP, the most effective treatment facility given the presenting problem, and how the treatment services will be paid for (third party or self-pay).

- Discussed at this point is how to get the IP to participate in the intervention. The group will almost always offer a manipulative ploy that is certain to start the intervention off on a bad note. The *surprise party* is not a good idea, and it gives the IP something to use against the group. With little discussion, the group is likely to see the value of honesty in simply asking the IP to come—to join the family in getting help for a problem that has been affecting the entire family. There is seldom resistance—in fact, there is often a sign of relief. In discussions with IPs after interventions, they often wondered: What took so long? The short answer to that question is that the SUD is a family disorder; if one person in the family changes, then, too, the other family members must change. A commitment to an intervention is a commitment to recovery for the entire family.

- Also talked about at this point is any possible resistance that the IP might present to avoid treatment, including walking out on the group. Excuses such as "What about my job?" "How about my dog?" or "I just can't go right now," are discussed and resolved. At the time of the intervention, any resistance that might be presented has already been anticipated in its preparation. Remember, ambivalence is a prevailing factor: I need help now, but maybe tomorrow is better!

- The intervention is planned and structured. It is training necessary to ensure the chance of a successful outcome. Everyone will know what is going to be said at the intervention because session two—the next session—is a rehearsal. There will be no surprises at the intervention.

- In all likelihood, the IP will agree to the wishes of the group and agree to treatment. But there are no guarantees, of course. He or she may refuse. This possibility must also be planned for, and the responses to this decision by the IP will also be discussed. If appropriate, a compromise in the LOC might be offered—if not inpatient, then outpatient. A friend may tell the IP that their friendship rests on this decision—that if this is his or her decision, then that relationship must change. Or the damage might be so bad that a divorce is threatened. Or an order of protection will be served. I had one participant tell her brother, "If you don't agree to treatment, you can never pick up my baby again." The baby was 18 months old and loved by the IP. The IP agreed to treatment. Other leverage includes withholding nonessential financial support, modifying levels of communication, involving child welfare services, and so on.

- It is nearing the end of the first session, and the group has accomplished a great deal. Using one or two examples, the interventionist discusses the assignment that needs to be completed between this session and the next: to modify the statements made earlier (what they would like to say to the IP if he or she were present), reframing and writing them to (1) communicate love, concern, and support; (2) cite behaviors, incidents, and events; (3) relate these data to the alcohol and drug problem; and (4) request that the IP join the family and accept help. These *data* may be represented with specific incidents, increases in use, deterioration of health, or changes in behavior. The participants are encouraged to start their comments off on a positive note (the way things used to be), be specific and current with data, and communicate how this problem is making the participant feel.

- A note about preparing the statements: There are several reasons why the statements are always written down. First, it is important that there are no surprises at the intervention—that everyone knows what everyone else is prepared to say. Second, an intervention is empowering, but it is also stressful. For this reason it is necessary that the formula be adhered to, eliminating the chance of forgetting something or nervously saying something regretful. Third, written statements have a greater impact on the IP. The fact that the participants have gone through all this preparation to help the IP is in itself a powerful message.

- The first session ends here, and the participants are provided guidelines to prepare their statements to the IP. The guidelines also review the intervention process and include sample statements and specific information about help for family members, such as Al-Anon and therapy options. The second session, preparation and rehearsal, is scheduled to be no more than 5 to 7 days away.

Session Two of Four The leadership role of the interventionist is as important here in session two as it was in the first session. This is also the rehearsal session, and the group is likely to be motivated and perhaps tense. The interventionist sets the tone for session two by reinforcing the progress that has been made and fielding any questions the participants may have. The IP's SUD is reviewed, and any interaction with the IP since the last session is discussed.

- The rehearsal is an essential function of the intervention process. It provides an opportunity to experience the intervention without the IP present. The participants are asked to read their statements (also called *letters*) in turn. This can be an emotional time. (Boxes of tissues should be available at all sessions.) It is a moving experience for everyone present—while the primary emotion for most of the participants throughout the progression of the SUD was likely to have been denial, avoidance, and fear, at this point in the intervention process hope and concern begin to emerge. The rehearsal, because it is the first reading of the statements, can be very emotional—even as emotional as the actual reading at the intervention might become. The rehearsal also provides the opportunity to discuss content and edit out comments that do not serve the objective. It has been our experience that participants religiously follow the guidelines they were given to take home, and the editing is usually minimal. Nevertheless, moral judgments, shaming, inappropriate anger, and punitiveness are discussed and modified or removed. Unnecessary redundancy of data by two or more participants is also addressed.

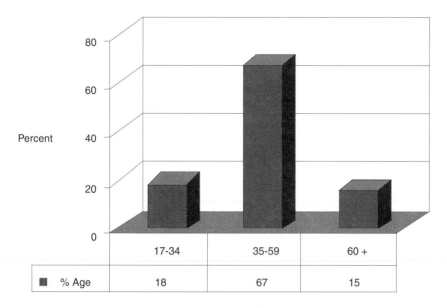

Figure 10.3 *Age at intervention.*
Note. Alcohol Dependence is a progressive illness, and an intervention can be conducted at any time. Most IPs were over age 30 (Scanlon, 2000).

■ The order of presentation is important. It is best to start off with a participant who can be rational and supportive. In most instances, it is best not to have a spouse or parent lead. A friend or favorite sibling is usually the safer choice. There are at least two reasons for such a choice: First, it is helpful if this person brings a kind of objectivity to the intervention that spouses, parents, and adult children usually cannot. Second, the lead person should be a loved one without a history of shaming, criticizing, or arguing with the IP. The order of presentation is based on the nature of the relationship and the content of the statements. The final participant to speak, for example, should have remarks that best sum up the event. The opening remarks should reassure the IP that it is safe, and the closing remarks should leave the feeling that this is all about love and concern.

■ Just as great care is taken in planning the order of presentation, the seating arrangements are also important. It is best if the IP has two trusted, nonthreatening participants within touching distance. As previously mentioned, the actual intervention can become emotional, and the ability to reach out and touch is very helpful. It is not unusual for a participant to get up, go right to the IP, and hold his hand while reading the statement.

■ Before the conclusion of session two, the intervention should have a mental checklist insuring that every detail has been addressed. These details include the following:

- Intervention time and place.
- Remind everyone to bring their statements.
- Who or how to invite the IP to the intervention.
- Who comes with the IP to the intervention location?
- Order of presentations has been determined.
- Seating arrangements have been determined.
- What happens if the IP walks out during the intervention?
- Make sure all the other "what ifs" have been addressed.
- Treatment program selection reservation.
- Second treatment options.
- Transportation: Who goes with the IP to the treatment program?
- Get a signed release to communicate with the program.

Session Three of Four: The Intervention The participants arrive at the intervention site before the IP. While the seating arrangements have been determined, it is best that the participants be standing, sitting, chatting, eating, and milling about in a fashion most appropriate to the setting and group. Knowing that the IP is not going to be surprised (he has been told of the meeting) lessens the anxiety for the group. This will *not* be a surprise party.

- When the IP arrives, he or she will be greeted and–depending upon the environment–invited to have a snack or soft drink. There are likely to be participants who the IP has not seen in some time, so socializing is expected. Although the entire intervention process is planned and structured, it is neither rigid nor inflexible. The mood of the group should be natural but not forced. This is an important event and the outcome can be managed but not controlled.

- At an appropriate moment, the host introduces the IP to the interventionist, stating, "I believe you know everyone else except John Smith [the interventionist]." The interventionist greets the IP in a professional and friendly manner, stating, "As you probably already know, I've been working with your family and

---

Cocaine and Alcohol Intervention

Evelyn was a 27-year-old Caucasian woman, using cocaine for more than 10 years. Her addiction had eventually affected her work, family, and social life; she was unemployed and beginning to drink heavily. The father was concerned that his own active alcohol problem would undermine his credibility as a participant. He thought she might walk out if he commented on her drug use. The father was urged to be there, and his comments to her were limited to "You're my daughter, and I love you. I know I haven't yet been successful in dealing with my drinking problem, but I'm trying. That's all I ask of you—that you join the family in helping each other. She stayed and just celebrated her 12th year of recovery. The father has 11 years of recovery.

friends on something that is a concern to all of them." (This is the participants' cue to take their seats.) "Each of them would like to share that concern with you, and they simply ask that you listen. You will have an opportunity to respond at the end. Will you do that?" The interventionist waits for an affirmative, walks the IP to his or her seat, nods to the first participant, and the statement reading begins.

The intervention is a major event that will forever change the relationships between the group members and the IP—for the better. Up until this point, the level of family dysfunction kept everyone on eggshells and the IP drinking or using drugs. The intervention is a turning point for the family. Although there still remains plenty of work to do, the first and most important step in that process has begun. A concerned individual—family member, employer, colleague, or friend—made the decision to face the problem head on and sought professional help. While this action is prompted out of concern for the IP, it is also a selfish action—selfish in a good way. The intervention benefits not only all who participate, but all who have been affected by the IP's drinking or other drug use. The person initiating the intervention is certain to be one of those individuals.

Session Four of Four This session is celebratory in nature. It is the beginning of a new phase in the IP's and the participants' lives. Whether the IP says "yes" or "no"—the IP will agree to treatment more than 80 percent of the time—this event will mark the beginning of recovery. The family has learned in just a few hours

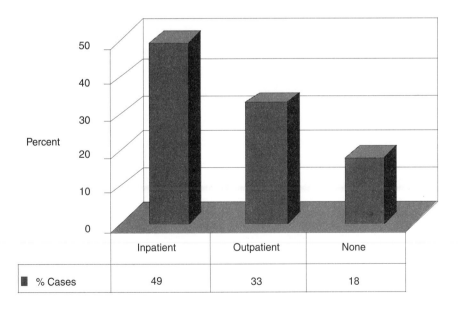

Total Cases (Men & Women)

Figure 10.4 *Postintervention treatment: Level of care.*
Note. Interventions are successful. Eighty-two percent of the IPs agreed to treatment (Scanlon, 2001).

that a serious family problem can be addressed with honesty and confidence. The secrets that have enabled the IP for far too long are in the past—albeit the recent past—and the opportunity to continue to practice openness is within reach. This is not to suggest that years of dysfunction can be reversed in 10 hours, but the intervention experience is so positive that it opens the door to continuing success. The intervention does not take much time to complete, but its impact does not end with the IP's decision. The family recognizes that recovery means recovery for the entire family, not just for the IP. Friends who have been concerned about the IP can now express their concern *to* the IP. The repressing mountain of feeling and concerns *not* expressed has been excavated with a single blow in the form of an intervention. The interventionist will continue to work both with the family and other participants and continue to play an active role in setting up continuing care plans.

The Systematic Family Intervention Model

While the focus thus far has been on the Ten-Hour model, which is a modification of the Johnson Institute model, there are other types of interventions that may vary in form or function. One such model that has developed in recent years is called *Systemic Family Intervention,* a model that focuses on the family and not on the IP. Developed by Speare and Raiter (2000), the Systemic Family Intervention model process is described as follows:

1. Preintervention: The family's focus is on their pain and the IP at this point.
2. Intervention Process Begins: The catalyst person seeks help.
3. Formal Intervention Process Begins: Catalyst contacts interventionist.
4. The Team Meets: The team begins to bond; the focus is still on the IP.
5. Family Sessions I, II: Healthy relationships begin to form.
6. Family Sessions III, IV: The Intervention Process; hope and trust starts.
7. Intervention Event: New boundaries emerge; the IP joins, invited to family.
8. Postintervention Apprehension: The group transitions from dysfunctional to functional.
9. Posttreatment Session: Everyone is on track; there is joy and gratefulness.
10. Ongoing Recovery: Family is cautiously optimistic; there are investments in recovery.
11. Relapse: Often, secrets impact recovery; there is relapse if not resolved (Speare & Raiter, 1997).

The Systemic Family Intervention model resembles short-term family therapy. It can be very effective in engaging the entire family in treatment, which may improve the IP's chance of successful recovery. This model does not encourage participation by nonfamily members, however. It is an approach that is best applied

Executive Intervention Checklist

- Team selection: A few key executives
- Shareholder interest: An important leveraging factor
- Ongoing communication: With selected heads
- Treatment providers: Must have executive experience
- Confidentiality and containment: No leaks
- Continued involvement: Interventionist continues to manage process (Fearing, 2000).

in a clinic setting and requires a greater commitment of time by the participants than other models.

The Executive Intervention

Executive interventions are different from family interventions. And that's because the world of work is different from the family. While there are some similarities in approach, there are additional dynamics and leverages that do not exist in the family. The intensity of denial might be just as great, and excuses just as prevalent, but deteriorating job performance is more easily observed. Absenteeism, tardiness, insubordination, poor productivity, and countless other indicators will flag personal problems such as SUDs. Financial leverage, career status, and job loss are powerful leveraging factors in corporate, executive, and employer interventions.

The Executive Intervention model is challenging in that the impaired person here is usually extremely bright and powerful. This is a model employed when the SUD affects a senior executive, up to and including the president and chief executive officer. A sharp executive can be intimidating and is quite effective in turning the tables and assuming control of the intervention. "Protective layers can make addicted executives difficult to reach," said James Fearing, PhD, founder of National Counseling Intervention Services. "Rank, power, money, or stature often insulate them from the natural and logical consequences of their illness" (Fearing, 2000). Experience and charisma are important prerequisites for the interventionist. With the impaired executive, the company's reputation and financial losses are also present—leveraging factors important to a successful intervention outcome. And instead of family members as participants, *selected* senior management and colleagues form the intervention team.

Executive Intervention Defined

Executive intervention is a process that allows the troubled individual to focus on his or her deteriorating functioning, identify the cause of the problem, and take whatever action is necessary to resume a normal, healthy, and productive lifestyle.

The CRAFT Intervention Model

One of the newest intervention models to arrive in the field is called CRAFT, which stands for Community Reinforcement and Family Training (Meyers & Wolfe, 2004). It is a program designed to reduce a loved one's substance use and encourage him or her to seek treatment. The research, so far, seems to validate this approach's effectiveness in getting loved ones into treatment. In one recent study, CRAFT was compared to the Johnson Institute model and to the Al-Anon approach in their ability to engage loved ones into treatment. The CRAFT approach resulted in two to six times more loved ones engaging in treatment than the other two approaches (Meyers, Miller, & Tonigan, 1999).

The goals of CRAFT are to improve the quality of a significant other's (SOs) life and to help make sobriety more attractive to the abuser than substance use. Making sobriety more attractive then substance use is achieved through modifying typical patterns of behavior between the SO and the abuser in order to achieve different results. By changing the way one reacts to the abuser, all subsequent reactions change as well. The first step is helping the SO to become aware of his or her existing patterns of interaction and then teaching him or her new and more effective ways of interacting.

For example, a common interaction between SOs and their substance abusing loved one is to nag, plead, or threaten. The CRAFT approach teaches effec-

---

A CRAFT Case Study

Ed had been trying for years to get Lydia to cut back on her drinking, but nothing worked. Nagging, pleading, threatening, cajoling—everything fell on deaf ears. Lydia wasn't a "falling down drunk," as she put it, and wasn't about to give up something that made her feel so good so fast when she got stressed. Ed, on the other hand, saw Lydia's drinking as a major problem as it resulted in her missing work, forgetting to pick up their kids from day care, and once driving home with the kids when she was drunk. Ed finally tried a different approach. He disengaged from the battle and, instead, mapped her drinking behavior and his responses to it. He outlined new behaviors for himself that would, in turn, elicit different behaviors from Lydia. For instance, when Lydia would come home from work complaining about the unfair treatment she received from her boss (a known drinking trigger), Ed would rub her shoulders and tell her how much he and the kids appreciated her even if her boss was a jerk. Then he'd tell her to enjoy a hot bath while he prepared dinner and make it clear to her that he really enjoys being with her when she is sober. Knowing that baths were one of her favorite stress-busters (next to liquor), Ed was able to sidetrack Lydia from the wine bottle long enough to defuse her mood, get dinner on the table, and shift her attention to more pleasant topics. The more often Ed was able to do this, the more positive experiences he and Lydia shared after work, and the more likely Lydia was to leave work anticipating feeling good when she got home. This positive anticipation, in turn, helped to defuse much of her work stress and made it easier for her to not drink (Meyers & Wolfe, 2004, p. 33).

tive alternatives. The central procedure for accomplishing this is called *behavioral mapping.* One first places effort into understanding his or her present unsuccessful interactions by writing detailed accounts of interactions in a sort of line-by-line script. The SO then learns to *remap* or revise that script for greater effectiveness. The script is revised to include interactions that will reduce substance using triggers and defensive or angry reactions and include rewards for sober behavior as well as consequences for substance using behavior. It places great emphasis on teaching SOs to be proactive rather then reactive. The more prepared the SO is for potential scenarios, the greater the effectiveness of his or her rehearsed interactions will be.

Improving communication skills is an important feature of CRAFT. Significant Others are taught to do the following:

- Phrase communications in positive terms. Rather than saying, "Don't embarrass me tonight," it would be more productive to say, "It would make me so happy if you drank soda tonight."

- Speak from the first person (I). Rather than saying, "You shouldn't drink tonight," say, "I would be so happy if you did not drink this evening."

- Be clear that you understand your loved one's position and care about his or her feelings. Rather than saying, "You're so selfish," try saying, "I understand how stressed out you are after work, and I want to help ease your stress without bringing more of it into our home."

- State your willingness to share responsibility for the situation, such as, "I know I sometimes react strongly to your drinking even when it's uncalled for. Let's work together to solve our differences."

Written activities and assignments are a large part of the CRAFT approach. Some of these activities and assignments include the following:

- Writing a detailed account of your last argument and ways you could have changed or controlled the outcome

- Writing a substance using map of your loved one's triggers, signals of intoxication, and consequences of use

- Developing a safety plan

- Establishing goals

- Identifying enabling behaviors

- Creating ways to reward behavior change

- Asking for help

- Rewarding self

- Working on problem solving skills

- Working on communication skills

The CRAFT model is a newly developed program that uses scientifically validated behavioral principles to reduce a loved one's substance use and to encourage him or her to seek treatment.

The Power of the Intervention

An intervention is not the first thought when alcohol- or drug-related problems begin to emerge—there is usually lots of inaction before that step is taken. Changes in behavior, deteriorating health, and family-related problems are likely to be ignored, rationalized, or minimized by friends and family. Poor management decisions and deteriorating job performance are often overlooked. Even when the problem is obvious to outsiders, those closest to the IP sometimes sit in silence hoping that "it's just something they're going through" and that "they'll get over it." Or the family may be very dysfunctional, and existing friends capable of orchestrating an intervention are few. Perhaps the personality of the IP might be too threatening to entertain the notion of an intervention. If the identified patient is a high-placed executive, he or she is usually capable of hiding his or her illness and covering up major mistakes. Family and social problems are insidious and sometimes difficult to quantify. Even health problems are often disregarded or not related to the drinking or drug use.

Perhaps there are SOs, but they may not be aware that there is such a thing as a structured intervention—or do not know where to look for an interventionist. Whatever the resistance or rationale might be, it takes a heightened level of concern to motivate family, friends, business associates, or colleagues into taking action. The three prerequisites to an intervention are *concern, knowledge,* and *risk.* There has to be *concern* for the IP—someone in the group must take a leadership role. This is usually the person who has *knowledge* about the concept of intervention. As for the *risk* of losing friendship, this is a notion that must be categorically dismissed. The risk is not in conducting an intervention, it is in *not* conducting an intervention—the consequences of an SUD can be devastating. At the very least, the IP's anger and despair will increase as the severity of the illness progresses. As drinking or drug use progresses to intolerable levels or as problems continue to mount, family becomes less accessible, and friends fall away. When the three perquisites are in place (*concern, knowledge,* and *risk*), an intervention is likely to happen. This also applies to executives who are in trouble with alcohol or other drugs. The risk in ignoring the problem can be costly—for the executive, for the company, and for all those affected by his behavior. Not only does the executive stand to lose his job and career, but also his family and health will not be far behind.

Whatever intervention model is employed, confidentiality, integrity, and professionalism should never be compromised. Family, friends, and employers should always use an interventionist who is referred by a reputable source—and has the credentials and experience to ensure the best possible outcome. The structured intervention is a unique experience that saves lives, jobs, and families. The power of this effort is evident in its results, as shown in the cited study. But equally important, the structured intervention marks a pivotal change in the family's thinking—a change that reinforces love and concern and moves toward the elimination of shame and blame. A well-planned family intervention is likely to both shorten the progression of addiction and provide a shortcut to the road of recovery (Scanlon, 2003).

References

Fearing, J. (2000). *Workplace intervention.* Center City, MN: Hazelden.

Johnson, V. E. (1973). *I'll quit tomorrow.* New York: Harper & Row.

Johnson Institute. (2005). http://johnsoninstitute.org/resources

McCourt, F. (1996). *Angela's ashes.* New York: Scribner.

Merriam-Webster's collegiate dictionary. (11th ed.). (2003). Springfield, MA: Merriam-Webster.

Meyers, R. J., Miller, W. R., Hill, D. E., & Tonigan, J. S. (1999). Community reinforcement and family training (CRAFT): Engaging unmotivated drug users in treatment. *Journal of Substance Abuse, 10*(3), 291–308.

Meyers, R. J., & Wolfe, B. L. (2004). *Get your loved one sober: Alternatives to nagging, pleading, and threatening.* Center City, MN: Hazelden.

Miller, W. R., & Rollnick, S. (1991). *Motivational interviewing: Preparing people to change addictive behavior.* New York: Guilford.

Scanlon, W. F. (1991). *Alcoholism and drug abuse in the workplace: Managing care and cost through employee assistance programs* (2nd ed.). New York: Praeger/Greenwood Press.

Scanlon, W. F. (2000). *Structured intervention: An effective pre-treatment motivational strategy* Unpublished Doctoral dissertation, Columbus University.

Scanlon, W. F. (2003). New data validate an old strategy. *Addiction Professional, 1*(3), 36–43.

Spear, & Raiter. (2003). Systematic family intervention training. Workshop presented at the Alcoholism Counsel of New York (ACNY).

Wheeler, G., & Dupré, D. (2001). *Before hitting bottom.* New South Wales, Australia: Du-Prevent Publishing.

CHAPTER **11**

Behavioral Change: Developing Essential Counseling Skills

arlier chapters focused on the assessment, diagnosis, and treatment of individuals presenting with Substance Use Disorders (SUDs). Without a clear understanding of the problems to be addressed, a successful treatment outcome is not likely. This chapter is aimed at developing effective counseling skills and treatment strategies. We will present a structured and organized way to effect addiction treatment counseling services. The first prerequisite in the delivery of such services is skills development. The addictions treatment professional will be only as effective as the limitations of his or her skills. We will also present a stages-of-change model for providing treatment. This will include a discussion on the strategies of treatment implementation, depending on where he or she is in the stages-of-change model. A discussion on group and individual counseling approaches will also be discussed in this chapter. Relapse prevention—the essence of effective treatment—will be introduced at the end of this chapter and covered in detail in the next.

There are seven essential counseling skills or traits needed by the SUD treatment professional:

1. Listening empathically
2. Understanding the stages of behavioral change
3. Educating the client
4. Resolving ambivalence
5. Knowing the available resources
6. Teaching coping skills
7. Preventing relapse

Listening Empathically

Empathy means listening attentively and fully without judgment or opinion. It means totally being there with the speaker or patient. It means making a commitment to understand what the speaker is trying to say. It means unconditional acceptance of where the patient is. Empathy does not mean that you agree with everything that the client says, but rather you are accepting his or her reality at the moment.

Often, we find neophyte clinicians doing more talking than listening. They often have the expectation that the clinician's main task is to provide solutions. It is dangerous to presume that the patient has not thought of the many solutions offered by the brilliant counselor. We suggest that counselors not offer advice until directly asked for it (Miller & Rollnick, 2002). If a patient wants our advice, he or she will ask for it! Stephen Covey, in his best-selling book *The 7 Habits of Highly Effective People*, states that, "Most people do not listen with the intent to understand; they listen with the intent to reply" (Covey, 1989, p. 239). Effective counselors listen with the intent to understand.

Giving advice prematurely can be counterproductive for the ambivalent patient. If a patient, for example, is conflicted about giving up alcohol use completely, and the counselor tells the patient that he or she should abstain completely or should make AA meetings daily, this may lead to patient resistance and treatment drop out. Furthermore, it may lead the patient to think twice about ever returning to treatment again.

Many clinicians believe they are empathic listeners. And many are. Many more of us, however, don't realize that our questions ("You used again?"), our nonverbal gestures (raised eyebrows, a look of shock), our apparent statements of help ("You need to leave that situation!") may all indicate a judgment. We become dismayed when a patient doesn't return to treatment after all we've done to help. "How dare they?!"

Miller and Rollnick emphasize the importance of empathic listening, suggesting that counselor empathy is a "significant determinant of clients' response to treatment" (Miller & Rollnick, 2002, p. 7). *The more the counselor uses empathic listening, the greater the likelihood of treatment success.* On the other hand, the more confrontationally one counsels, the less likelihood for change and the greater the chance for drop out from treatment.

Miller and Rollnick believe that the more resistance a patient displays, the less likely that change will occur. (Resistance will be explored in more detail later in this chapter.) We believe that empathic listening is the best way to minimize client resistance. Responses counterproductive to empathic listening include *arguing for change; presuming you know more than the patient; criticizing; shaming, blaming, labeling* (e.g., "You're an addict"); and *impatience*—being in a hurry to cause a change (Miller & Rollnick, 2002). For a more thorough discussion on how to develop empathic listening skills, the reader is encouraged to review *Motivational Interviewing: Preparing People for Change* (Miller & Rollnick, 2002).

Empathic listening is more than just a technique. It is a sincere effort to understand the speaker without judgment. "You're listening to understand" (Covey, 1989, p. 241). To gain a patient's openness and trust, the counselor must be able to convey *empathy, nonpossessive warmth, and genuineness,* as introduced by Carl Rogers (1959).

Covey underscores the importance of good listening, whatever your profession might be:

> When another person speaks, we're usually "listening" at one of four levels. We may be *ignoring* another person, not really listening at all. We may practice *pretending.* "Yeah. Uh-huh. Right." We may practice *selective listening,* hearing only certain parts of the conversation. We often do this when we're listening to constant chatter of a preschool child. Or we may even practice *attentive listening,* paying attention and focusing energy on the words that are being said. But few of us ever practice the fifth level, the highest form of listening, *empathic listening.* (Covey, 1989, p. 240)

Covey, educated in business management with an MBA from Harvard and a doctorate from Brigham Young University, goes on to describe empathic listening as listening with the intent to understand, that is, seeking first to understand—and then to really understand! Covey, who does not carry the credentials of clinician, certainly has a *clinical* understanding of the importance of listening—empathic listening.

Love as Empathy

M. Scott Peck, in his classic book *The Road Less Traveled* (2003), used a different term for listening to patients than what we are describing here as empathy. He simply called it *love.*

> We are now able to see the essential ingredient that makes psychotherapy effective and successful. It is not unconditional positive regard, nor is it magical words, techniques or postures; it is human involvement and struggle. It is the willingness of the therapist to extend himself or herself for the purpose of nurturing the patient's growth—willingness to go out on a limb, to truly involve oneself at an emotional level in the relationship, to actually struggle with the patient and with oneself. In short, the essential ingredient of successful deep and meaningful psychotherapy is love (Peck, 2003, p. 173).

For those who are concerned that loving a patient may lead to sexual relations between a clinician and patient, which would be unethical behavior on the clinician's part, Peck said, "It is out of love for their patients that therapists do not allow themselves the indulgence of falling in love with them" (Peck, 2003, p. 176).

While empathic listening is essential for making the patient feel cared for, it can also be draining. To feel the emotions of another in addition to your own is hard work! That is why it is important for counselors to avoid back-to-back sessions and allow time to debrief. It is also why it is important to take periodic vacations away from the office.

Once you feel confident in your ability to be empathic in your work—a precondition for effective counseling—you can then proceed to understanding the process of behavioral change.

Understanding the Stages of Behavioral Change

One of the most exciting advances in the field of substance abuse treatment over the past 20 years began around 1982 with the work of two clinical psychologists, James O. Prochaska and Carlo C. DiClemente. These men were determined to understand the factors involved in how people intentionally change behavior. Their work has revolutionized the treatment of addictive behaviors. In their quest to understand how people change behavior, they discovered new principles and challenged old ones. They set about making these discoveries by studying how people overcame problems of smoking, drinking, weight loss, emotional distress, and others (Prochaska, Norcross, & DiClemente, 1994).

Their most important discovery was that *all behavioral change is a process, with distinct stages along the path toward permanent change.* People do not suddenly change when they or someone else wants them to. Behavioral change takes time and effort. Prochaska and DiClemente sought to identify these distinct stages of change.

The notion of stages of change is not a unique one. Elizabeth Kubler-Ross formulated stages of change around the process of dying (Kubler-Ross, 1969). Carter-Scott discussed six basic steps toward executing change: awareness, acknowledgment, choice, strategy, commitment, and celebration (Carter-Scott, 1998).

Prochaska and DiClemente's model challenged the currently accepted model of change, called the *action paradigm* (Prochaska, Norcross, & DiClemente, 1994). The action paradigm suggests that people with undesirable behavior patterns (e.g., drug or alcohol abuse) quickly be taught the necessary skills to change the unwanted behavior (e.g., relapse prevention, coping skills). If a person does not change, then he or she is blamed for lacking the commitment to change. This traditional model assumes that people are ready, willing, and able to change at any time and can be expected to change quickly. Many managed care companies, subscribing to this belief, are denying treatment to patients for noncompliance because they are not taking immediate action steps toward change (e.g., going to 12-step meetings, obtaining a sponsor, remaining totally abstinent from substances). The researchers Prochaska and DiClemente discovered, however, that people do not change behavior immediately, but go through a set of internal stages before actual change occurs.

Prochaska set out to understand the process of human change. He did this by reviewing the common components of change available in all of the major psychotherapies. He was able to identify common processes of change found throughout different psychotherapies. Thus, he named his new approach the *transtheoretical approach,* encompassing common ideas found in all of the psychotherapies reviewed.

Prochaska soon collaborated with DiClemente and began studying cigarette smokers who stopped smoking on their own (self-changers). (An early realization was that the vast majority of former smokers quit on their own without any professional help.) They chose this group because of the easy access to a large sample size of former smokers.

Prochaska and DiClemente identified six distinct stages of change:

1. Precontemplation
2. Contemplation
3. Preparation
4. Action
5. Maintenance
6. Termination

The following is a brief overview of each of the stages.

Precontemplation

Precontemplation is a prestage to change in which a person does not perceive anything wrong with the behavior in question. It is debatable whether it's a distinct stage at all. In this pseudostage, there is no desire or concern for change. For instance, the cigarette smoker sees nothing wrong with smoking and has no intent to stop smoking, or the alcohol drinker is content with continued drinking and does not perceive any negative consequences from drinking.

Precontemplators rarely seek professional help on their own. Someone usually coerces the precontemplator into treatment, such as an employer, the courts, child protective agencies, or a spouse. Precontemplators are usually considered to be in denial of their problem. Others may perceive a problem with the precontemplator's behavior, but the precontemplator does not personally perceive the problem. Precontemplators perceive the behavior in question to be too beneficial to give up on their own.

This does not mean that the precontemplator will not give up the behavior in question. Under a powerful coercive force (e.g., loss of employment, prison time, loss of child custody, loss of spouse), the precontemplator will often give up the behavior. However, under this coercion, the precontemplator will resent giving up the behavior perceived as pleasurable, beneficial, or both. The precontemplator will often deny having this resentment out of fear of further punishment; once the coercive force is lifted, the precontemplator will often return back to the behavior in question. For example, the person who gives up marijuana use for fear of losing employment may return to marijuana use while on vacation where there is no fear of being drug tested. The parolee, fearful of violating parole, may return to cocaine use once the parole has been completed. The husband, fearful of losing his wife, may use cocaine when he knows his spouse will be away for several days. The homeless person living in a drug-free residence will return to heroin use once he or she obtains independent living.

Behavioral change for the precontemplator is transient and only maintained with the continuation of powerful coercive forces. This does not mean that the precontemplator cannot move on to higher stages of change. They are just not prepared or willing to change at the time someone else wants them to change.

Contemplation

The next stage of change is called *contemplation*. This may be the most crucial stage. This is the stage of *ambivalence*. On the one hand, the contemplator perceives problems associated with the target behavior; on the other hand, the contemplator sees pleasure and benefit from continuing the behavior. This internal conflict may occur indefinitely. Each side of the ambivalence may be stronger at different times and under different circumstances. For example, a contemplator, during the week, may be clear about the long-term consequences of continued drinking and, as a result, abstains from drinking. However, on weekends, the immediate benefits of drinking outweigh the anticipated long-term consequences, and drinking ensues. The cocaine user perceives the physical and emotional consequences of use following an event of cocaine use. This may lead to abstinence for several weeks. Over time, the ill effects of the last occasion of use begin to fade and the perceived benefits of use become stronger than the perceived consequences of use. A return to cocaine use follows.

Sometimes the benefits of the target behavior are not fully conscious to the person. We often hear patients claiming that they get no benefits from their substance use despite the fact that they continue to use. If a person were getting no benefits from a behavior, it appears highly unlikely that the behavior would continue. Patients are often unaware of their perceived benefits of use and need to become conscious of them in counseling sessions.

This is the stage when relapses occur frequently as a result of this ambivalence. One can often observe, during therapy sessions, the inner struggle and pain that the person is experiencing due to their inner conflict. The contemplator is on an emotional seesaw, battling between wanting to continue and to discontinue the behavior. Sometimes this conflict is not apparent to either the clinician or the patient. It is too painful for the patient to even admit to himself or herself. This patient continues to relapse without any understanding of why it keeps occurring. The contemplator continues this struggle, either consciously or unconsciously, until a significant event occurs to clearly give weight to one side of the ambivalence over the other. For example, when the contemplator loses a job due to the use of cocaine, or when the contemplator's wife leaves home after another alcohol relapse, or when a physician tells a cigarette smoker that he has emphysema. These events may finally tip the balance toward a resolution of the ambivalence.

Once a person develops the adequate level of motivation and commitment to change (once the ambivalence is resolved), the most difficult struggle toward change has been achieved. In 12-step lingo it's called *getting the first step*. This is not to say that the ambivalence may not resurface at some other time or in some other stage. It can resurface anytime the anticipated benefits of the target behavior outweigh the consequences of that behavior. However, resolving the ambivalence the first time is the most difficult and most important time of all.

Preparation

Preparation is the next stage of change. This is when the person makes the firm decision to discontinue or change the target behavior. As stated in the preceding, this usually occurs following a significant event that moves the person beyond the conflict of ambivalence. At this stage, the person prepares to make the behavioral change. This may involve preparing to change the usual routines involved in the target behavior, such as preparing to change friends, changing leisure activities, or changing one's responses to situations. "The more prepared one is to make the journey, the greater the chances of eventual success" (Marlatt & Gordon, 1985, p. 217).

This stage is usually considered a window of opportunity. It usually occurs following a significant event that upsets the ambivalence to change. Such an event may clearly tilt the scale away from continued substance use and toward the need for change. At this point, the person appears very motivated and committed toward change. Consequently, this becomes an opportunity for change. If at this point action steps are not pursued quickly, the person may soon revert back toward ambivalence and, ultimately, back toward the stage of contemplation.

Action

The *action* stage involves the process of discontinuing the target behavior. It involves steps taken to initiate change. This may include joining a 12-step group, entering a treatment program, purchasing a nicotine patch, or reading literature about stopping the undesirable behavior.

Entering the stage of action involves a clear commitment and desire for change. It involves a further weakening of the ambivalence toward change. As mentioned earlier, this does not mean that the ambivalence for behavioral change is completely eliminated at this stage. Ambivalence continues, but not to the degree felt in the contemplation stage. In this stage, the person is more resolved about his desire and commitment for change and often seeks support to implement a change.

Action steps must be differentiated from the steps taken by someone being forced to take action. For example, the person coerced into a treatment program by some outside force (e.g. courts, employer, spouse, etc.) may not yet be psychologically in the stage of action, despite its appearance. *One's internal state of readiness to change is more predictive of successful change than the outward appearance of readiness to change* (e.g., attending a treatment program, attending 12-step meetings, etc.). Others cannot force a person to reach the internal stage of action. It must be achieved through one's own process or journey. This is not to say that coerced patients cannot be helped along the way toward arriving at this stage. However, when handled improperly, this can actually cause the patient to increase resistance toward change. This will be further discussed shortly.

Historically, this stage has been given the most emphasis in the addiction treatment field. It is believed that taking action steps takes precedence over all other processes (the action paradigm). Consequently, most treatment programs center on teaching action steps such as coping skills training, relapse prevention skills, and the importance of following the twelve steps of AA. Twelve-step programs also emphasize action strategies, such as obtaining and calling a sponsor, attending 90 meetings in 90 days, and working on the steps. Managed care companies also focus almost exclusively on getting treatment providers to encourage their patients to follow these action strategies. However, following action strategies without the internal readiness and commitment to change is apt to lead to failure.

Unfortunately, most clinicians fail to understand that providing these strategies to patients before they have reached a sincere decision and commitment to change is like putting the cart before the horse. Providing these strategies prematurely may actually do more harm than good. For instance, the ambivalent client, who is a chronic relapser, may feel a greater sense of guilt and hopelessness after obtaining these skills and not exhibiting greater success. These feelings of failure and guilt can be so significant as to turn a minor occurrence of use into a full-blown relapse. (This will be discussed in the section on relapse.) Also, the person who continually relapses may drop out of treatment due to frustration with his or her lack of progress. The initial emphasis of treatment needs to be about getting the patient committed to change (as seen in the contemplation stage), not on action steps. Once this is achieved, the patient is ready to benefit from the cognitive and behavioral strategies commonly taught in traditional treatment programs.

We have often questioned if patients who complete treatment programs achieve success due to the treatment process or because those who complete treatment are the most compliant. It is often suggested, for those participating in 12-step meetings, that people make 90 meetings in their first 90 days of sobriety.

Do people who are compliant with this suggestion achieve success because they have made 90 meetings in 90 days or because only the most motivated and committed individuals are the ones who accomplish this task? Do patients who attend treatment programs get better because they learned cognitive and behavioral strategies and skills in treatment or because those who complete programs are the ones most committed to change? Possibly the most crucial element for successful behavioral change is the desire and commitment to change.

Maintenance

It is one thing to initiate an action step, but another to maintain it. Marlatt and Gordon believed the act of departure is only the *first step* of the recovery process. It is far easier to discontinue a behavior than to maintain behavioral change. The maintenance stage begins after behavioral change has been maintained for at least 6 consecutive months. As people who work in the addiction field know, maintaining abstinence from drug use is a very difficult task. The difficulty of maintaining behavioral change is apparent for any change undertaken. For instance, health clubs take advantage of this difficulty by getting their club members to sign up for lifetime memberships, knowing that the majority will not maintain their membership for very long. Weight loss centers use the same strategy in signing up applicants. "Without a strong commitment to maintenance, there will surely be relapse, usually returning the client to the precontemplation or contemplation stage" (Prochaska, Norcross, & DiClemente, 1994, p. 45). A person in this stage has made significant progress in working through his or her ambivalence toward changing the target behavior. Again, it does not mean that the ambivalence cannot return. One's commitment to change often wavers, but the more stable one's commitment is to change, the greater the likelihood of successful, long-term change.

The emphasis in our field has been on quitting the problem substance. Patients are regularly congratulated for successes in early recovery (less than 6 months). However, the person maintaining long-term recovery, which is much more difficult to achieve, gets little recognition except, perhaps, on significant anniversary dates. The person maintaining long-term change has clearly made a decision and commitment to change. If we can figure out how to maintain our clients' commitment and motivation to change, then we will have solved the greatest obstacle to maintaining behavioral change.

Relapse

"Relapse refers to a breakdown or setback in a person's attempt to change or modify any target behavior" (Marlatt & Gordon, 1985, p. 3). Relapse can occur during any stage of change. According to Marlatt and Gordon, over 85 percent of people attempting to change behavior have a relapse at some point. A person relapses because, for one reason or another, the benefits of the target behavior overshadow the consequences of the behavior. As cited earlier, these benefits are not always clear to the person choosing to relapse. The relapse may last as little as a moment, with a quick return back to the action stage, or it may last for months or years with a return back to the precontemplation, contemplation, or preparation stage. Fleeting relapses lasting only a brief time are often called *lapses* or *slips*. Lapses and slips can lead to full-blown relapses if not controlled in time.

Once a person relapses, he or she reverts back to an earlier stage of change and begins the cycle over again. It is like a game of Chutes and Ladders, in which you are moving around a game board only to land on a space that sends you back to the start. How quickly you return back to the place you were before depends on your ability to work through your ambivalence about change. We will be discussing the process of relapse in much greater detail later in this chapter and the next.

Termination

Termination is considered the final stage of change. It is believed to be the permanent end of an undesirable behavior, an exit out of the spiral of change. Termination implies that the undesirable behavior is gone for good. It is the ultimate goal. It seems to imply a cure, which is a controversial point in the field of addiction treatment. Does a person recovering from addiction ever reach a stage of termination?

There are a couple of questionnaires worth mentioning that have been developed for determining the stage of change that a patient is in. Prochaska and DiClemente (1984) developed the *University of Rhode Island Change Assessment* (URICA) for determining general stages of change. In 1990, William R. Miller developed the *Stages of Change Readiness and Treatment Eagerness Scale* (SOCRATES) to assess a patient's stage of change specifically related to drug and alcohol use. These are both objective questionnaires used for determining stage of change.

Key Points about the Stages of Change

Relapse Is a Part of Change Relapse is a return to an old behavior. In this model, it is viewed as a common part of the change process. It is believed that with each successive relapse, usually between three and seven relapses, the person will finally resolve his ambivalence toward the behavior in question and permanently stop the behavior. Relapse is perceived not as a failure but as an opportunity to learn and grow. Marlatt and Gordon (1985) used the analogy of a child learning how to ride a bicycle. Every time a child falls off a bike while learning to ride would not be considered a setback (relapse), but rather a learning experience through trial-and-error, leading toward acquiring a new behavior. Relapse is part of an evolution toward the cessation of an old behavior while being replaced by a new behavior (see Figure 11.1).

This is a different view of relapse than the traditional one in the field of addiction treatment. Clients have been regularly punished for relapsing. They have been demoted in programs. They have been stripped of their *clean time* in AA

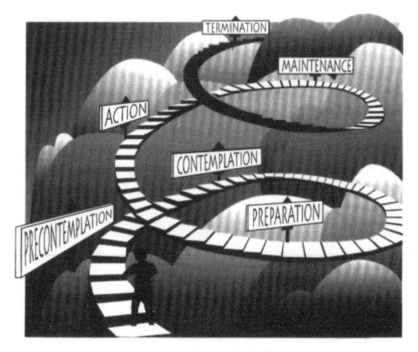

The Spiral of Change

Figure 11.1 *The spiral of change.*

meetings. They have often been involuntarily discharged from treatment programs. Managed care companies still commonly refuse to authorize treatment sessions for clients who relapse, citing noncompliance. And many employers continue to terminate employees after a single episode of relapse.

The Goal Is to Help Move Patients to the Next Stage of Change Whatever stage of change the patient is in, our goal is to help him or her reach the next stage. It is a *one stage at a time* philosophy. For example, if the patient begins treatment at the precontemplation stage, our goal is to help move him or her to the contemplation stage. If the patient meets us in the contemplation stage, our goal is to help him or her get to the preparation stage, and so on.

Individuals can only move one stage at a time. We cannot jump over stages, despite the wishes of others. We are often pressured by judges, employers, spouses, and case reviewers of managed care companies to get patients who have no desire to change (i.e., unaware of having a problem with drugs) to suddenly move into the action stage (i.e., discontinue the use of drugs). This is not practical. One individual may quickly go through the stages, while the next may get stuck at a particular stage for a longer period of time. Our goal as counselors is to help the patient get to the next stage of change as quickly as possible, not to leap over the stages of change.

This goal has been a source of relief for clinical staff trained by us. They do not feel the pressure of having to get all of their clients into the action stage. Instead, they feel a sense of accomplishment in seeing their clients' progress from one stage to the next. By relieving the pressure on clinical staff, we are also minimizing the occurrence of burnout, a common hazard in our line of work.

A final note is that individuals move through these stages with or without our help. The majority of people change behavior without the assistance of professional help. Cigarette smokers are a good example of this. We believe that, with our assistance, individuals will move through these stages more quickly than they would on their own. While it may take people 2 years to successfully evolve through the stages of change on their own, with our assistance they are expected to achieve the same results in a much shorter period of time.

Each Stage Involves a Different Set of Strategies for the Clinician to Employ *The stage of change that a client is in at the time of our interaction determines the strategies we will employ.* A patient beginning treatment at the stage of precontemplation will need a different set of strategies than the patient beginning treatment at the stage of action. *Each stage has its own unique needs and expectations.* Consequently, each stage has its own strategies for meeting these needs and expectations.

Precontemplators have the need to gain more awareness on how their behavior may be harmful to their lives. Contemplators need to resolve their ambivalence and make a decision whether to continue or discontinue the behavior. Individuals in the preparation stage need to know the options available to help discontinue a behavior and expect someone to direct them. Individuals in the action stage need to learn skills to change an undesirable behavior. Individuals in the maintenance stage need the skills to prevent relapse and require ongoing encouragement. The person who relapses needs support and encouragement to begin the process over again. The actual strategies to utilize in each of these stages will be reviewed shortly.

Client Resistance Suggests That We Are Employing the Wrong Strategies Client resistance indicates that the client is not keeping up with us. It suggests that we are moving too quickly for the client. It suggests that we are using inappropriate strategies. For example, using action stage strategies for a precontemplator will usually lead to client resistance. Telling a precontemplator that he or she needs to attend 90 AA meetings in 90 days or that he or she must enter an inpatient rehab center will usually lead to resistance. The precontemplator does not acknowledge having a problem with drug or alcohol use and, consequently, does not see the need for action strategies to stop the behavior. As a result, the client resists this prescription for help.

Client resistance has been categorized into four categories: *arguing, interrupting, denying,* and *ignoring* (Chamberlain et al., as cited in Miller & Rollnick, 1991, p. 103). Whenever we perceive an increase in client resistance, we must shift strategies. It means the client is not keeping up with us. Client resistance is an extremely useful tool in providing us feedback about where the client is. *Always be alert for client resistance.* This view of client resistance is very different from past views of resistance. Previously, client resistance was believed to be an inherent quality of the client. The client was either a resistant or a nonresistant client. This new formulation of resistance suggests that resistance is not a client trait, but a response to an interaction between two or more people. Resistance develops as a result of a person attempting to get another person to do something that he or she is not ready to do.

It Is Essential to Know What Stage the Client Is in at All Times *Knowing what stage your client is in will help keep client resistance to a minimum and aid in knowing which strategies to employ.* As the counselor, you are expected to be assessing client stages at all times. Not correctly identifying the stage of change that your client is in can lead to utilizing inappropriate strategies, which ultimately may lead to client resistance.

The first area to assess when initially interviewing a client is determining what stage he or she is in. By simply asking, "What brought you here?" you can accumulate important information about motivation and desire for change. For instance, the person who responds to the question, "What brought you here?" with "My job" does not appear highly motivated for change. This person, with further clarification, will probably be found to be in either the precontemplation or contemplation stage. The person who responds, "I'm sick and tired of being sick and tired" is more likely to be coming to treatment voluntarily. This person is more likely to be in the preparation or action stage.

Weighing the Benefits of Change All of the stages involve weighing of the benefits of continuing a behavior versus the benefits of changing the behavior. Movement through the stages involves changing one's perception as to the importance of change. In the precontemplation stage, the person clearly sees more benefits in continuing the behavior than in changing it. There is little importance placed on changing the behavior. The person in the contemplation stage is about evenly divided between the benefits of continuing the behavior and the benefits of change. This person is truly in conflict. The person in the preparation stage is leaning toward perceiving more benefits for change than in continuing the behavior. The person in the action stage clearly sees more benefit in change than in continuing the behavior. The person in the maintenance stage has the most clarity about the benefits of change versus the benefits of continuing the behavior.

Under certain circumstances, however, the weighing of these alternatives can change. During some particular moments or high-risk situations, the benefits of continuing the behavior outweigh the benefits of change. This often results in relapse. This will be discussed further in the section on relapse prevention.

As stated earlier in this chapter, the strategies to employ are based on the stage of change that your client is in during your interaction. We will have different treatment goals for a client in the precontemplation stage than the client in the contemplation, preparation, action, or maintenance stage. Thus, we will utilize different treatment strategies for each of these stages of change. This, hopefully, will provide the treatment professional with some concrete tasks and direction to take with your client on his or her journey toward behavioral change and recovery.

Educating the Client

Understanding which stage the patient is in regarding behavioral change is essential in determining how to approach the case. This section will discuss the strategies to employ for each of the stages.

Precontemplation Stage Strategies

People in the precontemplation stage do not see the need to change their behavior. They are quite comfortable with their current behavior. However, significant others (e.g., spouse, employer, probation officer, etc.) may not approve of their behavior. Precontemplators generally do not enter treatment programs by their own choice; others usually coerce them into treatment. Consequently, they are not very amenable to suggestions for change.

Demands for change are usually met with patient resistance and excuses for why it will not work. *The best approach for the precontemplator is to provide impersonal education and consciousness raising.* This is best accomplished in a didactic group involving information building with little actual therapy provided. Placing the precontemplator in a group full of acknowledged substance abusers is usually a set up for problems. Either the other group members get frustrated and angry at the stubbornness or intransigence of the precontemplator, or the precontemplator feels out of place with all of those *addicts* in the room, or both. It is best to place precontemplators in a specially devised group with other precontemplators.

The goal for the person in the precontemplation stage is to gain enough awareness of his or her problem behavior to begin contemplating a change in that behavior. This is best accomplished by increasing awareness in a nonthreatening manner. At Inter-Care, the author's outpatient program in New York City, there is a group called the *Early Intervention Group.* It is a precontemplation group. In other words, it is a group of individuals who have been mandated into treatment for testing positive on a job for some illegal substance or alcohol or arrested for a DWI or drug possession charge. After a thorough assessment (which includes administration of the Substance Abuse Subtle Screening Inventory [SASSI]), there may be no concrete evidence of Substance Dependence or even Abuse. However, there is enough evidence to suggest that the person may be at risk for developing an SUD. The person is told something like the following:

> Look, your job sent you here expecting you get some form of help. While there's no clear evidence of a Substance Use Disorder, your employer expects some type of intervention for you. I will not recommend treatment, but I will suggest some education around drug and alcohol use and awareness building. We have an eight-

week *Early Intervention* group that meets each week for one hour. Each week we discuss a different topic about drug and alcohol use and decision making. After eight weeks, I can give you a letter of successful completion and, hopefully, that's the end of this ordeal. You mentioned having children. These classes may, at the very least, be helpful when it comes time to provide them with useful information. What do you say?

This type of reasonable discussion usually leads the person to agree to enroll without much resistance. You then may add, "By the way, I would like to include weekly urine monitoring as a way to prove to your employer that there is no evidence of a Substance Abuse problem." Again, these mandated individuals usually agree to this out of fear that refusing to submit may be taken as a sign of active use.

At no time during these sessions are we placing any pressure on them to change their behavior, to speak in the group, or to admit to having a problem with substances. They bring about these tasks on their own just by being in a non-threatening and safe environment. The weekly sessions may include such topics as understanding the different classes of psychoactive substances; the symptom criteria for Substance Abuse and Substance Dependence; completing a screening instrument for SUDs, such as the SASSI; understanding denial; a review of the stages-of-change model; understanding the biology of addiction; and a review of the motivational components of change.

At the end of the eight sessions, we hope that the participants have gained a greater awareness of their use patterns and have moved closer to the contemplation stage. We also hope that the participants have had such a comfortable experience in the group that they would not hesitate to return on gaining further acknowledgment of having an SUD. In fact, all participants are encouraged to return if they run into any future problems around the use of a substance. Many of them do return at a later time, without coercion, after progressing to the preparation or action stage of change on their own.

Throughout the 8-week series, most participants submit to a weekly drug or alcohol urine screening. If any of the urine screens test positive for drug or alcohol use, this is used to further help the person acknowledge difficulty in abstaining from use and aids in moving the person closer to the stage of contemplation. Positive urine screenings may suggest the need for a higher LOC, including a more intensive treatment group, increased services, or the addition of individual therapy.

Resolving Ambivalence

Contemplation Stage Strategies

Resolving the ambivalence is an important function in this stage. The strategies employed for the patient in the contemplation stage of change are more complicated and involve greater skill than those used in the preceding stage. Most of the skills to be discussed in this section are techniques taken directly from the first and second editions of *Motivational Interviewing: Preparing People for Change* (Miller & Rollnick, 1991, 2002).

As stated earlier, a person in the contemplation stage is experiencing significant ambivalence regarding the target behavior. The person is conflicted about whether to continue the behavior. The person clearly sees the need to discontinue the behavior, only to be swayed the next instant by some conscious or subconscious belief as to the benefit of continuing the behavior. This internal struggle may continue indefinitely.

The goal of the clinician, in working with the contemplator, is to help resolve ambivalence one way or the other. It is usually not our responsibility to determine which way to resolve the ambivalence, only to help in resolving it. Sometimes patients resolve their ambivalence by deciding to continue the behavior that initially brought them into treatment. It is our job to raise the patient's consciousness about the consequences and benefits of each side of the ambivalence so that he or she can resolve that ambivalence for him- or herself. If we appear to be clearly taking one side of the ambivalence over the other, the patient may feel judged or pressured to do something he or she is not ready to do.

A skilled clinician can increase the speed by which the resolution of ambivalence is achieved. What may take years to achieve independently by the patient can be achieved in months by a clinician skilled in resolving ambivalence. When done properly, the patient may not even be aware of how the clinician helped him or her resolve the ambivalence. The patient may come to the conclusion that he or she resolved it alone.

Resolving ambivalence begins by gaining a clear understanding of the benefits and consequences of each side of the ambivalence. Many times patients are unaware of the benefits of their continued substance use. They do not understand why they keep relapsing. It is our task to help the client understand why a behavior is continued. Clients must also understand that they make a choice prior to initiating any behavior. Sometimes the choice is conscious, and at other times it is subconscious, but each action begins with making a choice. We must help the client understand why that choice was made. For instance, the client who picked up cocaine after abstaining for several months made a choice (conscious or subconscious) to use on that particular occasion. It is our task to help the client understand why he or she made that choice. It is also our task to help the client know if he or she would make that same choice again under similar circumstances.

Another task of the clinician is to point out discrepancies between the client's stated goals and the behaviors that impede those goals. A client who is intent on going to college may not be aware as to how the continued use of drugs is interfering with achieving this goal. The mother who has lost custody of a child to the foster care system must be reminded how her continued use of heroin impedes her ability to regain custody of the child. The employee who has been suspended from work due to alcohol use must be continually reminded that sobriety is needed in order to return to work.

It is important to gain a clear understanding of the goals and values of the client. We must then be on the constant alert for behaviors or verbal statements made by the client that seem to contradict these stated goals and values. This leads to consciousness raising in the client, an increased awareness of the motivations of one's behavior, and ultimately to resolving ambivalence.

It is not our job to judge the client's goals and values, only to help clarify them. It is ultimately up to the clients on how to resolve their discrepancies between their behaviors and their goals or values. We act only as *ambivalence-resolution specialists* without concern for the outcome. Our mission, in working with clients in the contemplation stage, is to resolve their internal conflict involving ambivalence.

Clinicians are encouraged to read *Motivational Interviewing* for a more thorough review of counseling strategies for working through ambivalence (Miller & Rollnick, 2002). These strategies include the use of reflective listening, summarizing, developing discrepancies, and eliciting change talk.

Because the contemplation stage is about working through ambivalence, direct advice giving during this stage is not suggested. At this stage, individuals are torn between two ways of acting (continuing or discontinuing the behavior). It is believed that advice giving by the clinician, at this point, would convey a judgment as to how to proceed. This would be counterproductive. For instance, if a client is ambivalent about ending a relationship with a physically abusive spouse and it is suggested that the client end the relationship, the client may suddenly discontinue treatment for fear of being pressured to leave the relationship. If a client, in another example, is ambivalent about giving up the use of alcohol, but the clinician demands he do so, the client may not return to treatment. In the past, this premature termination from treatment would have been blamed on the patient's denial rather than on the clinician's misinformed intervention. Today, we focus upon the clinician's intervention to see where the treatment may have gone wrong. Rather than providing advice and solutions at this point in treatment, it is much more effective to work through the ambivalence in a nonjudgmental manner. An empathic style of counseling is considered to be much more efficacious, at this point in treatment, than a solution-focused approach.

Clinicians periodically report resistance to utilizing this approach because they do not have the luxury of time to wait for a client to resolve his or her ambivalence. They assume that they can bypass this stage of change and go directly to the stage of action. *Attempting to bypass the contemplation stage and go straight to action increases client resistance, strengthens the side of ambivalence fighting change, and often leads to early termination from treatment.* The working through of ambivalence cannot be ignored if permanent resolution of the behavior is to be achieved. The primary goal of the contemplation stage is to help move the patient toward the preparation stage of change.

Knowing the Available Resources

Preparation Stage Strategy

The preparation stage is the stage in which the person prepares to make a change in behavior. It is important for the treatment professional to be fully aware of the treatment resources available. Marlatt and Gordon (1985) use the metaphor of preparing for a journey. The preparation stage is like preparing for departure. This stage usually follows some precipitating event, such as the loss of a job or a marital separation, which motivates the person to seek a behavioral change. The person begins to show signs of a readiness to change and takes preparatory steps toward change.

At this stage, the individual begins to seek information regarding change and appears more open to advice about change. Providing advice, at this stage, is acceptable if the client appears to be seeking advice. Clinicians are still cautioned not to provide advice until the client appears open to it.

The goal at this stage is to help the client prepare for change emotionally, logistically, and socially. Preparing the client for emotional change involves an exploration of the feelings anticipated regarding change, such as feelings of fear, sadness, anger, resentment, or insecurity. The clinician must help the client envision a successful future in the absence of the target behavior. Preparing for emotional change includes preparing for a possible grieving process involving separation from a loved one (the target substance). Emotional preparation may also include working through anger and resentment over giving up the substance. Emotional preparation may also include the fear of how to cope with life without the use of the substance.

Preparing for logistical change may include finding the right treatment approach for the client, making a treatment referral for the client, or finding other resources (e.g., housing, child care, etc.). Finding the right treatment approach for the client begins with giving the client a menu of options. "When a person perceives that he or she has freely chosen a course of action, it is more likely that the person will persist and succeed" (Miller & Rollnick, 1991, p. 34). Many times the client chooses the most convenient and easiest option despite our belief that he or she needs an alternate approach. This is the time to practice patience and tolerance. Unless the client directly requests our advice, it is best to allow the client to discover for him- or herself what works. Many times, to our dismay, we see clients succeed against our better judgment. In choosing the right treatment for the client, it is our responsibility to find services that are "acceptable to the client, accessible, appropriate, and effective" (Miller & Rollnick, 1991, p. 17). It is your responsibility as a clinician to become familiar with the different resources available in your area. In large cities, the variety of social service options may be overwhelming and overlooked. For small suburban areas, the variety of resources may be insufficient, requiring creative alternatives.

Social preparation for change may include providing sessions with significant others to discuss the plan for change and its impact on the relationship, obtaining support from other family members, and helping to develop new friendships with supportive others. The client's plans for change usually impact on the life of significant others. It is recommended that these potential changes be discussed with the client as well as with the significant others. It is important to get the support of significant others and prepare for potential obstacles to change. These obstacles may include who will care for children while the client gets involved in treatment, how to handle relationships with friends still involved in the target behavior, and preparing for any other potential obstacles for change. Change is never easy, but developing a detailed plan of action, including a list of the potential obstacles, can make the journey feel easier. Five techniques for strengthening commitment are discussed in *Changing for Good* (Prochaska, Norcross, & DiClemente, 1994):

1. *Take small steps.* This is especially true if the client is still experiencing significant ambivalence about change. Attempting to rush change and do too much at once can be counterproductive.

2. *Set a date.* Helping the client set clear dates of action strengthens commitment. It is important to discourage the client from changing dates or for finding excuses to delay a plan of action.

3. *Go public.* Conveying one's plans to others strengthens one's commitment to action.

4. *Prepare for a major operation.* Prepare for this behavioral change as seriously as one would prepare for any major operation. One must be prepared mentally, physically, and spiritually for change.

5. *Create a plan of action.* "To a large extent, success depends on using a plan that you and the client believe works; if you create the plan yourself, the belief becomes much stronger" (Prochaska, Norcross, & DiClemente, 1994, p. 158). Although we suggest that the client create the plan him- or herself, clinicians can assist in this process by providing the information, resources, and support needed by the client.

Teaching Coping Skills

Action Strategy

Teaching coping skills is an important function of this stage. The action stage occurs when a person takes concrete steps toward initiating change, such as purchasing a nicotine patch to stop smoking cigarettes, joining AA meetings to stop drinking alcohol, or entering a treatment program to control one's use of a substance or behavior (e.g., cocaine use, gambling, or eating disorder). Concrete steps are taken to help make the behavioral change. It is worth mentioning that some of these steps may actually begin in the preceding stage (the preparation stage), but, at that point, they are initiated in a more transitory and experimental manner, lacking any true consistency.

The action stage is the stage in which a person learns skills that will support and encourage behavioral change and obtains support for continuing the commitment to change. This stage has traditionally gotten the most emphasis. Most treatment programs emphasize the skills needed for this stage, while often neglecting the work needed for the other stages of change. This neglect of the other stages is sometimes referred to as the *action paradigm*. It is often falsely assumed that clients who enter treatment are ready to take action steps without any effort toward preparation for change or resolution of ambivalence. It is during this stage that the individual gets the most praise and encouragement from others (i.e., clinicians, family, friends, etc.).

It is important to emphasize that ambivalence does not disappear during this stage; it only weakens. The desire to return to previous substance use may strengthen at any time. It is vital that clinicians continually monitor the client's state of ambivalence. This is often not an easy task. Clients are not always conscious of their state of ambivalence and tend to minimize it. Also, clients often feel weak-willed if their ambivalence intensifies. As a result, they often hide these feelings from the clinician and others so as not to let anyone down. It is the clinician's responsibility to monitor the client's ambivalence as closely as a physician would monitor the blood pressure of a patient who has high blood pressure. Without adequate levels of motivation, no skills taught will be effective in preventing relapse.

The action stage teaches the skills necessary to initiate behavioral change and cope with the urges and cravings to return to the addictive behavior. Some general principles are taught, such as avoiding anything previously associated with the substance use patterns (e.g., people, places, and things), developing a positive social support network (e.g., 12-step meetings, obtaining a sponsor), and substituting new activities to replace old ones. High-risk situations and situations that are particularly difficult for the client to cope with without using substances are identified and explored. Essentially, the action stage, as well as the maintenance stage, is geared toward preventing relapse.

The action stage is the stage in which specific cognitive-behavioral skills are taught to break an addictive habit and to deal with life's demands without reverting to drugs and alcohol to cope. In the absence of effective coping skills, it is believed that the client will return to substance use to cope. The cognitive-behavioral model assumes that by learning new behaviors the client will be less vulnerable to relying on old coping patterns, such as getting high.

Presenting each of these specific cognitive-behavioral skills is beyond the scope of this book. To learn specific skills training exercises, we recommend reading *Treating Alcohol Dependence: A Coping Skills Training Guide*, by Peter Monti, David Abrams, Ronald Kadden, and Ned Cooney (1989). Another excellent resource for teaching coping skills is through the cognitive-behavioral coping skills manual developed by the National Institute on Alcohol Abuse and Alcoholism (NIAA), entitled *Cognitive-Behavioral Coping Skills Therapy Manual: A Clinical Research Guide for Therapists Treating Individuals with Alcohol Abuse and Dependence* (Kadden, 1992). There are more current resources available as well, and an internet search will reveal them, but we believe these two training guides are important additions to any treatment professional's library.

In the Monti et al. book, the skills to be taught are divided into two major categories commonly associated with poor coping skills: (1) *interpersonal factors*, such as how to develop social supports, how to deal with the pressures of marital or family relationships and work relationships, and how to deal with peer pressure to use substances; and (2) *intrapersonal factors*, such as managing thoughts about drugs or alcohol, relaxation training, increasing pleasant activities, anger management, managing negative thinking, and planning for emergencies.

In an ideal situation, we would assess the coping deficits of each of our clients and teach them only the skills they lacked. However, in most treatment settings, this will not be feasible. As a practical result, each of the preceding skills-training sessions would be taught in group settings with all participants learning each of them.

Preventing Relapse

Maintenance Strategies

An essential function of this stage is the development of relapse prevention skills. The maintenance stage begins after 6 consecutive months of maintaining behavioral change. It begins a stage in which the person is adapting to the new lifestyle. Thoughts of returning to the old behavior have been significantly weakened. Thus, the person is no longer obsessively thinking about using the problem substance. It is the stage in which ambivalence is minimally present. The person has significantly resolved his or her ambivalence to change. This does not mean that ambivalence cannot return; ambivalence can return at any time, which is why people can relapse even after many years of sobriety.

The central goal of the maintenance stage is to prevent relapse from occurring. This goal essentially begins in the action stage and continues through the maintenance stage. Logically, a critical task of the treatment professional is to assist the client in preventing relapse. If the client experiences a relapse, it will likely initiate a destructive spiral of change resulting in a return to the earlier stage of contemplation or even precontemplation. Although maintenance or relapse prevention is the last stage in the stages of change, it is by no means the least important. As stated earlier, relapse prevention is the essence of effective treatment. It is the development and application of skill sets essential to personal growth, lifestyle change, and successful recovery. It is such an import function of treatment that the entire next chapter is dedicated to it.

References

Carter-Scott, C. (1998). *If life is a game, these are the rules.* New York: Bantam Doubleday Dell.

Chamberlain, P., Patterson, G., Reid, J., Kavanagh, K., & Forgatch, M. (1984). Observation of client resistance. *Behavior Therapy, 15,* 144–155.

Covey, S. R. (1989). *The 7 habits of highly effective people.* New York: Free Press.

Kadden, R., Carroll, K. M., Donovan, D., Cooney, N., Monti, P. & Abrams, D., et. al. (1992). *Cognitive-behavioral coping skills therapy manual: A clinical research guide for therapists treating individuals with alcohol abuse and dependence* (NIAAA Project MATCH Monograph Series Vol. 3, DHHS Publication No. ADM 92-1895). Washington DC: U.S. Government Printing Office.

Kubler-Ross, E. (1969). *On death and dying.* New York: Touchstone.

Marlatt, G. A., & Gordon, J. R. (Eds.). (1985). *Relapse prevention: Maintenance strategies in the treatment of addictive behaviors.* New York: Guilford.

Miller, W. R. (1992). *Stages of Change Readiness and Treatment Eagerness Scale (SOCRATES).* Albuquerque, NM: Center on Alcoholism, Substance Abuse, and Addictions.

Miller, W. R., & Rollnick, S. (1991). *Motivational interviewing: Preparing people to change addictive behavior.* New York: Guilford.

Miller, W. R., & Rollnick, S. (2002). *Motivational interviewing: Preparing people for change.* New York: Guilford.

Monti, P. M., Abrams, D. B., Kadden, R. M., & Cooney, N. T. (1989). *Treating alcohol dependence: A coping skills training guide.* New York: Guilford.

Peck, M. S. (2003). *The road less traveled: 25th anniversary edition.* New York: Touchstone.

Prochaska, J., Velicer, W., DiClemente, C., & Zwick, W. (1984). *Measuring processes of change.* Unpublished manuscript, University of Rhode Island.

Prochaska, J., Norcross, J. C., & DiClemente, C. (1994). *Changing for good.* New York: William Morrow and Company.

Rogers, C. R. (1959). A theory of therapy, personality, and interpersonal relationships as developed in the client-centered framework. In S. Koch (Ed.), *Psychology: The study of a science: Vol. 3. Formulations of the person and the social contexts* (pp. 184–256). New York: McGraw-Hill.

CHAPTER 12

Maintaining Commitment: Relapse Prevention Therapy

Relapse Prevention Framework

While there is much information available on relapse prevention treatment (RPT), this chapter will primarily focus on the classic work of Alan Marlatt and Judith R. Gordon, *Relapse Prevention: Maintenance Strategies in the Treatment of Addictive Behaviors* (Marlatt & Gordon, 1985). There are, of course, other relapse prevention experts in the treatment of Substance Abuse Disorders (SUDs), but the work of Marlatt and Gordon is distinguished in both its originality and its approach. It is empirically based, lending it scientific credibility and establishing a foundation for further exploration and application. From their research has evolved specific cognitive-behavioral coping skills strategies that can be learned by SUD professionals and taught to clients in recovery.

Relapse Prevention Therapy (RPT) was originally designed as a maintenance program for use following the treatment of addictive behaviors although it is also used as a stand-alone treatment program (Marlatt & Gordon, 1985; Parks & Marlatt, 2005). In the most general sense, RPT is a behavioral self-control program designed to teach individuals who are trying to maintain changes in their behavior how to anticipate and cope with the problem of relapse (Parks & Marlatt, 2005).

Relapse refers to a breakdown or failure in a person's attempt to maintain positive change. Like other cognitive-behavioral therapies, RPT combines behavioral and cognitive interventions in an overall approach that emphasizes self-management and rejects labeling clients with traits like *alcoholic* or *drug addict* (Parks & Marlatt, 2005).

The Moral Model

Many theories have been offered to explain the etiology of addiction. One of those is humankind's sinful nature. Since it is difficult to show empirical evidence of a sinful nature, the moral model of addiction has been generally discredited by modern scholars. However, the legacy of treating alcoholism and drug addiction as sin or moral weakness continues to influence public policies regarding alcohol and drug abuse. Perhaps this is why needle/syringe exchange programs have been so strongly opposed in the United States (McNeece & DiNitto, 2005, p. 26).

Models of Addiction

Marlatt and Gordon write about three different models for explaining addiction. The first model, the *moral model,* explains addiction as resulting from a person's lack of moral character or lack of willpower to resist temptations to use a substance. The person is believed to have some type of moral weakness or failing. The second model, the *disease model,* focuses on "predisposing factors, presumed to be genetically transmitted, as the underlying cause of addiction" (Marlatt & Gordon, 1985, p. 6). In this model, the individual has no choice but to continue using once he or she picks up the psychoactive substance. The disease model believes that one is either in control through complete abstinence or out of control if one begins using a mood-altering substance. The third model views addiction as the acquiring of bad habits that can be modified or unlearned. This is called the *addictive behavior model.* Marlatt and Gordon subscribe to this last model. They believe that addictive behaviors "lie along a continuum of use rather than being defined in terms of discrete or fixed categories such as excessive use (loss of control) or total abstinence" (Marlatt & Gordon, 1985, p. 9). They believe that individuals can unlearn these maladaptive coping mechanisms.

Biological or Genetic Theories

The Disease Model

Biophysiological and genetic theories assume that addicts are constitutionally predisposed to develop a dependence on alcohol or drugs. These theories support a medical model of addiction. Their advocates apply disease terminology and generally place responsibility for the treatment of addicts in the hands of physicians, nurses, and other medical personnel. In reality, the medical model is generally practiced only during the detoxification phase.

Genetic factors have never been established as a definite cause of alcoholism, but the statistical associations between genetic factors and alcohol abuse are very strong. A great volume of research as been amassed in this area over the last several decades, and much of the evidence points toward alcoholism as an inherited trait (McNeece & DiNitto, 2005, p. 29).

We believe that all three models may play a role in the development of SUDs. Some individuals exhibit the inability to delay immediate gratification or control their impulses, thus failing to resist temptation. Others are spiritually empty and lack the will to avoid the temptation of immediate pleasure. Others have a genetic susceptibility to substances or a particular substance passed down from one generation to another, making control over their use of a substance impossible. Yet others have learned maladaptive coping mechanisms or have never learned adequate coping responses to control their use of substances.

Regardless of the etiology of addiction, this section will provide skills that can help explain the precipitants of relapse, as well as strategies for preventing relapse.

Relapse Prevention Defined

Let's begin by defining *relapse* and *lapse*. Marlatt and Gordon define *relapse* as a "breakdown or setback in a person's attempt to change or modify any target behavior" (Marlatt & Gordon, 1985, p. 3). What we typically see in a treatment setting is a *lapse,* "a slight error or slip, a temporary fall especially from a higher to a lower state" (Marlatt & Gordon, 1985, p. 32). Following a lapse, many clients pick themselves up, learn from their mistake, and become more resolute about their commitment to change, while others allow the lapse to escalate into a full-blown relapse.

According to Marlatt and Gordon (1985), the goals of relapse prevention are threefold:

- To prevent the occurrence of relapse after initiating change

- To prevent a lapse from turning into a full-blown relapse

- To maintain a balanced lifestyle

In the preceding chapter in the section on stages of change, we discussed how relapses usually occur from three to seven times before lasting change occurs. Rather than perceiving these relapses or lapses as failures, we prefer to perceive

Cognitive-Behavioral Theories

Addictive Behavior Model

The cognitive-behavioral theories offer a variety of motivations for taking drugs. One such explanation states that humans take drugs to experience variety (Weil & Rosen, as cited in McNeece & DiNitto, 2005, p. 27). The need for variety is demonstrated in cross-cultural expressions such as singing, dancing, running, and joking. Drug use is associated with a variety of activities—for example, religious services, self-exploration, altering moods, escaping boredom or despair, enhancing social interaction, enhancing sensory experience or pleasure, and stimulating creativity and performance. . . . Assuming that people enjoy variety, it follows that they repeat actions that bring pleasure (positive reinforcement).

The 90-Day Threshold

In general, about two-thirds of all initial lapses occur within the first 90 days following initiation of the cessation attempt across various addictive behaviors. (Marlatt & Gordon, 1985, p. 36)

them as steps toward lasting change. When Thomas Edison was asked what the key to his success was, he answered, "a thousand failures."

An important distinction must be made between a lapse and active use patterns. A lapse, as defined earlier, is a slight error, slip, or temporary fall. It is a return to a previous behavior following a voluntary choice or decision to change. Many times what we perceive to be a lapse may actually be a lack of commitment to change—or better defined as a state of *ambivalence*. This person is not having a lapse or lapses, but possibly just actively using at less frequent intervals. A person under some external pressure to discontinue cocaine use may have previously been using cocaine three times weekly. Because of external pressure, that person may now be using only monthly. We may choose not to define these monthly patterns of usage as lapses because he or she lacks a sincere desire to stop using cocaine; these monthly usage patterns are actually active use patterns, just with less frequency. Whatever they might be called, depending upon the ultimate goal of treatment, they could reflect a degree of success. *A lapse or relapse is a return to some previous behavior pattern following a sincere desire to discontinue that behavior pattern.*

Self-Efficacy

Let's look at the relapse process. The greater one's perceived control over a situation or one's confidence to handle a situation, defined as *self-efficacy,* the less likely relapse will occur in that situation. Self-efficacy refers to the individual's subjective expectancy concerning his or her capacity to count on a specific response, such as an effective coping response, in a specific situation or task (Bandura, 1977, 1981). This is the belief that one has the situation "under control" and "feels able to make it through or cope effectively with the situation without giving in to the temptation of the old addictive coping behavior" (Marlatt & Gordon, 1985, p. 75). When a person gives in to the addictive behavior, the belief that he or she cannot cope without the addictive behavior is further strengthened. "The longer the period of successful abstinence, the greater the individual's perception of self-efficacy" (Marlatt & Gordon, 1985, p. 37). This feeling of self-efficacy continues until the individual experiences a *high-risk situation.*

High-Risk Situations

A *high-risk situation* is defined as "any situation that poses a threat to the individual's sense of control (self-efficacy) and increases the risk of potential relapse" (Marlatt & Gordon, 1985, p. 75). The more effective one's coping response in a high-risk situation, the less likely relapse will occur.

According to Marlatt and Gordon, three-quarters of all relapses can be associated with three primary high-risk situations: negative emotional states, inter-

Relapse Prevention

Aversion Therapy: Early Efforts

> Attempts to disrupt alcoholic drinking by associating alcohol with some noxious stimulus—later called aversion therapy or a conditioned reflex treatment—began early in American history. Benjamin Rush's experiments with aversion therapy for alcoholism date from the 1780s. In the early 1800s, Dr. Kain used tartar emetic as an aversive agent to link the taste and smell of alcohol with nausea. In their separate reviews of the substances used to induce distaste for alcohol, Drs. J. D. Rolleston and Joseph Thimann named a number of substances, including rotted sea grapes, mole blood, and sparrow's dung. Some attempts involved elaborate procedures such as forcing the patient to drink wine in which a live eel had been suffocated or having the alcoholic consume powderized pork that had secretly resided in the bed of a Jew for nine days. Relatives of alcoholics have at various times been coached to place worms or insects into the alcoholic's bottle or to saturate with alcohol everything the alcoholic ate. Some specialists advocated that drunkards be forced to drink their own urine. The purpose of all such strategies was to induce a revulsion toward alcohol. (White, 1998, p. 105)

personal conflicts, and social pressure. *Negative emotional states,* which are associated with 35 percent of all relapses, involve "situations in which the individual is experiencing a negative (or unpleasant) emotional state, mood, or feeling such as frustration, anger, anxiety, depression, or boredom, prior to or at the time the first lapse occurs" (Marlatt & Gordon, 1985, pp. 37–38). *Interpersonal conflicts,* which are associated with 16 percent of all relapses, include "situations involving an ongoing or relatively recent conflict associated with any interpersonal relationship, such as marriage, friendship, family members, or employer-employee relations" (Marlatt & Gordon, 1985, p. 38). *Social pressure,* which is associated with 20 percent of all relapses, includes "situations in which the individual is responding to the influence of another person or group of people exerting pressure on the individual to engage in the taboo behavior. Social pressure may either be direct (direct interpersonal contact with verbal persuasion) or indirect (e.g., being in the presence of others who are engaging in the same target behavior, even though no direct pressure is involved; Marlatt & Gordon, 1985, p. 38). Negative emotional states are placed under a major subdivision called *intrapersonal determinants,* factors that do not involve other people (e.g., psychological, physical, or environmental factors). Other intrapersonal determinants include coping with negative physical-physiological states (e.g., withdrawal, chronic pain), enhancement of positive emotional states (e.g., celebrating), testing personal control (e.g., engaging in controlled use), and giving in to temptations or urges (using in response to cravings or urges).

Social pressure and interpersonal conflicts are placed under a second major subdivision called *interpersonal determinants,* factors involving the "significant influence" of others. These determinants may also include enhancement of positive emotional states primarily involving use in interpersonal situations (e.g., sexual situations).

The Coping Response

Before defining *coping responses*, let's define *coping*. Marlatt and Gordon use the definition by Lazarus and Launier, "efforts, both action oriented and intrapsychic, to manage (that is, to master, tolerate, reduce, minimize) environmental and internal demands and conflicts among them which tax or exceed a person's resources" (Lazarus and Launier, 1978, p. 311). They define *coping response* "as any response that enables the individual to get through (or around) a high-risk situation without experiencing a relapse. In simple terms, anything the person does that is successful in this sense constitutes a coping response. Coping responses vary in complexity and quality, ranging from simple avoidance responses (e.g., deliberately bypassing a specific high-risk situation) to complicated cognitive strategies" (Marlatt & Gordon, 1985, pp. 108–109).

Marlatt and Gordon sum up the necessity of adequate coping responses for averting relapse.

> The most important factor that serves to decrease the risk of an otherwise high-risk situation is the availability of an alternative coping response. If the individual has learned new ways of coping with stressful situations and has had the opportunity to practice these new skills without the aid of the former habit crutch, self-efficacy will be strengthened and the probability of relapse will decrease. Although other life experiences may render the person more vulnerable to temptation (e.g., an addictive lifestyle or a covert desire to resume the old habit pattern), the availability of an adaptive coping response will enhance one's perception of control in the high-risk situation. Every time a situation is dealt with effectively by the use of an alternative coping response, the desire for the old crutch decreases. Eventually the person learns that he or she can perform adequately without the aid of crutches and the situation can no longer be considered high-risk. (Marlatt & Gordon, 1985, p. 77)

Relapse Process

Let's look at the relapse process as explained by Marlatt and Gordon, using alcohol as the behavior in question. Let's first assume that the individual is internally motivated toward discontinuing the use of alcohol. He runs into a personal, high-risk situation that he feels unequipped to handle properly. He

Gorski on Relapse

> Relapsers need accurate information about what causes relapse and what can be done to prevent it. This is typically provided in structured relapse education sessions and reading assignments that provide specific information about the recovery and relapse process as well as relapse prevention planning methods. (Gorski, 1990, p. 130)

Relapse Case

John voluntarily entered AA meetings (internally committed to sobriety) after becoming sick and tired of his drinking consequences. He has been sober for 8 weeks. Yesterday was a particularly bad day for John. He was scolded by his boss for procrastinating on an important work-related project and also felt unsupported by his wife after telling her what happened at work (negative emotional state of anger, frustration, and self-pity). In the past, John would often escape his problems by drinking (negative coping response). A drink seemed like a good idea (positive outcome expectancy). John told his wife that he was heading to an AA meeting. On his way to a meeting, he passed a bar that he would often frequent (a seemingly irrelevant decision, to be discussed later). He gave himself permission to enter the bar just to see who was there. Once in the bar he believed he owed himself one drink for the miserable day he had (initial use of substance). After finishing the drink, John was overcome with guilt and conflict (abstinence violation effect). He continued to drink at the bar until he was asked to leave (lapse turns into relapse).

lacks the perceived coping response to feel self-efficacy (control) in this particular situation. If he also perceives some potential positive effect from using alcohol in this situation, known as *positive outcome expectancies,* the probability of use is greatly increased. "The combination of being unable to cope effectively in a high-risk situation coupled with positive outcome expectancies for the effects of the old habitual coping behavior greatly increases the probability that an initial lapse will occur" (Marlatt & Gordon, 1985, p. 41). Whether the initial lapse is followed by a total relapse depends on another mechanism defined by Marlatt and Gordon, called the *abstinence violation effect* (AVE). The intensity of the AVE is influenced by "two cognitive-affective elements" (Marlatt & Gordon, 1985, p. 41). The first is conflict and guilt. If there is "a disparity between the individual's cognitions or beliefs about the self (e.g., as an abstainer) and the occurrence of a behavior that is directly incongruent with this self-image (e.g., engaging in the forbidden act)," significant internal conflict and guilt emerge (pp. 41–42). The second cognitive-affective element influencing the AVE is what Marlatt and Gordon call a *personal attribution effect,* in other words, blaming yourself as the cause of the relapse due to personal weakness or failure. "Rather than viewing the lapse as a unique response to a particularly difficult situation, the person is likely to blame the cause of the act on such factors as lack of will power or internal weakness in the face of temptation . . . If the lapse is viewed as a personal failure in this manner, the individual's expectancy for continued failure will increase" (Marlatt & Gordon, 1985, p. 42; see Figure 12.1).

Let's provide an example of this relapse model:

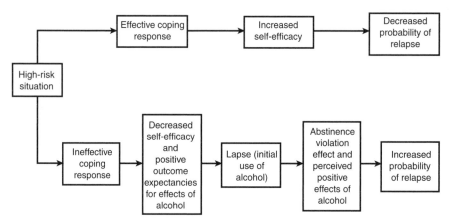

Figure 12.1 *Overview of Marlatt and Gordon's relapse-prevention model.*

Covert Antecedents of Relapse

Our patients cannot always anticipate running into high-risk situations. Consequently, clinicians must prepare their patients to cope effectively with these unexpected situations. We will discuss how to do this later in the chapter. On the other hand, high-risk situations are often planned or set up by patients in a subconscious, or what Marlatt and Gordon call *covert,* manner. The process begins with what Marlatt and Gordon call *lifestyle imbalances,* the lack "of equilibrium that exists in one's daily life between those activities perceived as external 'hassles' or demands (the 'shoulds'), and those perceived as pleasures or self-fulfillment (the 'wants')" (Marlatt & Gordon, 1985, p. 47). The greater the imbalance toward "shoulds" in one's life, the greater the "perception of self-deprivation and a corresponding desire for indulgence and gratification" (Marlatt & Gordon, 1985, p. 47). This lifestyle imbalance increases a desire for indulgence or a need for immediate gratification far outweighing "the cost of potential negative effects that may or may not occur sometime in the distant future" (Marlatt & Gordon, 1985, p. 46).

The desire for indulgence may be experienced as an urge or craving. An "*urge* is defined here as a relatively sudden impulse to engage in an act (e.g., an impulse to smoke a cigarette). *Craving* is defined as the subjective desire to experience the effects or consequences of a given act" (Marlatt & Gordon, 1985, p. 48). Both urges and cravings are assumed to be mediated by the positive outcome expectancies anticipated from the effects of the substance.

To complicate the situation further, the individual may be conflicted about consciously giving his or herself permission to use the substance. This conflict stems from the anticipated immediate gratification of using versus the potential consequences (e.g., social disapproval, self-blame, job loss, etc.). Consequently, through *cognitive distortions,* the individual sets up "an impossibly tempting high-risk situation" to avoid personal responsibility for the act. By covertly setting up a high-risk situation, one can justify use. Three primary cognitive distortions as-

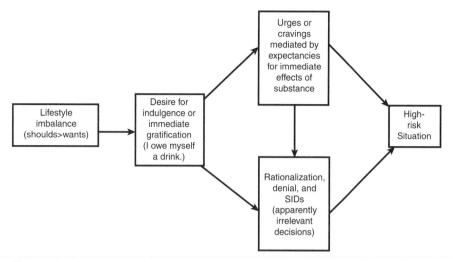

Figure 12.2 *Covert antecedents of a relapse situation.*

sociated with setting up the relapse episode are rationalization, denial, and seemingly irrelevant decisions. *Rationalization* is a cognitive rationale or an ostensibly legitimate excuse to engage in a particular behavior, for example, saying, "If you lived with her you would be getting drunk as well." *Denial* is a similar mechanism in which the individual denies or refuses to recognize selected aspects of the situation or set of events. *Seemingly irrelevant decisions* (SIDs) are a set of decisions or choices made leading up to the initial lapse and seemingly unconnected to the initial lapse, such as buying a bottle of wine "just in case guests come over." Seemingly irrelevant decisions were previously called *apparently irrelevant decisions,* but changed due to its acronym, AIDs, associated with acquired immune deficiency syndrome. Let's look at Figure 12.2 for a diagram of Marlatt and Gordon's covert antecedents of a relapse situation.

The following is a hypothetical situation of Marlatt and Gordon's model of covert antecedents of a relapse situation.

Covert Antecedent of Relapse

John is a 42-year-old married male with two young children. He has given up cocaine use essentially out of fear of losing his wife and children (*ambivalence*). His wife threatened to leave him if he continued using cocaine. He has not used cocaine for about 4 months. John is a hard worker who has been complaining that all he does is work (*lifestyle imbalance*). He feels life has been boring since he stopped using cocaine, but has been reluctant to find substitute, pleasurable activities to fill his down time. He occasionally admits to wishing he could use cocaine in a more controlled fashion (*desire for indulgence*). One morning, John's wife receives a disturbing phone call that her father had a heart attack and had to fly out of town immediately. She asks John if he can come along with her and the children. He claims it is impossible to leave work that week due to pressing commitments (*seemingly irrelevant decision*). On his way to work, John has urges and cravings to use cocaine (*urges and cravings*) and believes he had a right to use because he had been so good (abstinent) for so long (*rationalization, permission giving*). However, he knows he should not hurt his wife by using cocaine given her current circumstances. John goes to work, checks on his wife who arrived safely, and then leaves work earlier then usual, telling himself that he should take advantage of having the time alone (*seemingly irrelevant decision*). On the way home, John calls a friend, an active cocaine user, to see if his friend is free that evening to meet for a drink (*seemingly irrelevant decision*). The friend is available and agrees to meet at a local lounge. In retrospect, John claims he had no plan on using cocaine at this point (*denial*). After having a drink with the friend, the friend suggests they call for some cocaine. John states that he is trying not to use, but encourages his friend to call for himself (*SID, rationalization, denial*). Once the friend purchases the cocaine (*high-risk situation*), it isn't long before John gives himself permission to use, with the stipulation that the friend never reveal his use to John's wife. Because John fails to call his wife that night, she quickly becomes suspicious of his use and, soon after, requests a marital separation. Upon their separation, John quickly progresses into a full-blown relapse process, using more cocaine than ever before.

Relapse Prevention Strategies

Relapse prevention strategies are interventions employed at different points in the relapse cycle in order to break the cycle. Clients are first taught to become aware of their personal high-risk situations and avoid them whenever possible. If avoidance of the high-risk situation is not possible, clients are taught new coping responses to deal with them. Relapse prevention strategies are strategies to increase self-efficacy, improve coping responses, deal with high-risk situations, and improve a lifestyle imbalance.

The relapse prevention program should be an individualized approach whenever possible. It begins with an assessment, identifying potential high-risk situations and the person's unique coping responses. The information collected in the assessment is then used to develop a tailor-made program for the patient, selecting particular techniques and skills-building exercises.

Relapse prevention strategies fall into four main categories:

1. Identifying personal high-risk situations
2. Coping skills training methods
3. Cognitive restructuring strategies
4. Lifestyle intervention strategies

Before we describe the strategies for each of these categories, let's discuss a starting point. Patients should begin with understanding the theoretical overview of the relapse process as discussed in an earlier section. By understanding such a model, patients will begin to identify the variety of factors inherent in the process of relapse and also the many places to circumvent the relapse process once it is initiated. Understanding that many places are available to intervene in the relapse process brings relief for the patient and enhances self-efficacy.

Once the relapse process is understood by the patient, an individualized relapse prevention plan is initiated. This begins with identifying high-risk situations unique to each patient and also understanding how the patient copes with high-risk situations, the cognitive distortions used by the patient, and lifestyle imbalances unique to each patient.

Identifying Personal High-Risk Situations

"The first step to take in the prevention of relapse is to teach the client to recognize the high-risk situations that may precipitate or trigger a relapse" (Marlatt & Gordon, 1985, p. 53). Individuals should learn to identify their own high-risk situations and coping responses through an individualized assessment procedure. "Clients need to be trained to be on the lookout for impending high-risk situations and to take preventive action at the earliest possible point" (Marlatt & Gordon, 1985, p. 113). Let's discuss specific strategies for identifying potential high-risk situations:

Self-Monitoring Procedures This is a method of identifying potential high-risk situations. In this procedure, the patient maintains "an ongoing record of the target behavior as it occurs (e.g., a smoker can be asked to record each cigarette smoked, along with an indication of the time and setting, mood level prior to and after smoking, etc.). Self-monitoring can also be used to monitor urges or intentions to smoke, along with records of coping responses used (if any) and whether or not the urge was followed by an addictive act" (Marlatt & Gordon, 1985, p. 55). By self-monitoring, the patient can become more consciously aware of his or her potential high-risk situation, mood levels, and patterns of use behavior, thus reducing the chance of relapse. It is recommended that the client keep a diary, including the following information:

- Time—At what time did the drinking start?
- Setting—What was the environment, who was present, and what were the activities?
- Antecedents—What was the client doing and feeling prior to drinking?
- Amount Consumed—How much was consumed in specific quantities?
- Consequences—What happened as a result, and how did the client feel after?
- Time—At what time did the drinking end?

Total time spent drinking and specific quantities consumed should be tallied. Estimates of blood-alcohol concentrations (BACs) should be determined based on blocks of time spent drinking and quantities of alcohol consumed. While this may seem an unreasonable demand on a drinking client, it is important that it becomes an expectation of treatment. The treatment professional will help, of course, with the BAC calculations. The rule of thumb is that a standard drink contains enough alcohol to raise the BAC .02 percent, and the body metabolizes alcohol at the rate of .02 percent per hour. So if a person consumes two drinks in 1 hour, at the end of that hour their BAC will be approximately .02 (e.g., two drinks times .02 BAC per drink equals .04 BAC. Then, .04 BAC minus .02 BAC metabolized in 1 hour equals .02 BAC at the end of that hour). Body weight and gender are additional variables.

Self-Efficacy Ratings This involves presenting clients with lists of specific high-risk situations for relapse and asking them to rate their confidence in coping effectively in each situation.

Autobiography This is a homework assignment (5-10 pages) to describe the history and development of his or her problem. The objective is to understand the client's self-image associated with his or her addictive behavior, often romantically associated (e.g., "smoking is macho," "drug use is cool"). In the assignment, clients are asked to emphasize the following: description of parents' drinking and drug use patterns during the client's childhood; the first drinking or drug use experiences and first intoxication episode on their drug(s) of choice; the role of drinking or drug use in the client's development as an adult (during school years, in the military, and as part of important personal relationships); factors associated with the development of substance use problems; one's self-image as a drinker or drug user; and so on. It is also suggested that they write a brief description of how they would view themselves as an ex-user (Marlatt & Gordon, 1985, p. 103).

Descriptions of Past Relapse Episodes and Relapse Fantasies Ask clients to describe past relapse episodes. This can provide useful information on potential high-risk situations that need to be targeted for particular skills training. Ask, "What were the situational determinants, and how did you react to the relapse?" "Clients' attitudes toward relapse and their ability to control their own behavior will assist the therapist in structuring the intervention program" (Marlatt & Gordon, 1985, p. 103). Relapse fantasies include dreams involving drug use or responses to the probe: "I want you to imagine what it would take for you to return to the addictive behavior pattern."

The preceding strategies are used to identify personal high-risk situations that the client can utilize to increase awareness of these potential problem situations and avoid them. In the event that the client is unable to avoid high-risk situations, he or she is then taught procedures to cope with these potential situations.

Selected Coping Responses

Annis "focuses on having the client engage in homework assignments involving the performance of alternative coping responses in high-risk situations" (1990, p. 119). A hierarchy of progressively riskier situations is developed, and coping behaviors are developed for each situation.

Daley and Marlatt believe it is "helpful to have relapsers review their experiences in great detail so that they can learn the connections among thoughts, feelings, events, or situations, and relapse to substance use." Clients learn that relapse is a process and an event by reviewing the common relapse warning signs identified by recovering clients (1992, p. 537).

Gorski believes that individualized strategies for high-risk situations are usually needed to manage high-risk situations on situational-behavioral, cognitive-affective, and core issue levels. On the situational-behavioral level, the client often must avoid the people, places, and things that are high risk and learn to modify his or her behavioral responses (Gorski as cited in Fisher & Harrison, 2005, p. 163).

Coping Skills Training Methods

Coping skills training methods are used to improve one's coping responses to high-risk situations. If one is unable to avoid a high-risk situation, then one must be prepared to handle the situation effectively without reverting to an addictive substance to cope. Coping skills training is the teaching of skills to improve coping in high-risk situations. "Skills training methods incorporate components of direct instruction, modeling, behavioral rehearsal and coaching, and feedback from the therapist" (Marlatt & Gordon, 1985, p. 56).

Assessing for Coping Skills Deficits Prior to teaching the skills for improving coping responses, an assessment of the client's current coping skills or lack thereof when confronted with a high-risk situation is helpful for determining how one would respond. From this assessment, the clinician can choose which skills would be most helpful to teach the client in order to improve his or her coping responses.

Prior to teaching the coping skills necessary to avert relapse, we must first identify the coping skills *deficits*. The following are examples of methods to identify the deficits:

- Self-monitoring: Self-monitoring of coping responses or lack of coping responses is done on a day-to-day basis. This may include a daily journal for recording coping responses to high-risk situations. This could also include observations made by significant others about the client's responses to high-risk situations.

- Simulated High-Risk Situations: The client is presented with simulated situations (e.g., role-plays, staged encounters, written scripts, etc.) and asked to respond as if it really happened. An example of this procedure is the Situational Competency Test (Chaney, O'Leary, & Marlatt, 1978). The Situational Competency Test (SCT) asks clients "to provide an account (written or oral) of what they would do if they were in the high-risk situation described. This procedure permits an evaluation of their coping responses. Self-efficacy ratings and expected coping responses can then be examined to reveal an overall 'profile' of strengths and weaknesses across a variety of high-risk situations" (Marlatt & Gordon, 1985, p. 56).

■ Role-Playing: The client is asked to role-play his or her responses to a high-risk situation enacted by a small group of fellow clients or therapists (Marlatt & Gordon, 1985, p.112).

Training Methods Once we understand the coping skills deficits of the clients, we can determine which skills can improve their chances of dealing with a high-risk situation. An excellent resource for teaching specific coping skills is found in a book entitled *Treating Alcohol Dependence* by Monti et al. (1989). This book is discussed in the previous chapter on action stage strategies. Although the book is geared toward treating Alcohol Dependence, the skills discussed can easily be generalized to coping with other addictive substances. The book's central tenet is a coping skills approach. It provides empirical evidence that individuals "can be taught to use alternative methods of coping with the demands of living without using maladaptive addictive substances such as alcohol" (Monti et al, 1989, p. 1). The book provides useful exercises on teaching coping skills such as receiving criticism, drink or drug refusal skills, enhancing social supports, problem solving, anger management, and planning for emergencies. Other useful coping skills training methods include the following:

■ Covert modeling, also known as *relapse rehearsal:* The client is asked to visualize a high-risk situation "as vividly as possible and to experience the kind of thoughts and feelings that would occur if the person was actually in the situation" (Marlatt & Gordon, 1985, p. 118). The client then imagines practicing the coping response learned and on the successful outcome derived from the coping response (coping imagery). This method improves one's feeling of self-efficacy.

■ Relaxation training and stress management: These techniques are used to decrease fear and anxiety, which can interfere with adequate coping responses. It is used to increase the client's overall capacity to deal with stress. Such procedures as progressive muscle relaxation training, meditation, exercise, and various stress management techniques are extremely useful in aiding the client to cope more effectively with the hassles and demands of daily life.

■ Education about the immediate and delayed effects of the substance: Education is used to counteract the effects of positive outcome expectancies (a belief that the substance will provide benefit). It is hoped that educating the client about the deleterious effects of the substance(s) in question can help mitigate the effects of positive outcome expectancies.

■ Relapse contract, a contract limiting the extent of use once a lapse occurs, is important: The contract can include such items as fines or penalties for use, agreeing to delay use after an urge, agreeing not to use after a single dose, or delaying continued use after an initial lapse.

■ Reminder cards: These are carried by the client to remind him or her of emergency procedures to follow in the event of a lapse. The reminder card may include the reasons why he or she stopped using; the benefits that sobriety has brought; stop, look, and listen prompts—stop the flow of events, and look and listen to what is happening—reminders to keep calm and renew a commitment to sobriety; and phone numbers of those to call.

Cognitive Restructuring Strategies

Cognitive restructuring strategies are designed to provide the client with alternative ways of thinking, perceiving, and believing about the relapse process (i.e., to view it as a learning process). In this section we will be focusing on three critical cognitive mediating factors in the relapse process:

1. Self-efficacy

2. Positive outcome expectancies

3. Abstinence violation effect

Self-Efficacy Self-efficacy is a cognitive process because it deals with "perceived judgments or evaluations people make about their competency to perform adequately in a specific task situation" (Marlatt & Gordon, 1985, p. 129). If one does not perceive the ability to succeed in a specific situation, failure is likely.

You have often heard the phrase, "ready, willing, and able," but have you ever really thought about it? All three of these motivational factors must be met in order for change to occur. One must be willing to change (willing) and willing to change now (ready). However, without the third element (able), one will not succeed. The individual must believe he or she is able to change. In other words, the individual has confidence that he or she is capable of succeeding (self-efficacy).

"The probability of relapse in a given high-risk situation decreases considerably when the individual harbors a high level of self-efficacy for performing a coping response. If a coping response is successfully performed, the individual's judgment of efficacy will be strengthened for coping with similar situations as they arise on subsequent occasions" (Marlatt & Gordon, 1985, p. 133). Marlatt and Gordon state the results of a study, which found that "the higher the level of perceived self-efficacy at the completion of treatment, the greater the probability that subjects would remain abstinent throughout the follow-up phase or would remain abstinent for longer periods of time prior to relapse" (Marlatt & Gordon, 1985, p. 135).

From this conclusion, we suggest that a client's self-efficacy ratings regarding different situations should be taken regularly throughout the course of treatment to identify areas needing to be strengthened. An example of a self-efficacy questionnaire is the Situational Confidence Questionnaire (SCQ) (Annis, 1982). This questionnaire contains 100 items of common situations found difficult by alcohol abusers. The client is asked to rate each of these situations in terms of their confidence level to resist drinking in the situation on a scale of 0 (not at all confident) to 100 (very confident). Another questionnaire developed by the same author called the Inventory of Drinking Situations contains the same 100 items from the SCQ, but clients are now asked to indicate whether they drank in that particular situation on a scale from 0 to 4 (never/rarely/frequently/almost always; Annis et al., 1987).

The following are suggested techniques for increasing self-efficacy:

■ Coping skills training: Identify the high-risk situations that the client feels least likely to be successful in and teach them the specific coping skills discussed in the previous section that would improve their self-efficacy. By learning these new skills, clients feel more confident in their ability to handle difficult situations effectively.

■ Cognitive reframing: Reframe *failures* into *tries*. Explain how practice makes perfect and the importance of not giving up. Marlatt and Gordon speak about reframing the client's self-image from *victim* to *victor*, in other words, reframing helplessness into lacking the adequate coping responses to succeed effectively. Addiction is also reframed as a habitual behavior (to be broken) rather than as a self-image (who I am).

■ Relapse rehearsal: Practice how one would cope differently in a particularly stressful or high-risk situation.

■ Goal-setting: Set up short-term, attainable goals (e.g., learning a specific skill each week) through which the client begins to improve feelings of self-efficacy and self-mastery.

The following are some additional ideas from *Motivational Interviewing* for improving self-efficacy:

■ Reviewing past successes: Look for examples of a client's past successes in achieving change. For example, you could ask, "When in your life have you made up your mind to do something, and did it? How did you do it? What obstacles were there and how did you overcome them?"

■ Personal strengths and supports: Ask the client to list his or her strengths and sources of social support. "What is there about you, what strong points do you have that could help you succeed in this high-risk situation?"

■ Problem solving: Generate different ideas for dealing with high-risk situations (Miller and Rollnick, 2002, p. 114).

Positive Outcome Expectancies These relate to the beliefs about what the positive effects would be of taking the mood-altering substance (e.g., "I will feel more relaxed," or "I will no longer be bored"). Positive outcome expectancies are "associated with what the person 'knows' or expects to happen as a result of engaging in a given behavior" (Marlatt & Gordon, 1985, p. 137). Cravings and urges are the result of positive outcome expectancies. The first few days of discontinuing the addictive behavior are the greatest risk in terms of succumbing to cravings and urges. Marlatt and Gordon believe that positive outcome expectancies are more important than the actual effects of the drug in the decision to take the drug. What one believes will be the positive effect of the drug is often more consistent than the actual effects of the drug. Positive outcome expectancies arise from several sources, including classical conditioning, physical dependency, attitudes and beliefs, and situational-environmental factors.

Classical conditioning is something you may remember from a basic psychology course. The psychologist Pavlov did an experiment of ringing a bell every time he was ready to feed a dog. Eventually, the dog associated the bell to eating and would begin salivating (a physiological response) when hearing the bell in anticipation of being fed. Any people, places, things, events, and times often associated with substance use will often trigger a craving when someone is exposed to these conditioned cues. "Exposure to drug cues will elicit positive expectancies and an increased desire for the effects of the drug" (Marlatt & Gordon, 1985, p. 140). Positive outcome expectancies are more frequent in high-risk situations in which the person lacks sufficient coping responses and self-efficacy ("I could cope better with this situation if I only had a drink"). The good news is

---

Handling Urges

Reminder!

1. Urges are common and normal. They are not a sign of failure. Instead, try to learn from them about what your craving triggers are.

2. Urges are like ocean waves. They get stronger only to a point, and then they start to go away.

3. If you don't use, your urges will weaken and eventually go away. Urges only get stronger if you give in to them.

4. You can try to avoid urges by avoiding or eliminating the cues that trigger them.

You can cope with urges by doing the following:

1. Distracting yourself for a few minutes.

2. Talking about the urge with someone supportive.

3. *Urge surfing* or riding out the urge.

4. Recalling the negative consequences of using.

5. Talking yourself through the urge (NIAAA, 1994).

that, over time, if a person does not use substances when exposed to these drug cues, the conditioned responses diminish and eventually fade away.

Physical dependency clearly increases positive outcome expectancies. "I would feel a lot better if I only had one bag of dope." If one is raised in a culture or environment in which drug and alcohol use is regularly associated as socially acceptable behavior and with having fun and being cool, it is no surprise that one would have positive outcome expectancies associated with use. Finally, situational and environmental settings can often be associated with particular drug effects. For instance, we may associate drinking in bars with meeting a sexual partner, or smoking a joint at a concert as enhancing the experience of the event.

Strategies for handling positive outcome expectancies (i.e., cravings and urges) include the following:

- Identify triggers: Clients are asked to make a comprehensive list of their own triggers. This list will aid in determining what people, places, things, events, and so on that the client should attempt to avoid.

- Daily monitoring of cravings: Use a daily record of cravings listing the date and time of craving; the situation, thoughts, and feelings during the craving; the intensity of the craving (i.e., scale of 1 to 100); and how the client coped with the craving.

- Education about cravings and urges: Clients need to be taught that cravings are normal and expected and do not need to be acted upon. By not acting upon the cravings or urges, the intensity of future cravings or urges should diminish and eventually extinguish. They should be taught that cravings are time-limited and peak and dissipate in less than an hour. An explanation of conditioned responses and its association to people, places, and things can be very useful.

- Distraction: Have clients make a list of possible distracting activities to do (e.g., taking a walk, playing a sport, reading, watching a movie, etc.) if a craving arises.

- Stimulus control techniques: Clients are taught to avoid any stimuli that have been previously associated with use, at least for the first 90 days of their recovery, in order to reduce temptation.

- Labeling and detachment: Coping with cravings and urges by being able to label them when they arise (e.g., "I am having an urge to drink right now") and becoming a detached observer of them (e.g., "It is now peaking and will diminish shortly").

- Talking about craving: Enlist supportive others (e.g., friends, family, AA sponsor) to call in the event of feeling a craving. The therapist may need to train these supportive others on how to handle such a call.

- Coping imagery techniques: Teach clients to imagine the craving or urge as an ocean wave (urge surfing) that starts small, builds to a crest, and then subsides, or as a Samurai warrior who you must defeat. Use creativity in developing effective coping imagery scenes.

■ Recall negative consequences associated with use: Teach clients to recall why they decided to discontinue their substance use while having a craving. It is suggested that clients keep a reminder card in their wallet listing the negative consequences of their use to be read during a craving or urge.

■ Cue exposure: This is a debated technique of gradually exposing the client to drug cues (e.g., pictures, movies, actual settings) in order to desensitize him or her to cravings or urges.

Abstinence Violation Effect Another central, cognitive process discussed by Marlatt and Gordon is the abstinence violation effect (AVE). In summary, the AVE occurs when an individual encounters the following:

■ An individual is personally committed to abstinence from a particular behavior.

■ A lapse (substance use) occurs during this period of abstinence.

■ The individual feels conflicted and guilty about using (e.g., "I'm weak," or "I'm a failure"), attributing the cause to internal factors that are uncontrollable.

■ The individual continues to use to cope with his or her sense of failure and turns a lapse into a relapse.

Let's look at this process further. Marlatt and Gordon view relapse as a two-stage process. "The first stage consists of the initial lapse or slip; whether or not the lapse is followed by loss of control (leading to a full-blown relapse) in the second stage will depend to a large extent on the individual's perceptions of the cause of the first lapse" (Marlatt & Gordon, 1985, p. 169). If the person who lapses believes the lapse was the result of his or her own internal weaknesses, the AVE is more likely to occur. On the other hand, if the lapse is attributed to external factors (e.g., a difficult high-risk situation), the AVE is less likely to occur.

Marlatt and Gordon believe that the all-or-none requirement of the traditionalists sets clients up for the AVE. In other words, by believing one is either abstinent or not abstinent, there is no room for error; you are either succeeding or failing. Any use is equivalent to total relapse. Marlatt and Gordon believe in "degrees of relapse ranging from a single lapse to periods of no problem consumption and/or uncontrolled use" (Marlatt & Gordon, 1985, p. 170).

What the person believes is the cause of the lapse (attribution of causality) can either increase or decrease the probability of a lapse turning into a full-blown relapse. Attributing the lapse to external factors such as a high-risk situation or coping skill deficit *decreases* the probability of the AVE. Attributing the lapse to internal factors such as physical dependency, genetic susceptibility, poor motivation, or deficiency in willpower *increases* the likelihood of a lapse turning into a relapse.

It is helpful to educate clients about the AVE. But it is equally important that this construct not be used as an excuse to take a drink. In other words, teach clients that lapses are more likely to turn into relapses if the client attributes the lapse to internal and uncontrollable forces (e.g., lack of willpower, the *disease*) rather than external factors (e.g., coping deficit in a high-risk situation). While it is important that the client take appropriate action to avoid a lapse, it is equally important to explain that a lapse does not have to turn into a relapse.

It may also be helpful to *reframe* the lapse or relapse into what Marlatt and Gordon coined a *prolapse*—an opportunity for growth, understanding, and learning in similar situations in the future. It is also an opportunity to strengthen or develop new coping skills. Some other suggested reframes include the following:

- A lapse is similar to a mistake or error in the learning process.
- A lapse is a specific, unique event in time and space.
- The lapse can be reattributed to external, specific, and controllable factors.
- A lapse can be turned into a prolapse instead of a relapse.
- Abstinence or control is always only a moment away (Marlatt & Gordon, 1985, pp. 253–255).

Lifestyle Intervention Strategies

The final group of relapse prevention strategies to discuss is lifestyle intervention strategies. Marlatt and Gordon believe that relapse is more likely to occur if one's life is unbalanced. In other words, if one's life has too many *shoulds* or obligations in it and too few *wants* or pleasurable activities, relapse is more likely to occur. Without a balance of shoulds and wants in one's life, stress levels increase, intensifying the positive outcome expectancies of the addictive behavior (i.e., "A drink would certainly relax me now"). Too many shoulds in one's life is associated with self-deprivation and the need for self-indulgence or reward. A balance must occur between sources of stress and one's resources for coping with that stress. Without that balance, an individual is more likely to turn to addictive behavior to gain some relief or escape from his or her stress. Learning new ways to cope with a stressful life can reduce the need for addictive habits.

How does the individual currently cope with his or her stressful life? How balanced is his or her life between shoulds and wants? It is important to begin with an individualized assessment of a client's daily activities to ascertain the sources of stress and the current coping strategies to cope with them. Self-monitoring forms can be helpful and are not difficult to develop. They can be as simple as a daily listing of pleasurable versus stressful activities, or more sophisticated like the Daily Want-Should Tally Form developed at the University of Washington. Whatever method is used to monitor daily lifestyle activities, the objective is important: Get a clear view of your daily activities, measure their stress potential, and modify or change triggering activities and behaviors.

It is important to assess each client's global coping strategies currently being utilized. How does the client cope with stressors in his or her life? These global coping strategies can be divided into several key areas of lifestyle activities, including health and exercise, relaxation, interpersonal relations, and spiritual life. Clients who utilize these global strategies seem to handle stressful lifestyle situations better. Assessing how a client utilizes coping strategies in each of these areas of lifestyle activities can be beneficial in developing a lifestyle modification plan for improving overall lifestyle balance.

In the area of health and exercise, it may be useful to begin with a current physical examination to assess overall health status and pinpoint any potential obstacles to an exercise program. Reviewing current medications taken and the reason for taking them are important (e.g., to relieve stress). Assess the use of drugs for either self-medication or for recreation (getting high). To what extent does the client use caffeine and nicotine as a means of coping? A nutritional assessment is also helpful to ascertain eating habits, possible Eating Disorders, and the use of food to cope with stress. Exercise can be a very effective coping strategy. A review as to how exercise fits in with the client's normal schedule is important. Resistance to exercise must be explored. The goal is to improve exercise as a form of stress reduction in the client's life.

Another primary lifestyle activity that must be explored is how the client relaxes. What is the extent of substance use and use of medications to relax? Does the client use any formal relaxation procedures in his or her usual routine (e.g., meditation, yoga, etc.)? What are the client's typical recreational activities (e.g., watching TV, listening to music, reading, cooking)? When and under what circumstances do they participate in these activities? The goal is to improve positive forms of recreational activity to the client's life.

Interpersonal relationships can lead to significant stress or comfort. It is important to assess the quality of relationships in the client's life. Are these relationships contributing to or reducing the client's stress level? How is the client's sex life? Is he or she involved in social support groups such as 12-step meetings or church activities? The goal is to add supportive others to one's life and remove deleterious relationships.

The lack of a spiritual or religious connection can increase one's sense of aloneness and emptiness, often filled through the use of drugs and alcohol. On the other hand, improving one's spirituality can provide a powerful tool to overcome stress and fear. Consequently, it is vital to assess each client's attitudes and beliefs regarding spirituality and religion. Does the client view his or her addiction as a moral weakness? What is the client's general philosophy about life? What are his or her values? How much time does the client spend on spiritual growth or self-discovery?

By incorporating new and rewarding lifestyle activities into one's life, the client will obtain the following results:

- Add more balance into his or her life by including more wants than shoulds
- Reduce the feeling of deprivation resulting from giving up the addictive behavior
- Increase the feeling of self-efficacy and self-mastery
- Improve overall well-being

The goal of lifestyle modification is to add more healthy and pleasurable activities to one's life and to replace negative self-destructive behaviors with growth-focused positive ones. Recovery is a tall order and one that will usually involve several stages of change. But it will ultimately become a paradigm shift that begs the questions: How did I ever get there in the first place? While that question is certain to come up in both treatment and relapse prevention, a far more important question has been answered: What do I do to get myself out?

The Gorski Model

It is important to discuss another relapse-prevention model that is by no means a newcomer to the practice of relapse prevention therapy (RPT). Terence T. Gorski, founder of the Center for Applied Sciences (CENAPS) in 1982, launched CENAPS, which provides advanced clinical skills training for the addiction and behavioral health fields. A major focus of CENAPS is training health-care professionals in RPT. Where the Marlatt and Gordon's RPT assumes an addictive *behavior model* theory, Gorski's RPT subscribes to the *disease model* theory. And while there is plenty of common ground in both models, the differences are great enough to pack the house on at least one occasion when they had the opportunity to challenge each other. That was at the 10th Annual Dual Disorder Conference in Las Vegas where Marlatt and Gorski publicly debated the issue of whether addiction is a disease (Gorski, 2005). Gorski's approach is best summed up in his training course description, which follows.

Relapse Prevention Therapy (RPT) Training

Goal: *Identify and effectively manage the core personality and lifestyle problems that can lead to relapse in latter recovery after a stable recovery plan has been established.*

Objectives: *To develop in-depth clinical skills for completing the following:*

1. **Presenting Problem Analysis:** Teach your clients to create a list of their presenting problems, identify the relationship of each of those problems to their pattern of chronic relapse, project logical consequences into the future if noth-

ing changes, and make a commitment to change the core personality and lifestyle problems that cause relapse.

2. **Life and Addiction History:** Teach your clients to identify lifestyle problems that increase the risk of relapse by completing a detailed life and addiction history that includes childhood, adolescence, and adulthood.

3. **Recovery and Relapse History:** Teach your clients to identify factors leading to past relapses by completing a relapse calendar and a detailed analysis of relapse episodes.

4. **Warning Sign Review:** Teach your clients to identify the warning signs that lead from stable recovery to relapse by reviewing a list of common warning signs and identifying three personal warning signs.

5. **Warning Sign Analysis:** Teach your clients to identify the hidden warning signs that have led to past relapses by describing past experiences with his or her personal warning signs and identifying the thoughts, feelings, urges, and actions that comprise his or her self-defeating responses to those warning signs.

6. **Final Warning Sign List:** Teach your clients to develop a final list of personal warning signs that lead from stable recovery to relapse; identify the related irrational thoughts, unmanageable feelings, self-destructive urges, and self-defeating behaviors that drive those warning signs; and identify three critical warning signs.

7. **Warning Sign Management:** Teach your clients to identify and change the thoughts, feelings, urges, actions, and reactions that prevent effective management of the critical warning signs.

8. **Recovery Planning:** Teach your clients to develop a schedule of recovery activities that support the ongoing identification and management of core personality and lifestyle problems, test this schedule by identifying how each activity can be adapted to help him or her identify and manage those personality and lifestyle problems, and develop a final recovery plan that addresses all critical warning signs (Gorski, 2005).

As stated in the preceding, there is more common ground than differences in the Gorski versus Marlatt and Gordon models. But the differences that do exist are significant:

- Gorski subscribes to the disease model of addiction. Marlatt and Gordon do not.

- Gorski's recovery adheres closely to the 12-step principles of AA. Marlatt and Gordon do not view this as essential to recovery.

- Gorski emphasizes the physiological aspect of the disease. Marlatt and Gordon emphasize the behavioral.

- Gorski views one drink as a relapse. Marlatt and Gordon are likely to view it as a lapse.

- Gorski defines relapse as the process of becoming dysfunctional in recovery. Marlatt and Gordon view a lapse or relapse as a dysfunction in coping responses.

- In Gorski's model, admitting to an SUD is essential to long-term recovery. Marlatt and Gordon's emphasis is on the behavior.

As cited in Fisher and Harrison, Gorski states that the CENAPS model "integrates the fundamental principals of AA and the Minnesota Treatment Model to meet the needs of relapse-prime patients." He goes on to say that "The physical consequence of chemical dependence is brain dysfunction," and that it "disorganizes the preaddictive personality and causes social and occupational problems" (Fisher & Harrison, 2005, pp. 157–158).

Gorski delineates treatment from relapse prevention. That is, he differentiates clients who have completed the "primary goals" of treatment from those who have not (Fisher & Harrison, 2005, p. 158.). In other words, a relapse (and consequently relapse prevention) cannot happen unless the person understands or has already been in treatment or recovery. These primary goals are as follows:

1. Recognition that chemical dependency is a biopsychosocial disease.

2. Recognition of the need for lifelong abstinence from all mind-altering drugs.

3. Development and use of an ongoing recovery program to maintain abstinence.

4. Diagnosis and treatment of other problems or conditions that can interfere with recovery (Gorski, 1990, p. 127).

If we consider Miller and Rollnick's (2002) Stages of Change (see text box), based on Prochaska and DiClemente's (1982) legendary work, it is not difficult to understand Gorski's treatment prerequisite to relapse prevention. A person that

---

Stages of Change

Precontemplation—No awareness of problem and no desire to change behavior in the near future

Contemplation—Awareness of problem and seriously considering behavioral change but no action taken

Preparation—Intend to change behavior and have begun to take steps in that direction

Action—Actively working to change behavior or environment to overcome problem

Maintenance—Working to maintain changes in behavior that have already been achieved (Pizzi, 2004)

is using alcohol or other drugs and is in the precontemplation or even contemplation stage of change is not considered to be in relapse. Relapse is possible only after treatment has begun—or, based on the CENAPS model, after Gorski's primary goals of treatment are completed. One can argue that most persons with SUDs have probably attempted and failed to stop using before deciding to seek treatment, but this is an assumption. But in the Gorski model, the four criteria, including acceptance of the disease, is required before the CENAPS relapse prevention model is employed.

Selecting one model of relapse prevention over the other—Gorski versus Marlatt and Gordon, for example—is like selecting AA over cognitive-behavioral therapy. They are quite different from each other and both work very well. Twelve-step programs have helped millions recover from SUDs, while formal treatment models have helped millions more. And they are not mutually exclusive—in combination the results can be exponentially remarkable. Whether the client is in treatment for the first time or returning for relapse prevention therapy, there are many factors that determine outcome, including but not limited to the following:

- Motivation in terms of treatment readiness
- Skill and style of the case manager, counselor, and therapist
- Treatment program environment
- Client's diagnoses
- Existing support system

The stages of change consistently serve as the strongest predictor of treatment outcome. The greatest measure of success is movement, not from addiction to abstinence, but from one stage of change to the next. This is the road to long-term recovery.

References

Annis, H. M. (1982). *Situational Confidence Questionnaire.* Toronto, Canada: Addiction Research Foundation.

Annis, H. M., Graham, J. M., & Davis, C. S. (1987). *Inventory of Drinking Situations (IDS): User's guide.* Toronto, Canada: Addiction Research Foundation.

Bandura, A. (1977). Self-efficacy: Toward a unifying theory of behavioral change. *Psychological Review, 1984,* 191–215.

Bandura, A. (1981). Self-referent thought: A developmental analysis of self-efficacy. In J. H. Flavell & L. Ross (Eds.), *Social cognitive development: Frontiers and possible futures* (pp. 200–239). Cambridge: Cambridge University Press.

Chaney, E. F., O'Leary, M. R., & Marlatt, G. A. (1978). Skill training with alcoholics. *Journal of Consulting and Clinical Psychology, 46,* 1092–1104.

Fisher, G. L., & Harrison, T. C. (2005). *Substance abuse* (3rd ed.). Boston: Pearson Education.

Fisher, G. L., & Harrison, T. C. (2005). *Substance abuse: Information for school counselors, social workers, therapists, and counselors.* New York: Pearson Education.

Gorski, T. (1996). The disease model of addiction, edited lecture notes of October 4, 1996 [Posting].Retrieved June 20, 2005, from http://www.tgorski.com/gorski_articles/gorski_articles.htm

Gorski, T. (2005). Relapse prevention therapy training. Retrieved June 20, 2005, from http://www.tgorski.com/clin_mod/rpt/rpt.htm

Kadden, R., Carroll, K. M., Donovan, D., Cooney, N., Monti, P., & Abrams, D., et al. (1994). *Cognitive-behavioral coping skills therapy manual: A clinical research guide for therapists treating individuals with alcohol abuse and dependence.* Project MATCH Monograph Series, vol. 3. DHHS Publication No. 94-3724. Rockville, MD: NIAAA.

Lazarus, R. S., & Launier, R. (1978). Stress-related transactions between person and environment. In L. A. Pervin & M. Lewis (Eds.), *Perspectives in interactional psychology* (pp. 287–327). New York: Plenum.

Marlatt, G. A., & Gordon, J. R. (Eds.). (1985). *Relapse prevention: Maintenance strategies in the treatment of addictive behaviors.* New York: Guilford.

McNeece, C. A., & DiNitto, D M. (2005). *Chemical dependency: A systems approach* (3rd ed.). Boston: Pearson Education.

Miller, W. R., & Rollnick, S. (2002). *Motivational interviewing: Preparing people for change.* New York: Guilford.

Monti, P. M., Abrams, D. B., Kadden, R. M., & Cooney, N. T. (1989). *Treating alcohol dependence.* New York: Guilford.

Parks, G. A., & Marlatt, G. A. (2005). The national psychologist. Vol. 14, no. 3 May/June, 2005 from the September/October, 2000 (vol. 9, no. 5).

Pizzi, A. (2004, August). *Building treatment readiness for substance-abusing positives.* Paper presented at the Ryan White CARE Act Grantee Conference, Washington, DC. Retrieved June 23, 2005, from http://www.psava.com/rwca2004/workshoppdf/159%20Building%20Treatment%20Readiness%20for%20Substance-Abusing%20Positives.pdf

Prochaska, J. O., & DiClemente, C. C. (1982). Transtheoretical therapy: Toward a more integrative model of change. *Psychotherapy: Theory, Research and Practice, 19,* 276–288.

White, W. L. (1998). *Slaying the dragon.* Bloomington, IL: Chestnut Health Systems/Lighthouse Institute.

INDEX

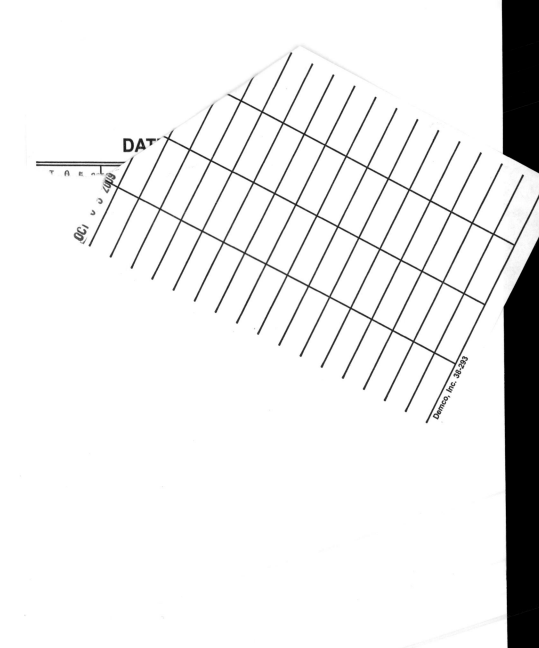